FRANCE ON THE BRINK

FRANCE ON THE BRINK

JONATHAN FENBY

ARCADE PUBLISHING • NEW YORK

FIRST U.S. EDITION

Material from Chapter 13, 'A French Life', first appeared in different form in the *Guardian* 'Weekend' magazine in 1995.

Map by Neil Hyslop

Library of Congress Cataloging-in-Publication Data

Fenby, Jonathan.
    France on the brink / Jonathan Fenby.
        p.   cm.
    Includes bibliographical references and index.
    ISBN 1-55970-488-8
        1. France—Economic conditions—1945– 2. France—Social
conditions—20th century.   3. France—Politics and government—1945–
4. Social values—France.   I. Title.
HC276.2.F44   1999
944.083'9—DC21   98-49658

Published in the United States by Arcade Publishing, Inc., New York
Distributed by Time Warner Trade Publishing

10 9 8 7 6 5 4 3 2 1

B P

PRINTED IN THE UNITED STATES OF AMERICA

To the memory of
Alter and Fanny

CONTENTS

Preface
ix

Map
xiii

1
SOMETHING SPECIAL
1

2
BEHIND THE MASK
54

3
VANISHING MADELEINES
81

4
COUNTRY LIVING
95

5
MODERN TIMES
120

6
BUSINESS MATTERS
143

7
ANOTHER FRANCE
179

8
SPECTRE AT THE FEAST
209

9
'FOG OVER CHANNEL'
243

10
DIVIDED WE STAND
267

11
THREE MEN AND A COUNTRY
318

12
FRIENDS OF FRANÇOIS
343

13
A FRENCH LIFE
366

14
THE JAWS OF VICTORY
387

15
ON THE BRINK
420

Bibliography
435

Index
438

PREFACE

The first time I went to France, I didn't like it much. My god-mother had invited me to join her on holiday in Britanny to look after her children. I have two memories of the trip: daringly calling out '*Ah, les flics!*' at the police on the seafront, and trying to learn to sail on a boat with a grizzled Frenchman who kept yelling about '*le foc*' – the mizzen sail, not a Breton approximation of a four-letter swear-word.

Forty years later, I was sitting in my office by the harbour in Hong Kong, having edited the *South China Morning Post* through the territory's return to China. It had been a breathless summer, with no time to think of anything except work. One Wednesday in August, I was seized by a single thought. My wife was in France, taking the waters at an obscure spa in the wilds of the Cévennes. In three days' time, she and three of our closest friends would drive to a favourite restaurant and hotel in a medieval village by the Aveyron river. My diary was embarrassingly empty. So I booked a ticket for that night, flew to Paris, changed airports and boarded a little plane to the town of Rodez. Once there I hired a car, drove twenty miles, and was sitting in the garden by the river when they drove over the hump-backed bridge on Saturday afternoon.

France gets you that way. Its lure is the reason for this book. I had wanted to write an account of the state of France for some time; what got me started was the virulence and scale of the protests that were set off by President Chirac's decision to resume nuclear testing in the summer of 1995. Why, I wondered, did France arouse such strong emotions? What is it that is so unusual about this nation and its people? And then, looking at the morosity which spread across the country from the mid-1980s, how does one reconcile the superior sheen which France displays to the world with the realities of double-digit unemployment, a rampant extremist party of the far right and a people who reject the elite that has ruled them for decades?

Without a healthy France, there is no Europe. That is why the state of the land between the Atlantic and the Rhine, the Mediterranean and the Channel matters so much, and why, for all the pleasures and stimulation it offers, France needs to get a grip on itself.

For a foreigner to try to grapple with such matters may seem arrogant. But I hope that three decades spent either living in France or watching it closely from abroad have enabled me to take the pulse of the nation, though I know that many friends living in Paris, the Berry or the Auvergne would disagree with my concerns about their country. My starting-point is certainly not that of a Francophobe; rather more that of a lover who entertains some fundamental worries about the object of his affection.

That affection comes from personal experience, encounters and observation as well as from my work as a journalist in France for Reuters, *The Economist*, *The Times*, the *Guardian*, the *Independent*, the *Observer* and other publications in Britain and the United States. I could never have undertaken this book, let alone finished it, without the help of my wife, who has given me roots-by-marriage in France and whose assistance has been as invaluable as it has been rigorous. Hundreds of people have contributed to my knowledge of France and given me material for this book. I owe a special debt to my colleagues in the French press and broadcasting; in particular to *L'Express*, *Le Monde*, *Libération*, *Le Figaro*, *Le Nouvel Observateur*, *Le Point* and RTL. I have indicated their specific contributions at various points in the text, but, beyond that, they have given me a far broader insight into France over the years as friends and colleagues.

Louis and Lya Wartski and their children have been an invaluable well on which to draw since the mid-1960s. Roger Galéron was a particularly moving witness of one day in 1942. The late André Passeron was my first and best guide to French politics, while Louis Marcerou opened windows on to France that I could never have found elsewhere. Paul Webster was an essential companion at historic moments in the 1990s as well as unearthing valuable material on the saga of François Mitterrand, which he generously made available.

I owe a special debt to the inhabitants of Mourjou and Calvinet in the Cantal, and in particular to our generous and ever-dependable host in the chestnut country, Peter Graham. Among the Anglo-New Zealand tribe to be found in those parts, Keith Walker, Brian Oatley, Peter and Win Campbell have provided information and food for thought over the years in the Place de l'Église. Ginette Vincendeau has been both a valuable source of material and a stimulating verbal sparring-partner. Bernard Edinger has always been there when facts needed to be checked or leads followed up, while Simon Caulkin, Jack Altman and David Lawday have been friendly sources of ideas through more years than any of us would like to acknowledge.

I would also like to thank the following, for their often unwitting contribution over the years: Jacques Attali; Raymond Barre; Jean-Philippe Béja; Pierre Bérégovoy; Luc and Annie Besnier; Jean-Louis Bianco; the Baron Bonnefous; Denis and Geneviève Brulet; Claude Cheysson; Jacques Chirac; Mary Dejevsky; Roland Dumas; Albert Duroy; the Estienne family and others who stayed on in the village of Saint-André-de-Rosans; Nicole and Michèle Fagegaltier, and their father; Philippe and Claire Ferras; Anne Freyer; Marie-France Garaud; Valéry Giscard d'Estaing; Jacques and Annie Hudès; Denis Jeambar; Serge July; Pascal Lamy; Jean-Marie Le Pen; Jean-Yves and Michèle Libeskind; John Litchfield; Gerald Long; Serge Marti; Dominique Moïsi; Christine Ockrent; Micheline Oerlemans; André Poitevin; Louis-Bernard Puech; Martine Schultz; Dominique Strauss-Kahn; Margie Sudre; the Vincendeau family and John Vinocur.

The chapter on the National Front draws, in part, on Alexander Fenby's thesis on the party, and Sara Fenby kept me up to date on the latest relevant French writings while I was on the other side of the world. In Hong Kong, Winnie Tam, Joseph Leung and other colleagues helped in producing the manuscript, for which deep thanks to them.

Though our paths diverged, Faith Evans set the ball rolling, and Gillon Aitken gave valuable advice. Paul Theroux suggested a vital connection. Christopher Sinclair-Stevenson's enthusiasm made all the difference. I am grateful to Philippa Harrison for having decided to publish the book, and to Andrew Gordon for his expert editing and backing. But, in the end, it all comes down to Renée, without whom none of this would have been possible. That's why one flies from the other side of the world to sit by a river in the Rouergue.

April 1998

FRANCE

Kilometres
0   50   100 150 200

Note

French spellings have been used for the names of towns and cities throughout, although geographical or administrative regions (e.g. Brittany, Burgundy) take the English name where there is an accepted Anglicised version.

Because of movements in the currency markets, French francs have not been converted. Over the past two or three years the exchange rate has fluctuated between five and six francs to the American dollar.

I

SOMETHING SPECIAL

France occupies an exclusive place in the world, and could accept nothing less. It is, its President declares, a beacon for the human race. The nation and its people may be loved or hated, but they can never be ignored. This, after all, is the land which gave the planet *Liberté, Égalité, Fraternité*, Charles de Gaulle and Gérard Depardieu, the Musketeers, Madame Bovary and Cyrano de Bergerac, Brigitte Bardot and Joan of Arc, claret and the cinema, the Cancan, denim and champagne, the theory of deconstruction and Édith Piaf, the Statue of Liberty and the modern totalitarian revolution, liposuction and the vegetable mixer, the sardine can, striped bathing costumes, the Impressionists, disposable razors and babies' feeding bottles. In 1998, its soccer team beat the odds to win the World Cup. Who could ask for anything more from a nation – and who could deny its uniqueness? The French have a term for their particular position – *l'exception française*. In case anybody should be tempted to miss the point, the country's Head of State had a mother-of-pearl button sewn on his suit jackets to attract the eye when he stood in group photographs with other world leaders.

France is central to the future of Europe, and, it sincerely believes, to the globe as a whole. With the fourth biggest economy, nuclear weapons and a permanent seat on the United Nations Security Council, it can claim to rank behind only Washington in international reach and ambition. Since General de Gaulle restored the country's faith in itself after 1958, the national psyche has sprouted a self-confidence which is not always becoming, but which leaves no doubt that it offers the rest of the world something out of the ordinary.

Not for the French the small opt-outs or grey compromises which satisfy others; they wield vetoes and strut the stage with a panache rare in the late twentieth century. Their vision of history is unabashedly Francocentric. The supreme monarch, Louis XIV, didn't win many wars, but no European doubted that his Sun King court at Versailles was the centre of the Universe – and just imagine what would have happened if his successors hadn't made a hash of the Anglo-French wars of the mid-eighteenth century and had emerged dominant in North America. The most famous Corsican of all time may have ended up in poisoned exile on an island in the Atlantic, and become an overblown inspiration to dictators and press barons alike, but Bonaparte could still appear to Hegel as the master of the world, inspire an estimated 45,000 books and set Beethoven to write the 'Eroica' Symphony, even if the composer did withhold the dedication in what may have been the awakening of the Romantic movement to reality. Charles de Gaulle could be, in the words of an adviser to Franklin Roosevelt, 'one of the biggest sons-of-bitches that ever straddled a pot', yet his style of national leadership equalled Napoléon's in coining a new adjective for the world. Wherever they go, the French take their country with them – from Corsican restaurants in Indochina to their unrivalled network of *lycée* schools around the world, which ensures that French children follow the central cur-riculum from Bonn to Beijing.

Lenin and Mao may have overthrown empires, but they were johnnies-come-lately in the revolutionary stakes. The uprising of 1789 set the template for getting rid of tyrants, and the national anthem still urges citizens to take up arms to defend the day of revo-lutionary glory. That being the case, the French are nurtured in the knowledge that they belong to the mother of modern republics, erected into a lay religion in the nineteenth century and epitomised in every mayor's office by the bust of the young woman Marianne, with her revolutionary headgear and exposed bosom. The fact that the bust is modelled on the most beautiful actress of the day helps: for the his-torian Emmanuel Le Roy-Ladurie, it is enough that 'France is, first of all, a woman. A beautiful woman.'

The people of the country called the Hexagon – bounded by the Channel, the Atlantic, the Pyrenees, the Mediterranean, the Alps and the Rhine – feel they do not have to bother overmuch about what the rest of the world thinks of them; simply being French is enough. They have little time for multiculturalism – foreigners and emigrants from other nations should count themselves lucky to be allowed inside the tent, and should conform to French ways and culture. After all, which other nation can boast such a baker's dozen of writers as Rabelais, Molière, Corneille, Racine, Stendhal, Flaubert, Balzac, Hugo, Zola, Baudelaire, Proust and Dumas *père* and *fils*? Feydeau set the template for farce and, even if his creator originated from across the border in Belgium, Commissaire Maigret was quintessentially French. When it comes to painting, the list is equally impressive – from Poussin and De la Tour through Corot and Cézanne to the Impressionists and on to Matisse and Braque. Henri Cartier-Bresson may be the century's greatest photographer, and the whole world knows the Hunchback of Notre Dame, the horrors of Bluebeard, the adventure of *Around the World in Eighty Days*, the Cannes film festival and the Paris fashion shows.

It is not only that France feels no concern about standing apart: the urge to be different is, in the words of the commentator Dominique Moïsi, a fundamental part of national existence. As the novelist Julian Barnes puts it, the French embody 'otherness'. We are almost perfect, declared a Tourism Minister, though she also urged her compatriots to be more welcoming to visitors since 'even the most attractive girl needs a bit of make-up to seduce'. The French are conceited rather than vain, in a phrase used by the British politician, Roy Jenkins, about De Gaulle. Two centuries ago, Napoléon hit a note for the nation to live up to: 'My power depends on my glory, and my glories on the victories I have won. My power will fail if I do not feed it on new glories and new victories.' Or, as *le Général* remarked: 'The French need to be proud of France. Otherwise, they fall into mediocrity.'

This nation's special character looms far larger around the globe than any country containing only 1 per cent of the planet's population has the right to expect. Presidents of the Republic play on their double role as head of state and head of executive government to impress the world. As they travel abroad, they carry Europe 'on the soles of their shoes', one French minister declared. France was the last

Western nation to test nuclear weapons, and one of the first to take serious action in Bosnia, where seventy of its soldiers died. In the post-colonial world, it maintains territories stretching from the North Atlantic to the South Seas, not to mention its shared suzerainty over the tiny tax haven of Andorra, high in the Pyrenees. Its natural position as the leader of Southern Europe puts it at the head of 175 million people from Portugal to Greece. Long after decolonialisation, Paris retained a *chasse gardée* in Africa, from where half a dozen rulers looked to the banks of the Seine for guidance and protection. France ranks ahead of Britain, Germany, Japan and the USA in the proportion of its gross national product devoted to overseas aid, and has produced a truly great humanitarian organisation in Médecins Sans Frontières.

Open the record book and the achievements come tumbling out. French women have the longest life-expectancy in Europe; until her death in 1997 at the age of 122, the world's senior inhabitant held court in an old people's home in Arles, making rap recordings and complaining about the food. At the other end of the age scale, Étienne Bacrot became the youngest-ever chess grandmaster at the age of fourteen. France has the world's largest opera house, one of Europe's most extensive and least crowded road networks, and as big a railway system as Britain and Italy put together. Only the United States house more nuclear power stations. The French go to the cinema more than other mainland Europeans, and their film industry produces the most full-length features on the continent. They eat high levels of butter and eggs while maintaining a low rate of heart disease and – until recently at least – an obesity level one-fifth of that of Americans. A Europe-wide investigation reported that their children were the most healthy on the continent.

This country grows the most expensive potatoes on the planet, nurtured on seaweed and once sold for 3,000 francs a kilo. It is the world's biggest exporter of apples, and bred the first hybrid tea rose. France houses what may be the world's earliest work of art in the form of a 32,000-year-old cave painting, and the most ancient walnut, an 8-million-year-old fossil discovered in Burgundy in 1995. It produced the greatest court diarist in Saint-Simon, and witnessed the first parachute descent, two centuries ago from a balloon above the Parc Monceau in Paris – the intrepid jumper had prudently tried it on his dog beforehand. A Frenchman sailor was the first man to make a solo crossing of the Atlantic. A seventeenth-century prelate, Pierre de Fermat, set out the theorem which took three centuries to prove and Albert Binet invented the intelligence test. On a less elevated tone, France has given the world the first men's underpants with a horizontal fly; a toilet which keeps users locked inside until they have washed their hands; and lavatory paper printed with short articles on culture, geography and the European Union. For other sources of information, the French may suffer from having a weak national press, but Canal Plus runs Europe's biggest cable television operation and *Elle* magazine claims to be the highest-selling international women's publication.

It was French agents who finally captured the terrorist Carlos the Jackal in the Sudan. Rugby players from the south-west and France's colonies give Gallic Grand Slam style to the Five Nations, and a French athlete won the gold medal in the 200 metres at the Atlanta Olympics after competing 'just for fun'. A Frenchman holds the world record for staying under water without breathing. Two others set new standards for speed eating of snails – 275 in 15 minutes – and shucking oysters – 2,064 in an hour. Their compatriots are both champion pet-owners (42 million household animals for 58 million people) and leading carnivores (just 1 per cent of the population is reckoned to be vegetarian).

The town of Condom is living up to its name with the world's only contraceptive museum, while the Mediterranean port of Sète has the first museum devoted to the sardine. The Tour de France cycle race is watched each year by more on-the-spot spectators than any other annual sporting event on Earth, and is televised in 163 countries. When it comes to literature, the French count the largest number of Nobel Prizes; their authors include one who wrote a whole book without using the letter 'e' and another who, suffering from 'locked-in syndrome' after a severe stroke, dictated a memoir by blinking his eye as an amanuensis read through the alphabet. What other state can boast a President who flew to a summit meeting reading poetry and another who repaired to a garden on election eve with a slim volume of Japanese *haikus*? Which other people could have prompted a 235-page academic treatise on their gestures, from the Phallic Forearm Jerk to the Ambiguous Gut-Punch? And a best-selling book even claims that Christ was buried in France.

France's armed forces, according to a report by the Royal United Services Institute in London, are outdone only by the US and China in 'martial potency'. Its people feel that they belong to a thoroughly modern, powerful nation. Their Post Office set up the first on-line data network available to households throughout the nation, and their government took the lead in developing the supersonic airliner. Their high-speed rail service was so successful that double-decker carriages have been introduced on the main link between Paris and Lyon to handle the flood of passengers – and the *Train à Grande Vitesse* so outdid Britain in its bullet links to the Channel that railway executives across the narrow sea were reduced to making jokes about the virtue of giving travellers time to appreciate the Kent countryside.

France entered 1999 with an annualised inflation rate of 0.3 per cent, wage settlements are low, and the government insisted that events in Asia and Russia would not seriously dent its growth forecasts. Strong exports and limited imports have boosted the trade performance since 1992, with 1997 producing a record surplus of 231 billion francs. The budget deficit was officially forecast to fall to 2.5 per cent of gross domestic product by 1999 – just over half its level in the mid-1990s. As the decade progressed, the franc grew so muscular that the specu-lator George Soros was reported to believe that it might be the key European currency of the future rather than the Deutschmark. When the US dollar and sterling showed their own muscles later in the decade, exporters reaped a dividend that compensated for low domes-tic demand. Such was the international confidence in the economy that, at one point, France was able to pay lower interest on bonds than Germany.

The value of the Paris Bourse has soared, with the trading volume rising by 39 per cent in 1998. Pursuit of shareholder value by a new breed of managers attracted foreign funds in their billions – non-French investors accounted for half the turnover on the stock market. Overall, France became the fourth biggest recipient of foreign invest-ment in the world, as companies such as IBM, Motorola and FedEx developed their operations – and, most significantly, Toyota decided to build a 4-billion-franc plant in Valenciennes rather than in Britain.

French companies are world leaders in tyres, cosmetics and yoghurts. Air France is the fourth biggest international carrier. The state is a major force in the highly successful European Airbus consortium, whose development is being steered by a Frenchman. A hundred space rockets have been launched from the base in French Guyana. Électricité de France is by far Europe's biggest exporter of power. A French firm has built the world's largest flight kitchen at Hong Kong's new airport; another has installed almost half the new telephone lines in China. The AXA–UAP group is the second largest asset manager in the world. The Société Générale bank has snapped up one of the last City investment houses, Hambros, and France's second largest insurer, AGF, has managed to enlist German backing while keeping its French nature. At the same time, the luxury goods firm LVMH established itself as a top world player with its growth round the globe and its assault on Italy's Gucci. The French state even found itself owning a Hollywood film studio.

France is the world's favourite holiday destination, attracting over 70 million visitors in 1998 and earning 175 billion francs from tourists. After all, which other country can offer the châteaux of Versailles and the Loire, the walled city of Carcassonne and the papal palace of Avignon, the jewel church of Vézelay and the Romanesque beauties along the pilgrim trail towards Compostela, the hilltop fortresses of the doomed Cathar heretics in the Pyrenees, the cathedrals of Chartres, Reims or Albi, the central square of Nancy or the Dominican church and hidden medieval town-houses of Toulouse, the Spanish-accented charm and Fauvist colours of the anchovy port of Collioure on the Mediterranean and the turn-of-century elegance of Deauville on the Channel? From the rough beauty of the Cévennes and the towering peaks of the Alps to the lavender fields of the Drôme and the softness of Anjou, from the wild horses of the mountain plateaux of the Spanish border and the pink flamingos of the Camargue to the storks nesting on the rooftops of Alsace and the seagulls wheeling over the vast D-Day invasion beaches of Normandy – no country of comparable size, perhaps not even those of much greater size, can equal such variety of landscape and life.

Its capital offers an unparalleled range of architecture, history and personal memory, from the Roman relics of the Arènes de Lutèce to the Renaissance mansions of the Marais around the Place des Vosges, through Baron Haussmann's nineteenth-century construction of a city centre, and on to the legacy of steel, glass and concrete bequeathed by François Mitterrand. Its most popular attraction, the

Centre Georges Pompidou in the Beaubourg district, lured five times as many visitors as originally planned, and had to close for two years to repair the resulting wear and tear. It has some of the most famous monuments and open spaces in the world – the Eiffel Tower, the Louvre and Arc de Triomphe, the Place de la Concorde and the Bois de Boulogne. But it also has a uniquely private aspect with its court-yards, alleyways, hidden buildings and concierges who long ago learned that information was power. From China to Argentina, cities in search of glamour call themselves the 'Paris of the East' or the 'Paris of the Americas'. Though London's rebirth as the most lively city in the world hits magazine covers once a decade, it is Paris which clocks in with unbeatable regularity in the top league of the world's most beautiful and exciting capitals. Despite all those tales of outrageously priced cups of coffee on the Champs-Élysées, it is not among the most expensive to visit; and its famously abrupt inhabitants are as likely to be in a hurry as rude. There is something pretty obnoxious in the advertising slogan of Poland's airline for Warsaw as a place of 'quaint little Parisian cafés without the Parisians', for there would be no Parisian cafés without the Parisians – but then, as we will see in a later chapter, scoring points off the French is a worldwide sport.

Charles Lindbergh became a hero when he landed at Le Bourget airfield in 1927 and, for more than a century, the City of Light was the magnet for artists and writers, and for political exiles ranging from White Russians and Jews, to Communists and the Duke and Duchess of Windsor in their memento-filled villa in the Bois de Boulogne. Reporting on the Dreyfus case for a Vienna newspaper set Theodor Herzl on the road to Zionism. The men who were to become Ho Chi Minh and Pol Pot studied Marxism and Leninism in France's cap-ital. For decades, Paris was at the cutting-edge of modernity. One of the troop of foreign writers and artists who came to live there, Walter Benjamin, called Paris the capital of the nineteenth century; a bit later, another resident foreigner, Gertrude Stein, dubbed it 'the place where the twentieth century was'. It was home to Picasso and Modigliani, and a last refuge for Oscar Wilde and Marlene Dietrich. Ernest Hemingway and Scott Fitzgerald sized up their penises in a Left Bank café lavatory. Paris and France adopted Josephine Baker and Sidney Bechet. Fats Waller got a chance to play the 'God box' in the organ loft of Notre Dame, and jazz musicians fleeing American racism found a home from home in the Hôtel Louisiane on the Rue de Buci. In a different musical mode, Jim Morrison's grave is still a pilgrimage spot for Doors fans on the northern slopes of the city.

A Paris publisher was the first to print Joyce and Nabokov. George Gershwin sailed home in 1928 with a collection of Paris taxi-horns to use in *An American in Paris*. Eugène Ionesco and Samuel Beckett wrote in the language of their adopted country; asked why he lived in Paris, the Irish playwright replied: 'Well, you know, if I was in Dublin I would just be sitting around in a pub.' Cole Porter made April the city's month. Gene Kelly and Fred Astaire gave it the sheen of musical romance for cinema audiences around the globe. Humphrey Bogart comforted Ingrid Bergman in *Casablanca* by assuring her, 'We'll always have Paris.' Even Hitler had to admit that, while levelling London or Moscow would not have disturbed his peace of mind, he would have been greatly pained to have had to destroy the capital of France.

Not to be outdone, other cities, towns and regions have attracted their stars, too. The still two-eared Van Gogh drew his inspiration from Provence. Salvador Dalí proclaimed Perpignan station to be the centre of the Universe. Medieval popes took up residence in Avignon. Deng Xiaoping worked in a provincial factory which branded him 'unsuitable for re-employment'. Chopin made beautiful music with George Sand in the dank flatlands of the centre. Robert Louis Stevenson trekked through the Cévennes on a donkey. Madonna named her daughter after the pilgrimage shrine of Lourdes, and Yul Brynner's ashes were laid to rest in a monastery in the Loire Valley. As for the Côte d'Azur, Scott Fitzgerald's 'pleasant shore of the Riviera' became such a mecca for the smart set of the 1920s that they could believe they had invented it; later, Somerset Maugham held lugubrious court in his villa at Cap Ferrat; and Graham Greene denounced the local political mafia as he saw out his last years in one of the less fashionable towns of the coastline.

For all the rivalry from across the Channel and from the New World, France's food still sets the international benchmark (despite such aberrations as *foie gras* sushi). The world is ready to buy everrising prices for the great Bordeaux and Burgundy wines, not to mention the export of 100 million bottles of champagne a year. Though it has become fashionable to decry the static nature of French cooking, the criticism is, for the most part, misplaced since it consists of taking France to task for not doing as others do – which is rather like attacking Chinese cuisine for not including *salade niçoise*. Plain steak and chips may be the favourite national dish, and some foreign food entrepreneurs may have attracted the smart set in Paris, but, as we will see, the allegation that French chefs have become stultified and boring simply ignores the widest-ranging gastronomy on Earth, and one which has a completely different dimension to all the seared seabass with Thai spices on a bed of curried Californian lettuce. When a top French chef lays down his chopping-knife, it is news around the globe, and a guidebook noted as if with surprise that there was only one world-class table to be found between Bordeaux and Tours, a distance amounting to all of 350 kilometres. No other country has as many different cheeses or wines; not to mention a 100-kilogram pumpkin grown by a gardener east of Paris, a 16-foot-wide quiche made from 1,928 eggs and the world's longest tripe sausage – all 150 feet of it. Champagne can legally come only from France. Smart eateries off the Champs-Élysées may adopt Americanised names, and you may stumble across a Tex-Mex restaurant on the Place de la Bastille, but a French name denotes quality eating around the globe: New York has Le Cirque, Los Angeles Ma Maison, London Le Gavroche and Tante Claire, and both Stockholm and Hanoi L'Opéra. Tokyo's Ginza shopping avenue is swamped with French outlets, and Japanese gourmets can spend a fortune eating the potato purée of three-star chef Joël Robuchon in a full-scale replica of a Loire Valley château constructed with stone imported from France. Across the sea from Japan, North Korea marked the elevation of a new Great Leader by ordering 66,000 bottles of French wine for the occasion, while China's biggest city has a Café de la Seine on the riverfront and a brasserie called Chamselisee (say it fast with a Shanghai accent and all becomes clear).

France may no longer produce the unchallenged leaders of world fashion – its top couture houses employ British, Italian and Russian designers to give them that end-of-century edge – but these designers still want to work for the top houses in what, for the global imagination, remains the city that epitomises high style. Boutiques from Oslo to Osaka call themselves by French names in the quest for smartness. Rag-trade workshops around the world stitch in 'Arc de

Triomphe' or 'Tour Eiffel' labels. Paris still means fashion, even if the frocks are financed and dreamed up by people who can't speak to the limo driver on the way home. It was, after all, Christian Dior who invented international *haute couture*, and his successor, Yves Saint-Laurent, who carried on the tradition – even if, as his lover and manager once said, he was born with a nervous breakdown.

The great figures of French history have a universal dimension. Make what you will of Napoléon – a mountebank chancer or the ultimate meritocratic inspiration – but the sheer scale of his achievements remains unequalled: commanding some of the greatest military victories the world has seen while reforming the legal code and the educational system, establishing a national police system, rebuilding his capital, encouraging arts and science, introducing the sugar beet to beat the British blockade, conducting tempestuous love affairs, and ruling an empire whose power stretched across a continent – even if he only got a bargain basement price for Louisiana. Joan of Arc is the symbol of the defiant heroine, invoked to describe everybody from Aung San Suu Kyi in Burma to Paula Jones. Marie Curie stands for the triumph of women in science. Brigitte Bardot is the most natural sex-symbol the cinema has known.

France fascinates, irritates and intrigues. It has a unique capacity to be brilliant one moment, self-destructive the next. Nowhere is this more apparent than in its global dealings, particularly when it is pursuing selfish interests under cover of higher principles. As a nation which thinks of itself alone as having proclaimed a universal message – liberty, equality and fraternity – it can only be deeply resentful that the American model of democracy and markets has stolen the show. Its great solo artist of international politics of the post-war era, Charles de Gaulle, didn't give a damn who he annoyed in expressing his 'certain view of France' on the world stage. His country must be 'dedicated to an exalted and exceptional destiny', and had no value, particularly in the eyes of Frenchmen, without a world responsibility. Others might use less sonorous words, but if anybody expressed France's view of itself, it was the man who saved his nation's honour twice in a lifetime.

The tone was set in 1940, when he insisted on his Free French command in London being the only Allied European force not to be integrated under the British. For the next four years, he struck a belligerently autonomous pose, even if his Free French crusade depended on the readiness of his allies to continue fighting. In 1945, he tried to make London choose between Paris and Washington, with predictable results. For more than a decade of the Cold War from 1958, Gaullist Paris presumed to act as a bridge between East and West and denounced the division of Europe, if only because it had been enshrined at the Yalta summit of 1945, to which De Gaulle had not been invited. It insisted on freedom to target friend and foe alike with its nuclear force. In 1963, France vetoed Britain's entry into the European Common Market for the first time, mocking poor Prime Minister Macmillan from across the Channel and acting, in the eyes of London, with almost unbelievable rudeness. A little later, the President simply left the French chair at Common Market meetings empty for months when he didn't like the way the embryonic Community was going.

Independence from Washington has been a constant theme, from De Gaulle's withdrawal from Nato's integrated military structure and his attacks on the Vietnam war to more recent differences over Iraq and support for an exchange rate regime to contain the dollar. But there was also solidarity, from backing for Kennedy over Berlin and the Cuban missile crisis to the current project for a joint US-French mission to Mars – not to mention the Foreign Minister's dismissal of the Clinton impeachment as a backward step for democracy. Cutting corners is no problem when the occasion demands it. On a visit to French Canada, De Gaulle told his hosts at Montreal city hall he would like to address the crowd outside. They pointed out that this was impossible because no equipment was available. So De Gaulle's bodyguard sidled out to the balcony to set up a microphone without consulting anybody. That enabled the General to stride outside and set off a storm with his headline-grabbing declaration: '*Vive le Québec Libre*' ('Long live Free Quebec'). Very French.

Under Presidents of right and left alike, the Gaullist heritage has been an enduring element in France's relations with the rest of the world. The repertoire has always gone much further than simply asserting independence from Washington, vital though that is. In a single press conference, the founder of the Fifth Republic managed to dismiss Britain's application to join the Common Market, support a return to the Gold Standard, criticise the Israelis as 'an elite people, self-confident and dominating', and refer to Quebec as a sovereign state. Three decades later, France was, at one point, simultaneously trying to set a line of its own over who should become the next Secretary-General of the United Nations (Paris insisted on a French-speaker), who should command the southern flank of the Nato alliance (Paris insisted on a French general), over Central Africa (France insisted it should make Western policy), the Middle East (which Paris insisted must be less of a US domain) and US-led international embargoes (which France insisted it had every right to break without endangering international solidarity). Paris led Western dissent from US plans to attack Iraq at the beginning of 1998. Britain's Foreign Secretary, Robin Cook, called it the odd man out in Europe on the issue, but the President's standing jumped in the opinion polls. At the same time, not content with having a French civil servant reorganising Asian economies at the head of the International Monetary Fund, it engaged in simultaneous lobbying to get its men installed as head of the European Bank of Reconstruction and Development and, even more important, to run the European Central Bank. Asked if this wasn't a bit rich, the Finance Minister responded that he was the kind of man who liked to have a cheese course as well as dessert.

Coherence, or rather lack of it, is not a problem. The first President of the left caused concern in Washington by taking Communists into his government, but then gave determined backing to American missile policy in Europe. His successor from the right cancelled summit meetings with some of France's closest partners for alleged lack of solidarity with Paris, but then announced a major reorganisation of the armed forces which affected its allies without prior consultation. And, all the time, linguistically and philosophically the French obfuscate behind a thicket of subjunctives and conditional tenses. They can be 'masters of splendid ambiguity' as Britain's former Foreign Secretary, Douglas Hurd, noted. Margaret Thatcher wrote – in evident exasperation – of a President 'speaking in paragraphs of perfectly crafted prose which seemed to brook no interruption', while US Secretary of State Madeleine Albright recalled the inscrutable comment of a French diplomat about the interaction of the various European organisations: 'It will work in practice, yes. But will it work in theory?'

'The French are by nature inclined to bully the weak and to fear the strong. Although they are boastful and vainglorious, as soon as an

enterprise becomes difficult they abandon it; they are better at starting things than following them through.' That was the judgement of
Marquis Tseng, the Chinese minister in Europe, who negotiated with
the French over Vietnam in 1881. Echoing the familiar description of
the French cavalry as being magnificent when it advances but ragged
in retreat, this is a verdict which many, including some friends of
France, would regard as an apposite piece of Oriental wisdom. But
when I put the notion to a French professor, she gave me a Gallic
response from a 1930s film: 'The locomotive of your ignorance runs
on the rails of my indifference.' *Et schlack* – so there!

   The international self-confidence is not hard to understand. All
over the world, traces of France pop up. Archaeologists reckon that
the greatest symbol of Britain's prehistoric past, the stone circle at
Stonehenge, was probably the work of invaders from Brittany. The
remains of a tenth-century monastery transposed from Saint-
Michel-de-Cuxa in the Pyrénées-Orientales department stand above
the Hudson River in New York; down below, the Statue of Liberty
was a gift from France, and the televisual *Friends* have a poster of a
park in northern Paris on their wall. Frederick the Great named his
palace in Potsdam Sanssouci, and his successors called their supreme
military medal *Pour le mérite*. The French architect Joseph Ramée
was the progenitor of the American campus plan with the Union
College of Schenectady. Bonaparte 'discovered' Egypt's ancient
civilisation for the outside world, and a French team freed the
Sphinx from the sand. Louisiana is home to half a million Cajuns
descended from French settlers who were ethnically cleansed from
their Acadia in Nova Scotia by the British, and who keep the language of the Hexagon alive on the bayous 250 years later. Lenin had
a French mistress; Japan has its version of the Eiffel Tower; and a
reproduction of the Alsatian town of Colmar is being built above the
tropical forests of Malaysia. The most expensive hotel suite in Korea
is modelled after the Palace of Versailles. An Indochinese sect counts
Louis Pasteur and Victor Hugo among its saints, and Cambodians
smoke cigarettes named after the actor Alain Delon. Schools on the
resort island of Phuket in Thailand learn to play pétanque, and
Madame Mao (somehow Mrs Mao doesn't sound right) plotted the
Cultural Revolution from a villa modeled on a Louis XIII manor
house in Shanghai. As for the classic Coca-Cola bottle and the

Lucky Strike packet, a Frenchman redesigned them both.

Bitter opposition to France's nuclear tests in 1995 did not cause the Australian Prime Minister to abandon his hobby of collecting French clocks, or stop a Japanese firm tripling its orders of Beaujolais Nouveau. The head of one of the world's largest media and entertainment companies keeps a copy of the Albert Camus novel *L'Étranger* in his office in New York. In the 1960s, an aged African dictator tried to get his country turned into a department of France. Another African President called Charles de Gaulle 'papa', and the leaders of the Indian Ocean island of Mayotte announced that they wanted to become part of France 'like the department of the Lozère'. Duke Ellington defined himself as a drinker of Beaujolais; James Dean found solace in Saint-Exupéry's *The Little Prince;* and Ella Fitzgerald was once spotted reading a book by Jean-Paul Sartre in her dressing-room.

This country invented the pressure cooker, the sewing machine and the non-stick frying pan which gave Ronald Reagan his Teflon nickname. French surgeons conducted the world's first graft of a hand in the autumn of 1998 just as Paris put into service the first major underground railway line without drivers or conductors. Voltaire dreamed up Candide and Panglosse, and Beaumarchais provided Mozart with Figaro. Ferdinand de Lesseps would have added Panama to his canal-building triumph at Suez if the terrain in Central America and corruption in Paris had not interceded. In more relaxed mode, the Club Méditerranée set the model for informal, all-inclusive holiday resorts, and it was a Parisian who commercialised the bikini swimsuit, employing a nude dancer to show it off after the regular models refused to wear it. Frenchmen invented the first non-iron pure cotton shirt, and have developed a year-round oyster that defies months without an 'r'. A muddy spring in the south discovered by Hannibal in 218 BC and rediscovered by a crippled Englishman twenty-one centuries later has become synonymous with fizzy water in countries where '*eau*' means nothing.

Nicéphore Niepce invented photography in Burgundy, and, if they cannot claim the first motor-car, French manufacturers did make two landmark vehicles. In 1955 Citroën unveiled its DS (the initials sound like the French word for 'goddess') with front-wheel drive, disc brakes, spaceship looks and self-levelling suspension. Seven years earlier, the same firm had turned out one of the world's most practical conveyances, the Deux Chevaux, on the specification of being able to transport 2 people and 50 kilos of potatoes at 60 kilometres an hour on no more than 3 litres of petrol per 100 kilometres – the ability to carry eggs over a ploughed field without cracking them and to leave enough room for hats to be worn inside were added later. Despite their flapping canvas roofs and self-motivated folding windows, they were wonderful cars. A friend of ours had a thirty-year-old 2CV which had been driven to Kenya and back; it still sat for a week in the snow at Orléans railway station and started with one turn of the ignition – or three, at most. But the coming of the motorway and the desire for a car in which you could sit in comfort meant the end of Deux Chevaux production – in France, at least. Some years after manufacture stopped in France, Chrysler had one of the cars shipped across the Atlantic, took it to bits and used it as the model for a people's car for China, India and South America, made of plastic. A Citroën spokesman agreed that imitation was the sincerest form of flattery.

The Lumière brothers made the first moving picture. Marcel Carné's *Les Enfants du Paradis* regularly figures high in lists of the best films ever made. One French author provided the inspiration for both *The Bridge on the River Kwai* and *Planet of the Apes*; two others served up the plot for *Vertigo*, and *films noirs* have become a Hollywood genre. French films have been a highly fruitful pillaging ground for a string of Hollywood vehicles for Arnold Schwarzenegger, Sharon Stone, Steve Martin and others. 'Another week, another Hollywood remake of a French movie,' as the *New Yorker* remarked. Although patriotic French *cinéastes* decry the process and insist that *Trois Hommes et un Couffin* is far superior to *Three Men and a Baby*, the studio bosses may not always be wrong in their remaking frenzy. French directors and actors do not, as a rule, work well in Hollywood. In France, Disney's cartoon version of *The Hunchback of Notre Dame* was a major hit, while France's biggest-ever home-grown success, *Les Visiteurs*, grossed just $36,732 across the Atlantic.

A pair of Frenchmen created two of the world's longest-running musicals; Claude François, a French singer who subsequently electrocuted himself in his bath, was responsible for the music of 'My Way', while another, Sacha Distel, co-wrote that alternative saloon singer's anthem, 'The Good Life'. Though linguistic backwoodsmen in Paris are up in arms about the spread of the English language, French terms still permeate the globe: if anybody sat down to calculate whether more words of French origin are used in English than vice-versa, French would come off much better than its fearful defenders might think. Chic, after all, is smarter than smart. *Faute de mieux*, invitations in London or Hong Kong come marked RSVP or Pour Mémoire. Generals have *aides de camp*, newspapers call their foreign offices bureaux and America's greatest artistic gift to the world probably takes its name from the use of the chattering verb *jaser* by Creole speakers in New Orleans. Louis Pasteur, Joseph Guillotin and the Marquis de Sade bestowed their names on posterity. The caped cloaks of the Limousin region of France provided the synonym for motor-cars with hoods. Extreme patriots and opponents of women's rights take their label from an enthusiastic Napoleonic veteran, Nicolas Chauvin. Gymnasts somersault more easily thanks to the garment invented by the trapeze artist, Jules Léotard. Disciplinarians should flick their whips towards Colonel Martinet for the strict order he imposed on Louis XIV's infantry. Napoléon's name, albeit bereft of the acute accent, was used by Conan Doyle to describe his master criminal, and by the US Secret Service as its code-name for Frank Sinatra. The extremely grand Vicomte de Turenne, on the other hand, might be less than charmed to know that, outside the history class, his name is perpetuated by his habit of using his helmet as a soup bowl.

In filmdom, even producers like to be called *auteurs*. Gourmets eat in restaurants, tourists buy souvenirs, bourgeois folk gather at table for dinner, and may make a rendezvous at a café afterwards. Negligees and culottes may no longer be in style, but women wear brassieres every-where except in France itself (where they prefer the *soutien-gorge*). Hotel concierges and waiters the world over address women as Madame. The French are even credited with things to which they would never wish to lay claim: French toast or the goo called French dressing across the Atlantic. As for French beans and French kisses, even the most ardent disciple of M. Chauvin would hardly pretend that they were exclusively national property.

At first sight, there seems to be no end to the aura created by this nation, no reason to doubt its claims to enduring greatness. So long, that is, as you do not look too carefully in the mirror, or stray too close to the brink of the apparently settled plateau of national existence. Keep to the surface, and everything seems in order. Lift the curtain, and things become very different. '*Tout va très bien, Madame la Marquise*,' as the butler told his employer over the telephone in a famous French comedy song. The château and the stables are burning down, your favourite mare is dead, your husband has killed himself, but, apart from that, everything's all right, Ma'am: *tout va très bien, tout . . . va . . . très . . . bien.*

The song has been highly apposite because this has been high-anxiety time in the Hexagon. After laying out all those reasons for pride, just consider the contrasts between the message from the top of the lighthouse and the reality below, between the glossy image and what people actually see when they glance into the national mirror.

France has a barometer of the national mood which swung from pessimism to optimism for the first time for a dozen years after the World Cup win. Spending on drugs to soothe the nervous system is 50 per cent higher than in Britain and twice that in Italy. The number of workers subject to the strains of 'just in time' production has doubled in ten years. In one supermarket studied by sociologists, 42 per cent of the check-out cashiers took sleeping pills – two-thirds of them were aged under thirty. At a plant in Brittany which put together fashion goods for top Paris houses, the manager paced the floor with a stopwatch shouting at the seamstresses that they were 'bitches, tarts, piles of shit'; he was only dismissed when the company's financial fortunes dipped.

A barometer of public opinion shows that people regard eleven of the years between 1980 and 1995 as having been 'bad times'. In surveys between 1973 and 1990, only 12–13 per cent of the French said they were 'very satisfied' with their lives, compared to more than 30 per cent in Britain, Denmark, Belgium, Ireland, Luxembourg and the Netherlands. The magazine *Le Nouvel Observateur* reported in 1992 that a help-line in Paris was getting 15,000 distress calls a year. Polls in the mid-1990s showed a steady 55 per cent expressing pessimism about the future. The suicide rate is among the highest in developed nations: more than 150,000 French people try to kill themselves each year, and 12,000 succeed – an increase of 50 per cent in two decades. In Paris, 500 police officers had to be put on light duties because of their mental condition in 1996. A quarter of the population lives alone, double the figure of thirty years ago. Six million people are reckoned to suffer from excess noise.

National spirits rose after an initially more easy-going Socialist government replaced hair-shirt Gaullism in 1997, but there was a big legacy of depression to deal with. One survey in the mid-1990s reported that 45 per cent of the French could see themselves falling into clinical depression. Hard times breed introspection, and a growing selfishness. More and more people admit to sympathy with racism – a European poll at the end of 1997 showed the French classing themselves as the second most racist people in Europe, topped only by Belgium. After falling for three years, crime rose in 1998, with minors accounting for 20 per cent of offences. France has 70 per cent more murders than Britain – a quarter are unsolved despite the country's 255,000 police. Fear of a breakdown of law and order is gaining ground and support for the return of capital punishment is increasing. The criminal justice system is in crisis and enjoys low public esteem. A poll for *L'Express* showed that only a fifth of those questioned believed justice was independent. The prison population has risen from 30,000 to 51,000 since 1975, and 40 per cent of those in jail are awaiting trial. Crimes committed by minors have soared: even offences by children aged thirteen or under have risen by 57 per cent in ten years. The traditional belief that child abuse was an Anglo-Saxon vice was blown apart when police rounded up 600 suspects in 1997 in an investigation into paedophilia. Polls show anxiety levels about drugs at more than 90 per cent. Scare rumours, often involving tales of outrages by immigrants, whip round the country. The National Front piles up votes in areas which hardly see a dark face and where crime is low. Once a haven for those seeking political asylum, France now has some of the tightest controls in Europe, taking in only a quarter of the refugees it had accepted at the start of the 1990s. While proclaiming their attachment to justice and the rights of man, Gaullist and Socialist governments alike took their time allowing French soldiers who served in Bosnia to testify at war crimes tribunals.

'There is too much violence in our country, too much insecurity – in schools, on public transport, in the streets,' the President of the

Republic declared in his New Year message for 1998. 'Every day new limits are broken beyond which our society will disintegrate.' The news broadcasts that night echoed his concern. In France's Euro-city of Strasbourg, rioting youths set alight fifty-three vehicles, smashed twenty-one telephone boxes, damaged thirty-two bus shelters and threw fire-bombs at three schools. In Mulhouse in the east, Saint-Etienne in the centre and Perpignan in the south-west, youths set cars on fire and destroyed telephone booths and bus shelters. Seventy vehicles were reported to have been set alight in the suburbs round Paris. A year later, fresh outbreaks of violence marked the end of 1998, and the Interior Minister was moved to speak of establishing special detention centres for young delinquents and of suspending welfare payments to their families.

As the Chirac presidency got into its stride after 1995, one former member of right-wing governments compared the national disenchantment with the ruling elite to the run-up to the revolution of 1789. A one-time Interior Minister saw a country on the eve of revolt, while another former senior minister spoke of a pre-Fascist climate fanned by scandal, unemployment and alienation between the people and the power structure. Bookshops were full of volumes enquiring into what was wrong with the country. An apocalyptic essay on the coming elimination of the working man by a woman writer better known for her romantic novels sold 350,000 copies in a year. News weeklies reported how the best and brightest of the nation's youth were fleeing the constipated world of French business; a former presidential adviser, Jacques Attali, warned that in today's mobile world, 'Hotel France could find itself empty'. The title of a book by the head of France's Institute of Demography asked simply, *Will France Disappear?* while an annual social analysis identified 'a collective depression, an angst and a refusal to change'. A Gaullist deputy wrote of a national nervous breakdown, and a leading political commentator, Jean-Marie Domanech, depicted France as resembling a more successful Soviet Union, prisoner to grand plans that never work but which draw attention away from current difficulties – and which end up sinking its people into a mass version of Madame Bovary's dreamy self-deception.

The election of a left-wing government in the summer of 1997 lightened the national mood. The impact was compounded by the

World Cup victory and a cyclical European economic upturn. It was all very encouraging, particularly since the unfolding comfort blanket meant that basic problems could be avoided, for the time being at least. The future remained more problematic.

Self-confident as they like to appear, the French have increasingly fallen back on artificial comforts. They imbibe more alcohol than any other people in Western Europe: 2 million of them are estimated to be completely alcohol-dependent, and between 30,000 and 60,000 die each year from drink-related illnesses. One-third of the population soothes itself with nicotine. Between 1 and 2 million are thought to use cannabis on a regular basis – one report estimated that as many as 7 million people had tried marijuana at least once while the number of people picked up for drugs offences has doubled in five years. On a different drugs front, the Tour de France bicycle race was tarnished in 1998 by a string of doping scandals.

Medical spending has shot up, and not simply as a result of the cost of new equipment. The French still keep a close watch on the state of their livers and worry about being caught in a draught, but nobody seems to have a common cold any more; they suffer instead from the much more serious-sounding *rhino-laryngite*. France has more psychiatrists than any other European country, four times as many now as in 1980. The number of people working in the health sector doubled between 1970 and 1988 and pharmacists grow rich on the endless prescriptions with which doctors soothe the national hypochondria. In some prisons, half the inmates are on pills. A study published in 1998 put the number of overweight people at 16 million – blaming stress and psychological problems as well as fast food and lack of exercise.

Though the Pope attracted a million young Catholics from all over the world to a mass at Longchamp racecourse in 1997, seeking comfort in orthodox religion does not seem a popular remedy. While four-fifths of the French have been baptised, only 17.5 per cent are counted as practising Catholics; infant baptisms have fallen from 92 per cent of babies to 58 per cent in the last forty years, and only half the French get married in church today compared to 77 per cent four decades ago. In the mid-1980s there were 40,000 Catholic priests; ten years later, there were 22,500. But 40,000 just happens to be the estimated number of people now offering a different kind of pastoral care as psychiatrists, psychologists and other 'psys'.

The French pride themselves on being pioneers of rational thought and Cartesian logic, but only one-third of them disagree with the proposition that success in life is pretty much determined by forces outside an individual's control. The national on-line data system, Minitel, offers hundreds of services providing astrology, tarot readings and other guides to the future. A survey by a government organisation reports that just over half the French believe in healing through the laying-on of hands, one-third think dreams predict the future and a quarter are prepared to put their faith in soothsayers and palm-readers. The main monthly astrology magazine reports that readers used to write in with queries about love, but now ask about un-employment. Demand has been rising for the services of the eighty exorcists recognised by the Catholic Church. Cults thrive, with police registering between 150 and 170 main sects and 800 satellites, ranging from a well-behaved Japanese group in a château outside Paris to the Solar Temples on the Swiss border, where forty-eight people died in a mass suicide and killings in 1994.

There are, it must be said, plenty of precedents. An early article of faith among French Christians was that a martyr executed in Paris walked ten kilometres to his burial ground in the suburbs with his sev-ered head in his hands. In the fourth century, St Martin of Tours avoided being crushed by a falling tree by making the sign of the cross, and Simplicius, the Bishop of Autun in Burgundy, used the same device to root local oxen to the ground, thereby converting four hundred awed locals to Christianity. Joan of Arc was guided by voices from above. The repeatedly rediscovered French seer known as Nostradamus is said by his true believers to have predicted the death of Elizabeth I, the execution of Charles I, the French Revolution, the rise of Hitler and the spread of Islamic fundamentalism. Several royals fell for charlatans – even the great unifying king, Louis XI, spent his last years listening to a guru in a cave outside his château on a hill above Tours. Bonaparte said that he took counsel on important deci-sions from a 'little red man'. Christian Dior depended on a clairvoyant up to the day he ignored her advice and went on a slimming cure in Italy to render himself more attractive to his boyfriend, only to col-lapse and die in the process. More recently, France's leading astrologer drew up charts for President Mitterrand on his political opponents.

Despite all this supernatural assistance, doubt is everywhere. Successive governments have worried about one of the most basic elements of all in national life – the number of people living in France. If it were as densely populated as England, France would have three times as many inhabitants as the 58 million who actually live in the Hexagon. At the beginning of the nineteenth century, France had a population two and a half times that of Britain; today, the two nations are about equal. There are many explanations for this, ranging from the idealisation of a small family nurtured by that seminal reactionary, Jean-Jacques Rousseau, to the huge death-toll of the First World War. The French, according to a recent survey, have intercourse more often than any other people on Earth and their governments have traditionally awarded large payments to couples who procreate – still, the population remains obstinately low.

Even as solid a national institution as the country's ninety-five thermal resorts, with their baths of mud- and mineral-enriched waters, has been pronounced by a minister to be 'in a state of crisis'. And the French snob's bedside book, the *Bottin Mondain*, which lists 44,000 of the social elite, has felt the need to include a section on table manners. So what have things come to when high society needs to be told not to eat *foie gras* with a knife?

Move from the personal to the practical, and there too some of France's most prized achievements turn out to have a darker side. The motorway network may be among the best in Europe, but twice as many people die on the roads each year in France as in Britain, and in 1997 Paris was the scene of the world's most famous car crash ever. Closer to the wallet, 80 per cent of its motorways impose tolls, compared to a free ride in Germany and Britain. The size of the network and the cost of high-speed trains helped to make the SNCF railway service one of the world's biggest loss-making enterprises in the mid-1990s – though the deficit was slashed in 1997. Proud as successive governments have been of all those nuclear power stations, the Socialists and their Green partners decided in 1998 to close down France's major fast-breeder reactor. Quite apart from the 10-billion-franc cost of the seven-year operation, this raised the decidedly tricky question of what to do with its radioactive contents – and there was also an awkward report in the *British Medical Journal* suggesting that children who swam in the sea near another nuclear plant ran a higher risk of contracting leukaemia than those who bathed elsewhere.

If France remains the world's top tourist destination, it seems to attract some pretty economical guests: the 45 million visitors to the United States in 1996 spent more than twice as much as France's 62 million tourists. Overall, tourist revenues fell by 5 billion francs in the first half of the 1990s. The most popular paid-for tourist attraction in France is no longer the Eiffel Tower or the entrance-fee sections of Notre Dame, but the European Disneyland, which was denounced by the Parisian elite as a 'cultural Chernobyl' when it opened. The Club Méditerranée plunged into loss in 1996, and was revealed to have kept dossiers on clients who indulged in affairs when on holiday. Denouncing the amateurism with which the holiday village chain had been run ('140 clubs around the world and one at its Paris headquarters', as the *Financial Times* put it), the man who had made Disneyland work in France moved in and watched impassively as the founding family walked out in protest, talking vaguely of starting a new resort concept – for the elderly.

Lift the velvet curtain at many of those châteaux, manor houses and dovecotes set back from the roads of rural France, and one finds a less than perfect fabric. An estimated 400,000 historic buildings do not have protected status. Many are crumbling away. It was not until 1957 that the first twentieth-century building was recognised for its architectural value. The Romanesque church of the Burgundian village of Vézelay may be classed as a world heritage site by Unesco and attract 800,000 visitors a year, but the local mayor had to threaten to shut its doors before the state coughed up 10 million francs for badly needed repairs. It was a Japanese television network which paid to provide the *Mona Lisa* with a room of her own in the Louvre in 1998. The government spokeswoman might speak lyrically of the Roman amphitheatre of Arles, but there was no money to stop it falling to bits. The newspaper *Le Figaro* estimates that state spending on the 40,000 classified sites falls more than 25 per cent below what is required, and that some 700 million francs needs to be spent on the far more numerous, if smaller, unclassified sites. The director of the national heritage foundation says that it would take about the same amount each year for the next quarter of a century to restore 1,500 major monuments. At a time of tight budgets, that can only sound like whistling in the wind.

The divisions of inheritance under the legal system bequeathed by the Napoleonic Code has split up country estates. But it is not only families who sell off their country jewels to divide the proceeds between brothers and sisters. The Defence Ministry put up for sale the eighteenth-century fort at Verdun, the army's headquarters in the First World War battle in which 340,000 French and German soldiers died. The cottage where Joan of Arc was born has been covered with yellow paint which leaves it, in the words of one newspaper, looking like a slice of bread and butter. The French, it has been said, treat their national heritage as they might an ageing mistress: 'Occasionally with indulgence, more often with neglect.'

Or, too often, with concrete. Much of the Riviera has been blotched with ugly but highly lucrative developments. It was only in 1997 that the city council of the turn-of-the-century resort of Biarritz on the Atlantic coast revolted against plans to build yet another tourist complex, and drew up a list of the town's architectural gems to be saved from destruction. In Paris, one bank of the Seine has been ruined by the express road system where the Princess of Wales crashed to her death. The presence of an environmentalist in the Cabinet did not stop the 80,000-seat stadium built on the edge of the capital for the 1998 World Cup being made mostly of PVC.

François Mitterrand's new opera house at the Bastille was the apple of the President's eye in his last years, but it has been battered by the dismissals of a string of directors, money troubles, politics, bad acoustics, a set collapse which killed one person and injured forty – and a tribe of striking musicians, *viz*, 'What is the difference between the Bastille Opéra and the *Titanic*? The orchestra on the *Titanic* actually played.' Between them, the 'People's Opera' and the stately theatre at the Palais Garnier in the centre of the city take subsidies that work out at around 700 francs per seat. On top of which, Mitterrand's pride and joy had to be wrapped in netting to protect passers-by from bits of falling masonry.

Paris still likes to think of itself as the world's cultural centre, though most non-French observers would look elsewhere – across the Atlantic or even, perish the thought, over the Channel. This is not to say that artistic endeavour is not alive and well on both banks of the Seine, just that much of the status which France and its capital assume to be theirs is based more on the past than the present. 'In France, they want to always keep things the same,' as Angelin Preljocaj, a controversial choreographer who grew up in an immigrant ghetto outside Paris, puts it. To repeat Gertrude Stein's remark, Paris may be where the twentieth century 'was', but the accent is now on her tense – and the century is almost over, anyway. Here, as in many areas we will visit in this book, France is torn between the realities of the late twentieth century and the traditions and achievements of its past. Its enormous cultural heritage buttresses the nation's place among the great civilising influences of world history, but it also raises some awkward questions for the present in both popular and high art, and in the more general field of learning.

True, the government spends a lot of money on the Culture Ministry, whose occupant has been a high-profile figure since De Gaulle appointed André Malraux to the job in 1959. One of Malraux's successors, the Socialist Jack Lang, was able to make such a splash in the job that he ended up as the second-ranking minister. But the aura of French culture is waning. There are important theatrical and dance troupes, the Odéon and Bouffes du Nord playhouses in Paris, the Lyon Ballet and the Avignon Festival. But where are the new internationally-respected authors and artists? Who is replacing Édith Piaf or Yves Montand or the clutch of singer-poets led by the classic southern troubadour, Georges Brassens? The new dandy philosopher may pose for *Paris-Match* in a silk shirt, while his peers seek to dazzle with assertions that 'the Gulf War never happened' or with comparisons between the mathematical symbol for the root of minus one and an erect penis. They may, in the words of the writer Pascal Bruckner, 'take, endlessly, the beautiful risk of thinking', but can they claim to be worthy heirs of Jean-Paul Sartre and Raymond Aron? A piercing analysis of current French philosophy by an American and a Belgian academic has shown pretty convincingly that some of France's leading thinkers haven't got much of a clue what they are writing about, and hide their vacuity behind a thicket of meaningless prose.

As for more approachable culture, James Cameron's Oscar-winning *Titanic* took just thirteen weeks to become the most-watched film in

French history, topping a domestic comedy which had held the record for thirty years. Is it a pure accident that great international entertainment successes created by the French in recent years have drawn on classics like *Cyrano de Bergerac, Le Retour de Martin Guerre* and *Les Misérables*? France's last Nobel Prize for Literature was in 1985; for a winner before that, you have to go back to the 1960s. Forty per cent of books borrowed from French libraries are comic strips. France could take pride in having a singer who had the largest number of albums released in Britain in 1996, but he was the old crooner Charles Aznavour. To celebrate French cultural vibrancy, an American news magazine uses ghetto rappers for its cover, not novelists or painters. When France's perennial top rock star, Johnny Hallyday, who says he only takes cocaine these days when he is working, played Las Vegas, he laid on a fleet of charter planes to fly in French fans to make sure the house was full.

And when it comes to the culture of education, the record is far less impressive than might appear from the national pride in the *lycée* system. Yes, children carry up to 10 kilos of textbooks to school each day, and a comparative survey showed that 86 per cent of French pupils said they wanted to do well at school as against only 66 per cent of English children. Yes, a national spelling competition is broadcast live on prime-time Saturday night television. But, reflecting the centralising quest for national order which we will come across time and again, rote learning forms the backbone of French education. Committees in Paris, on which national unions have a large voice, allocate teachers to schools across the country. Though they provide one of the biggest blocs of Socialist voters, those teachers are, themselves, a bulwark of conservatism; when the Education Minister tried to loosen up the system in 1998, he provoked a strike.

But defending the current system grows increasingly difficult for anybody who does not earn a living from what the minister in question described as 'the fat on the mammoth'. France did not make it into the world top twenty when nations were ranked by the numeracy of their nine-year-olds. A test in the mid-1990s found young teenagers making two and a half times as many spelling mistakes as their peers in the 1920s, and doing far less well in solving maths problems. A quarter of pupils entering secondary school do not know how to count; 15 per cent cannot read. Three-quarters of those who sit the *bac-*

calauréat school exit exam pass, but the Education Ministry has let it be known that examiners should be 'indulgent' to ensure a good success rate: one teacher of English who was judged too severe was sent home. In a comparison of examination results in forty-one countries, France finished thirteenth in maths and dropped to twenty-eighth place when it came to science. Only 44 per cent of university students stay the course to get a full degree. An official report found that 35 per cent of young unemployed people on training schemes could not read a simple newspaper article all the way through. An international study of literacy standards in the mid-1990s would have revealed that 40 per cent of French people aged between sixteen and sixty-five had difficulty reading and understanding everyday texts, had not the report been deemed so shaming that the government insisted on all mentions of France being cut from the published version.

This is particularly serious because language is a particularly serious matter for France. In the 1970s, President Georges Pompidou declared it was the French language which made his nation more than just another country in the world. In pursuit of purity, the 'immortal' members of the venerable Académie Française spend years dancing on pinheads, reflecting in all their pomp the strength of a conservatism which goes far deeper than politics, and which we will encounter throughout this book. They epitomise the deadly combination of an over-riding faith in codification and a distrust of change which permeates too much of French life. The members of the Académie know, of course, that they are – in the words of one of their members, Jean d'Ormesson – only immortal while they are alive. But this realisation makes the mission of laying down the rules for the future all the more imperative. This is not a scholastic ivory-tower affair. Language has long been a matter for official meddling – it took legislation at the turn of the century to authorise the abandonment of the imperfect subjunctive mood. Ministers fight to hold back the tide of English and American words flowing into French. A linguistic defence association is trying to keep English off French-based Internet sites. In an increasingly fluid world, all this looks horribly like a sign of a profound lack of national self-confidence in the ability of the French tongue to stand up for itself, to adapt and to digest foreign terms when they are useful.

Domestically, the Académie has a running battle with women

members of the government who wish to be called 'Madame *la* Ministre' rather than the traditional 'Madame *le* Ministre'. The ministers argue that their sex entitles them to a feminine definite article, while the Academicians, including a woman historian, point out that they have got it all wrong and that, since French does not have a neutral gender, the masculine is used for neutral cases. But the Académie's real target is the spread of English, and here it flies in the face of the everyday reality of international crossbreeding. While the French absorbs terms from English, *The Times* heads its superior secretarial jobs section 'La Crème de la Crème', and airports signal that planes are En Route rather than On Their Way. In London, a louche entrepreneur who enchants his coterie with his soi-disant joie de vivre is dropped off at his pied-à-terre in Beauchamp Place by his blasé chauffeur who manoeuvres his flamboyant limousine into its garage at the end of a cul-de-sac while his wife has a rendezvous for a tête-à-tête with a chaperone – and a distinct sense of déjà vu. In Paris, meanwhile, un dealer d'Ecstasy drives le break from le parking to pick up une top-model for un week-end avec le jet-set. Bridge players in London finesse a trick while tennis men in Paris drop un lob to the back of the court. What is worse for the socially ambitious: finding yourself hors de combat as a fait accompli in Britain or being blackboulé by l'establishment in France?

The Académie's criteria are not always very clear – the latest edition of its dictionary bans le cash-flow and le deal but allows le dead-heat and le boom. And the French have always been adept at inventing terms out of English, from La Walterscottomanie of the 1820s to les rugbymen of today. Nightclub denizens of the 1960s showed their style by ordering 'un baby' Scotch. Le footing is less in fashion than it once was – what's wrong with a promenade, after all? But, if you are seeking Le Standing, you might be tickled to receive a card known as un Bristol telling you to wear un Smoking at a black-tie dinner party. A magazine writes about a manager being 'scotché' to his desk; a radio presenter calls Louis Armstrong 'un scatman'; a redesign is known as 'un relookage'; and an airline is 'surbooké'.

But, for the powers that are in France, language is too precious to be left to the ordinary people. So the government limits the number of foreign songs that can be played on the radio, and issues a 74-page list of 'foreign terms or improper terms to avoid or replace'. Not content with its domestic crusade to keep English at bay, France spends a lot of money promoting its own language abroad, through an organisation known as La Francophonie. Since its foundation in 1986, the association's membership and character have followed unexpected paths. Some of the countries which lined up to join, such as Bulgaria and Moldova, were not exactly known as buzzing French-speaking centres. On the other hand, Israel, where there are reckoned to be almost 1 million French speakers, was kept out after Lebanon waved its veto, while Algeria – with the second largest population of French speakers outside Europe – decided to boycott La Francophonie and to declare English its second language after Arabic.

The organisation needs members wherever it can find them. Despite the extravagant claims from Paris, only 2 per cent of the world's population speak French, putting it in ninth place in the language stakes. Just 6 per cent of pupils and students around the globe learn French as a foreign language. Five hundred million people live in countries which belong to La Francophonie, but only a fifth of them are reckoned to speak French fluently. The gap between illusion and reality was shown vividly when forty-nine member nations of La Francophonie gathered for a summit in Hanoi at the end of 1997. Paris put up 75 million francs to help stage the meeting. For a few days, the old colonial capital of Vietnam took on the patina of a Francophone city; thousands of waiters, hostesses, porters and drivers underwent crash courses in French, and signs in French suddenly appeared in the streets. The illusion was spread, but the truth is that fewer than 1 per cent of Vietnamese speak French. When I visited Hanoi in 1995, I came across only two men who could converse in the language, both in their seventies. At the main French-owned hotel, English reigns, and the taxi meters are set in US dollars.

That did not deter the proponents of La Francophonie. Having failed to save him his job at the United Nations, France enrolled the ousted Francophone Secretary-General, Boutros Boutros-Ghali, to head the organisation. Mr Boutros-Ghali told the Hanoi meeting that he saw the future of the association in 'cultural diversity and multi-lingualism, which constitute the true quality of the human heritage'. What that boiled down to was an attempt to set up a counterweight to the power and influence of the United States. Nothing new in that as far as France is concerned. The snag, however, was that the enterprise was sailing under false colours, and involved some pretty nasty associates. How heavily Mr Boutros-Ghali's rhetoric weighed in the hearts and minds of the warlords of Cambodia or the despots from Africa who mingled with President Jacques Chirac in the Vietnamese capital was questionable. The hosts showed their devotion to diversity by pulling the plug on French broadcasters who mentioned a damning report about human rights in Vietnam – and cynics noted the French businessmen hovering on the sidelines of the discussions about culture and multi-lingualism who were busy snapping up contracts for telephone lines, a water supply system and a cement works.

Closer to home, there was bad news on the European front for the champions of French: a two-year survey which leaked out early in 1998 revealed that, for the first time, more European Union documents were translated into other EU languages from English than from French. Only two of the eleven countries applying to join the Union in 1998 put their bid in French. Even Romania, a member of La Francophonie, preferred English. One linguistic chauvinist has a simple answer to this. A bow-tied anti-American French aristocrat, with the appropriate name of Hervé Lavenir de Buffon, has set up a Centre for European Study and Action which wants the European Union to adopt French as its single official language and the United Nations headquarters to be moved to 'the centre of the world' – i.e., Paris. There are plenty of precedents for such a view. Victor Hugo once told two English ladies who sympathised with his ignorance of English: 'When England wishes to converse with me, it will learn to speak French.'

If the French language is punted on the kind of rancorous base proclaimed by the likes of M. de Buffon, the result can only demean the land of Rabelais, Flaubert and Jacques Prévert, of the invention of Raymond Queneau and *Zazie dans le Métro* and a language which distinguishes between its varieties of prostitutes with a dozen different terms depending on the way they ply their trade. One might have thought that a tongue with the cultural baggage of French could look after itself. But the protection of French linguistic virginity is a well-established intellectual industry which foreigners query at their peril. Still, it was striking that, for all the rhetoric in Hanoi, the new Prime Minister of 1997 forgot to assign the ministerial portfolio for La

Francophonie to anybody when he took office.

In a further departure from inward-looking orthodoxy, the most vibrant linguistic growth is taking place among people who couldn't give two hoots for the scriptures of the Académie. Young city-dwellers have developed a whole new patois known as *verlan*, from *l'envers* (opposite), in which syllables are wrenched around to produce new words – thus a woman, *une femme*, becomes *une meuf*, while a policeman, *un flic*, turns into *un keuf*. France's linguistic ayatollahs had better seek solace on the line to Madame la Marquise. This is, after all, a world in which the number of French people who emigrate in search of work is rising steadily, and for many of those who jet off in search of a job, the English language is as important as a passport.

If the French still see their language as a badge of international pride, and like to talk about the radiant influence of their culture on the world, it is, in part, because theirs is a country still coming to terms with its post-imperial place in the world. The twentieth century began with France possessing the second most important empire on Earth, spread across large tracts of North and West Africa, through the rubber and opium fields of Indochina to a collection of scattered outposts from the South Seas to the North Atlantic. For the powers that were in Paris, it was a cultural as well as an economic and polit-ical exercise: France wanted to spread its ideas, its language, to turn Africans or Indochinese into French-minded people worshipping at the altar of the Republic. An extremely thin upper-crust did, indeed, feel as comfortable on the boulevards of Paris as they did at home, but the motivation for a Vietnamese rice farmer or a Senegalese teacher to become French in mind and spirit was tenuous, to say the least. Now only the outposts remain, reclassified for more correct times into overseas departments and territories, known as Dom-Toms (Départe-ments d'Outre-Mer/Territoires d'Outre-Mer) – the Caribbean islands of Guadeloupe and Martinique; French Guyana, on the shoulder of South America; the islands of Réunion in the Indian Ocean and Saint-Pierre-et-Miquelon off the east coast of Canada; French Poly-nesia, New Caledonia and Wallis-et-Futuna in the South Pacific; plus French-held frozen wastes in the Antarctic.

Ministers speak of these places as part of a worldwide destiny, and extol the nation's responsibility to people who, even if they live on an atoll on the other side of the world, are officially regarded as being as French as if they were eating tripe and onions in the bistros of Lyon. The overseas departments and territories have twenty-two seats in the National Assembly between them, some with tiny electorates – the Gaullist who won Wallis-et-Futuna in the far Pacific in 1997 got in with 7 per cent of the number of votes that returned the new Prime Minister near Toulouse. The truth is that the Dom-Toms are not a comfortable appendage for a modern nation. Few could survive without handouts from Paris. Most have high unemployment. Guyana, once considered only good to house the Devil's Island prison colony, now draws half its tax revenue from the space launch base at Kourou, spends sixteen times as much on imports as it earns from exports, and has seen 1,000 companies go bust in two years. Guadeloupe is mainly notable for having spent 121 million francs on a cycling stadium which is used once a year. On the other side of the globe, French Polynesia has relied on funds poured in for nuclear testing on the atoll of Mururoa: in a corruption case involving a million-franc bribe to a local official from a private clinic, the court said the episode had led to the belief that, in Polynesia, anything could be bought. These territories are stuffed with civil servants who are paid large bonuses to compensate for the high cost of living – that is to say, the cost of buying French goods tens of thousands of miles from the Hexagon. Why, one might ask, should the taxpayer of Clermont-Ferrand or Rennes stump up to keep a middle-rank pen-pusher in a soft life under the palm trees? But that question never seems to be put, and when the government tried to do something about it on Réunion, a couple of protests from the functionaries involved was enough to produce an unseemly retreat.

Not that all the inhabitants of these territories seem grateful for being gazetted as part of France. Presidents in Paris talk emotionally about France's brother citizens spread around the planet, but some recipients of fraternity presume to agitate for independence. Bloody incidents in New Caledonia, including one in which four gendarmes were killed and twenty-seven taken hostage in an attack on a police station in 1988, have paved the way for the gradual introduction of self-government though Paris will keep control of justice, law and order and the currency. With an unemployment rate put officially at

40 per cent, Réunion is constantly referred to as an island volcano waiting to erupt. Guyana was hit by riots after the arrest of separatists. At the 1995 presidential election, 42 per cent of the overseas electorate showed how interested they were in French politics by abstaining.

More significant than the Dom-Toms has been France's involvement in Africa. For decades, this enabled Paris to see itself as playing an important role in an area from which other big powers were absent. The French began to grant independence to their colonies in the 1950s, but, in many cases, the old links stayed. The interests flowed both ways. Big companies and political parties used friendly former colonial states as handy screens for below-board activities: smaller entrepreneurs set up all manner of businesses – from garbage collection to personal security. A special ministry was set up under De Gaulle to handle Africa; when the Foreign Ministry tried to take it over in 1995, African heads of state protested and the President publicly reaffirmed its independence. For decades, France backed its favoured dictators with 8,000 troops stationed across the continent and an equal number on standby at home. In all, they have intervened on more than two dozen occasions since the 1960s to put down rebellions and mutinies, to prop up France's friends, and to perpetuate what the *Wall Street Journal* dubbed a 'virtual empire'.

Three decades after France gave its African conquests their independence, the neo-colonial web which offered protection to dictators in exchange for influence and raw materials looked distinctly tattered, but it took Paris a long time to re-evaluate its role. At the height of the Rwandan tragedy, France helped to supply weapons to the massacring Hutus, who came to be known by the French term of '*les génocidaires*', and sent in troops to provide safe havens for the killers. There were persistent reports – denied by Paris – that the missile which ignited the tragedy by bringing down the plane carrying the Presidents of Rwanda and Burundi came from a French armoury, and that French troops turned a blind eye to the massacres. But then Paris had never been squeamish about the clients it picked – no less a person than the third President of the Fifth Republic had accepted the big-game-hunting hospitality of the mad self-appointed Emperor Jean Bedel Bokassa, whose refrigerator was reported to have contained the bodies of his enemies stuffed with rice.

Bokassa, a former sergeant in the French colonial army, had been authorised to seize power in the Central African Republic by one of the most enigmatic figures of the Fifth Republic, Jacques Foccart. In the early days of decolonisation, the rotund, multi-chinned Foccart acted as paternalistic patron and guide to a succession of African rulers who were encouraged to see themselves as the children of the wise father-figure in the Élysée Palace. He allowed, or encouraged, a coup here and the suppression of a revolt there. All the while, the former colonies were tied closely to Paris through the presence of French troops and a franc-based monetary system, which enabled the ruling elite to export its money to safe havens abroad at highly favourable rates of exchange. In post-De Gaulle days, a string of visitors from former colonies continued to take the lift to Foccart's ornate apartment in central Paris, where a grey parrot kept this man of the shadows company. There, they received advice on how to run their countries and, above all, on the need to repel any attempt by Washington to influence the continent. It was said that some of them entrusted Foccart with standing orders allowing French troops to intervene – only the dates were left blank. When he died in 1997, the great manipulator who listed his occupation as 'exporter' was seen off with military honours in the courtyard of Les Invalides, close to Bonaparte's last resting-place. Eight heads of state and government from Africa joined the President of the Republic at the funeral.

From Morocco to Zaïre, Foccart and Paris have definitely not been on the side of the angels. In early post-colonial days, that may have reflected sheer realism at a time when nobody cared much about what despots got up to south of the Sahara. Africa provided a happy hunting-ground for French business, and its votes were useful in showdowns with Washington at the United Nations. Arms sales to apartheid-era South Africa – sometimes via client African states – helped the trade balance. But, in time, an inevitable conflict developed with the ideals France made much of promoting elsewhere. How to reconcile support for Václav Havel or *glasnost* in Moscow with backing rulers who shot demonstrators and looted their national treasuries? Naturally, François Mitterrand blamed others. 'It's an inheritance nobody has ever talked to me about,' he complained at a meeting of ministers in 1990 when the matter of Africa's aspirations for democracy were mentioned. 'For the past two years, no minister has presented me with a report asking that things change! There has been a misunderstanding between us. I am surprised and pained to hear what I hear.' As if Mitterrand had had no idea of the nature of his host when his helicopter deposited him on the deck of a dictator's yacht with its forty-place dinner setting in rose crystal, or when the President enjoyed the sun with his friend the King of Morocco, who kept his opponents in some of the worst jails in the world. The one Socialist minister who had wanted to stand up to the dictators had been quickly ditched, leaving the framing of African policy at the Élysée Palace in the hands of Mitterrand's son, Christophe, who became known by the nickname of '*Papa m'a dit*' – 'Dad's told me'. Some years later, *Le Figaro* quoted Mitterrand as having said that, in countries like Rwanda, genocide wasn't such a big thing.

But in the end, even Mitterrand abandoned his hypocrisy and threw his lot in with the good guys, urged on by one of his aides, the Goncourt literary prize-winner Éric Arnoult. 'Given its responsibilities, France cannot remain silent much longer. An announcement of a plan to back the concrete installation of democracy would be welcome,' Arnoult wrote in a note in 1990. 'We cannot continue much longer to struggle openly against the opposition to the ruling regimes, and to expel opposition figures from France as soon as they open their mouths.' At a French–African summit in a resort town on the French coast, the President finally pronounced the word 'democracy'. His guests were not impressed. As *Le Monde* put it, only the sound of the wind on the sea broke through the silence with which they received his plea for the 'universal principle' of democracy. One head of state made it clear that he was more concerned with why French troops had not put down a mutiny by his own soldiers. Others were ready to hold elections – on condition that the outcome could be written down in advance. And, for all his protestations, the President went on aiding and protecting the *génocidaires* in Rwanda.

Mitterrand's successor, a man who liked to put himself forward as somebody who understood non-European values and considered that democracy was not incompatible with a one-party system, was, therefore, more likely to be to their taste. But by the time Jacques Chirac became President, other factors were coming into play. France had already tugged at the monetary carpet by devaluing the Central African Franc by 50 per cent, which forced the countries involved to face up to international competition. Some of the old tyrants were losing their grip. Above all, it was becoming increasingly embarrassing for France to be seen as a principal backer of horror figures like the President, Marshal, Guide and Helmsman of Zaïre, Mobutu Sese Seko, one of the world's leading kleptocrats, described by one French minister as 'a walking bank balance with a leopard-skin cap'.

Zaïre had been a colony of Belgium, not France, but it was also for many years the biggest French-speaking nation outside the Hexagon, and Mobutu's loyalty to Paris was never in much doubt so long as France made sure it was in his interest. He bathed in French perfume, and spent a slice of his pillaged fortune on a sumptuous Riviera property. Whenever he was in Europe, Mobutu was visited by French officials who hurried to his hospital ward when he was treated for cancer and paid court on him on the Côte d'Azur. Even in his campaign for national 'authenticity' he stayed linguistically faithful; when the wearing of suits was banned, the replacement native garment was called an 'abacost' – from the French words 'à bas le costume'.

France stuck by Mobutu to the last. There were reports of French help in despatching Serbian mercenaries to try to prop up his regime. But, in the end, all the efforts of Foccart's successors could not keep the Guide-Helmsman on his throne, though even after he was deposed, some old stagers could not give up the ghost: the deputy to France's ambassador in Kinshasa doggedly kept up contacts with members of the old regime who were trying to stage a comeback – and was expelled for his pains. France's obtuse and murderous policy in Zaïre followed by Mobutu's fall in the summer of 1997 marked a death-knell for the traditional French presence in Africa. Paris had few friends there any more. As a French academic close to African policy put it: 'We had this notion that dictators were good for us and Africans didn't deserve any better. We have been behaving like slobs, and finally we have to pay the bill.'

What made things even worse was the way the Americans weighed in after decades during which Paris had aimed, above all, at keeping Washington's nose out of Francophone Africa. The great anti-American seer, Jacques Foccart, was gone. Africa was no longer France's backyard. The US Ambassador to Zaïre told journalists that France was incapable of imposing its will in Africa, that the Cold War was over and that 'it is no longer a matter of supporting dictators just because they are pro-Western'. As if that was not enough, President

Clinton's first Secretary of State made the Washington view perfectly plain, declaring that 'the time has passed when outside powers could consider whole groups of countries as their own private domains'. Soon afterwards, Jacques Chirac told a French–African summit that it was no longer the role of any non-African country to interfere in the continent's affairs. That took a little time to materialise: French troops went into the Central African Republic three times in eighteen months to put down anti-government mutinies. A President of the Congo Republic who had favoured American oil interests over a French company was overthrown – but the main role was played by other African countries rather than by Paris. Whatever Gaullist nostalgists might feel, the die was cast: the Socialist government elected in 1997 decided to cut its forces in Africa from 8,000 to 5,200, and to shut down its base in the Central African Republic. Ministers insisted that the new force would be more mobile and more modern, and would still enable France to make its presence felt when needed. The government reformed aid policy, in part to fight corruption, and the Prime Minister spoke of a new partnership with Africa, which would demand respect for human rights and growing democratisation. Apart from anything else, as France struggled to meet the European budget criteria, the cost of maintaining a post-colonial empire across Africa had simply become too expensive.

Nobody made this plainer than France's most important dictatorial friend of the past quarter-century. Jacques Foccart had picked the name of Omar Bongo from a list of potential Presidents of Gabon in 1967. His country is France's single biggest source of oil. As we will see, Bongo's regime has vital and dubious links with the Elf Aquitaine oil company, French intelligence and French politicians. One of his remarks had for years been taken as a motto for the relationship between Paris and its former colonies: 'France without Africa is like a car without petrol. But Africa without France is like a car without a driver.' Thirty years after Foccart put him in power, Bongo struck a rather different note. 'It is high time for Gabon to erase this image of being France's private hunting-ground [and] to turn towards a partner like the United States, which is more open and more understanding towards it,' he wrote. Bill Clinton might not be too thrilled at such an endorsement from a despot for whom a bad election is one in which he gets only 90 per cent support. France's post-colonial edifice had clearly reached the end of its life. The dictators might find it harder than they expected to live without the unquestioning support of the Foccart machine, but France could no longer presume to be puppet-master of vast tracts of Africa. Its horizons had contracted: it was, in another of Bongo's phrases, just a medium-sized power to which, by implication, its former colonies would no longer look for protection, let alone guidance.

France's post-colonial experience provides one glaring contradiction of its national motto of *Liberté, Égalité, Fraternité*. But there are also some striking exceptions closer to home, for instance involving the treatment of just over half the population.

The richest non-royal woman in the world may be French (the L'Oréal cosmetics heiress Liliane Bettencourt). The symbol of the Republic may be female; French women writers may stand out as feminist icons; more women may be more highly educated than men; and a masculinist movement claiming 30,000 members may protest at the 'feminisation' of French society. But French women feel hard done by, and with reason when it comes to being in a position to affect the way the country is run. Until the legislative election of 1997, the National Assembly had the lowest proportion of women of any parliament in the European Union, ranking seventy-second in the world. The only woman to have become Prime Minister, Édith Cresson, calls French politics a 'closed men's club'. Élisabeth Guigou, a former European Minister who later became Minister of Justice, has complained of the 'below-the-waist jokes' directed at her in parliament: she once stared down a macho male minister when he suggested that she could increase her popularity by wearing crimson lingerie. A former Environment Minister recalls the time when a deputy responded to a female colleague with the name of a rap group which means, literally, 'fuck your mother'; on another occasion, a male member of parliament interrupted a female speaker during a debate on rape to assure her that she wasn't at risk. Hunters demonstrating against one of her successors in Paris in 1998 waved placards reading: 'Dominique, get back to your housework and leave us alone.'

Disrespect for women can be traced, like so much else in France, back to the supposed new dawn after the fall of the Bastille. British writers deplored the political influence of women in eighteenth-century France and the first political movement run by women for women, Les Citoyennes Républicaines Révolutionnaires, was established in Paris in 1793. But the Revolution gave rights to just about everybody except women and slaves. Emancipation of the latter only came after the restoration of the monarchy; French women had to wait rather longer. Napoléon declared them to be 'the property of man as a fruit tree belongs to the gardener', and his legal code gave men power over their wives that lasted for more than a century. Up to 1938, French wives needed the permission of their husbands to get a passport, and it was only in 1965 that they gained the right to join a profession without his authorisation. The Revolution may have proclaimed equality for all, but women did not get the vote until 1944: twenty-five years later, Charles de Gaulle was said to have ridiculed a suggestion that he should establish a ministry for women, by wondering if he should also set up a ministry for his wife's favourite occupation of knitting. Asked when France would have a woman president, Édith Cresson, now a European Commissioner, replied: 'Not in a hundred years.'

Cresson also recalls that when she went to business school, there was a section for '*jeunes filles*'. 'We were told that we would become confidantes to our bosses: "Everybody will be jealous. You'll have to be impeccable." I was about to explode. The boys were going to be the bosses. And they still are.' Women on average earn significantly less than men. For those who succeed professionally, a stereotype has been drawn up of the strong, upwardly mobile female who lives a barren personal life, sacrificing the traditional values of husband and children, the warm family hearth and tasty traditional dishes on the altar of ambition, with its consequent stress, empty relationships, snatched holidays and heartache in the early hours of the morning. French men like their women to look good, but they also like them to know their place. 'Swimming teachers concentrate on the times of boys and the style of girls,' according to Élisabeth Guigou. 'Faced with competition from women, men feel obliged to act like fighting cocks,' says France's champion woman cyclist, Jeannie Longo. 'The most unjust thing is that even mediocre performances by a man get applauded, while a woman has to pull off a real exploit to get noticed.' She knows what she is talking about: Olympic gold medallist and a leading world cyclist for fifteen years, Longo is less well known than any flash-in-the-pan Tour de France competitor.

There have, it is true, been strong and popular women ministers on both the right and left. But, until very recently, they have been notable by their rarity, and by the way in which they were kept to certain domains – welfare, social affairs, the environment. In 1995, the right-wing premier Alain Juppé appointed twelve women ministers, who immediately became known as '*les Jupettes*' (the miniskirts). His technocrat heart hardly seemed to be in it. Christine Chavet, one of the twelve, recalls that the Prime Minister called her in, asked her which languages she spoke, and told her not to leave Paris. Soon afterwards, she learned from the radio news that she had been appointed Junior Minister for Trade. Some months later, she and the other Jupettes were summoned to the Prime Minister's office in the middle of the afternoon. 'It was like a dentist's waiting room – people were waiting everywhere. Given the crush in the ante-chamber, I guessed why we were there. It was like a Feydeau farce with the doors opening and closing. Some came out in tears. One woman read *Le Monde* out loud to calm herself. Then she ordered tea – there were cups everywhere. Juppé just told me: "I'm sorry. I bring bad news." Not very elegant, that's the least one can say. Afterwards, we arranged meetings among ourselves because we hadn't even had time to say goodbye. We had been shipped out.'

Eighteen months later, Juppé was calling for positive discrimination for women and declaring France to be a lopsided democracy which 'only advances on one leg'. A radio commentator of the time quipped that the role of women in French public life was only slightly better than under the fundamentalist Talebans in Afghanistan. And then there was a frisson when a collection of letters appeared in which the feminist icon, Simone de Beauvoir, called herself a little loving frog and promised her American lover, Nelson Algren: 'I will do the washing-up. I will sweep the floor. I will buy the eggs and rum cakes myself. I will not touch your hair, your cheeks, your shoulders without permission.'

Still, change is in the air: the number of women sitting in the National Assembly nearly doubled in 1997 to sixty-three; forty-two of them are Socialists. That was still pretty lopsided given that women make up 53 per cent of the electorate. But the new government of the left had a woman, Martine Aubry, as its deputy leader and another, Élisabeth Guigou, at the Justice Ministry, one of the most sensitive posts in the Cabinet given the tide of politico-business scandal sweeping France. The Mayor of Strasbourg, Catherine Trautmann, became the government spokesperson. One day, maybe, sexual equality at the very top of politics might prove a vote-winner: that, alone, could sway the old masculine establishment. Some think that Martine Aubry could prove Édith Cresson's presidential prediction wrong by almost a hundred years. But she still had to struggle to escape from typecasting as the daughter of the perennially popular Jacques Delors to establish herself as a formidable political presence in her own right.

Nowhere have the end-of-century realities confronting France been felt more forcefully than in the economy. It is here that the basic circle of discomfort was closed, boosting the Pessimism Index and the consumption of tranquilisers. From one point of view, France's performance since the mid-1980s has been a success with low inflation, a strong franc and leaner companies. But, for many of the French, economic revival translated into more than a decade of low growth, declining morale and, above all, persistent double-digit unemployment. Though they grew more cheerful with the expansion that set in during 1997–98, French managers were for years less optimistic about the future than their Western European peers. Even some of those who earned the praise of the international financial community recognised the extent of the social dangers the country faced.

The state planning commission has forecast that France needs annual growth of 3.5 per cent to bring the jobless toll well into single figures. That is way above anything achieved in recent years, and even the hopeful Socialist government could not set its sights above 2.7 per cent for 1999. The Organisation for Economic Co-operation and Development (OECD) puts the level of structural unemployment in France at 10 per cent, and the expansion needed to achieve a really significant reduction looked so unattainable that the new Socialist government elected in 1997 grabbed at the mirage of a shorter working week and artificial job-creation as the answer to the challenge of mass unemployment. Meanwhile, some 750,000 of the unemployed are living below the official poverty line for a single person. No wonder that the Finance Minister, Dominique Strauss-Kahn, was greeted at the World Economic Forum in Davos in 1998 by an American businessman who told him: 'You have the worst job in the world.' Indeed, were it not for the public sector and changes in the methods of calculating the jobless total, the employment picture would be considerably worse: while Britain and the United States were cutting the number of state employees and expanding private employment, jobs in the public sector in France increased by nearly a fifth between 1980 and 1995. As for the unemployment figures, they were subject to frequent massaging which managed to keep them from soaring away from the 3 million mark. A European forecasting unit puts the true level of unemployment among under-25s at almost 30 per cent. France's main planning body put the number of people in economic difficulties at 7 million – it also reported that the proportion of householders aged under thirty who were living in poverty had doubled since 1984 to 18.5 per cent. Polls show a huge majority of people expecting unemployment to remain at its record levels, while few put any faith in job-creation schemes – their pessimism seemed to be borne out by a parliamentary report which said that less than a fifth of jobs conjured up under such programmes involved real productive work. Even those in employment could feel less and less secure: nearly one-third of French workers are on limited-time contracts, and the head of the country's young employers' association talked of creating 'a sub-proletariat'.

Setting aside such personal pain, the scene behind the curtain is not as rosy or France's standing quite as high as the boosters would have it. The state debt has doubled since 1990. Taxes and social security contributions take a higher proportion of national wealth than in any other major European Union nation. The number of pensioners will rise to one-fifth of the population by the end of the century, as will the ranks of students: both groups will be increasingly expensive to look after. The steadily ageing population contains a financial time-bomb: by the year 2030 there will be fewer than two workers for every pensioner, raising big questions about funding the country's traditionally generous retirement payments. The Paris Bourse has made great strides but its turnover is less than half that of London, and it was excluded from a major link-up between the London and Frankfurt markets in 1998. By one comparison, the value of publicly held shares in high-tech companies in Silicon Valley, alone, approaches that of all publicly traded French shares. Among international currency markets, France ranks only eighth, dwarfed not only by Britain, the US and Japan but also by Singapore and Hong Kong. France may have done well in attracting venture capital, but luring Toyota's new European plant and its 2,000 jobs to the depressed northern city of Valenciennes involved subsidies that could run to half a billion francs. France will remain a major trading force, but if domestic demand does grow, the boost to imports – allied to the effect of the slump in big export markets in the Far East – could put a brake on the boom in the trade balance.

Despite the significant business potential in some major mergers of recent years, and the advent of some thoroughly modern managers, international listings show a distinct pattern of just a handful of companies from the Hexagon among the biggest players: the Elf Aquitaine oil group was the only French enterprise to figure in the *Financial Times* ranking of the global top one hundred for 1997. Despite the country's worldwide ambitions, no French company appears among the top dozen multinationals. When it comes to profit or returns on earnings or assets, not a single French business figures among the world's top fifty performers. State-controlled enterprises have cut their combined deficit from the horror levels of the early 1990s, but still managed to be 11 billion francs in debt in 1996. Nor did all those telephone lines in China save the company in question from plunging deeply into the red – when the *Financial Times* polled top managers to find Europe's most respected companies, only four firms from France made the top thirty, compared to twice as many from Britain, and when *Fortune* carried out the same exercise worldwide, just two French enterprises finished in the top hundred. A survey by the Economist Intelligence Unit in 1998 ranked France only sixth as the most attractive European country in which to do business.

In some sectors, as we shall see, France has gone through several corporate nightmares, and nowhere more so than in its highly overcrowded and frequently misguided financial sector. While the farmers' bank, the Crédit Agricole, has been a great state-assisted success story, only one French financial institution – the insurance group AXA – figures in the world's top ten by any measure, and only one French bank makes it to Europe's top twenty by capitalisation. While foreign fund managers have been buying into the Bourse, the outflow of French capital to purchase foreign stocks and bonds has also soared. In a sign of the times, an American investment bank overtook national financial institutions to top the French mergers and acquisitions table in the mid-1990s. Even the state's ownership of MGM ended in tears: it came about as the result of a big bank falling for an Italian swindler, and cost taxpayers a billion dollars.

As for cutting-edge industries, France is a minor player. After a costly struggle, the state gave up the fight to make its Bull company a major international computer firm. Figures at the end of 1998 showed France lagging behind Germany and Britain, not to mention the US, Japan and Singapore in per capita ownership of personal computers. A campaign to provide every school pupil with a PC ended in fiasco when lobbying by domestic manufacturers led the government to drop plans to use Apple in favour of a French computer, which proved unable to do the job. France is justly proud of the Post Office's Minitel electronic information network, which delivers 26,000 services to some 6 million terminals in homes, offices and post offices across the country, but its very success encouraged the French to stay with an expensive, limited technology dating from the 1980s rather than moving into the Internet age in a major fashion, though the state telecommunications company has pledged to catch up in cyberspace as it partially privatises itself. Only 5 per cent of France's corporate bosses have an e-mail address. Visiting the President of the Republic, Bill Gates could not refrain from remarking on the lack of computers at the Élysée: Chirac did not get his own e-mail address until 1998, and he specified that his replies to electronic messages would be sent by ordinary post. When it unveiled its programme, the Socialist government of 1997 made no mention of the new electronic world – and an American expert has calculated that only 2 per cent of material on the Internet is in French.

The economic pain of recent years has translated into political disillusion on a major scale. France is now questioning the way it is ruled. The angst set off by the downside of apparently relentlessly applied economic orthodoxy saps the nation's confidence. Those who once worshipped together at the secular altar of Marianne's unitary republican state are split in two. A swelling army of people fearful of losing their position in life confronts an elite which they see to be acting against the best interests of its people. The classic democratic means of effecting change proved empty for too long: in five major elections from 1988 to 1995, the people voted but it was the technocrats who reigned. 'If it is the Bank of France and the financial world which set the law, what value does the vote of the French people have?' asks a union leader. Rather than putting their faith in their representatives in the National Assembly, Frenchmen with a grievance prefer direct action in the streets. Demonstrations are a hallowed element in the national tradition, but the success of lorry-drivers, farmers, fishermen and others in staging sometimes violent protests and getting what they want undermines conventional politics and raises a major concern about the use of force in a modern democracy.

Into this questioning there comes, crucially, the matter of Europe. Properly, the French see themselves as pillars of the community. The bargain struck in the 1950s between French agriculture and German industry has provided the very practical scaffolding for the construction of a new continental system which made a repetition of war between Germany and France impossible. It has brought great economic advantage to France, particularly when Paris fell from fifth to ninth place among contributors to the European Union budget. Sixty per cent of French exports go to the European Union, a higher proportion than for Germany, Britain or Italy. Still, the French cannot escape the challenge which remaining at the forefront of Europe has posed to some of their most cherished national habits as it put millions of their compatriots in an economic vice that bred anger, fear, disenchantment and extremism.

For the first time since the foundation of the Common Market four decades ago, the domestic price of increased European unity came to figure on the central fault-line in French society. An opinion poll in the spring of 1998 showed that 48 per cent of those questioned felt integration threatened their national identity. Views are polarising – while a majority of the French support a European Central Bank and a common currency and oppose a federal European system, the number of those in favour and those against rose significantly in all three cases between 1994 and 1996, with the don't-knows more than halving. One best-selling author, who condemns the European Union as being nothing more than a vehicle for 'Anglo-Saxon ways of doing business', has likened the anti-European sentiment in France to the popular resentment that gave birth to the Revolution of 1789. An easy linguistic jibe adds spice to the mix: who can ignore the similarity between '*franc fort*' (strong franc) and 'Francfort' (Frankfurt), the city where the bankers of Germany lay down the monetary law for Europe? The contrast between the Euro-technocrats and the suffering little people of France is too tempting not to be picked up. 'Rather than the sect of the strong franc, I prefer the France of small shop-keepers, farmers, small and medium-sized firms which create our wealth,' declared the deputy Secretary-General of the Gaullist party in 1996.

The concern is sharpest among the poor and the unemployed, among public-sector workers who fear for their privileges and quail before the opening of national frontiers to competition, and among farmers afraid of losing their subsidies. But it also extends more widely as the years go by. Two-thirds of a group of senior civil servants said they saw the growth of European institutions as threatening the authority of the state on which the Republic rests. In a reflex action during the 1995 presidential election campaign, Jacques Chirac suggested holding a referendum on Europe, despite the fact that one had taken place only three years earlier, and he had backed the successful campaign for a 'yes' vote. 'Everywhere, people are asking themselves what interest there is in building a Europe on the ruins of the welfare state,' writes the editor of the left-wing review *Le Monde Diplomatique*.

The European engagement has come to mean bearing the full price of a market economy run on classic 1980s lines, and that hurts. But raise the possibility of France travelling anywhere other than in the locomotive of continental progress, and you'll be met with a snorting refusal even to entertain the idea. Still, the French gave an early indication of the way their bile was rising when they almost rejected the Maastricht Treaty on Europe at a referendum as long ago as 1992. Five years later, 55 per cent told pollsters they would probably vote against the agreement if given a second chance. A few months after that, they had the opportunity to express themselves at the ballot box when Jacques Chirac called a snap election to get backing for economic policies designed to ensure that France met the Maastricht criteria.

Faced with a choice between a government committed to budget-cutting to keep up with the Germans and a Socialist Party which

promised to put job creation first, voters delivered a stinging defeat to
the President and the orthodox policies he had adopted in 1995 after
telling them that he would bring something new and different to the
party. The Socialist Prime Minister whom he was forced to appoint,
Lionel Jospin, came into office warning that, if French interests were
not served, Paris might not go along with the path agreed at
Maastricht. With a government dependent for its parliamentary
majority on Communists, Green environmentalists and left-wing
Socialists who disliked the idea of a capitalist, market-oriented Union,
France suddenly appeared to have the potential to strike out on its
own.

Proclaiming the beginning of a new employment model not just
for France but also possibly for Europe, the Labour Minister launched
plans to cut the working week from thirty-nine to thirty-five hours
without loss of pay by the end of the century, though nobody was
quite clear about how this was to be achieved or what the effect
would be: the French already worked fewer hours than the
Americans, Japanese or British, but still had far higher unemployment.
The decision provoked a major crisis with the employers' federation,
whose chairman felt obliged to resign. Jospin's problem was that the
idea of a reduction in working hours as a panacea for unemployment
had become such a mantra on the left – and such a cause for his popular Labour Minister – that the government had been obliged to act,
whatever the private doubts of some of its leading figures. As a
European Prime Minister put it to me, Jospin was a Protestant who
thought he had to do what he had promised: he also could not risk a
split within his own ranks. On other fronts, however, it was easier to
allow at least some of the old logic to re-assert itself.

After an audit of public finances had shown that the deficit would
be some way above the Maastricht level, the new Finance Minister
introduced a 32-billion-franc package of deficit-reduction measures.
Sure enough, they were politically slanted, consisting largely of
increases in corporate taxation and a squeeze on the middle class. But
the point had been made that, under the left as under the right,
France was still aiming to hit the 3 per cent level laid down in the
treaty. A couple of months later, despite the Prime Minister's doubts,
the Bank of France moved in step with the Bundesbank in raising
interest rates in a foreshadowing of what lay ahead. Polls showed a

large majority of the French wanting their country to join monetary union from the start. They might vote for Jospin, but that did not mean they would countenance moving out of the continental driving seat; a European Commission poll published soon after the left's victory showed that the balance of opinion in favour of a single currency was still well above the average for the nations involved. The result of the National Assembly election of 1997, which took everybody except the most optimistic left-wingers aback, showed just how tightly the spring of popular anger had been wound against the way the country was being run, bringing Communists into government for the first time for thirteen years and producing the ultimate paradox that it was a dyed-in-the-wool Gaullist nationalist – Jacques Chirac – who nailed his colours to the Euro mast. Naturally, the Socialists and their partners put the best gloss on their prospects while, with five years of his term to run, the President bided his time. The resulting sense of relief sent approval ratings for both Chirac and Jospin to above 50 per cent. But fundamental problems remained below the euphoria, even if both men gained a fresh boost to their popularity as the glow of France's World Cup victory rubbed off on them.

One of the left's main election cards had been to promise to create 700,000 jobs. Helped by an upward turn in the economic cycle, the unemployment rate did fall, but, 18 months after Jospin took office, it was still above 11 per cent, and the 35-hour week initiative had produced only 10,000 new jobs. The government faced recurrent protests over unemployment, and a major outbreak of demonstrations by high school students in 1998. Regional elections that year produced a muddy result, without much progress for the left. Divisions within the coalition held up reforms on everything from the audio-visual system to taxation of stock options. The Prime Minister distanced himself publicly from tough law-and-order measures proposed by the Interior Minister to combat a sudden rise in the crime rate, and the government parties ran sharply competing tickets for the 1999 European elections.

The right-left cohabitation remained popular with the public, but at what price? 'France has come to a halt,' the editor of Le Monde wrote at the beginning of 1999. The choice was between the incessant changes of government seen over the preceding decade or a near paralysis as Chirac and Jospin jockeyed for position for the presidential poll in 2002 while the factions in the broad coalitions below them settled their internal scores. It risked becoming the longest election campaign France had ever seen, and raised the question of whether the Republic which De Gaulle founded in 1958 was reaching the end of its useful life.

Society is changing around the world. The transformation is never easy, but a rough-and-ready distinction can be drawn between those who look forward with hope and those who look fearfully over their shoulders at what they may be about to lose; between those who believe they can turn the next century to their advantage and those who would like to stop the clock right now – or preferably ratchet it back a couple of decades. In France, the great shift in social conditions that occurred from the 1950s onwards is ancient history. It is hard to remember the days when less than a third of homes had a bath or shower and under half had a lavatory of their own (by 1990, only 7 per cent had neither). What is happening now is a moving pattern which continuously reinvents and reinforces itself. Below the coverlet of *la France éternelle*, national life has changed out of recognition. Families have shrunk since the years of the 1960s, when governments worried about falling natality rates and threw money at couples to reproduce. Now, as those babies enter middle age, life expectancy grows and the birth-rate falls, France is becoming an ageing country. There are not enough young people to keep the population at its present level in the next century, but nobody outside the pro-family lobbies seems to care very much. If more young adults are staying in the family hearth, it is simply because they cannot find a job to pay for a place of their own.

Traditional morality is crumbling year by year, which is a cause for lament by some, but a reason for rejoicing by others as the old bourgeois hold on French society wanes. The number of marriages fell by 35 per cent between 1970 and 1995 – if the trend changed in the mid-1990s, it was a temporary blip for tax reasons. The number of couples outside marriage has risen fivefold, and two out of five births in France are now born outside wedlock – and there is no shortage of prominent examples – actresses Catherine Deneuve, Isabelle Adjani, Emmanuelle Béart and Sophie Marceau have not seen the need to marry the fathers of their children, nor have two of France's leading television news presenters. The First Secretary of the Socialist Party and the Junior Minister for Education have had four children without visiting the register office. Homosexual couples have been given the tax and legal benefits of heterosexuals, and qualify for the same fare reductions on the state railway. The country, according to its President, is entering an era when 'test-tube babies will be surfing the information superhighway'.

These trends fit France's nature as a modern nation, but they run up against a backdrop of doubt that suits the country less well. The plummeting status of the political class has shown through in election after election. Abstention rates rise steadily, and electoral support for mainstream parties of left and right has fallen from 85 to 67 per cent in a decade. In municipal elections in 1995, fewer than 55 per cent of the registered electorate went to vote in Lyon, Metz, Nancy and Rennes. In the regional poll of 1998, 41 per cent of voters stayed away. Two-thirds of the French say they expect their politicians to lie to them. The best-placed politician in an end-of-year national popularity poll in 1997 – Jacques Chirac – finished only thirty-third, one place ahead of his Prime Minister. Another survey of faith in national institutions gave the justice system 38 per cent, parliament 32 per cent and the presidency 29 per cent. In a study of twelve European states, the French ranked only ninth in expressing faith in their nation's democracy. Asked if they were being told the truth about the way public money was being spent, three-quarters of those questioned said no.

Such deep disillusion shows through in the bounding scores of the National Front. At a series of national elections of the 1990s, voters have given between 12.5 and 15 per cent of the first-round vote to a party whose followers distributed a leaflet during riots on a housing estate in the Loire Valley asking: 'Why do rats wear roller-skates in Tours?' Answer: 'To clean out the dustbins quicker than the Arabs.' Though the proportion of immigrants is about average for an industrialised country, many people feel they are in danger of being swamped by brown and black foreigners. At the last National Assembly election, the National Front won almost as many first-round votes as the Gaullists, and finished ahead of the other main orthodox right-wing group. In regional elections in 1998, in which it got 15.5 per cent of the vote, the Front topped the poll in Alsace and went away with 27 per cent of the vote in Provence-Alpes-Côte-d'Azur in the south-east. The once ragged party of Jean-Marie Le Pen joined the Socialists, Gaullists and the loose centre-right Union pour la Démocratie Française (UDF) as one of France's four big political movements, only to tear itself apart with an internal war that raged through 1999. The conflict between Le Pen and his former dauphin, Bruno Mégret, drew on the violence and passion which had always characterised the party. 'Our adversaries want to kill us,' one Front official told a meeting during the glory days. 'Our backs are against the wall, and we're going to be very, very nasty. National militants are treated like dogs, like pariahs. This situation can only be ended by us reacting vigorously. One must kill one's enemies. I don't want to say that the President should be killed, but we must stop being considerate and respectful. This is a combat we have to fight, and we can't fight it with kid gloves.' He was applauded, and the idea of reaching at least a tacit understanding with the National Front has intrigued more mainstream right-wing politicians than would like to admit it.

The bad temper which fuels the Front springs from many wells – unemployment, the tensions of late-century life, Europe, immigrants, indisciplined youth or simply the difficulty some people find in getting on with each other. But those springs well up, too, across the country among people who – as yet, at least – would not think of voting for an extremist party. Setting aside the providential, and temporary, feel-good factor of sporting victory in the summer of 1998, Europe's most self-confident people had become the inhabitants of a nerve-end society with declining faith in the future. Is the problem that France is just 'a medium power which exists only because it clings to Germany, which has always beaten it on all fronts', as its one-time dictator-client President Omar Bongo of Gabon declared? Or is it that the French put their faith for too long in an elite which was not up to the job? Has the destruction of the checks and balances of national life in pursuit of executive omnipotence reached a point at which rational resolution of national problems has become impossible, making each policy lurch more extreme than the last? Has the disenchantment with scandals lapping around everything from the national railways to medical charities produced such a degree of cynicism that the country can no longer believe in anything? In each case, the answer, to varying degrees, has to be yes. The common good which was the cornerstone of the Republic is fading and social cohesion fragmenting, while France watches its old totems crumbling and feels that the only way to preserve them is by a big step backwards – a step it cannot take if it wants to remain a major force in the world.

The conservative strain in French life has always been far stronger than the revolutionary images suggest. Now, it is more paramount than ever, with the ultimate paradox that governments of the left are elected because they are seen as bulwarks of economic and social conservatism in a nation which cannot accept that it does not have a God-given right to be an exception in a globalised epoch. Survival at the top is rarely a comfortable matter. Unlike Tony Blair across the Channel, Lionel Jospin does not have a Thatcherite past on which to build. France has put off its days of reckoning for so long that it cannot bring itself to face the realities of the coming century. That is part of its charm, of its uniqueness. This special place not only stands apart, but takes a positive pride in so doing. Year by year, the stakes grow. This home of logic is embarked on one of the highest-risk and most irrational games of any nation in the world – a game in which it is, in essence, playing with itself. Forty years after Charles de Gaulle gave it a new lease of life, France is again a nation at risk.

2

BEHIND THE MASK

Diminishing faith in leaders is a general phenomenon in the West, but it has a particular impact in France because of the quasi-monarchical status of the nation's supreme guide. The President of the Republic has more power than any other elected official in an advanced democracy. With a seven-year term, he is both Head of State, Executive President of the Republic, and boss of a major polit-ical party which usually forms the biggest group in the legislature. He names the Prime Minister, and approves the composition of the gov-ernment. He runs foreign policy and any other domains which attract his attention – one former minister told me that he was blessed because the President of the time had no interest whatsoever in his field of responsibility. He commands the armed forces and sits atop vast acres of patronage. The state apparatus at his disposal is extraor-dinarily pervasive and excessively powerful. He can call a referendum whenever he wishes as a means of rallying the country behind him. And his influence is not just a matter of politics: speaking of one of his grand cultural projects in Paris, François Mitterrand put it in a nut-shell: 'I choose, I decide, I build.' A quizzical presidential look at the colour of the desks in the new opera house at the Bastille was enough to get them replaced. In what may not be an apocryphal story, another President was told on a trip abroad that his country no longer had a leading world novelist. 'When I get home, I'll call a ministerial meeting to deal with the matter,' he replied. It is not surprising that commentators speak of 'our president-monarchs' and note how many of the trappings of power that surrounded the kings of Versailles are echoed in more modern form at the Élysée Palace, even down to a mistress and her child under the longest-reigning President.

It may be all too much for a single human being, and calls for discrimination in the exercise of power which can hardly be expected of men who have spent their lives fighting their way up the political ladder. The experience since the mid-1970s certainly argues in that direction, as the men France chose turned out to be incapable of rising to the heights expected of them while the interplay of the party and electoral systems repeatedly excluded those best fitted for the job. The concentration of power might be acceptable if it was exercised in the true broader interests of the people, but national politics has become the domain of self-interested clans which put their own struggle for power above everything else. The periods of *cohabitation* between a President of the left and a government of the right, in 1986–88 and 1993–95, underlined the way in which everything is subordinated to the pursuit of electoral victory – in each case, the Prime Minister's main concern was to become President at the end of his term as premier. From 1997, Lionel Jospin had five years to consider if – or rather how – he would follow the pattern.

Faced with the huge task of reviving the nation from the ruins of the Fourth Republic, liquidating the cancer of Algeria, quenching military revolt and avoiding a repetition of his post-war defeat by the political establishment, it was not surprising that Charles de Gaulle opted for an imperial presidency modelled on his vision of the nation when he returned to power in 1958. He had to hold the divided, dispirited country together and provide the leadership needed to take it into a new dimension. His success marks him as the greatest French leader of the twentieth century. But, a decade after riding roughshod to power, the General was an old man clearly incapable of driving the great presidential engine he had constructed. So, adopting the logic underlying the Gaullist system, the people turfed him out in a referendum in 1969. After a five-year interlude of pragmatic conservatism, France embarked on another adventure, with the brilliant, conceited and ultimately fragile Valéry Giscard d'Estaing, who ended his term dragged down by rising unemployment, vicious in-fighting on the right and allegations that he had accepted jewellery from a notably unsavoury African dictator. The man who vanquished him in 1981 enjoyed a De Gaulle-like monopoly of the levers of power – the Élysée Palace, a faithful Prime Minister, an obedient Cabinet, an adoring party, and control of the National Assembly. He could, personally and politically, speak about it being a time for dreams. To nobody's surprise, the fervently anti-Gaullist François Mitterrand, who had once denounced the permanent *coup d'état* of the Fifth Republic, found that, once in power, the presidential raiment suited him very nicely indeed.

But Mitterrand misplayed his hand in a domain he took pride in knowing nothing about – the economy. As a result, his presidential leadership was rapidly undermined by a rolling crisis which led to one of the greatest policy U-turns seen in modern Europe. Although most of it was hidden at the time, the regime was also being sucked down into a mire of scandal, which reached from the everyday business of raising political funds to the destruction of the anti-nuclear ship, *Rainbow Warrior*, by French agents in New Zealand. Mitterrand held on to the Élysée in 1988 thanks to clever tactics and the widespread distrust of his main opponent. But, almost as soon as his second term began, the *après*-Mitterrandist jockeying started, and the President devoted himself to playing favourites with his courtiers and ordering up grandiose building projects worthy of the Sun King. Once again, France had found that the man of its choice could not live up to its hopes. Seven years after his first victory, the first President to claim to come from the left confided that he had 'learned to distrust dreams'.

Some of Mitterrand's achievements will last – the commitment to Europe, the abolition of the death penalty, the encouragement of culture, the renovation of the Louvre Museum, and the great buildings he commissioned. Above all he showed that France did not have to be ruled eternally from the right, and that an alternance of power was possible. But he also led France to the edge of disaster and, when he went, the country deserved a new start. What it got was Jacques Chirac.

The new President was hardly a fresh face: he had been a junior minister at the time of the 1968 general strikes and student riots, when he was said to have attended a secret meeting with union leaders in a prostitutes' hotel in northern Paris with a revolver in his pocket – presumably none of the labour bosses made the Mae West joke about him being glad to see them. Up to his election to the Élysée, Chirac's career went in twos – two spells as Prime Minister and two presidential bids while holding the twin roles of Mayor of Paris and Gaullist party boss. Two years seems his natural span – each premiership lasted that long; so did his time as 'president in waiting' from 1993; and so did his parliamentary majority as Head of State. Multiply by ten and you get his basic political support, which has fluctuated around 20 per cent for two decades. Once, it is said, a soothsaying princess in Africa told him he would fail twice in his ultimate quest. 'On the third attempt,' she said, 'you will succeed – to your great unhappiness.'

The paradoxes of his character are enough to give a psychiatrist a lifetime's work. His energy and charm co-exist with periods of detachment and depression. He combines a grasshopper attention span and nerve-end impetuousness with grinding long-term ambition. He revels in grand occasions, but harbours contempt for what he once called the 'salon hamsters' of high society. He operates through a mix of loyalty and ruthlessness. A fervent Gaullist, he was among those who prepared the way for the General's downfall, and is now portrayed by some commentators as a throwback to the despised Fourth Republic. His attachment to republican legality is not in doubt, but he can also play the poor man's Bonaparte and cultivates semi-clandestine networks of influence which have always been a hallmark of Gaullism. A man of the right, he organised his party on Leninist lines. In the 1995 presidential election, he portrayed himself as an outsider ready to put right the wrongs of French society, but he has lived for so long in the palaces of the regime that the editor of *Le Monde* punningly baptised him '*le Résident de la République*'.

For all this, nobody knew what made up the *real* Jacques Chirac – or if, indeed, there was such a thing. The first time his wife met him, his legs jiggled so much under the table that she concluded he must drink too much coffee. After beating Chirac in the 1988 presidential election, Mitterrand told an aide: 'Basically, this man is mad, and does whatever comes into his head. He may get elected after me, but he'll soon be the laughing-stock of the whole world.' Chirac's gung-ho image is set for life as a man whose tastes stop at peasant food, Western films and military music. In fact, he has greater depths – passionate about primitive civilisations, he refused to have anything to do with the 500th anniversary celebrations of Columbus' voyage because of the havoc wreaked on the people of South America. Adoptive father of a Vietnamese child, he is a man who would hide a volume of poetry in a copy of *Playboy*, remarks the journalist Françoise Giroud, who served in one of his governments. But show him a crowd and he rises to the surface at the first handshake. On his emotional bottom-line, he seems to fear failure above all else, and he knows plenty about it. In the 1988 presidential election, he was humiliated by Mitterrand. The French, his wife is reported to have told him at the time, just didn't like him. That was something he simply couldn't bring himself to accept. Following him at election meetings and on the streets seven years later was to witness a man who was, literally, reaching out for support each time a hand came into view, a man who longed to be loved and had to prove that he could surmount the final hurdle – he should have appropriated the Paul Anka-Claude François anthem of doing it his way before Frank Sinatra got hold of it.

So, to fill its imperial presidency, a post requiring massive vision and deliberation, France found itself with a man who picks up ideas like lint and who cannot resist going after the gallery. As a former Premier put it: 'For him, thinking is, first of all, thinking about what others think.' Back in the 1980s, when Chirac was out of national power but still an important figure as Mayor of Paris and leader of the neo-Gaullist party Rassemblement Pour la République (RPR), I had breakfast with him at his office in the Hôtel de Ville. He was going to Bonn later in the day, so we spoke about Franco-German relations and I wondered if, in the spirit of greater co-operation, there might be some scope for Paris to offer the Germans a finger on the French nuclear trigger. It was a silly idea – there was nothing Germany wanted less than to be involved in nuclear weapons. But that evening, the television news reported that, on his visit to the Konrad Adenauer Foundation, Chirac had suggested that the Germans might like to share in turning the key that would set off France's contribution to an earth-shattering war.

Given the natural vim and vigour of the man who moved into the Élysée in 1995, it was entirely natural that the new presidency began on a high, sweeping away the cobwebs of the Mitterrand era as Jacques Chirac zoomed to unprecedented heights in the polls and upstaged the much younger Bill Clinton and John Major when they gathered for their first summit with him. France is back, alive and kicking, was the message. *Vas-y, fonce*: crack on, and damn the consequences. So it was also entirely predictable that one of Chirac's first major acts was to arouse and ignore world opprobrium by resuming nuclear testing in French Polynesia. And, as night follows day, the new President's popularity slumped after the initial honeymoon. Plans for welfare cuts and proposals to reduce the huge losses of the state railway system, where staff were entitled to retire on a full pension at the age of fifty, brought hundreds of thousands of protesters out in the streets. The nation's pessimism reached the levels of the darkest days of François Mitterrand. Scandals began to swirl around the new administration. Unemployment rose to a record level.

Achieving the goal of his political life at the third attempt might have induced a certain serenity in another man. When things began to turn sour, another politician might have sat down and drawn up a long-term plan to make the maximum use of his seven-year term. In philosophical mode, Chirac once reflected that political life was 'a succession of reflections on life and on oneself'. But the ups-and-downs of his own career have produced a deep insecurity that sits uneasily with the office he had won at long last. After his defeat by Mitterrand in 1988, he was, aides recalled, physically present at meetings but his mind was absent. His victory in 1995, confounding opinion polls which had cast him initially as an also-ran, restored his manic side. So the decision to meet the rising tide of discontent head-on by calling a premature parliamentary election in 1997 was in character, but also doubly dangerous.

Not only did he risk defeat, he also created a formal blurring of lines between two great institutions of state, the presidency and the legislature. Presidents had always thrown their prestige into parliamentary elections to aid their own party, but this time Chirac was, in effect, putting the presidency on the line for his Prime Minister. It was sheer folly to expect a grouchy electorate to supply the shot in the arm he was seeking. France was fed up with its rulers, annoyed that yet again they had failed to come up with a miracle remedy as promised by witch-doctor Chirac two years earlier. Voters were deeply worried about unemployment and the social cost of Europe, and felt that the men in power did not understand – or even care – about the fears that kept them awake at night. So it was not surprising that Chirac's gamble went horribly wrong, that the right lost its comfortable majority in the National Assembly, that the President was forced to appoint the Socialist Lionel Jospin to head the second government of his septennat, and that the National Front established itself as the electoral arbiter in more than sixty constituencies.

In many ways, the whole episode provided a sharp snapshot of the trouble with France – an out-of-touch elitist leadership, an electorate grasping for straws from politicians it had decisively rejected only a few years earlier, an ominous rise of extremism, and widespread disenchantment reflected in a 31 per cent abstention rate. Far from making matters better, Chirac had only aggravated the state in which France found itself. His predecessor at the Élysée had been able to survive defeat for his party in two legislative elections, and to maintain the status of the presidency even when the right-wing government of 1993–95 was riding high in the polls. But Chirac had tied himself too closely to a lost cause. It wasn't as if France had suddenly fallen back in love with the left. Jospin, described by the editor of the newspaper *Libération* as having the temperament of a provincial Swedish curate, did not enjoy an electoral sweep similar to that of Tony Blair's New Labour in Britain, and was only able to form a government with the help of the Communists, the Greens and a left-wing Socialist group. Rather, voters acted negatively against the very man they had chosen to lead them only twenty-five months earlier. The politics of rejection ruled. Year by year, spurred on by the incompetence of its leaders and the vagaries of its people's character, France was being forced back on itself, bereft of the inspiration it so vainly sought from the top.

The disenchantment is all the greater because the French were shielded for so long from economic reality by inflation, corporatism, self-defensive politicians, a provident public sector and the belief that the state and its servants will always look after them. They acquired a sublime confidence in their God-given right to survive and prosper during the three decades after the Second World War which became known as *Les Trente Glorieuses* (The Glorious Thirty). The nation floated on an inflationary cushion. Prosperity brought telephones and washing machines to almost every home; rat-infested city buildings were replaced by tower blocks; France walked tall on the world stage.

As the Glorious Thirty slipped seamlessly into what were later dubbed the Lazy Ten, other countries were marching to a different drum. Margaret Thatcher was doing her utmost to change Britain. Ronald Reagan was altering America. Germany was pushing its productivity to new heights, and Japan was leading Asia's economic charge. But the French refused to change, and when the crunch came at the end of the 1970s, they blamed their President for the threat to their comfortable way of life posed by the oil price crises, the shifting shape of the world economy and growing cost of the welfare state. And when Giscard d'Estaing rightly noted that the country was caught up in a world crisis, he was ridiculed for seeking to evade the blame, as if any French Head of State worth his salt should be able to buck international trends.

The narrowness of Giscard's defeat in 1981 showed that France was not all that convinced of the merits of swinging to the left, but the temptation to reject his stern medicine proved irresistible. So France flew out of the window of reality on a rip-roaring expansion jag which all too soon slammed with sickening inevitability into the tough monetarist wall of the Ten Fearful Years of deflation.

After more than a decade of fear and belt-tightening, George Soros was far from alone in admiring the way successive Finance Ministers of right and left kept to the straight and narrow anti-inflationary path. France's trade balance with the rest of the world rose to record levels of surplus as the 1990s progressed. In a country which had never been entirely at home with modern business (and often preferred to leave finance to Protestants or Jews), market capitalism became the flavour of the decade. The head of a pharmaceuticals company told me that the crisis 'makes one more intelligent'. It also enabled managers to award themselves large pay rises and plentiful share options. French workers, on the other hand, have been classed as the most insecure in Europe, with the lowest identification with their companies and the least positive relationship with their employers. The fact that unemployment soared under a government of the left elected to usher in economic expansion was an irony which many find hard to stomach.

The combination of deflation and high unemployment, lack of convincing leadership, mounting social tensions and gnawing uncertainties at home and abroad has encouraged the process of fear and contraction to feed on itself. Those in work save an ever-larger proportion of their earnings year by year as a hedge against losing their jobs and hard times ahead. Two-thirds of the French say they regularly cut back on household expenditure. *Le Figaro* reported that 10 per cent fewer people ate out in restaurants in 1997 than in the previous year. And when people spend less, demand falls and companies shed thousands more jobs, as the monetarist circle is joined in one of its more unlikely homes with high real interest rates and a stagnant property market – think of all those bargain rural properties British visitors have been buying up for less than the price of a semi-detached former council house. For all its natural expansiveness, the Hexagon found itself crammed into a straitjacket which stunts growth and saps the gaiety of the nation. In a deeply worried society, holding on to what you've got becomes the main priority in life.

Anxiety has a freezing effect, and the greater good ceases to have much meaning. Private-sector employees live in fear of the sack from employers struggling to compete internationally, in part because of the excessive social security payments they are required to pay. Public-sector workers demonstrate *en masse* against any threat to privileges which cost more than the country can afford. Journalists strike to defend a special 30 per cent tax break for their profession introduced in the 1930s by governments anxious to get a good press. Once individualism was a cause of chuckling approval – consecrated in what is known as 'system D', for '*débrouille*', or getting round the rules, preferably by crafty methods. Now, nobody laughs: they're too busy elbowing their way to the front of the queue.

No, public morality ain't what it used to be. The ranks of role models are shrinking. France's most socially-aware bishop was removed from his post by the Pope, and is reduced to preaching brotherhood over the Internet from his one-room apartment in northern Paris. An official report a the end of 1998 finally revealed widespread secret sterilisation of the mentally handicapped. The nation's principal saint-in-waiting, a Benedictine priest called L'Abbé Pierre, who has spent his life helping the poor and has been regularly voted the most popular person in France, ran into trouble for defending the author of a book which talked about the 'false and arbitrary figures' given for Jewish victims of the Holocaust and which called *The Diary of Anne Frank* a myth. The Catholic Church rebuked him, and the eighty-three-year-old priest fled to an Italian monastery. Emerging after a month's retreat, he hardly helped his case by blaming the Church's attitude towards him on media pressure 'inspired by an international Zionist lobby', and accusing the Jews of having committed a genocide of their own in Palestine eleven or twelve centuries before Christ.

A few months earlier, a cancer research charity which had enjoyed about the same high repute as the abbot was revealed to have spent only a third of its donations on medical work, and to have funded political parties by the back door. Its seventy-year-old president, who used to appeal for donations on television surrounded by pale children, was accused of having diverted tens of millions of francs from the charity, known by its initials as the ARC. As the net closed around him, Jacques Crozemarie had a heart attack; he was charged with fraud in his hospital bed. The charity had attracted around 600 million francs each year in donations. It paid out a billion francs to contractors without requiring any tenders: in return, kickbacks running into tens of millions of francs flowed to the men running the ARC. One was said to have received 10 million francs and free holidays in the South Seas. Evidence emerged that some of the donations ended up funding Crozemarie's hunting estate and his holiday villa. If this scummy scandal seemed to show that nothing was sacred, it was promptly followed by the disclosure that nurseries of Paris were buying milk from corrupt suppliers in exchange for bribes.

Champions of the homeless and cancer charities should be above reproach, but, as realists, the French do not expect their politicians or businessmen to be as pure as the snow on the Alps, though they do anticipate that they will take pains not to be caught. There has always been politico-business sleaze, from the great scandal over the financing of the Panama Canal at the turn of the century through the high-rolling swindlers who helped to undermine the Third Republic in the 1930s to the darker shadows of the Gaullist period. The first two decades of the Fifth Republic saw the kidnapping of a Moroccan opposition leader on the Boulevard Saint-Germain with French connivance; the murder of one minister and the mysterious death of another; a long-running controversy over whether the head of the

Communist Party had gone voluntarily to work in Germany during the war; awkward revelations about how little tax one Prime Minister had paid; the treacly matter of state-subsidised repairs done to a château bought by one of his successors; and the affair of jewels given to Giscard d'Estaing by Emperor Bokassa of Central Africa. At a less elevated level, the funding of political parties has always been opaque, and the interplay between local authorities, the state and the private sector over major infrastructure projects has given rise to accusation of many a mutually advantageous deal over the decades.

What has come to light recently has been, in part, a continuation of business as usual – mayors demanding kickbacks for public-works tenders or accepting a car from a friendly contractor, companies slipping local officials plane tickets for exotic holidays or giving their relatives jobs. Some regions have a long tradition of graft: one French commentator, Alain Minc, talks of the Mediterranean stretch from Marseille to the Italian frontier becoming like Naples or Sicily, with local government linked to the underworld, laundered cash being pumped into real-estate and a growing population of dodgy foreigners (including Russian mafiosi). The state audit court found 'serious irregularities' in the management of public finances of the southern Bouches-du-Rhône and Gard departments. In the nearby Var department, which has become a battleground for gangs fighting over prostitution, slot machines and protection rackets, a National Assembly deputy, Yann Piat, who had started out with the National Front but then moved to the more orthodox right, was gunned down by a man on a motorcycle as she drove along a rural road in 1994. Piat had declared war on the local mafia. Two years before her death, she had written a letter mentioning a local senator and a gang boss, 'in case of mortal accident to her person'. Soon after her death, two brothers with whom she had been associated were found dead in a car in their garage. A tube ran from the exhaust pipe into the car, and the verdict was suicide. Since the evidence was quickly destroyed there was seen to be no point in reopening the case, which was very convenient since it emerged that no fumes had been found in the tube; that the bodies were held in place by seatbelt; that the garage door was held shut by a vehicle parked outside; and that one of the dead men had blood on his shirt. In 1997, on the evidence of a man who appeared to be either a manipulator or what the French call '*un mythomane*', or both, a book appeared which claimed that Piat was killed to stop her disclosing a plan to sell military land to the mafia, and implicated two leading right-wing politicians referred to as 'squid' and 'scooter'. That led to a flurry of outrage, law suits, heavy fines and accusations of political dirty tricks – and helped to explain why the Var is the only French department to have elected a parliamentary deputy from the extremist National Front who is also mayor of its main city.

Apart from providing fodder for the far right, what has changed is that the local corruption has become the target of sustained legal assault and media attention. A dozen political figures from the Var, including seven mayors, have faced prosecution. An eighty-year-old former president of the departmental council was sentenced to two years in prison and a million-franc fine over the payment of bribes for a public construction project. Eastwards along the Mediterranean, the Mayor of Cannes, once known as 'the Kennedy of the Croisette' after the resort's sea-front boulevard, was unable to check a roller-coaster of corruption accusations even when he went on hunger strike and was taken to hospital. In succession, Michel Mouillot was handed a suspended prison sentence and a large fine for corruption. He was also charged with having demanded a bribe of 3 million francs to allow slot machines to be installed in a British-owned casino, and investigated on allegations that he had received 10 million francs from a property company for agreeing to expropriate occupants of buildings on the Croisette so that a casino could be put up in their place. After spending six months in jail, Mouillot had the good grace to resign from office; by then, he was being investigated not only for corruption and influence-peddling but also for misusing corporate funds and falsifying documents. Another Riviera boss who liked to call himself 'the Godfather' and was arrested for taking kickbacks amounting to 1.8 million francs, put up the ultimate defence. 'I did not demand money,' he said. 'I was offered it.'

In this southern gallery, nobody could rival Jacques Médecin, the swaggering, high-living Mayor of Nice, a one-time Minister of Tourism, an all-too-typical scion of a local political dynasty, author of an excellent cookbook and escort of starlets in see-through blouses. Médecin was put under the spotlight in the early 1980s by one of the more eminent Englishmen to have chosen to live on the Riviera:

Graham Greene accused him of running a mafia system in his city. Once, telephoning me after lunch on a Sunday, Greene rambled on about former torturers from French Algeria working for the mayor's camp. When I later tracked down the man Greene fingered as the secret underworld boss in Nice, he turned out to be a petty criminal who appeared to have crossed one of the author's local friends. Still, there was little doubt that the Médecin system was deeply rotted by kickbacks, corruption and flirtation with the far right. Naturally, Médecin blamed the left which, he once told me, was after him because he was 'the most offensive' politician in France (his English was not as good as he thought it was). Eventually, the dashing, mousta-chioed mayor fled to South America, but returned to be jailed for skimming millions of francs from municipal funds. On his release, he went back to Uruguay, where he sold hand-painted T-shirts and died at the end of 1998, lamented by the National Front's Jean-Marie Le Pen as a man who 'was no more guilty than others'.

Some of this could be written off as what Alain Minc calls 'a Latin predisposition to deals and fiddles'. But what has come to light in France is a much wider and more pervasive network of scandal which threatens to undermine confidence in the system as a whole. Underlying the web of deceit and corruption is an enduring belief by politicians that they can act above the law – and get away with it. For many years, they did. But now a new breed of judicial investigators has combined with the politicians' own arrogance to make their com-fortable old system vulnerable. From the viewpoint of public morality, this is admirable. What it does for public trust in the governing class is quite another matter.

As the Gaullists sought new national figures for their Chiracian revival in the 1980s, no two politicians better represented the coming spirit of the party than Michel Noir, from France's second biggest city of Lyon, and Alain Carignon, from the Alpine showcase of Grenoble. They were each thoroughly modern men, mayors, good communi-cators and managers who could hope to rise to the very top of government. Tall and handsome, Noir became Minister for Foreign Trade and earned much moral credit by preaching the need to resist any temptation to flirt with the growing forces of the far right. But in 1995, he proved to have feet of clay. After a sensational trial, he was given an eighteen-month suspended jail sentence for a political funding affair centring round his flashy son-in-law, whose pharmaceutical franchising business he helped to promote – the affair was given added appeal by the involvement of the presenter of France's main nightly television news programme who, unlike Noir, kept his job.

Alain Carignon was even more of a star than Noir. Grenoble had become a showplace for French modernity before he was elected as its mayor in 1983. Carignon's election seemed to mark a neat fit between the man and the place. The dapper mayor was appointed Environment Minister at the age of thirty-seven, and was spoken of as a potential Prime Minister. Behind the scenes, some more old-fashioned games were being played. A local official recalls meetings at which the mayor fixed the distribution of the spoils of sleaze – the Gaullists got as much as the Socialists and Communists combined. (This official, himself, received a monthly salary from four construction firms which worked for the city.) As Carignon's self-confidence grew, he doubled his party's take, and accepted a rent-free flat in Paris, plane tickets, holidays and finance for his campaign newspaper from a lobbying company representing a big public-works group. He billed the city government for trips of doubtful value to Grenoble, and kept the councillors of the surrounding Isère department sweet by doubling their stipends.

In 1995, Carignon was arrested and held for 200 days in the jail cell in Lyon once occupied by the Nazi war criminal Klaus Barbie. While there, he went on receiving a special monthly allowance of 20,000 francs for his promotional activities for Grenoble. When he was put on trial, his supporters declared their love for him from the public gallery and a group of stars, including actor Gérard Depardieu and philosopher Bernard-Henri Lévy, issued a statement in his defence. It did no good. Carignon was convicted of having accepted 21 million francs in return for awarding a water supply contract to one of France's biggest companies. He had also interfered with witnesses, the court ruled. The once dashing hope of Gaullism was sentenced to three years in prison, a term later increased to five years. He was the most senior French politician to be jailed under the Fifth Republic.

As the number of big political scandals rose above thirty, the reputation of the establishment came under threat: 'Other countries have political crises, we have scandals,' a former high official reflected.

Sleaze oozed out of the very summit of power. The Socialist Party which came to office in 1981 promising new ethical standards was found to have been taking widespread pay-offs for public-works contracts – there were even suggestions that it was François Mitterrand himself who had dreamed up the scam. The President of the National Assembly Finance Committee was sentenced to a suspended eighteen-month prison term, fined 30,000 francs and deprived of his civic rights for two years after being found guilty of being involved in the scheme to raise money for the party through false bills issued to firms which got contracts for public works in Socialist-run towns. A Socialist minister and his chief of staff plundered 20 million francs from a fund set up to help pay for a Franco-African summit. A year after moving into the Élysée, Mitterrand established a 'black box' police cell which carried out secret missions for him, without any legal status whatsoever. Some leading party figures appeared to bear political responsibility for delays in testing HIV-contaminated blood in the national blood bank which infected 1,250 haemophiliacs. The first President of the left liked to denounce the immorality of money and of all who sought it, but it turned out that his oldest friend had used his position to wring commissions out of French state contracts, to sell his near-worthless company to the state for a hefty price and to use privileged information for insider dealing. In a move which even some of his loyalist followers found hard to stomach, Mitterrand invited a rogue in recurrent trouble with the courts and the tax authorities into the Cabinet. Two of the President's closest associates killed themselves. Illicit telephone tapping from the 'black box' unit at the Élysée targeted 1,500 people, including the Aga Khan and the President's mistress. The allegations continued for years after Mitterrand's death. At the beginning of 1999, a former secret agent said $2.5 billion had disappeared from a secret Saudi loan to France in 1983 – he thought it had been used for both personal and polictical enrichment. At the same time, a businessman being questioned in another scandal said he paid Françoise Sagan 9 million francs to induce her friend the President to rescue an oil deal in Uzbekistan – the writer issued a categorical denial. (Beside all this, news that Mitterrand's Defence Minister had been a KGB agent in the 1950s and 1960s was almost conventionally reassuring.)

On the other side, allegations swirled about the way Paris was run under Jacques Chirac and the funding of his neo-Gaullist RPR movement. A magistrate raided party headquarters and received tantalising documents allegedly taken from secret police files which appeared to relate to allegations that the RPR had received kickbacks from public-works firms through Swiss bank accounts. It was revealed that Alain Juppé, Chirac's right-hand man in Paris, who moved up to be his Prime Minister in 1995, had enjoyed a low-rent apartment owned by the city in a smart Left Bank street, and that the President's successor as mayor, Jean Tiberi, had arranged for his children to occupy other grace-and-favour flats. Tiberi's wife came under investigation about how much work she had really done on a 36-page report on development aid commissioned by a local council run by a Gaullist, for which she was paid 200,000 francs. To show how serious the case had become, the government unavailingly sent a helicopter to search the Himalayas for a holidaying judge who could block the proceedings. Tiberi himself was questioned about whether he had negotiated his wife's fee, and was investigated for possible complicity and misappropriation of public funds. As if this was not enough, it was then revealed that Air France had paid a million francs to his son over a period of three years after the young man had left his job at the state airline to act as a ministerial aide. Not surprisingly, polls showed a majority of Parisians expressing scepticism about the cleanliness of city politics. In her private diary, Tiberi's wife wondered rhetorically why her husband was taking so much of the flak rather than Chirac and Juppé. She did not have to wait too long for the net to widen. In August, 1998, a magistrate put Juppé under formal investigation over allegations that the City of Paris had secretly paid the salaries of staff of Chirac's Gaullist party – setting off a debate about whether the President of the Republic, himself, could end up also being hauled in by the law.

The flurry of scandal on both left and right showed up the close-knit nature of those involved. Just as Mitterrand was surrounded by a court which depended on him for its place in the sun, so Jacques Chirac sat at the centre of a web of men who had worked together for long years, who knew one another's secrets and who marched to his drumbeat. Leaving Tiberi to run Paris, Chirac took the key players of his municipal team off to the Élysée Palace with him – while Juppé became Prime Minister, another close associate, Jacques Toubon, took over the key post of Justice Ministry. Toubon had family problems, too: his stepdaughter was put under investigation for her activities as chairwoman of a ski resort which appeared to treat its directors particularly well. But, as the President said, 'he'd jump through the window if I asked him to'.

The broader question is whether, as well as protecting the ruling class, the hermetically sealed groups that run so much of France actually encourage corruption. The head of France's fraud squad reported in 1997 that nearly 500 politicians had been indicted in scandals – though he quickly added that only 10 per cent of them had been accused of personal enrichment. On the right and left, small groups of men and women work together for decades at the junction of politics and business, beyond the control of the electoral process. The widespread practice of a politician holding several offices at the same time – mayor, regional councillor, member of the National Assembly – extends their ambit and limits the number of players. At the same time, the way in which bureaucrats move between politics and business creates another layer of mutual understanding. As a former Socialist minister who later sat on a top administrative court put it: 'In the relatively narrow world of the administrative universe, everybody knows one another.' Sometimes, this may lead to the past coming back to haunt the great and good: the chairmen of two major state companies found themselves under investigation for alleged involvement in scandals during their previous incarnations as senior civil servants.

The parade of smartly suited businessmen and politicians wending its way through the courts underlines the extent to which France, though priding itself on being a meritocratic society, has an extraordinarily impermeable ruling class, rigorously selected from the common run of mortals and lifted to a pedestal which encourages a distorted view of life and engenders social divisions that make a mockery of the national slogan about equality. As a former minister has reflected: 'We make fine speeches about equality of opportunity, but France is the European country where the selection of elites is the fiercest, and the division between good and bad pupils perpetuates the cleavage between social classes.' When the 'good pupils' are seen to fall short, the rest of the class inevitably begins to wonder why they are up there in charge of things. At the least, that breeds an unhealthy degree of corrosive cynicism; at worst, it could lead to a desire to tear down the temple of the elite which rules the nation.

Britain has Oxbridge, America the East Coast college mafia, France the Grandes Écoles. Once again, France is different. You may get an intellectual sheen and start to build up networks at Oxford or Harvard, but you are not specifically educated to take charge of a nation. Margaret Thatcher read chemistry; Bill Clinton law. Neither of them was set on a course of administrative and political power, as such. But that was precisely what was laid out for Presidents Jacques Chirac and Valéry Giscard d'Estaing, and for Prime Ministers Édouard Balladur, Michel Rocard, Alain Juppé, Laurent Fabius and Lionel Jospin when they emerged from the final oral examination for the hundred bright young people who graduate each year from the leading finishing school for the elite, the École Nationale d'Administration, known by its initials from one end of the country to the other simply as *l'ÉNA*.

In all, there are 184 establishments under the umbrella of France's network of administrative finishing schools, the Grandes Écoles, with some 65,000 students. From there, the future mandarins of France enter one of eleven *corps d'état*, which group the men and women who really run France. They are a select body. To take one example, the *corps des mines*, which is more concerned these days with management than mining, has around 600 of its members active at any one time. In 1998, they included the bosses of such companies as the Total oil group; the Usinor Sacilor steel firm; Saint-Gobain, the glass-maker; and Péchiney, in aluminium. A French luncheon guest explained to a *Financial Times* reporter that a big takeover of a state conglomerate had gone in favour of one company rather than its competitor because it had been able to boast an *Ingénieur des Mines* among its top brass: it was a joke, but only just. Another graduate of the École des Mines became boss of the Peugeot car company in the autumn of 1977, and the careers that he and his predecessor followed were good illustrations of the opportunities open to such men. Jean-Martin Folz had gone through the Industry Ministry, the Rhône-Poulenc chemicals group, Péchiney and the Eridania Béghin-Say food firm before being hired by the Peugeot family to head their enterprise. His predecessor, Jacques Calvet, had moved from ÉNA into the civil service in 1957, ending up as chief of staff to the Finance Minister and then moving on to the Banque Nationale de Paris, where he became chairman before spending fifteen years in charge of Peugeot.

The aim of ÉNA is to teach its students how to order and present their ideas, how to produce a seamless presentation on any subject under the sun in which style vies with substance. From any set of data, a true graduate of ÉNA, or Énarque, should be able to extract a convincing case for either side in an argument. The system is hermetic – and not by accident. Set up after the Liberation by De Gaulle's fervent follower, Michel Debré, the aim was to produce an irreproachable mandarin sect whose only duty would be to serve the nation above and beyond partisan politics or personal advancement. The rankings of students on leaving the college would provide an objective, scientific gauge to who was capable of running the administration of France, in contrast to the way in which pre-war civil servants and Vichy collaborators-to-be got their jobs through social and family connections at interviews which they attended in morning coats and white gloves. As Debré's master, the General, told the students of 1959: 'You are called by your vocation to exercise the most important and most noble function which exists in the temporal sphere – I mean, the service of the state.'

'We are defined by our jobs,' one ÉNA graduate who rose through the civil service to the summit of the French business world reflected. Some break free – one Énarque became Le Monde's presidential correspondent, and another, a businessman called Marc de Lacharrière, came out of a ruined provincial aristocratic family to put together a major conglomerate with a turnover of 8 billion francs. Not that either lacked the contacts which an ÉNA background helps to nurture. The journalist's dinner parties were truffled with top civil servants with whom he had studied, and he was France's principal presidential scoop merchant for many years. As for M. de Lacharrière, he has known Jacques Chirac since the 1970s, is a good friend of the head of the Gaullist party, funds a social body set up by the second-ranking minister of Lionel Jospin's government, employs former leading aides of ministers of left and right, and funds the classic politico-literary monthly, the Revue des Deux Mondes.

Around 4,000 Énarques – 20 per cent of them women – are at work in France: three-quarters in the civil service, 600 in senior positions in public-sector companies, and 200 in private firms. They run state banks and arms companies, private-sector firms and planning bodies. They guide the country's political destiny from ministries and parliament, conduct its diplomacy, and offer counsel in weighty tomes of futurology. At the very top of the tree sit 400 *Inspecteurs des Finances*, a band of super-auditors whose job is to find out how public money is spent. To become an *inspecteur*, one has to have finished in the top 10 per cent of an ÉNA class. Having achieved that, as *The Economist* put it, 'they hand each other plum jobs in the public and private sectors without any sense of shame; they are, after all, the best'.

As De Gaulle instructed them to be, these technocrats are ecumenical servants of the state. The importance of *l'État* in France is something we will come to in more detail later: for the moment, it is enough to say that the legitimacy of this elite class is based on the Republic which they are meant to serve through thick and thin. They could not exist without the republican state; nor it without them. The result is a sealed circle which leaves little room for self-examination but which risks imploding or exploding if it does not live up to its own proclaimed expectations of itself.

François Mitterrand, who finished his education before ÉNA came into being, and who wouldn't have got in anyway, had four Énarque Prime Ministers – two each from the left and the right. When one graduate, Michel Rocard, challenged his leadership of the Socialist Party in the late 1970s, another old boy, Jean-Pierre Chevènement, rode to the rescue at the head of a Marxist faction – and then went on to show the seamless adaptability of the true power-player as a fiercely left-wing Industry Minister, a patriotic Education Minister and an anti-Gulf War Defence Minister before becoming Interior Minister in Lionel Jospin's government. (He is also said to have invented the term 'Énarque'.) When the right lost its parliamentary majority in 1997, one Énarque succeeded another at the prime ministerial office at the Hôtel Matignon, not far from the college's Paris headquarters. Lionel Jospin's new government contained the highest proportion of Énarques for a decade, and his own 35-strong staff included twenty-five graduates of the finishing schools for France's rulers. The most senior

of them was reported to have justified his refusal to offer a suitably elevated job to the head of the national planning office by observing,
'That's normal, he's not even an Énarque.' When the Socialist Prime
Minister confronted the leader of France's employers over cutting the
working week, the two men could look back to the time they
spent together at ÉNA in the early 1960s – their class also included
the Socialist Interior Minister and the Gaullist Justice Minister in the
previous government.

Even at the most egalitarian stage of Socialist rule in the early
1980s, nobody had the President's ear more than another Énarque,
Jacques Attali. Attali's brilliance was constantly on display: everybody knew that he could talk about everything, but, equally,
nobody knew if he was actually capable of doing anything. That
wasn't the kind of petty matter to worry an Énarque, however.
Didn't François Mitterrand say that Attali had so many ideas that if
one turned out to be any good from time to time he would have
earned his keep? Subsequently, the directors of the European
Investment Bank proved somewhat less indulgent towards this owlish
gadfly, who cost them a fortune turning their institution into 'the
Glistening Bank' with its marble halls and expansive expense
accounts. Showing the true confidence of his breed, Attali once
invited me and two other journalists to breakfast at the Élysée
during a currency crisis, and planted a false story about France
being ready to sell its gold reserve to defend the franc without
having bothered to consult the Finance Ministry: he must have
thought it was a good idea at the time. On another occasion, he
defended himself against accusations of literary plagiarism by saying
that, since he got up at four in the morning to write his books, he
must be excused if he copied out some of his notes from other
works verbatim. When the Socialists returned to government, they
gave him the mission of finding a way to bridge the gap between the
Grandes Écoles and the less elevated universities across the country.
Naturally, it was a job for an Énarque.

Politicians can be voted out of office; not these fellows. One day a
ministerial adviser; the next, in charge of a big company. As one
graduate told me, ignorance about a new job was a positive blessing,
since it meant one was not saddled with preconceptions. 'ÉNA creates
a self-reproducing caste which has completely conquered the key

political positions and confiscated the apparatus of the state, making politics very technical with the same approach by left and right,' according to the author of a recent study carried out for another elite college, the École Normale Supérieure. Or, as a member of the 1986–88 government puts it: 'The big failing of top civil servants is their superiority complex towards ministers. Their class, made up of technocrats and technicians of governments and administration, only really respects the President of the Republic.' They are the experts – why search any further? 'When one looks for people who can understand industry, public finance or the reform of the social security system,' observes a former chief of staff at the Prime Minister's office, 'one quickly turns to the pool which provides the administration – for ever.'

Despite the array of graduates who have become Presidents and Premiers, relatively few Énarques actually go into party politics; they hardly need to. Their role is more likely to be exercised behind the scenes, and there have been notable examples of their survival capacity in serving ministers of different political camps with equal aplomb. One ran a major state firm through eight governments of different political complexion; another served as the spokesman for a President of the right and then headed the state broadcasting authority for six years under a Socialist Head of State. In the public mind, they can almost make politics and its practitioners irrelevant, which may be one reason why the people take directly to the streets rather than trusting their elected representatives in parliament to make their concerns felt. When the Prime Minister of a neighbouring country expressed concern about the zigzags of Jacques Chirac's European policy in the 1995 presidential election, a French elder statesman reassured him that, whatever the politicians might say in public, the officials had laid down the unalterable tracks for the future behind the scenes – and so it proved.

At any one time, half the chairmen (they are all men) of France's top 200 companies are likely to be from ÉNA. A few have failed in an embarrassingly public fashion: it was an *Inspecteur des Finances*, no less, who presided over the biggest losses in French banking history. The growing ranks of critics of this elite relish the occasion to shrug their shoulders and exclaim, '*Ah, encore un Énarque*' as though that explains everything. François Mitterrand complained mildly that they used too many adverbs. More trenchantly, the business magazine *Le Nouvel Économiste* asked in a cover story, 'Should we kill off the nation's elite?' A populist former Interior Minister, Charles Pasqua, suggested a novel way of doing down France's economic rivals: 'We should export half our ÉNA graduates. And send them to our main competitors.' Or, as the arch free-marketeer of the right, Alain Madelin, told an election rally: 'Britain has the IRA, Spain has the ETA, Italy has the Mafia – and we have the ÉNA.'

A group of less elite civil servants has set up an association called Against the ÉNA System, whose rallying cry is, 'Yesterday the Bastille, today the ÉNA.' The sociologist and historian Emmanuel Todd compares their attitude to the flowering of the authoritarian, Catholic tradition in the wartime Vichy collaborationist years – for them, he adds, 'The infallibility of the central banks has replaced the infallibility of the Pope.' The far right delights in alternately denouncing and ridiculing the tyranny of the ivory-tower technocrats. In his man-of-the-people mode, Jacques Chirac dismissed a Socialist who came to challenge him in an election in his rural stronghold as 'an Énarque no better known than Mitterrand's Labrador dog' – ignoring the fact that he, himself, went to ÉNA and was surrounded by an army of its best and brightest at the Élysée Palace. One of Chirac's deputies tabled a bill for the college to be abolished, on the grounds that its graduates have become a self-interested caste and 'we can no longer accept Martians making laws for earthlings . . . We need a ritual sacrifice.' Drawing a comparison with the Japanese civil service, that fan of the strong franc, George Soros, worries about 'the French elites who listen to themselves talk and pay no attention to the real world, not even to the state of mind of their fellow citizens. They think they know better than the people what is good for them. There is too much statism in France. Too much value is placed on the management by brilliant pupils, reared in elite institutions.'

Or take one of the recurrent crop of Énarque jokes.

A young man stops his car beside a field. He goes over to a farmer he sees walking on the pastureland with his dog and a flock of sheep.

'If I can tell you how many sheep you have here without counting them, will you give me one?' he asks.

'Okay,' says the farmer.

'Eighty-one,' says the smart young man.

'That's amazing. How did you know?' asks the farmer.

The young man does not reply. Instead, he picks up an animal and walks back to his car.

'Now, let *me* try something,' says the farmer. 'If I can tell you where you were educated, will you give me my animal back?'

'Of course,' says the young man disdainfully.

'You're from the ÉNA,' says the farmer.

'How did you know?'

'Because that's my dog you have under your arm.'

ÉNA is, as it happens, beginning to reform itself. In a symbolic piece of decentralisation, it has split its activities between Paris and the Euro-city of Strasbourg. The transfer of its students into top jobs for life is no longer quite so automatic. Prominent graduates like former Prime Minister Laurent Fabius have come out of the closet to acknowledge the unhealthy nature of a system which picks up bright young people in their early twenties and anoints them as rulers for life, and some of the top students of recent years have recognised its failings.

But, still, when a people feels unhappy, it seeks a target to blame for its frustrations. Inevitably, the bureaucracy figures high on the grouse list. At an everyday level, the French rail against the weight of administrative controls, the fiscal burdens that constrain small businesses from growing, the uneven application of valued added tax, and, behind all the daily irritations, at the technocrats who run the nation through an ocean of directives and controls. The topsy-like growth of official paperwork seems unstoppable – the main social security form now has twenty-nine separate boxes compared to two ten years ago. Sitting on top of the pyramid, the Énarques risk becoming like eggheads in 1950s America or social workers in Thatcherite Britain: figures to be viewed with suspicion and ridicule, held up as the worst examples of the one-track mindset, *la pensée unique*, which bedevils France. There was great amusement, for instance, when it became known that the move of part of the college's activities from Paris to Strasbourg had been so mismanaged that it took more than twice as long as planned and ran 70 million francs over budget. It was a perfect example of the imperial caste which could not run itself with the standards it demanded of others.

But if the college is an irresistible populist target, the criticism it is attracting may be yet another evasion of responsibility. Abolishing ÉNA would be only a ritual sacrifice, like killing off social workers or eggheads. It would, in itself, not change the way the French elite thinks and operates. Although half the college's intake comes from an executive or professional family background, the other half includes the sons and daughters of workers, school teachers and even a smattering of farmers. If it disappeared tomorrow, the upper civil service might become even more restricted in its social background and ways of thought. ÉNA has become a convenient symbol as the French, emotionally rather than rationally, sense that their seamless, self-preserving master-class is coping poorly with the challenges of the late-twentieth-century world. When things were more comfortable, the elite could take the credit; now, it cannot escape the blame, and its responsibility cannot be narrowed down to a single college which has become a facile demon figure for those who seek easy targets and avoid a deeper reality.

What is clear is that the technocrats have not re-thought their role and outlook. On a higher plane, the growing concern about Europe jeopardises the elite's reputation for infallibility if only because it is so closely identified with the restrictive, strong-franc policies of the past decade. An Énarque at the head of the Bank of France can produce analytical demonstrations of interest rates till the cows come home, but, as one magazine noted, a word which seems to have no place in the discussion is 'unemployment'. Economic and social engineering does not take account of either the deep changes the world is going through, or the alienation and anger being felt on a deeply personal level. In the mind of the Énarque, everything can be resolved by the exercise of logic and reason. That is not exactly the way a man who has never had a job, or a single mother limping by on welfare, sees things. Nor are the international fund managers who invest in France too happy when they watch their cash going down the plughole of a bank run like a branch of a Grande École. As one of Chirac's close friends, the author Denis Tillinac, points out, the mindset of ÉNA graduates would be fine for a country with a 6 per cent growth rate, but it is inappropriate for a nation in a monetarist vice. Or, as the President of the Republic himself noted: 'Our technocrats are neither amoral nor incompetent: they are the heirs and guardians of a thirty-year-old system. They knew how to manage a stable society, whose sustained growth ensured social progress. But this society no longer exists. The society of the 1990s is shifting and divided. To govern it, old reflexes have to be wiped out. The intellectual effort needed for renewal will be great: it will not come from technicians.'

None of which seems to faze those concerned. A poll of Énarques published by *Le Monde* showed a remarkable degree of self-satisfaction. Only 8 per cent felt that they might have too much power in carrying out decisions for the state – and 28 per cent thought they did not have enough.

France's mandarins see little need to prepare public opinion for the tablets of wisdom they hand down from the administrative heights. Did Confucius worry about public relations? The people are told what is good for them, and should gratefully accept. But now the superior style grates and proves counter-productive, setting off a call-and-response pattern in which the orders from the summit are met with popular revolt. Everything then either runs into the sand or ends with one side backing down. Though they would shudder at the very thought, the Énarques and their peers are, in their way, part of a disjunction at the centre of French life. Seen in historical terms, they are playing out a game which repeats the themes of the Revolution of 1789, and in which they represent the rulers against whom the people rise up. They are also natural heirs to the philosophers and revolutionaries of the eighteenth century who believed that intellectuals can reshape society: in his black frock-coat and powdered wig, Robespierre would have made a tip-top *Inspecteur des Finances*.

Within six months of Chirac's election, his Prime Minister and fellow ÉNA man, Alain Juppé, known as 'the computer' for his lack of the human touch, had come to personify all that the French disliked about the self-assurance of the elite. When Juppé sprang on the country his programme to slash welfare spending, shrink the heavily-indebted railway network and reduce social benefits in the public sector, the people knew their part, too. The sacrificial lambs were trotted out, from train-drivers to priests who were to be made to pay the same social security charges as salaried workers. The streets were filled with protesting crowds; the provinces attacked the metropolitan elite in Paris; the railway unions evoked the heroic figure of the train-driver getting his passengers safely into the station on time. And the

Prime Minister duly became a national hate figure. In a typically inept reaction, he told Cabinet colleagues not to be seen smoking cigars in public for fear of a negative popular reaction, and then sat down to write a 120-page book to show that he was 'capable of emotion, love, passion and tears'.

Everything Juppé proposed was long overdue, but the egghead from ÉNA quickly became the most unpopular politician in France. He was feared not only by those who would suffer from his proposals; millions of others saw him cutting away at the comfortable mattress on which France had lain for so long with all the lack of feeling that personifies his breed. Worst of all, he retreated on key issues, and was doubly damned for that. So, in another joke of the times, two blind animals try to identify each other by touch. The first one quickly nails down the second beast as a sheep by its woolly coat and four legs. The sheep then feels out the second animal – a snake. 'Ah,' says the sheep, 'you are smooth and cold and you have no balls – you must be Alain Juppé.'

As for the mindset of the Prime Minister, a former aide remarked that 'Alain has nothing but contempt for those who disagree with him. He thought they were either stupid or involved in an anti-Juppé plot.' Such a frame of mind was all too typical of a caste which has lost touch with the nation it presumes to govern as a matter of right.

The irony is that, more than ever in its history, France is looking for guidance. But, given the gulf between the people and the elite which Juppé came to epitomise, the natural tendency is to fall back on the past, on the old comforts of national life that predated such convulsions. More than most nations, France lives with its traditions – but they are no longer a suitable guide for the twenty-first century. As the economist Alain Minc puts it: 'Our political culture, our history predetermine us. But they will not prove eternally right against the whole world.' Particularly since the bedrock on which France has lived for so long is ebbing away. The result is a national identity crisis with which France lives, usually unconsciously, each day. The French may want to seek refuge from the present in the past, but, once they get into the cork-lined room, they find that the little cakes of history which they seek are crumbling away.

3

VANISHING MADELEINES

Modernists and technocrats may scream, but a set of images defines France – the beret and the café, dark pungent cigarettes, the baguette breadstick and red wine, the accordion, garlic and the Seine. Air France put a beret on top of a globe for instant national recognition in its advertising around the world. A compact-disc compilation of French songs by a British record firm is subtitled 'the garlic and Gauloises world of French accordionists and singers'. At the reconstruction of the citadel at Verdun, where hundreds of thousands of French soldiers perished repulsing the German advance in 1916, the table is laden with baguettes and bottles of red wine. Nothing stirs as much nostalgia for the older French as the evocation of the *bals musette,* the popular dances at which lovers sway to the strains of the squeeze-box. No film would be complete without a scene in a café – and every documentary about Paris has to have a long, lingering shot of the Seine and its bridges.

So now we move from the general to the particular, and consider the symbols of everyday life which are seen as reflecting France's character – in its own eyes, as well as those of the rest of the world. Their current condition tells us much about the shifting sands of national life.

Start at the top. Stone carvings from the Middle Ages show French beret-wearers. More recently, Jean-Paul Sartre sat at Left Bank café tables philosophising with one on his head. Picasso, a Spaniard turned French resident, painted in one. France produces a million of them each year, and the beret-making city of Pau in the Pyrenees plans to introduce beret motifs on its lamp-posts and bus stops. The stereotype seems firmly in place.

But, though berets may be more common in France than bowler hats are in Britain, you could drive from Calais to Cannes without seeing one. (The only beret-wearer I know lives in Berkshire.) A third of the berets produced each year are for the French army. France now has only three beret-making factories, one-tenth of the number before the Second World War. All three turn out what are known as *bérets basques* – though, confusingly, they are located around Pau in the Béarn region, rather than in the neighbouring Basque country. Employing a grand total of 180 people, these companies have only survived by diversifying into wool caps and 'event headgear' emblazoned with logos and decorations – a 'Just Married' (in English) model for newly-weds or an Eiffel Tower version for tourists.

Then take the baguette. Again, things seem well-settled. Three-quarters of the bread produced in France comes from outlets that call themselves bakers – compared to one-third in Britain. While the amount of 'industrial bread' rises each year, it only accounts for 16 per cent of the 3.6 million tonnes sold each year.

But dig below the crust. A celebrity chef who appears on a popular knock-about radio show has made a speciality of denouncing frozen, pre-constituted dough from which even baguettes are made these days. He has a point. The baker who stays up all night kneading dough and supervising its passage through the oven has been overtaken by more convenient and financially rewarding methods, even among self-proclaimed *boulangeries*. The process of making dough from flour, water, salt and yeast can take up to three hours by the traditional method. After that, the dough is divided into sticks and fermented to increase its volume before going into the oven. The longer the dough is left, the better it is; but that takes time, and time is money. So the baker uses frozen dough containing two or three times the normal dose of yeast. Intensive kneading, as it is known, increases the end volume by up to 30 per cent, but produces inferior dough. At the next two stages of production, the mechanical shaping of the dough sticks toughens the inside of the baguette, while modern hot-air ovens do not give a thick crunchy crust.

Traditional bakers remain, mainly in the country and in up-market city enterprises. On the southern slopes of the Massif Central, an Auvergnat bakes his bread once a week in the oven in his farmhouse, and drops the big round loaves off to grateful friends in big flour bags. But the industry as a whole faces long-term decline. As people grow richer and more urbanised, they eat less bread. A century ago, the average French person consumed 219 kilograms a year. By 1967, that was down to 82 kilos; in the 1990s it fell below 60 kilos. Parisians now average only 36 kilos a year, and the national record for bread-eating is in the deeply rural south-western department of Gers. Not surprisingly, the number of small bakers has nearly halved from 54,000 in 1960 to a little over 30,000 today. Bread makes up only about 50 per cent of their takings, compared to cakes, chocolates and pastry.

This is more than the decline of a cottage industry. Bread has a resonant place in French life. Members of the Annales school of social historians would say that its price was more important than which nobleman happened to be Foreign Minister under King Louis the Whatever. The theft of a loaf of bread by Jean Valjean set off the saga of *Les Misérables*. For most French people, it is difficult to start a meal without a chunk of baguette by the plate. Bread plays the same role as rice for Asians: it is more than a simple means of calming the pangs of hunger or mopping up sauce. Not quite the staff of life in the late twentieth century, perhaps, but still a food with deep social roots.

In terms to warm Annalyst hearts, a leading Paris baker, Lionel Poilâne, calls bread 'the key to social peace and stability for every French government'. This star *boulanger* of the Rue du Cherche-Midi on the Left Bank marks his loaves with a trademark square indentation: in its lack of concern for bread, he warns, France is spinning off the rails. Poilâne's proof: 'I went to give a talk to young people about becoming bakers, and most of them got up and left the room.' To prevent such terrible occurrences, the government swung into action. Only bakers who made their own dough were to be allowed to call their establishments *boulangeries*. A scheme was launched to give the best bread a special stamp. Bread served to children with school meals was improved to catch them young. An apocalyptic television commercial thundered, 'If you don't eat bread any more, one day there won't be any!'

All this showed how close bread is to France's idea of its own identity. And in national symbolism, bread means, above all, the baguette, preferably with its crust still warm from the oven. Sandwich shops around the world sell themselves on the idea of its appeal (even if they are run by English or Asian entrepreneurs). As part of the overseas aid effort, an expert from eastern France teaches bakers in developing countries how to make French bread. In the Élysée Palace, Jacques Chirac eats one and a half baguettes a day, and a hundred bakers compete each year for the Grand Prix de la Baguette and the honour of supplying the President with his daily bread. Crunching his crust, Jacques Chirac stigmatises industrial bread as 'not even a Christian food'. An author of a book called *Vive la Baguette* says the breadstick should sound like a drum, and 'flatter the palate with its slightly-caramelised hazelnut flavour'. But how many French people these mornings have the time or inclination to walk down to the *boulangerie* to buy a freshly-made baguette to flatter their palate while the coffee is percolating? One survey shows that the French idea of really good bread is round *pain de campagne* loaves or bread studded with nuts, not the crunchy stick of national imagery. Another cliché bites the dough.

Now drop in at the greatest French social landmark of all, the café. For Balzac, it was 'the parliament of the people'. A century later, the novelist Nathalie Sarraute sat writing at the same table every morning for forty years. The café was hailed by the poet Léon-Paul Fargue as the soundest of French institutions: no revolution, he wrote, had been able to rock its foundations. That was in 1946. Seven years later, Robert Doisneau took one of the great photographs of everyday French life at the Bouillon Tiquetonne café in the Paris market dis-trict of Les Halles. A man in a thick jacket and cap stands in front; an accordionist is on the right by the wall-sized mirror; a stout gesticu-lating woman fills the middle ground; empty glasses and wine bottles sit on every table. The French would like to believe that nothing has changed since then. But the reality of today is a long way from Fargue's post-war world. Surveys report that half the French hardly ever set foot in a café.

In 1910, France had 510,000 cafés and bars for 38 million inhabi-tants: by the mid-1990s, there were one-tenth of that number for 50 per cent more people. Between 1960 and 1995, the ratio of cafés to people fell by a factor of five. Three thousand close each year, up to half of them in Paris. Knocking back a quick calvados on the way to work or propping up a zinc bar while downing a *pastis* or three on the way home is no longer in fashion. Ingeniously, the president of a café-owners' association blames the decline in spirit-drinking on the better quality of coffee now being served. 'It used to be so undrinkable that it encouraged customers to lace it with a small glass of calvados, kirsch or rum,' he says. 'Nowadays, the coffee you get served is of such high quality that anyone adding a dash of spirits to it would raise an eyebrow or two.' As for another icon in the Doisneau photograph, despite the invention of 'rock-musette' combining accordions with heavy bass-lines and a few retro-restaurants complete with strolling players, you have to go a long way to hear an accordionist in the flesh these days. France's principal accordion factory, in the central town of Tulle, now produces just 800 instruments a year compared to 6,000 before the Second World War. One of the last heroes of 'the piano of the poor', Jo Privat, ended his days as a born-again star in Japan after work dried up in France.

Television keeps people at home in the evening. The exodus from the land has deprived thousands of country cafés of customers. Villages which once had three are lucky to have one – and some of those only exist thanks to a subsidy from the local council. An inhabitant of a village without a café in the south-west was reduced to petitioning a visiting British Prime Minister in a bid to get one opened. For speedy eating, people flock to fast-food outlets. The arrival of a hamburger establishment is estimated to cut the trade in nearby cafés by up to 35 per cent. Even the tax system is tilted against the café: the food they serve is subject to value added tax at the maximum rate of 20.6 per cent, whereas take-aways are hit for only 5.5 per cent.

Of France's 2,300 fast-food outlets, 1,200 are *'hamburgeries'*. Around 550 of these are McDonald's, which counts France as its sixth biggest market in the world. One estimate reckoned that the French spend three times as much on hamburgers as on eating at restaurants with rosettes in the Michelin guide. Purists may sniff into their *boeuf bourguignon*; parents in the south-eastern town of Romans may protest when the local McDonald's lays on a free bus service to take schoolchildren to lunch. The Paris authorities had to stop the golden arches being erected on a building where Picasso and Matisse once bought their paints. But the traffic is not all one-way. The food chain has introduced a 'French-taste' hamburger with a sauce featuring pepper and mustard, a thicker tomato slice, a non-shredded lettuce leaf and onions. And nobody except the most gastronomically chauvinistic economist or politician could gainsay the 25,000 jobs which McDonald's created. If things go on at the present rate, the model Frenchman of the twenty-first century will not be emerging from a café in a *pastis* haze but leaving a fast-food joint with his take-away burger in one hand and a packet of sliced bread in the other.

The pungent smoke of another cliché has wafted through national life for most of this century. Tobacco entered the French conscious-ness after the ambassador to Portugal treated his injured cook with a patch made from a herb imported from the New World in 1559. News of its therapeutic qualities got back to France and the ambas-sador was soon supplying the court with tobacco grains. The Queen used them against headaches, and such was their popularity that Louis XIV restricted worshippers at mass to only one sniff of the stuff from the spiritual staff. By the beginning of the eighteenth century there were 1,200 snuff and tobacco establishments in Paris; the smartest still exists in the Place du Palais Royal. In 1818 the special property of tobacco was given a name, inspired by the original ambassador to Portugal, Jean Nicot. Three centuries after his discovery, the manu-facture of cigarettes began after French soldiers came across them while fighting in Spain.

Tobacco is estimated to cause 45,000 premature deaths a year in France, one of the highest rates in the industrialised world. Among men, lung cancer is the leading cause of early mortality, well ahead of alcoholism. Overall, deaths from lung cancer are reckoned to have nearly doubled since 1970. It is a particular killer among the working class, but a killer which has long been close to the Finance Ministry's heart. Tobacco taxes came in under Cardinal de Richelieu in the seventeenth century, and a state monopoly followed. As well as the tax takings, the state cigarette company, Seita, provided large revenues to the public purse in three decades of nationalisation: today, privatised Seita ranks as one of the country's dozen biggest agro-food busi-nesses. In a country which looks after its agriculture, tobacco is an important crop and is given appropriate government protection.

It was not until recently that French politicians had any reservations about being photographed dragging on a cigarette in a way that would have been unacceptable in, say, the United States. A classic photo-graph of the Tour de France from the 1960s shows a cyclist giving a team-mate a light from his stub as they freewheel at the head of the pack. At a time when the rest of the developed world was cutting down, the number of cigarettes smoked in France rose from 85.7 bil-lion to 97.1 billion during the 1980s. Twenty per cent of men smoked more than fifteen a day. Then, in 1991, the government got tough.

There had always been isolated pockets of anti-tobaccoism. If a client at the restaurant run by the godfather of modern cuisine, Fernand Point, was seen lighting up during a meal in the 1950s, coffee and the bill were immediately brought to the table, even if the crayfish or *poularde en vessie* had not yet been served. Some anti-smoking measures were introduced in public buildings in the mid-1970s. When these were extended to provide for no-smoking areas in restaurants and cafés, they were much honoured in the breach. One café in the Paris suburbs put up a notice proclaiming that its owner would rather go to prison than infringe his customers' right to smoke; another designated a single table in the middle of the premises as the no-smoking area. When my wife asked for the tobacco-free zone in a Left Bank restaurant, she was told simply: 'Outside' (the owner insisting that the odour of perfume was far more detrimental to the enjoyment of food than tobacco fumes).

A serious-minded Socialist Health Minister banned smoking in canteens, public areas in hotels, lifts and offices containing more than two people. Offending individuals or employers were threatened with fines or imprisonment – the state railway was found guilty of failing to put up big enough anti-smoking posters at a station in Lyon. Cigarette advertising was outlawed. An opinion poll said 84 per cent of people supported the measures. The consumption of cigarettes fell steadily through the 1990s, and the Jospin government announced plans to increase taxes on cigarettes and tobacco – not, of course, to raise rev-enue but as a way of discouraging young people from smoking. But, if the French are smoking less, where the cliché really comes apart is in what they actually puff.

For decades, there was something exotic about French cigarettes; even the brand-names were peculiarly resonant. As cigarettes swept the nation at the turn of the century, smokers could choose from 242 different products. There was a name for everybody to identify with –

Odalisques and Jockeys, Boyards and Havanaises. The Hongrois brand changed its name to Gauloises in 1910 and became the market leader ten years later. Gitanes-Vizier put a woman on its packet in 1927, the year it dropped the Turkish second half of its name. The Belle Époque brand, *élégantes de luxe*, turned butch after the First World War by altering its name to Amazones. For chauvinists there were Celtiques, Royale and, most simply, Les Françaises; those with more distant horizons could buy packs of Congo, Maryland or Égyptiennes.

Despite the range of choice, French cigarettes were epitomised for decades by Gitanes and Gauloises, in conventional white paper cylinders or more exotic maize paper. Gitanes had a characteristic flat box that opened like a drawer; Gauloises were tapped out of a soft packet with a card-shuffling motion. No French film was complete without a cloud of smoke round Jean Gabin or Jean-Paul Belmondo; no existentialist nightclub or corner café was authentic without the tobacco haze; no Paris taxi ride was real without a throat-twitching, stomach-churning stink wafting back from the driver. In the early 1970s, when the Head of State appeared on the cover of a biography with a thick dark French cigarette clenched between his lips, *les brunes* accounted for 86 per cent of sales. The songwriter Serge Gainsbourg, who lived in a perpetual cloud of smoke, appeared quite content when Catherine Deneuve told him in a duet that, while God puffed Havanas, 'you are only a smoker of Gitanes'.

Now, as with the café and the baguette, things are different. Law suits have been launched against cigarette companies for allegedly giving insufficient warnings of the health dangers of smoking. An illustration on a stamp of the writer and former Culture Minister, André Malraux, was doctored to eliminate the cigarette between his lips. 'Given the law, we had no choice,' explained a spokeswoman for the postal service. The traditional French brand which Malraux was smoking in the photograph was still the individual national favourite with 20 per cent of sales, but, overall, dark tobacco cigarettes are now outsold two to one by light tobacco ones. *Blondes* put out under the Gitanes mark sell almost as many as its *brunes*. When Marlboro went on sale in France in 1924, it was as a niche product aimed at women, complete with a red tip to go with their lipstick. Seven decades later, the brand takes 17 per cent of the market, and even the President of the Republic smokes Virginia-style cigarettes. Foreign brands account for almost half total sales; filter-tips rule. Perhaps that is why French films seem to show less smoking these days. Gérard Depardieu drawing on a Stuyvesant wouldn't be quite the same as the gangs of the great *films noirs* plotting their heists in a pall of smoke you can smell off the screen. And even the packet for Gitanes Blondes has taken on a new look from the other side of the globe. Its new fliptop box with a little yellow figure dancing against the traditional black gypsy silhouette on a stonewashed jean background is the work of a Japanese designer. But then, a baker born in Portugal won the Grand Prix de la Baguette in 1998, and a sommelier from Japan has carried off the top prize at the Bordeaux wine fair.

If brown tobacco, breadsticks and cafés are three essential elements in the traditional image of France, another is red wine. But here, too, late-twentieth-century reality chips in. The French still drink more wine than any other people on Earth, and there are restaurants where you are automatically brought a litre of rough red with your set menu. But just as it is rare these days to see a zinc bar topped with a row of glasses, the number of people who drink wine every day has almost halved since 1980. Even Jacques Chirac makes no secret of his preference for beer (although, after being elected, he at least had the patriotic decency to switch from his preferred Mexican brew to Kronenbourg). By 1995, 45 per cent of the population were regular drinkers of mineral water while only 27 per cent took wine with their meals each day. The worst offenders were the young, only 17 per cent of whom drank any wine at all on a regular weekly basis.

The world's largest wine-producing region is near the Mediterranean coast in south-west France, where a few good wines are swamped by a multitude of *vins de table*. But France's vineyards cover only one-third of the land they occupied before they were devastated by the phylloxera disease in the mid-nineteenth century. The number of people employed in making wine has halved since 1970. Sales of soft drinks rise year by year, and 70 per cent of 14- to 25-year-olds say they never touch ordinary wine. This is a matter of taste, the result of savvy marketing and a fashion trend. There is also a serious survival issue involved: despite still holding records for alcoholism, premature deaths due to drink are waning. A couple of glasses of wine may help ward off heart attacks and reduce the chances of cancer or senile dementia, but even the French have been shocked to learn that 40 per cent of their fatal road accidents involve drunken driving.

Worst of all, some of France's own experts have rounded on the quality of some of the home-produced drink. Most French wine is excellent, and no country has a greater range of regional vineyards, each with its own distinctive taste. However, the head of the institute which monitors standards acknowledged at the end of 1995 that even wines bearing labels attesting to their status as coming from an Appellation d'Origine Contrôlée (AOC), which is supposed to guarantee quality, were sometimes undrinkable. On occasion, they were even 'scandalously bad'. There should have been nothing too surprising about this. Anybody who has drunk any quantity of reasonably priced wine in France or anywhere else will have come across poor bottles. Whatever their labels may say, some wines will always turn out to be below standard in some vintages. Real or apocryphal stories have been around for years about tanker lorries filled with cheap southern (or even North African) plonk turning up in Beaujolais and Burgundy to add strength to the produce of up-market vineyards in thin years. The pursuit of higher yields, sometimes by late watering which makes the grapes swell, has jeopardised quality in some areas. So has the addition of sugar to the fermenting grape juice to raise the alcohol level. More seriously, questions have been raised about pesticides getting into the wine from the wooden barrels at one leading Bordeaux chateau, and about the practices of some top Burgundy growers. But the local committees of growers rarely deny the AOC label to their neighbours; one estimate puts the failure rate at only 2 per cent.

When the consumer magazine *Que Choisir* detailed some of these failings, it aroused a storm of protest – not from drinkers but from the wine industry which tried to get the article withdrawn. The official who acknowledged the scandalous quality of some growths had to resign. Faced with the pesticide revelations, the growers' association said it was best to treat this as a private matter since the public might not understand the complexities involved. The French may drink less wine than they once did, but the renown of their national drink has to be defended come what may.

This raises a real problem. The French believe that their wines are the best in the world, and they are right. Though they sell a smaller proportion of their output abroad than Spain, Italy or Germany,

France's vineyards still account for almost half the world's exports, measured by value, and a French company is busy taking the message to the other side of the world by planting 3,000 hectares of quality grapes in China to nurture the nascent wine industry there. Led by the great growths of Bordeaux and Burgundy, and by legally ring-fenced Champagne, wine sales abroad rose by 16 per cent in 1997 to 42 billion francs, with claret racing ahead by 40 per cent. Ranking second only to aerospace as an earner of foreign currency, annual exports of wines and spirits were the equivalent of the sale of 135 Airbus planes or 560 high-speed trains. Prices of the finest French growths spiralled beyond reason as Americans increased their purchases by one-third and Asian buyers circled Bordeaux. The Saint-Emilion vineyard, Château Cheval Blanc, was sold for 860 million francs by French and Belgian businessmen at the end of 1998. A case of 1945 Château Pétrus which had been bought for the equivalent of $42,000 fifteen months earlier went for $75,000. Prices at the annual auction in the Burgundy wine capital of Beaune shot up 47 per cent at the end of 1997 as the speculators gathered. Rare French wines were a great new market, even for Muslims who never sipped alcohol. 'Wine is going to become the hobby of a few specialists,' warned one Burgundy expert. More likely, it looked like a sure-fire way of making money for people who couldn't tell a Corton from a Corbières.

Such inflated values will not be achieved by any New World wine. Still, any market leader has to look over its shoulder. France cannot ignore the competition on the international scene from the New World. In 1998, the highly respected wine critic of the *New York Times* declared the best reds of California and Oregon to be worthy rivals of the great Burgundies. Australian wine exports have risen tenfold in a decade. Cloudy Bays from New Zealand and the best of the Napa Valley can even be found in timid corners of the wine lists in some French restaurants: one sniffily entitles the section '*Vins d'ailleurs*'. Simply saying that French is best is no answer. Some producers in the Hexagon have actually learned from methods used in California and Australia, while the American producer Robert Mondavi set up a company to make wines in Languedoc specially designed to appeal to US palates. Domestic consumption may remain resolutely national, but there is a battle to be fought abroad for everyday wines which ordinary drinkers can afford to take home in the evening. Being special is one thing; being affordable and reliable is another.

All right, so things are changing, but one fact about the French is surely unshakable – they stink of garlic. Indeed, they may be so imbued with the vegetable that they don't notice its aroma: a gourmand academic from London, Keith Walker, once ate a whole chicken stuffed with forty cloves and rode the train back to Paris from Orléans without anybody pursing his nose. The truth is, however, that France does not even rank in the world's top half-dozen producers or consumers of the vegetable. Yes, there is an association devoted to its folklore and promotion in the middle of France, whose members parade at jolly ceremonies wearing hats shaped like the clove. But the leading academic expert on garlic is in the United States, and the South Koreans use far more of it than the French. The self-proclaimed garlic capital of the world is Gilroy, California. The International Garlic Information Centre is to be found in East Sussex. New York has a Garlic Seed Foundation. At an 'officially regulated tasting' of a dozen varieties held there in the autumn of 1995, there was a French entry, but Spain took the prize.

One by one, the landmarks crumble, change, or are not quite what they seem to be. The madeleine on display at the house in the country town of Illiers-Combray which has been turned into a museum to the memory of Marcel Proust's most famous novel turns out, inevitably, to be made of plastic. *Foie gras* is imported from Central Europe and snails from as far away as Taiwan. That essential element in traditional French hygiene, the bidet, is now installed in fewer than 10 per cent of new bathrooms. The famously rotund Michelin Man, Bibendum, was slimmed down for his hundredth birthday in 1998. France may still be the world centre of pétanque, but the world championship was won in 1997 by Tunisia. Money and crooks ain't what they used to be, either: preparing for the European common currency, the national mint has stopped producing franc coins and banknotes while a top cop, Robert Broussard, says the old race of hoods has been replaced by a more discreet, more intellectual, more financially astute class of criminals, 'who live in smart districts and send their children to the best schools'. As for the prostitutes with gold-plated hearts who have been part of the popular imagination from Manon Lescaut through Toulouse-Lautrec's easy ladies to Irma la Douce, they are being banished to the outer reaches of cities or replaced by students who advertise their attractions electronically. Modern society and fear of AIDS have even undermined the image of the headstrong French lover – in an opinion poll men expressed their preference for a partner who would bring a condom along with her in case he forgot his rather than for an impromptu unprotected coupling. There has even been an offensive from across the northern border on one worldwide French icon, claiming that French fries are actually a Belgian invention. The home team, however, appears to have a good defence on this score, pointing out that Thomas Jefferson spoke of 'Potatoes, Fried in the French Manner' thirty years before Belgium even came into existence as a country.

Once-sacred traditions like the business lunch and holidays have been affected by the shifts in society, and the caution generated by living in a high-unemployment economy. Business meals eaten in restaurants are reckoned to have fallen from 48 million in 1980 to 19 million in 1995: in part that was due to changing lifestyles (mineral water and a salad instead of Cahors and *cassoulet*) but cost also counted – bills running into thousands of francs no longer go through the accounts department so easily. A travel agent offers stand-by tables at top restaurants with menus at half-price. Chefs are no longer otherworldly figures who care only for the freshness of their vegetables or the texture of their sweetbreads. 'Before I make money, I have to pay overheads,' as one three-rosette cook involved in the stand-by scheme put it. 'Maybe I won't make a profit tonight – but at least I won't lose money.'

As for holidays, the month-long vacation in August is becoming less sacrosanct, with people ready to go away for shorter periods. The new boss of the Club Méditerranée has added one-day breaks in France to the organisation's traditional offering of long stretches in exotic places. Executives can get twitchy sitting on a beach when their companies may be heading for restructuring. Money-conscious holidaymakers have been avoiding the Riviera and frequenting cheaper areas of the country. Those who still go south rent simple *gîtes* away from the coast. The mood swung against the conspicuous consumption of the Côte d'Azur in favour of the more bracing and less polluted west coast, against the gilded palaces, intensive suntans and over-priced lounging chairs on the beaches at Nice and Cannes in favour of woolly jumpers, sailing and family walks through the wind-swept Celtic heather. When Lionel Jospin took a brief break from his first months in office, it was to breathe in the sea breezes on an island off the Atlantic coast, and even Princess Caroline of Monaco was sighted in the same area. The change of scene was not just a matter of the amount of cash spent – Brittany can be as expensive as the Mediterranean – but more a matter of mood. 'I see in this fashion the generation of those in their forties who have done it all,' says the publisher of magazines for the smart set of the south and the west coasts. 'They want a return to the family, which is even more sacred to them because they are often starting out for the second time after a divorce. They remember the quiet family holidays in Brittany during the 1950s. For years, they made fun of them, but now they realise they weren't so bad after all.'

In a final cliché challenge, the river along whose banks lovers traditionally stroll on the screen, in romantic imagination and in real life, may even be misnamed. The Seine rises in Burgundy, hundreds of kilometres from the capital. On its way to Paris, it joins another Burgundian river, the Yonne, at the town of Montereau. Their waters are, from then on, known as the Seine. But the custom is that when two rivers meet, the one which has the largest volume of water gives its name to the combined flow. And the flow rate of the Yonne at the junction is 105 cubic metres per second while that of the Seine is only 75 cubic metres. The Mayor of Montereau has no doubts: 'The rivers are of different colours. It is easy to see that the Yonne beats the Seine.'

In this moving set of stereotypes, however, one thing seems certain: the name of France's best-known river will not be altered. But plenty else is changing in the countryside where the Yonne, the Seine and all France's other great rivers flow, for the most basic of all madeleines is undergoing a metamorphosis which is more crucial to the nation than all the Virginia cigarettes, Euro banknotes or McDonald's in the world.

4

COUNTRY LIVING

If there is one thing which the French have long held particularly dear, it is the rural land that covers some 90 per cent of the surface of their country. Agriculture is a major element in the wealth of the nation, but the status of the countryside is not to be reduced to mere economics. The pull goes far deeper than that. The rural world is a pole around which national sentiment has revolved ever since the Romantics saw fields and lakes as more than a way of scraping a life from earth and fresh water. But now it, too, is changing more than the French would wish to admit. Ninety per cent of rural households do not contain anybody working in agriculture. Farms are being deserted, villages are emptying. Pig factories flourish while the streams are empty of crayfish. *Foie gras* is as likely to originate from Eastern Europe as from a farm in the Périgord. The seeds for Dijon mustard come from Canada. Traditional evenings around the village fountain exist only in books and on the screen. Hypermarkets are killing off rural shops. All of which is so disorienting because what is vanishing is crucial to the nation's idea of its own basic character.

Country life has deep roots in the French imagination. The tale of a harassed town-dweller escaping to peace and contentment in a rural idyll is a constant theme of popular books and films. France has a set of diverse and thriving regional cultures. Many of its greatest writers have drawn on their direct link with a country region – Balzac with the Loire Valley, Flaubert with Normandy, Mauriac with the Bordelais, Mistral, Giono and Pagnol with Provence. As Jacques Chirac has pointed out, the regional appeal in fiction lies in 'the rediscovery of a source of popular memory which the French are afraid of losing for ever'. Up-market pop singers record hymns to their native corner of the land, and regional cultural centres keep traditions alive, if sometimes rather artificially. A remarkable encyclopaedist, Marcel Lachiver, has collected 45,000 rural terms in a book running to 1,816 pages. In the heart of France, the annual literary fair of Corrèze draws 100,000 people to the departmental capital of Brive. For some who have risen to the summit of power and glory, the essential link with the countryside is one which harks back to an innocent childhood. Through his long political career in Paris, François Mitterrand never shook off the sentimental appeal of his native region of the Charente, which his fellow south-westerner, François Mauriac, described as 'an unchanging landscape where I can still believe I am an adolescent'.

French townspeople have more country homes than any other Europeans. Nearly 70 per cent of France's 12.5 million gardens have a vegetable plot. A million and a half people count themselves as hunters – 150,000 of them marched through Paris in February 1998 to proclaim their right to shoot migrating birds. Scratch an urban French man or woman and they will speak nostalgically of the village or small town where they grew up or where their parents hailed from. Their taxes pay for services which would be hard to find in many other advanced economies – for the electricity network which takes no account of distance or inaccessibility, airports that handle a hundred or so travellers a day, the country train network with its neat little stations, and the highly efficient postal system which supports rural offices with annual turnovers of just 50,000 francs. In person or through television, many more join the great annual celebration of the French countryside that is the Tour de France, as riders sweep across the plains, climb the mountains, swoop down on the coasts and rocket through a hundred villages in *la Grande Boucle* which brings the nation together.

In a country which has always appreciated feminine virtues of an old-fashioned kind, the land is essentially a woman. There is plenty of stereotypically rugged masculine mountain terrain on the edges and in the middle of France. Still, the traditional image of the rural lands echoes the remark by the historian Emmanuel Le Roy-Ladurie about France being, first and foremost, a beautiful woman. This is '*la douce*

France' immortalised in Charles Trenet's songs. Today's writers shrink from genderised descriptions, but the inventor of the modern French novel had no inhibitions. For Balzac, his native Touraine was 'a woman going to meet her lover'; nature resembled 'a woman rising from her bed' and the Loire estuary became an older woman 'swollen with all the disappointments and tribulations of life'.

In the national imagination, stock characters pop out from the hedgerows: the ruby-cheeked priest preaching to a tiny congregation of old women, and the earnest left-wing teacher trying to instil republican values in a class of bored children; the dried-up widow in black peering at passers-by from behind her curtains and the amply-breasted, loosely-dressed village flirt who leads the farm boys off into the long grass; banquets without end on market days and the old-fashioned farmer eating his soup as his wife stands humbly behind him; the poacher lying in the bushes watching for rabbits on the edge of the local hunting estate and the gamekeeper who waits till the owner has driven back to town before inviting his friends round for a feast behind the château. It is not all a matter of imagination. In one village we visit regularly, an old woman sat for many years watching the passers-by from behind her curtains, and the priest drinks cheap wine from tumblers as his housekeeper serves his meagre supper. Bernadette Chirac recalls that, when her husband began campaigning in the Corrèze in the 1960s, local dignitaries held dinners at which their wives remained standing behind them after serving the dishes – now, in her role as a local councillor in the department, she, herself, soldiers through the eight-hour annual banquet of the local firemen. Some years ago, I spent a long Sunday at an open-air banquet in the grounds of a hunting estate amid the forests and lakes of the Sologne region, where the increasingly drunk gamekeeper denounced his employers, opened their finest wines and terrines of *foie gras* – and ended the day by lurching off into the woods with his wife.

France is a patchwork of local *pays*; *paysans* are not peasants but the people of their stretch of the land. Frenchmen living ten thousand miles from the Hexagon define themselves as Berrichon or Provençal as much as French. As La Rochefoucauld put it: 'The accent of the country where one is born remains in the spirit and the heart as it does in the language.' Roots count, up to the very summit. Though born in Paris, Jacques Chirac talks of his adopted homeland in the

Corrèze as though it were more important to him than the Élysée Palace.

The untranslatable expression '*la France profonde*' refers not just to areas like the great central region stretching from the Limousin through the volcanic peaks of the Massif Central to the Cévennes. It is not just a matter of geography, of what a Parisian friend used to refer to as 'the French desert'. Rural France is a state of mind. Towns breed politics and division; farmers get on with life in a down-to-earth manner, and stand together in adversity. 'With bare arms and pure hands, we will go to clean up Paris,' proclaimed a pre-war quasi-Fascist rural movement, the Green Shirts. Sixty years later, the President of the Republic speaks feelingly of 'a land peopled by humble, brave, honest and hard-working folk'. Though the Île-de-France region around Paris was, as its name suggests, the kernel of the nation from the Middle Ages, there is a lingering and unshakable feeling that the real France lies in the countryside, not in the capital.

Farmers, proclaims Jacques Chirac, 'are the gardeners of our country and the guardians of our memory'. Provincial, rural knowledge is a natural gift as opposed to an acquired skill – folklore rather than culture, a natural wisdom absorbed from the ebb and flow of the seasons instead of being learned from books. The country is a place where people have proper old French names rather than being called after American film stars, where the tombs in a graveyard by the Aveyron river deep in the Rouergue region commemorate Albertine and Armand, Baptiste and Blaise, Calixte and Célestin, Firmin, Germaine and Marise, and where the living old folk get a twice-yearly free banquet of soup, asparagus quiche, stuffed veal, duck, cheese, dessert and cakes at the Michelin-rosetted restaurant opposite the church. Like Bouvard and Pécuchet, Gustave Flaubert's classic couple of city-dwellers who think they have found paradise in a crumbling farmhouse in Normandy where the vegetables wither, the cabbage is inedible and the neighbours mocking, the French stand ready to be swamped by a rural idyll.

On this hymn-sheet, city people are bad-tempered, materialistic seekers after money and slaves of empty fashion who jostle one another on the pavement, have heart attacks in traffic jams and only escape from their concrete jungle by roaring out on multi-lane motorways at murderous speeds. In contrast, country folk are easy-going and friendly, ambling up leafy lanes behind their herds of cattle, or driving their old cars gently along empty roads bordered by poplar trees. This view is not confined to the French. 'Parisians,' declared a letter-writer to the *Independent*, 'are rude, ignorant and in a hurry. Provincial people are pleasant, attentive and relaxed.' The contrast is seductive, as the creative directors of advertising agencies know when they conjure up rural images to sell processed food. In 1981, Mitterrand's presidential bid was greatly boosted by a poster showing him against a soft-focus village complete with church tower. Thirteen years earlier, it had been fitting that the great urban student revolt and general strike of 1968 should have been brought to a peaceful and mutually profitable conclusion by a head of government who hailed originally from the iconic-sounding Auvergnat village of Montboudif.

Much of this is rubbish. 'The land is tough,' as a local landowner remarked to Bouvard and Pécuchet while their haystacks burned down. Less so today than when Flaubert wrote, but there are few lotus-eaters on the land, and the idea that proximity to the earth brings with it a sunny disposition is strictly for the birds. Many more people die on country roads than on motorways. Farmers are notoriously aggressive demonstrators, and there has never been any shortage of village money-grubbers. Rural folk are as likely as anybody to name their children after pop stars and film idols. The highest rates of suicide are in largely agricultural areas of the north-west. The countryside's good sense often equates to reactionary conservatism.

Still, the ideal provides a mattress and a vital prop for the nation. The politicians in their ministries in the far-away capital certainly recognise the need to keep the non-urban world happy. Almost 20 per cent of voters are reckoned to depend for their livelihood on farming and the countryside in some way. Nearly one-third of French mayors are farmers. Few government posts are more sensitive than that of the Agriculture Ministry. An attempt by the left to alter the power structure of the farm organisations in the early 1980s ended in farce when the minister was marooned in a muddy field by demonstrators who prevented her helicopter from rescuing her. (The appointment of a woman to deal with such a chauvinistic group of men as the farmers was seen as either a provocation or a massive miscalculation, or perhaps both.) Later, when he wanted to do down a rival, Mitterrand put him into the Agriculture Ministry and dared him to do something about subsidies. On the other hand, Jacques Chirac's stint in the job in the early 1970s made him the farmers' friend for life – his vehemence in defending their interests led his German counterpart to advise him to see a psychiatrist. A quarter of a century on, the farm vote kept Chirac in the presidential race in 1995, ahead of the distinctly unrural Prime Minister, Édouard Balladur, whose inability to hold a lamb in such a way that it would not urinate over him caused much mirth among the farmers when he visited the Agriculture Minister's south-western town of Rignac. Once installed at the Élysée, Chirac the born-again Correzian repaid the compliment by devoting five hours to visiting the Paris agriculture show; in all, 200 politicians went to the exhibition that year to pay their respects to the farming world.

The countryside counts not only in politics and the national psychology, but also where it really matters – in the stomach. Food in France is linked to the land in a way that is not the case in many other nations. This, after all, is a country where an academic writes a 152-page treatise on one sort of Auvergne cheese and where, for many years, food pirates found it worth their while to buy cheap brown lentils from the Cantal department, die them green and pass them off as the prized pulses from the neighbouring Haute-Loire. Paris has excellent chefs, but it is the regions, the *pays*, which make French cuisine what it is. A 440-page compendium of national menus by the Maîtres Cuisiniers de France contains only half as many pages on the Île-de-France region around the capital as on Brittany, Guyenne or Languedoc. Pollution may have driven the famous *sandre* from the Loire river, and the *boeuf bourguignon* served up for dinner may have been produced on an industrial estate, but food remains rooted in the countryside, and most of the top restaurants are still located in the provinces. Each product has its specific local link. The best butter comes from the meadows of the Charente, the sweetest melon from Cavaillon in the south, and your favourite wines from any one of a hundred individual vineyards, each with its own taste. Those green lentils from Le Puy have an Appellation d'Origine Contrôlée to honour and protect their excellence, as do poultry from the wetlands of the Bresse east of Lyon, nuts from Grenoble, potatoes from the Île de Ré in the Atlantic, and the olive oil from Les Baux-de-Provence and from Nyons in the foothills of the Alps. These are national treasures, as much a part of France's glory as Notre Dame or the nuclear strike force. The AOC accolade has even been extended to a foodstuff not consumed by humans, the 100,000 tonnes of hay harvested each year on the plain of Crau at the mouth of the Rhône which is exported as far away as Hong Kong for the delectation of thoroughbred racehorses.

To illustrate how the countryside and village life imbue French gastronomy with its real strength, let us take a short tour around three sides of the great Massif Central mountain range. To the north-east lies the village of Saint-Bonnet-le-Froid, a lost place in the Haute-Loire department known mainly for its annual mushroom fair before it became the home of a great cook. Son of the local café-owner, Régis Marcon wanted to be an artist but turned to the kitchen instead. After travelling to London and learning his trade under the Roux brothers there, he returned to his native village and transformed the family café into a restaurant and simple hotel – at the same time running the village petrol pump. He used the extraordinary natural local ingredients, and made a few mistakes along the way – his cèpe mushrooms in vinegar were inedible back in 1986. But by the mid-1990s, Marcon was a deserved gastronomic star. His food remained rooted in the countryside around him. He constructed an annexe to his hotel in the glitzy style French chefs seem to enjoy, but his menu built on local fungus was a marvel worthy of a brace of rosettes. And, if Marcon's Auberge des Cimes was full, you could always stoke up on the seven-course menu of solid country food at the café across the road for 65 francs.

To the south, up a winding road in the Cévennes mountains, lies the village of Vialas, where another son of poor parents, Patrick Pagès, has reinvented a string of local dishes. There have been periodic food fads in Paris for outlandish gastronomic combinations which usually don't work because, however clever they may appear to the chef, they taste awful. But Pagès took the invention which used to be essential to make cheap, repetitive rural food interesting all year round, and gave it a quality flip. He serves mushrooms with chestnuts, lamb sweetbreads with thyme flowers, pig's trotters with apples. Fish with the juice of sausage meat or dishes incorporating old bacon may sound distinctly unappetising, but they are very good indeed. These are, or were, poor people's ingredients: backward villages in the Cévennes didn't get much in the way of lobster or caviar. The original versions of these dishes may have been horribly effective – sausage juice off-setting rotten fish, tart apple sauce sharpening the gelatine of the trotters. In the hands of such a cook, they become both delicious and a reaffirmation of rural values through the gut.

A couple of hundred kilometres north-west from Vialas across highlands and through deep folds in the hills, the Fagegaltier sisters have carried out a similar transformation in one of the most beautiful villages in the whole of France. Their establishment in the deeply rural department of the Aveyron used to be a simple café run by their rock-like father, who still sits quietly on a straight-backed chair at the top of the steps leading up from the street to the restaurant. Born on the plateau overlooking the valley of the river which gives the department its name, he started out building roads and other public works, and rose to become a foreman. 'I had a place in life,' he remembers. 'I could have gone away. But then I met my wife by chance. We were mature – I was thirty, she was twenty-eight. We decided to stay here.' They ran the café by the old bridge across the Aveyron, specialising in frying the little fish plucked fresh from the river outside. One day, a retired miner came to stay, and began fishing in the river. Before long, he returned, and fished some more. Eventually, he became a fixture, spending the last fifteen years of his life in the village, where he was remembered years later as 'the king of whitebait'. One day, father Fagegaltier recalled, a party of a dozen people turned up unexpectedly – 'and within fifteen minutes, we'd caught enough fish to feed them all'.

Like him, his daughters could have moved on – they have dipped a toe in the celebrity chef circuit with an expedition to Tokyo, where the jet-lag was a problem. But the excellence of Nicole Fagegaltier, the sister who does the cooking, would be unthinkable away from their roots. The food is so good that one guide named them the best-value restaurant in the whole country. Nobody who has eaten there would argue, and Nicole received a supreme local accolade when she won a cookery competition and was rewarded with her weight in prunes. Still, she remains properly down-to-Aveyron-earth. 'A cook,' she says, 'may be an artist and a dreamer – but also needs to be a good manager.' Again, it is the rural-based dishes which make their mark – cèpe mushroom tart, salt cod, veal and lamb with varia-tions of herbs and berries in the sauce, stuffed cabbage, cream of bacon to accompany the sweetbreads, all washed down by Marcillac wine from over the hill. For the big menu, you need a solid appetite – on one occasion, this might mean artichokes and asparagus with truffles and powdered ham, red mullet with sweet onions flavoured with anchovies, duck liver with young turnips and a sauce made from a local liqueur, sweetbreads, local cheeses and four desserts; on another, crispy potato cake with shrimps and cèpe mushrooms, sea bass and leeks with cèpe oil, grilled duck's liver with green beans and a sauce using a Marcillac liqueur, pigeon breast in breadcrumbs with garlic and rosemary oil, local cheeses and four desserts. At one recent Sunday lunch, every table except ours was taken by local family parties, and several of them were eating the big menu.

In times of trouble, the country is a source of valuable supplies: one of the staple Second World War tales is of food being smuggled into Paris, preferably involving a squealing pig which has to be kept quiet while the police patrol passes by. At such moments in history, the contrast between town and city becomes all the sharper. While food was hard to come by in the occupied capital, a marriage banquet in an isolated village in the centre of the country consisted of a *macédoine* of vegetables, ham and butter, home-made *foie gras*, rolls of ham with cream, guinea fowl in sauce, chicken with truffles, vegetables, turkey with watercress, cheese platter, apple pie, almond cakes and fruit, with red and white wine, champagne and liqueurs.

For some, at moments of great danger, the countryside provides an even more important succour as a haven to escape into the vastness that is rural France. The isolated town of Le Chambon-sur-Lignon, with its reserved Protestant inhabitants, won fame for sheltering thousands of Jews from 1940 onwards. When the German army swept by on its regular patrols, the refugees were hidden in the rough countryside of the windswept plateau that surrounds the town. After the war, Chambon was offered a Garden of Thanksgiving in Israel but, in its modest manner, refused the honour.

Two hundred kilometres to the east, it was the snow on the foothills of the Alps that dazzled a five-year-old girl who didn't know what she was escaping from. 'We arrived in the village in wintertime,' she recalled half a century later. 'Snow covered the countryside. I was five and tired from the long journey. My father carried me on his shoulders up the path that led to our new home, the farm of the Vieux Colombier which we had rented in the Free Zone to escape from the persecution in Paris. Years later, the family would repeat my first words when we got there: "Oh, look at the white snow, it's like pre-war snow." I had heard everybody saying, when they saw anything good, that it was like before the war – so I guess I thought that was the best thing I could say about the snow.'

Her father had been taken prisoner by the Germans in 1940, and had escaped from his camp. His wife and two children avoided deportation from Paris to Auschwitz by a mixture of hiding and good luck; some of their aunts and cousins died there. In 1942, they decided to flee the city. The little girl was entrusted to her nine-year-old brother. The two children were taken to a group of *passeurs*, people living by the demarcation line between the occupied zone of France and the Vichy-run 'Free Zone' where the Germans had not yet arrived. Some *passeurs* took Jewish children to safety in the south; others sold them to the Nazis. This brother and sister were lucky. Their mother travelled separately to join them in the Free Zone, hiding in a crate of coal on a goods train from Paris. Before it left the capital, police with dogs searched the train for people like her fleeing death, but they did not find her. When she emerged from the crate and met relatives in Grenoble, they could not help remarking on her face. At such a tragic time, how did Fanny have the vanity to put on mascara? It was coal dust.

In the Alps, life was different. The father came from rural stock in Poland: he told rousing stories about repelling bandits and riding through the family forests with a rifle in his hand. In Saint-André-de-Rosans, the war was far away. 'Our farm was one kilometre from the village,' the daughter recalls.

We lived in the back of the building. A family from Marseille and then a group of resistance fighters were in front. We had a garden and a courtyard where the poultry ran. One evening my brother and I gave the chickens the wine left over in the glasses from supper. They tottered about, completely pissed. On one side of the building was a mysterious room; later I was told it was occupied by a member of the collaborationist militia.

My brother, five years older than me, went to the village school, and learned to talk the local patois with his mates. Once, I remember, the whole village was gripped by fear: word spread that a German was marching across the square. But it was only a teenager who thought it was a good joke to dress up in a Wehrmacht uniform – where he got it from we never knew.

The family pretended to be Turks and called themselves Vartil rather than Wartski. Not that the demons stalking France at the time would have been fazed by a name. Appearance counted for more, and there they were fortunate in their father.

One day, the schoolteacher came up to our farm. He'd slung a satchel over his shoulder so that it would look as though he was out hunting, or picking berries. 'They're here,' he warned. My mother, my brother and I ran up the hill to hide in another farm. My father stayed behind, working in the garden. The Germans, who were retreating from Italy, stopped and said they had been told that Jews were being sheltered in the area. At a time like that, all they could think of was rounding up some more of us. With his green eyes and white hair, my father looked like a Kirk Douglas Jew. He shook his head and said no, he didn't know of any Jews in the area. So they drove on, and nobody in the village betrayed us.

But even far away in the countryside danger remained ever present. The Wartski–Vartil parents kept an empty tube of toothpaste in their barn with rolled-up banknotes tucked inside. They told their young son: 'If anything happens to us, take the money and look after your sister – and God help you.' North-east of Saint-André, an anonymous tip-off in March 1944 led the Germans to a farmhouse near the mountain village of La Martellière, in which eighteen Jews were staying with a resistance group led by a rabbi. All were sent to a transit camp on their way to their deaths. One escaped. The others were deported to Auschwitz, where all but one died. Fifty-three years later, a plaque with the names of the dead was unveiled in the village – and still nobody knew who had tipped off the Germans.

★

In view of all the emotional investment in the idea of the land and those who live on it, nobody should be surprised if France's stout defence of the European subsidies paid to its farmers is more than a matter of money and votes. One of the key tasks of the central government is to protect the rural fibre which underpins the nation: ministers may deplore violence against prefecture buildings and the blocking of roads by tractor barrages, but they cannot afford to be seen to be hostile to the *paysans*. When farmers spread manure in the streets or pelt officials with rotten fruit, they find an echo which would be unthinkable across the Channel. Town and city dwellers see their compatriots in the countryside as victims of modernisation who deserve support, not as subsidy-absorbing leeches on the tax structure. They view them as giving something to national life that goes well beyond their economic contribution – though, since France is the world's second biggest food exporter and accounts for nearly a quarter of agricultural output in the European Union, their weight as wealth-producers is very considerable indeed. 'Tillage and pasturage are the two breasts of France,' a royal official declared in the seventeenth century. The economic statistics may indicate that this is still the case, but, behind the billions of francs earned by France's farms each year, the mother's milk is turning somewhat sour.

Take, as an example, a series of snap shots over thirty-five years. In the 1950s, the woman who had sheltered in Saint-André went back to live in her wartime haven 600 metres up in the southern foothills of the Alps. 'In the summers then, Saint-André-de-Rosans was always busy,' she recalls.

> The women gathered around the fountain to gossip and exchange secrets as they did their laundry in the public wash-house. Farm-hands sipped *pastis* while they waited their turn to play pétanque in front of the three cafés round the main square. On summer evenings, the young people danced to the music on the portable gramophone – *le pickup* – set up outside Madame Roland's café down the main street: the priest warned us we were courting damnation. In the winter, after supper, we wandered from house to house, chatting and listening to the old folk recounting their memories in the local Provençal dialect. Our favourite stopping-off point was the post office, where Madame Estienne had a wireless for us to listen to the

hit shows from Paris. The schoolteacher taught all his pupils in a single class. Those who graduated to secondary school moved to the town down on the plain to study.

At weekends, we sometimes went to visit relations in nearby villages for lunches that stretched on till the evening. Each commune and village had its own fête, held in August when the harvest was in. The day-labourers who moved around from village to village would join in before going on to their next place of work. We danced late into the night under lanterns in the trees. The music was by little country bands in which the accordion-player was always the star.

Once a month, the travelling cinema came by. A white sheet was hung on the wall of the mayor's office and the whole village trouped in, everybody bringing their own chair. The sound and picture sometimes got out of sync. The noise of the projector drowned out the actors' voices. There were gaps while the projectionist changed the reels. None of that mattered. It was always an evening to remember.

The food sprang from the earth, and I can still taste the flavours to this day. The salad of big shallots with walnut oil from Léon Jean's farm. The gratin of wild herbs which Granny Augustine collected on the slopes above the village in the skirt of her apron held out in front of her as far as her arms could reach. The thrushes and rabbits which the Estienne boys brought back from their poaching expeditions . . .

Now fast-forward to the 1970s. Like the rest of France, Saint-André has been modernised. The houses have running water. The jolly Madame Estienne is delighted that she no longer has to press the nuts and olives from her garden: she can buy her oil ready-made in a plastic bottle. Washing machines have destroyed the convivial gossiping round the communal wash-house, but have made life easier for the women of the village. There is only one café in the square now: it serves meals for tourists as well as *pastis* for the locals. Most of the elderly people have died or moved to old folks' homes. Madame Roland is as alert as ever in her café. Every year, she goes on a package tour for pensioners, once all the way to Ibiza. The young people have left to work in the town on the plain, or farther afield. Several are in Marseille; others in Lyon or Paris. Some come back in the summer with their families to spend their holidays with their parents. The village fête is still held in August. One year, we meet two of the Estienne sons there. At night, one of them leads half a dozen of us out on the ridge beyond the farthest-flung farm, from where there is a superb view of the Milky Way. The other son is the life and soul of the party, organising beds for visitors and roasting a whole lamb on a spit in the garden of a mill he is rebuilding nearby. Following in the footsteps of his father, Venance, he has become a postman. Venance delivered the letters on foot across the hillside, winter and summer in snow and sunshine. The son drives the mail in a van in the Paris suburbs.

In the early 1980s, the ruin of a chapel opposite Madame Roland's café was declared a historic monument and added to the official route of the Romanesque churches of southern France. By then, the village had so few inhabitants that many of the fields were left untended. But the remaining villagers nurtured the dream that the tourists visiting the ruins might stay, seduced by the beauty of the place. They could walk in the fields, climb the neighbouring rocky outcrop of Mont Risou and write postcards to their friends in Paris congratulating themselves on having found an undiscovered corner of paradise in the Hautes-Alpes. A potential new source of revenue seemed to be there for the taking: Madame Roland installed showers in the rooms below her café. But tourists these days want swimming pools and tennis courts, good food and service – not stuffy rooms in the basement of a village café run by an eighty-year-old.

So the visitors stopped, looked and drove on. Before they left, some wandered through the narrow, winding streets between the crumbling stone houses with their collapsed beams and heaps of fallen masonry on the floor. We were told that we could have a fine old ruin if we simply paid the legal fees. But there was nobody around to rebuild the houses, install bathrooms and kitchens and make sure the walls weren't going to fall in. And who wants to live in a place where the only distraction is a village fête once a year and where the remaining inhabitants are dying all around you?

'It's so sad,' lamented the woman who had first gone to Saint-André as a little girl in the war and took me back there after we married. 'Saint-André is one of the most beautiful villages on Earth. When we were feeling energetic, we used to climb Mont Risou and light bonfires on the top for the festival of St John. You could see the glow from far away.'

On the paths around the village, the scent of lavender still hung heavy in the air – ancient, straight-backed Mélanie gathered it to sell to the perfume-makers of Grasse down south. Up the hill, in the farm to which my wife and her mother and brother had fled when the Germans came through, Monsieur Richard dispensed his home-made *pastis* and advises against a third glass – can it be the long-banned absinthe that drove Verlaine crazy? On the slopes below, the goats munched the wild herbs that give their special flavour to the cheese made by the bachelor brother and spinster sister, Marcel and Marcelline. At the bottom of the ravines, the river water was as fresh and pure as ever.

Some years later, we revisited Saint-André one day in August. That used to be the busiest time of year. But now all was silence. The square was deserted. The big old building which had housed the Estiennes' post office, the school where my wife learned to read and write, and the mayor's office was boarded up. The walls were peeling, ugly amid so much natural beauty. The clock on the top floor from which the children had learned to tell the time had stopped long ago. The café had closed when the owner's wife left him and he went to a teaching job in the town down the hill. The school bus no longer came up the hill; there were no children to collect any more.

As we stood in the shade of the trees in the square where *le pickup* once played and the men tossed boules outside the café, Marcel and Marcelline walked by, bent with age. Madame Roland still kept her café, but there was nobody to sit at her two tables. The earth mother, Madame Estienne, was in an old people's home in the Rhône Valley, said to be in poor health.

'The others?' my wife said. 'Dead – like my old village.'

Rural depopulation is not a new trend. The appeal of urban jobs, a falling birth-rate and the loss of life in the First World War reduced the population of some country regions significantly from early in the century. But the outflow has generally speeded up since 1960. The quintessentially rural Creuse department, for instance, has lost half its population since 1901. Forty per cent of those have gone since 1960, and the numbers are still falling year by year. It is now the least populated department in the country. In 1929, France had almost

4 million farms; by the 1950s, that number had halved and now the total has dropped below three-quarters of a million. More than a million agricultural jobs have vanished since 1970 – the rural contribution to unemployment should not be underestimated. Farmers and farm workers make up less than 7 per cent of the active population, only one-third of the level of the early 1970s. Over the same period, more than 50,000 shops and small rural businesses have shut down. The French have a word for the emptying of the countryside, la désertification – not that the wide open spaces of the middle of the country bear any resemblance to the Sahara. The official definition of this is a population level of thirty people or less per square kilometre. That makes half the land area of France into a green desert.

Itinerant farm labourers who were a feature of life at harvest time in a thousand villages like Saint-André have virtually disappeared. So have the bands of rural artisans who developed particular skills and roamed the country offering their services – masons from the Limousin, tree-cutters from the Forez region around Roanne, chimney-sweeps from Savoy, wet-nurses from Burgundy. Those who stay on the land are progressively older. In the Creuse, one-third of the people are aged over sixty; in the Auvergne region to the south, nearly half the farmers are over fifty-five, and in the Indre department of central France the number of people over sixty-five is double the national average. The French may cherish the idea of the rural bourg with its weekly market and its links with the surrounding countryside, but the population of towns of under 20,000 inhabitants has been declining steadily. Most telling of all, despite buoyant prices in some northern areas, the average price of agricultural land fell continually after 1980: in 1995 it was only just over one-third of the level of twenty years earlier.

There has also been a dramatic change in how rural people earn their living. A study published in 1998 by two official research institutes showed that only 20 per cent of their jobs are in agriculture. The countryside is becoming the setting for small-scale industry and services, and 2.6 million people commute to work in towns. Back on the land, the nature of farming has changed as the balance of production has shifted from animals to cereals. The old image of France as a nation of small farmers eking out a living has been overtaken by intensive agriculture – just as rural backwardness has been punctured by consumer goods, one of the best rural road systems in Europe and the Minitel data terminal network, which brings train timetables and sex on-line to the most isolated of farms. In the north and the east, huge grain and beet fields are farmed as efficiently as anything in Britain or Germany. Agriculture is a compartmentalised business. Once regions aimed to be self-sufficient: now they are part of a global market, and concentrate on what they do best. The west contains half of France's dairy farms. Brittany houses 60 per cent of the country's pig plants and grows most of the nation's cauliflowers. Paris is at the centre of a great grain belt. In the east, fortunes are made from sugar beet, not to mention champagne. One-third of south-western farms concentrate on maize and oilseeds (and the poor uplands of the centre have made a speciality of living on European subsidies). Wine-making has become a science as well as an art. The old regional languages of the land have been submerged in a common glossary of terms for agricultural machinery and scientific aids to greater productivity: a whole list of traditional names for farm implements no longer appear in the dictionaries of today. And, in a tiny village in the middle of the country, the grave-diggers drive to the churchyard in a Toyota four-wheel-drive land-cruiser with a large Coca-Cola logo on the bonnet.

Off the coast, farming at sea has run into rough weather. The fishing fleet has been halved since 1988, to around 6,000 boats. Even oyster producers have been hit by disease and lack of breeding space. It is not that demand is lacking – French fishermen provide only half the 600,000 tonnes of fresh fish France eats each year. The trouble is that domestic trawlers cannot compete on price with East European fleets. On top of which, the mark-ups along the wholesale and retail chain make fish a relatively expensive dish without benefiting the fishermen too much. A French magazine which priced a kilo of cod at the various stages between Brittany and a Paris fishmonger found that the fisherman got only 10 per cent of the final selling price. Trawlermen from north to south express their anger in the habitual way by blocking the entry to ports for foreign boats, pouring oil on imported mackerel and attacking lorries carrying rival catches. The government reacts by giving in. It doles out money and imposes health tests that ensure foreign fish goes rotten by the time it gets to market. None of this does any good. On sea as on land, the small harvesters of food face a future of decline.

Still, it is the old agricultural ways which loom large in the national mind, and the countryside still calls to the city-dweller. Some follow the rural siren. An Air France executive gave up his career at the age of thirty-five, spent seven years moving from farm to farm to learn the ways of the land, and then set up in Normandy to raise goats and ducks, and make cheese, *foie gras*, sausages and pâté. A fertiliser salesman from a big multinational bought a vineyard in the Rhône Valley and now sells 110,000 bottles year. Such experiences warm the French heart. When there is good news from the deep heart of France, everyone cheers. So visit the small village of Calvinet, perched 600 metres up in the very south of the Cantal department, between the blustery heights of the Massif Central and the sunny uplands to the south.

On the face of it, Calvinet should have had no more reason to survive than Saint-André-de-Rosans. It lies in a region known as 'chestnut country', because the nuts used to be its main resource – they were the staple ingredient in the local flour. Today it remains much as described by a local carpenter, Joseph Lavigne, in a 26-page memoir he wrote in a notebook discovered after his death in 1994 at the age of eighty-two:

> My parental home was by the pastures. The silence was broken only by the crow of the cockerel or the snorting of the cows. My commune stood on the rise of a hill and it got the first light of day. To the south were the big fields where the wheat rippled like a rough sea. To the east and west, there were chestnut trees under whose shade the cows passed by. To the north were the poor people, scratching a living from the soil. There, too, were sheep grazing amid swarms of bees sucking the honey from flower to flower. In the village, the houses were mostly white, low-standing and with slate roofs. They looked charming from a distance; a group of homes with a bell tower in the middle, a schoolhouse and the big lime tree on the square, known as the tree of liberty.

Calvinet has gone through many changes since then. It was rent by a long and searing battle between reactionary Catholics and a pioneer of lay education: a *Romeo and Juliet* saga was played out between two young people from either side. In the 1930s, peddlers hawked their wares in *patois* at the market: '*Boutous de braguas, de comijias, de couls, de giletas, de broguetas.*' (Sixty years later, there were still vestiges of the local dialect. The nearby fifteenth-century village of Marcolès put up signs for visitors in both French and *patois*. Walking through a farm-yard on the hills one spring day, my wife and I were surrounded by a pack of dogs. We implored them in French to leave us alone. They took no notice. Then the farmer came out of a barn and shouted at them in *patois*. The dogs turned tail and ran off into the woods.) During the last war, a local inventor built a bicycle made of wood, but his plans to commercialise it came to nothing. The population declined, and the village became increasingly dependent on subsidies from Brussels. Around 1980, several of the younger men decided to take its destiny into their hands. While they had no intention of demanding any less in the way of European funding, they believed that Calvinet should avoid becoming another rural basket-case.

'It would have been easy to have sat back and done nothing, and watched the young people leaving for the town, and their parents being reduced to watching the television because that was all there was to do,' said one of the younger generation. He, himself, works in the departmental capital of Aurillac, forty kilometres away – but the road has been widened and improved and the journey takes half the time it used to. Calvinet is part of the wider world: there was even talk of building a branch of the Auvergne motorway in the hills down towards the Lot river.

The son of the local *charcutier* went off to learn to be a cook in Toulouse. He returned with a host of new ideas and ambitions, but was sage enough to draw on his mother's old recipes and his father's ham and sausages. Soon he was in the national guidebooks. He mar-ried the daughter of the local chemist, and they undertook the renovation of the hotel above the restaurant. Foreigners started coming for their holidays, and one day a fleet of bright red Ferraris called by for lunch on a sponsored rally through the region.

The village now has five places to eat or drink. The main square has new curly lamp-posts and a wooden notice-board with a large guide to the surrounding area. The main restaurant has won a Michelin rosette. There are two tennis courts in the woods by the camping site, a convenience store and a swimming-pool of sorts in the reservoir. The baker still serves up good old-fashioned bread. Naturally, Calvinet is not free from complaints, or concerns. The farmers worry not simply about the age-old uncertainties of the weather, but also about how well they are being defended in Brussels, and what trickery the Americans are up to in world trade talks. A local producer of *foie gras* once told me that, if this delicacy were banned in the USA, it would not be because the Americans really thought force-feeding was cruel – who could imagine any such thing? – but as a non-tariff barrier aimed at France, which should ban McDonald's in retaliation. As for the matter of mad cows, a farmer outside Calvinet was convinced that it was all a plot dreamed up by Washington to boost exports of American beef to Europe – ships full of transatlantic cattle were, he assured me, heading for Spain at that very moment, ready to be driven over the Pyrenees and supplant the Salers cattle in the fields below him. Another shook his head when the name of Jacques Chirac was mentioned. 'He thinks he can count on us, but he doesn't do anything,' he said, adding ominously: 'There are others who will look after our interests better.'

The strong franc is another cause for complaint – it is helping competitors from Italy and Spain to sell their produce. Oh, and don't forget the Arabs: they used to import a lot of local lamb but they aren't buying any more. When I mention the way in which farm incomes have been rising, I get a dismissive shrug and expulsion of breath: as a city-dweller, not to mention a foreigner, how could I possibly understand that, whatever the statistics may say, France's farmers are always on the edge of disaster? That, Monsieur, is a fact with which nobody had better argue.

If its rural roots still permeate France, the general mood of worry and self-absorption may be simply a translation of countryside concerns into the national bloodstream. Here in Calvinet, familiar national obsessions punctuate the conversation about falling beef prices and the grand wedding being held next Sunday on the street known as the Avenue de la Grande Armée because a couple of retired military officers live there. The restaurateur expostulates against the tax system which, he insists, makes it impossible for him to expand, and may encourage him to go back to his father's trade as a *charcutier* since VAT on cold meats is a quarter of the rate on cooked meals. Still, I say, he must be happy with his Michelin rosette. Yes, but his reply is complex. He reckons that he got the award for his traditional local dishes, like his mother's recipe for duck in a secret thick sauce (which I think contains both blood and bitter chocolate). Those are what the customers want when they drive up with the red guide in their cars. But what he'd like to be famous for is more adventurous recipes. Still, I say, things are going well in Calvinet. In return, I get a grudging *oui, mais* . . . the undefined 'but' which could mean that the weather may turn bad tomorrow, the crops may fail, the cattle may fall ill, the volcanoes may erupt, the world may come to an end.

On a ridge outside the village, a sharp-faced weather-beaten farmer sits at a huge wooden table and keeps watch on the herd in his cow-shed via closed-circuit television. He went to Paris once, but found the city so dirty and airless that he had to get home fast. His farm-house has walls a metre thick. In the courtyard outside, there is a hundred-year-old drinking trough hewn from a solid block of vol-canic rock. In the big, stone-floored main room, a stuffed fox stands on a ledge, copper cooking utensils hang on the wall, a grandfather clock reaches to the ceiling, three hunting rifles are racked over the huge fireplace and a big old television set sits on a dresser. By the door, a pair of horns has been mounted on the wall. The farmer's strongly-built, smiling wife explains that they belonged to a cow which was a treasure at the farm, never caused any trouble, but which went berserk when taken to the slaughterhouse. The farmer and his wife shake their heads at the memory, as though the cow was an inexplicably wayward child.

We had telephoned that morning for a couple of rabbits for dinner. The farmer's wife couldn't supply them immediately because her hus-band was out harvesting, and she had nobody to hold the animals while she killed them. By afternoon, she had found help, and she brought the cut-up meat in on a plate from the pantry. Over our protests, she added a large chunk of stuffed cabbage – layers of veg-etable and minced meat with herbs – and half a dozen eggs. Then her husband led us out into the kitchen garden, looking out on to a horseshoe-shaped wood and an endless vista of countryside all the way down to Rodez. He gave us a handful of cucumbers and a couple of big courgettes, and told us that what he really needed was a good downpour. On the way back to the house, we passed the rabbit hutches, two of them empty and with their doors open.

Down the road, the local nobleman shows me round the wood-panelled rooms of his château one evening, and then sits and sips whisky and talks about his daughter's wedding, and about a young man from the village who went to Paris after the Revolution and made a fortune out of floating brothels on the Seine. He won respectability as a banker to the First Empire and developed the big park on the Buttes Chaumont in the north of the city. A century ago, the nobleman's family held aloft the clerical standard in Calvinet; they boycotted the village council when their lay opponents replaced the cross in the main square with a statue representing the Republic. After peace had broken out, the baron became mayor of the village, and used his social and political contacts to ensure that Calvinet got a bite at any financial cake on offer from the region. Now, he has given up the post, but his presence is still felt, standing in the queue for the checkout desk at the local self-service store with a roll of kitchen paper towels under his arm or sitting at a window table in the restaurant for Sunday lunch, a bottle of Bordeaux on the table in front of him. 'Oh, Calvinet will always be here,' he says at the end of our evening conversation. 'We just have to make sure it is in as good shape as possible.' He accompanies me to the door of the château. As I motor up the long driveway to the road, I see the baron in my rear-view mirror, urinating against the wall of his ancestral home. It is an image from a book of clichés about rural France, but a cliché that seems alive and well.

There may be a hundred re-awakened Calvinets across France; still, the waning of country customs cannot be denied. The annual killing of the pig and the use of every morsel down to the ears and tail for food has been supplanted by preserved cold cuts in cellophane from the local supermarket. A professor remembers how, in her childhood in the Vendée region, a rope was traditionally hung between two houses after church weddings with a jar of sweets attached to it; the mother of the bride then took a long pole and broke the jar with heavy symbolism for her virginal daughter as the children ran forward to scoop up the bonbons; today, in the same area, old church confessionals are being sold as big bird cages.

Much as the farmers welcomed Jacques Chirac's presidential election victory, the Head of State can do little to slow down the change in rural life, even if he wants to, and some might even wonder if the countryside really deserves special treatment and over-representation in the National Assembly, when so many industrial areas are feeling such pain. At a time of low inflation, farm incomes rose at more than 10 per cent a year in the mid-1990s. Whatever the rigours of their daily lives in some areas, the farmers, in general, remain a protected class. Their social security payments have gone up more slowly than those of the rest of the population, and taxes on their production have fallen by 10 per cent. In three years, the subsidies they received more than doubled to 50 billion francs: France easily heads the list of recipients of payments under Europe's Common Agricultural Policy, to the point that its growers of wheat and colza are reckoned to have had an over-payment of up to 14 billion ecus from community funds.

This treasure was all the more valuable to those who got it, since it was spread among a diminishing number of people as the big farms got bigger and the small ones died out: an average grain farm in the Oise department north of Paris can rake in subsidies nearly three times the national average, while a dairy farmer near the Channel coast gets only half the general level. Agriculture has produced its share of boutique farmers, grafting together wild and cultivated strawberries for a new fruit called the *mara des bois*, pressing exotic vegetable oils or raising silkworm cocoons in the Cévennes. There will always be a market for increasingly expensive fine fish, and France has become a big producer of kiwi fruit. Some 4,000 'bio' farmers cultivate their vegetables and raise their cattle without using any chemicals. Down south, in the Hérault department, the 430-inhabitant village of Avenge-les-Bains sells 2 million sprays made from its local waters in Japan each year. In Le Puy in the Auvergne, the number of lentil-growers exploiting the unique combination of volcanic soil, altitude and climate has doubled in a decade, and, down by the Lot river at Port d'Agres, a market gardener does a nice line in Asian vegetables for adventurous restaurants.

Still, the clear trend is for the big boys to grow bigger and the small folk to go to the old people's homes, or to be bought off active farming by a handout from Brussels. In one quintessentially rural village, a plump farmer's wife with tree-trunk arms who used to drive the fly-infested cattle to and from the fields lived placidly for years with her hard-drinking husband until he died, at which point, by coincidence, the European Union decided that it had too many cows, and would pay her and others like her to get rid of her beasts. This she duly did, using the money to refashion her house, buy a smart little car, have her hair done, and generally appear happier than she had ever been, free at last from the tyranny of the land.

As the average size of French agricultural holdings has doubled in the past thirty years, banks have taken to arranging seminars for their urban customers on the attractions of putting spare cash into the soil. Financial institutions buy up agricultural land as a good investment for themselves or their clients. Some farmers who rent their land have never seen the owner. The nature of farming changes year by year to meet the requirements of the bottom line, and maximise the return on capital for owners who would not know wheat from barley. For all the small farmers who dump their produce on the roads and drive their tractors in noisy demonstrations, the agricultural union is controlled by the big operators in the north who make sure that they reap a double benefit from high prices and rising productivity. Intensive pork and poultry farmers of the west saw their revenues go up by 50 per cent over only two years; at the same time, earnings of cauliflower-growers fell below the levels of the 1980s – and they were soon out blocking the roads of Brittany in protest. Ducks now provide far more livers for *foie gras* than geese because they are easier to force-feed with machines. Proclaiming that scientific advances did not always bear 'the mark of the devil', the government lifted a ban on growing genetically modified maize, boosting France's position as the European Union's biggest producer of the plant. Increasingly, farm houses are sold separately from the land to city-dwellers or foreigners, and then the fields are amalgamated into larger holdings.

All of which exacerbates the conflict between the way agriculture is going and the image the nation cherishes of its land. It is difficult to wax sentimental over a grain baron from the Beauce, south-west of Paris, who runs his fields with a computer, buys genetic crop strains from a Swiss drugs firm and flies off to an exotic holiday twice a year. And equally difficult to expect a twenty-year-old son of a hill farmer to remain on the land. 'I can't wait to move to the town,' a youth in Calvinet said at the football pitch one afternoon. 'Except that I won't find a job there, will I?'

Some resist. Deep in a forest off a main north–south route, but light-years from the world of motorways and high-speed trains, a farmer in his thirties lives in a muddy, fly-infested hovel at the end of a track. He ekes out a living with his wife and three children, tilling a small plot of earth and tending a herd of goats which produce fine cheese. It looks a miserable existence but, he says, 'I am from the earth. I live with my beasts. This is my life.'

As the rural world meets the twenty-first century, that life becomes rarer. The identification between the countryside, agriculture, tradition and the nation is breaking down into an economic bargain. One demographer has worked out that active farmers make up only one-fifth of the 15 million people who live outside towns and cities. Farmers, one of their leaders remarked, have believed for too long that the countryside belonged to them alone. Now, if they want to survive and prosper, they have to jump on the latest bandwagon, drawing the maximum in European subsidies and convincing the banks that they are a step ahead of the market. The new race of rural entrepreneurs approaches the countryside with the logic of modern business. One year they grow grain; the next, maize. One year they raise battery poultry; the next, they go for calves. Behind them, they leave breeze-blocks and corrugated iron, drained fields and an abandoned work-force. 'Farmers are their own worst enemy,' remarked a landowner whose locality had been devastated in this manner. Tradition fades, and another divorce develops between a vital element of national life and the way the French actually live now. And as the icon of the small farmer at the heart of France dissolves, we should turn to look at the condition of the other pea in the national pod.

5

MODERN TIMES

The country which invented the modern popular revolution naturally gave its working class and its urban life a historic place in society. Now, as with the traditional rural world, the rush of present-day realities cuts deeply into the fabric of town and city life while the industrial transformations of the past decades have eaten into the cherished old ways.

The Great Revolution may have been directed by the bourgeoisie and petty nobles, but the storming of the Bastille has gone down in history as a defining moment of popular passion, and the legitimacy of France's Republics through five manifestations over the last two centuries is based on the people. A rolling saga of revolt carried on from the Revolution to its more timid successor in 1830 and a rising by Lyon silk workers seeking a minimum wage, which left hundreds dead the following year. In 1848, another revolution brought in the Second Republic and inspired Karl Marx. The violence of the Paris Commune of 1871 terrified the middle classes and helped to ensure that, despite its greater tenors of the left, the Third Republic was their regime for nearly all of its seventy years. In this century, the nation's greatest sacrifice of lives was by millions of working-class men from both urban and rural France in the trenches of the First World War.

In the 1920s and 1930s, mass culture celebrated the workers; the icons of the age were not just popular but populist – the actor Jean Gabin in his vest; the actress Arletty making the most of her Parisian street accent; the songs of husky-voiced women bewailing the loss of their men; Marcel Pagnol's moving trilogy of plays and films about Marseille port life; Jean Renoir's cinematic celebrations of everyday existence; and the imperishable photographs of cafés with accordion-players, of a family picnicking on a river bank, of a narrow suburban street under a railway viaduct. Amid the tumult of the 1930s, the granting of the right to holidays with pay to workers – *congés payés* – has a historic resonance which may seem strange beyond French borders. The arrival of crowds of city workers and their families on hitherto middle-class beaches symbolised a social revolution. If the trains from Paris to the coast of Normandy were not quite a new storming of the Bastille, they came close in their way. As the eminent British historian of France, Douglas Johnson, has put it: 'It was dramatic. There were those who saw the sea for the first time. There were children who at last met their grandparents. Men whose families had come to Paris to find work visited the countryside their forefathers had cultivated. And there are other memories. Bourgeois families who had enjoyed the privilege of using certain beaches . . . were invaded by "louts wearing caps" and their followers.'

The Popular Front governments of 1936–38 which introduced paid holidays were a political and social watershed, bringing together Socialists and Communists, cutting the working week, nationalising the Bank of France and trying to show that France did not always have to be ruled from the right or the bourgeois centre. They certainly scared a lot of proper-thinking people. Charles de Gaulle's deeply reactionary mother described the Socialist leader Léon Blum as an agent of Satan, and a right-wing refrain of the time proclaimed 'Better Hitler than Blum'. In many ways, the left lacked a true cutting-edge. It let down the Republican peers in Spain, and quailed before the rampant slanders of the right. But it bequeathed an imperishable mark on society which France would not forget. When Blum was released from imprisonment at the Liberation, he took a suit to the cleaner. When he collected it, he found a handwritten note in one pocket: 'Thank you for the *congés payés*.'

The military importance of the French Resistance to the Nazi Occupation is open to debate: Hitler's architect, Albert Speer, once responded to a question on the subject with a scornful: 'What Resistance?' But the fact that some did stand up to the Nazis was essential to the salving of national pride after the Liberation. The

Army of the Shadows was the essential counterpoint to the civil service collaborators who did not even have an ideological excuse for
what they did. While there were resisters from the right, the domestic fight against the Occupation was primarily a movement of the left,
particularly after Hitler invaded Russia and thus freed the Communists
to participate; the murdered Resistance chief, Jean Moulin, was even
suspected by some Gaullists of being a secret agent of Moscow.

The left's role in fighting the occupiers gave the working class a
special badge of respectability after 1944, and led some alarmists to
fear a Marxist coup. In some cities, Communist Resistance leaders
seemed poised to take power. But General de Gaulle used his position
as the Great Liberator at the head of a Government of National
Unanimity to carry out a ruthless amalgamation of the Resistance
with the regular army and to exert control. He also showed a distinct
lurch to the left in preaching the virtues of the public interest, of using
national wealth for the benefit of all, and of the right of everybody to
live, work and bring up their children in security and dignity. To show
that this was not a matter of empty rhetoric, his government nationalised coal, gas and electricity, banks, insurance businesses and some
major industrial companies. Family allowances were introduced,
together with unemployment and sickness pay, and women finally got
the vote. Soon afterwards, long-term state planning was instituted
at the behest of the future Father of Europe, Jean Monnet. Implicit in
the Resistance and the victory of 1944 was a rejection of the static
conservatism that had contributed so much to the shame of 1940. The
Fourth Republic, which came into being with the Liberation, would
degenerate into a regime far more splintered and impotent than its
predecessor, but the bright dawn of 1944 gave it a socialist–statist
base which became entrenched in national life. Much as foreigners
might scoff at France's political instability, and De Gaulle might rail
at his successors after he lost power in 1946, the inflationary, state-
cushioned economy that ushered in the Glorious Thirty Years
represented a triumph for a system which catered to the desires of
France's workers under the guidance of powerful trade unions.

When the General returned to office and changed the political
system in 1958, the economy and the position of the working class
altered little. Ministers might be Gaullists rather than members of the
myriad small parties of the previous Republic, but managers and

workers went on cutting easy deals in both private and public sectors. De Gaulle's Premier, Georges Pompidou, ended the nationwide strikes of 1968 with the simple expedient of a budget-busting pay agreement. Labour leaders were great national figures, and a former union official called Jacques Delors became a top-level governmental adviser with new-fangled ideas about industrial relations and worker participation in companies. De Gaulle sprang from the old-fashioned right, but he drew support from voters on the left – even the Communists liked his independent attitude towards Washington. In its early years, the Fifth Republic bound French society together and, though more in appearance than in reality, offered the working class a stake in society.

The politics of the 1980s changed all that. Not that anybody would have guessed it while the crowds danced in the streets to celebrate the Socialist victory of May 1981, and the newly-elected President proclaimed it to be 'a time for dreams'. As frightened businessmen smuggled money across the border to Switzerland, the Social Security Minister announced that her job was to spend money without bothering about the accounts. The government decided on the most expensive and inefficient way of nationalising a dozen key companies, followed by a deeply misguided attempt to build up stand-alone French production chains overseen by that Énarque of the left, Jean-Pierre Chevènement. It was all done in the name of the workers, even if there were more teachers than labourers among the Socialist Party faithful.

When three rapid devaluations of the franc, a bounding trade deficit and out-of-control inflation woke the President from his reverie, it was those workers who suffered. After the Socialists were forced into their economic volte-face in 1983, redundancies ripped through coal-mining, textiles and ship-building. François Mitterrand returned from a visit to the United States and said how impressed he had been by the automated steel plants he had seen there: in the ensuing years, job cuts in the great mills of Lorraine ran at 8 per cent or more a year, and those thrown out of work could only look for employment across the German border to the east. Robotisation of factories hit France with a vengeance. Unemployment shot up in the industrial bastions of the north and centre and along the Mediterranean, where the presence of large numbers of immigrants and of former settlers from Algeria exacerbated social tensions and gave the far right its deepest wells of support. Parisians grew accustomed to seeing teenage beggars huddled in doorways. The solidarity proclaimed by the Socialists in 1981 gave way to selfishness: it was increasingly difficult to be a good Samaritan if your job might no longer be there when you got back from helping one of your less fortunate fellow men on the other side of the road.

As the crisis bit ever deeper, and poverty became a way of life among the one-time workers of the old industrial areas, a reporter for *Le Monde*, Corine Lesnes, travelled to the northern mining basin and brought back a telling piece of reportage from a typical town of brick houses and paved streets. In Fresnes-sur-Escaut, 800 were out of work and 200 families lived on welfare. To save money, dozens had moved out of their homes and into old, abandoned caravans. One woman cooked for a community of fifteen living in a Second World War blockhouse.

'A woman of thirty-four died after her lungs were contaminated by toxic fumes: she burned rubbish and electric wires to recover the copper inside and sell it,' Lesnes wrote. 'The four children of last year's Father Christmas at the parish church are in care; Santa Claus spent five days in prison for a tax debt of 1,800 francs. Women get pregnant younger and younger – the children's allowances are like a wage for them.

'The most common way of making money is to collect scrap metal and sell it to the foundry for 3 francs a kilo. Anything goes – skeletons of cars, railway tracks, drain covers and even, last year, the railings of the bridge in the neighbouring town. Misery has a particularly black tone here.'

One woman, Nadine, divorced from a drunken husband, had seven children aged from one to seventeen, one of them a chronically ill truant of a teenager. The children did their homework by candlelight because it would take two years to pay off the debts to the electricity company. An older woman, Marcelle, lived on 15 francs a day, dropping in at neighbouring houses at mealtimes and watching for the days when rotten apples were thrown on the local dump. 'All one can do is to share their worries as winter comes and applaud the government's ritual anti-poverty plan,' Lesnes wrote. 'Or re-read Zola and Dickens. And flee.'

Under succeeding governments led by Socialists and Gaullists, things only got worse for the working class. With the number of jobs falling in three-quarters of France's regions, 9 million people were unemployed or in part-time posts or 'precarious' jobs. Star industries stumbled. Household names took the shears to labour costs: the loss-making appliance firm which gave the world the vegetable mixer (under the slogan 'Moulinex frees women') shed a quarter of its full-time jobs. Even the smile of the pneumatic Michelin man couldn't save 15 per cent of the tyre firm's workers from getting the chop. The French term for downsizing – *dégraissage* – moved out of the kitchen and on to the factory floor. Four former homeless men marketed social problems with a board-game in which players had to dodge dole queues, debt, alcoholism and the police to reach the ultimate prize of a job – it was packaged in the brown cardboard from which street sleepers make their shelters.

Moving to the upper end of the working class, the number of office staff and white-collar employees signing on for benefit doubled over five years. The slowdown in hiring meant there were fewer and fewer jobs for young people, and those who did get work found it mainly in small firms and on short-term contracts.

The process which started with a series of political decisions by an administration which had come to power supposedly to promote the interests of the working class rapidly took on a life on its own, arching beyond politicians. Because they could not control events, ministers could not explain what was happening to their voters – or, more painfully for the Socialists, to their own party members. The language of the early 1980s became archaic as the habits of past generations were blown away. The working class was abruptly removed from its sentimental pinnacle and made to feel useless. The old notion of long-term relationships between workers, managers and owners evaporated in the face of the pursuit of survival, as the old anchors were pulled up and the ship of everyday existence was cast to the winds. Take three examples from urban life – shops, cars and the party which claimed to stand for the workers of France.

In the panoply of French working life, small shopkeepers, tradespeople and artisans have long been a key element in the nation's daily existence. They give many city streets an essential part of their character. In the countryside, they served a far-flung community out in the fields and villages. Before the Germans destroyed it in 1944, the small town of Ouradour in the middle of France counted around fifty family or one-man enterprises – hairdressers and butchers, shoe- and dress-makers, bakers and iron merchants, carpenters and dealers in agricultural produce, a dentist, a tailor who also sold insurance, and a bunch of weavers – plus six cafés. In the capital, even the smartest districts have traditionally been alive with a variety of small shops that made them self-sufficient: a 200-metre stretch of a street on the Left Bank of Paris where I lived in the 1980s contained three butchers, a stationer, a greengrocer, a dry-cleaner, a cheese shop and an outlet from the Félix Potin chain of grocers.

Launched in 1844, the Potin chain made its reputation by promising honestly weighed goods, quality products bought by the founder in person and a low profit margin. The firm established the first French food-processing factories owned by a retailer, and pioneered home delivery. Its clients included the Élysée Palace. The main Potin factory in the north of Paris stretched over four hectares. The shops were a unique kind of enterprise. Though small in size, they used bulk-buying and a standard range of goods to undercut stand-alone rivals. They were mini-supermarkets and, as such, overcame smaller competitors. Yet, being neighbourhood establishments, they carried with them none of the looming size and power of the hypermarkets which were to follow. They kept a local feel, and a family atmosphere. They were often run by a couple whom customers knew by name; in the early days, employees had to obtain the firm's permission before getting married. Many of the managers lived in company flats above their shops. And there was a fine nostalgic resonance of their founder's first name: very few French baby boys are called Félix these days.

In 1956, self-service was introduced to the 1,200 Potin outlets. Soon after that, two revolutions shook up French retailing for ever. The first saw a boom in the mail-order business. The second involved the huge growth of giant out-of-town shopping centres. France has more hypermarkets per head of population than any other European country. Municipal authorities made the most of the planning powers devolved to them under decentralisation measures to attract shopping centres. Consumers are estimated to buy 90 per cent of their groceries from such places. In services as well as retailing, big chains took more and more of the market. From McDonald's to exhaust-pipe fitters, franchises spread across the nation. Five per cent of small hairdressers go out of business each year, while the head of one chain of franchised salons, Jacques Dessange, sits back in his mansion at the foot of the Champs-Élysées and says he gets 3,000 requests a year to open an outlet. Overall, small shops now account for less than 45 per cent of the retail market. Take one example – Avallon in Burgundy, famous as a town where Napoléon spent a night on his way to Paris from his first exile on Elba. In the past two decades, the number of butchers in the town has dropped from twelve to two for a simple reason – a shopping complex run by the appropriately named Mammouth chain which opened just outside the town. As well as offering cut-price goods, the complex has become a focus of social activity, in a reversal of the old image of shoppers hailing one another and chatting as they move from one small shop to another. 'Mammouth has become the town centre,' says an Avallon fishmonger. 'People go there to meet their friends as well as to do their shopping.'

Social intercourse apart, shops like the Félix Potin chain simply could not compete on price; and, if there was one thing that ruled in France in the 1990s, it was price. 'Bargain hunting has become a way of life,' the magazine *L'Express* concluded in a cover story on the wave of discounting sweeping the country. A new Anglicism even emerged: 'les hard discounters'. It was not just the poor who flocked to them; plenty of middle-class mothers sorted through the cheap clothes, cut-price food and do-it-yourself gear on offer. A sociologist from the College of Political Science in Paris, Denis Stocklet, dubbed bargain-hunting a national sport, and an author has compiled a 564-page guide to factory outlets which sell brand-name goods cheap, complete with restaurant-style star ratings.

There had, of course, always been stores which piled the goods high and sold them cheap. The Tati chain, set up by an immigrant from Tunisia in a former brothel in the down-at-heel Barbès area of Paris, had the atmosphere of an Arab market as their customers, many of them immigrants themselves, sorted through goods heaped on counters before taking them away in the chain's distinctive pink gingham-pattern shopping bags. 'Keep the thieves out of my shops, and you'll take away part of my clientele,' the founder once remarked.

He knew how humiliating it could be for poor people to ask superior shop assistants for the price of goods which they might not be able to afford, so he did away with the assistants and let his customers check the prices themselves before taking them to the cash tills. At its height, the chain attracted some 25 million customers a year in nine cities. Then other retailers noticed how keen the French had become to save money on clothes. By 1996, one-third of garments were being bought at discount houses or in sales. Smarter stores which had once let Tati have their unsold stock at knock-down prices began to sell it cheap themselves. Turnover slumped in Tati's souks. To restore its fortunes the chain looked overseas, and cashed in on its kitsch image with disposable cameras in shades of its trademark pink, a Fifth Avenue store in New York, and a jewellery outlet on the smart Rue de la Paix. Everybody was in the cut-price game now, and, as the lines of hypermarkets grew for kilometre after kilometre on the edge of provincial cities, Denis Stocklet reflected that, without realising it, the French had gone back to nineteenth-century Catholic ways of parsimony and economy. That made a few people very rich indeed: three of the country's half-dozen largest fortunes belong to big retailers.

Governments have tried to check the mega-stores, but with scant success. The bottom line rules, and the bigger the store, the greater the profit – takings per square metre in the country's 1,100 hypermarkets are double those in the 7,300 supermarkets. When predatory pricing was banned to try to protect small shops, one supermarket boss reacted with glee to the news that he would not have to offer bread at below cost price to lure customers. Jacques Chirac thundered about the 'extraordinarily negative' effect of supermarkets in drawing people to 'unfriendly' suburban centres; but his Prime Minister promptly presented a business award to the head of one of the monster chains. A move to make planning permission more difficult for new hypermarkets only set off takeover battles as the bigger chains sought to grow ever larger by acquiring their weaker brethren. For all the rhetoric of regret for the cosy past and the place of small shops in the social blanket, the die was cast. Even if they shudder at its social cost, one thing successive governments have pursued with success is low inflation, and the discounters help to achieve that – the harder the better.

Some of the cut-price retailers see themselves as playing a positively crusading role in forging a better way of life for their compatriots. One cut-price pioneer, Édouard Leclerc, has been deeply hurt by official criticism. 'We're attacked like the Jews once were,' he says. 'They used to be held responsible for everything that went wrong. Now it's us.' Leclerc is a phenomenon of post-war France. Born into a poor family of thirteen children, he opened his first shop after the war in the west of Brittany, selling chocolates, biscuits and sweets at half the artificially high wartime rates still charged by other stores. The secret of his success was simple: 'I sold retail at wholesale prices.' As Centres Leclerc sprouted throughout the country, small shopkeepers demonstrated against him and his methods. Local farmers refused to sell him milk or vegetables. Leclerc, a man who loves to upset established ways, relished the battle. Sometimes things turned violent. Lorries were stopped by force; a leader of protesting shopkeepers was hit in the face by a rock and lost two teeth. Then Leclerc had the idea of selling discount petrol to attract car-owners to his stores. Once there in their Renaults and Peugeots, what could be more convenient than to load up with goods from the adjoining store? A believer in astrology, Lerclerc adopts a quasi-religious approach to retailing. 'He taught us that the only thing that counts is our intellectual capital,' one of his sons says. His local managers are known as disciples or adherents.

Though the founder has never taken much money out of the business, his followers do very nicely. Lerclerc often gives his managers an ownership stake in their enterprises, and insists that they share the takings with the staff. They are invited to conferences to listen to his vision of the future. 'As the years have gone by, one has seen them turning up in thicker and thicker furs, with bigger and bigger rings and in more and more powerful cars,' one observer of the Leclerc phenomenon told *L'Express*. 'Édouard is their god. It isn't a limited company he set up, but a movement. A man who lets you build up such a business for yourself without asking for anything in return except that you follow certain moral rules (don't rob the customer, sell as cheaply as possible and distribute a quarter of the profits to the staff) is unique.'

So, in an age when families drive scores of kilometres to shopping centres for a Saturday expedition, eat lunch on the spot, fill the car with goods and go home feeling they have passed a day well spent, shops like Félix Potin found their backs to the wall. The founding family sold out, and the new owners realised that inner-city property prices meant the real-estate value of their assets might well outweigh the revenue to be earned from retailing. Little by little, the stores were hived off for development. At the end of 1995, the remaining 400 Potin shops received a terse note from the central management: 'You can stay open until December 31 at 20.30.' Given that New Year is a more important occasion for celebration than Christmas in France, it was a Christmas carol from a Gallic Scrooge, a death knell for an institution.

The French love affair with the motor-car has been charted by writers, lyricists, photographers and academics. The greatest modern French novelist, Albert Camus, died in a road crash; a far poorer writer, Roger Limier, won fame as 'the French James Dean' for dicing with death – which finally caught up with him – in fast cars. The revolt of shopkeepers and small businessmen led by Pierre Poujade in the 1950s would not have been possible had its leader not been able to drive about the country from one village meeting to another. The reputation of the novelist Françoise Sagan as a symbol of modernity was inflated by the way she ignored speed limits. Despite the efficiency of French public transport, 82 per cent of local trips are still made by car. France has more motor dealers than any other European nation. In 1973, a French sociologist was moved to write an article entitled 'Automobile Accidents and the Class Struggle'. The philosopher Roland Barthes devoted an essay to the semiology of the Citroën DS. An American academic, Kristin Ross, entitled a study of post-war French society 'Fast Cars, Clean Bodies', noting that, after the 1950s, a revolution in attitudes towards mobility and displacement had permeated every aspect of life with 'the dismantling of all earlier spatial arrangements, the virtual end of the historic city, in a physical and social restructuring'. So it is not surprising that France's main car manufacturer should have played a key role in national life, going beyond the mere construction of vehicles, and that its history should tell a story about the evolution of French industry and those who worked in it.

For six decades, the Renault plant on the Île Séguin on the Seine in a suburb of Paris was France's greatest industrial citadel. Built in

1929 by Louis Renault, 'Fortress Billancourt' sprawled over sixty-five hectares. It brought major assembly-line production to France, and was immortalised as an industrial monument and shrine of the French working class in photographs, books and even poetry. In the 1930s, the town of Boulogne-Billancourt became a treasure-house of modernist buildings by the urban pioneer Le Corbusier and a dozen other leading French architects. During the German Occupation, the plant was turned over to the Nazis, who used it to produce military vehicles – Allied air-raids killed more than 1,000 workers. After the Liberation, Louis Renault was arrested for collaboration, the company was nationalised and the Communists turned the factory into a union stronghold. Before she discovered silk stockings, Cyd Charisse's Ninotchka put a visit to Billancourt high on the list of things she had to do on her first visit to Paris. Édith Piaf moved into a villa across the river. Renault set the norms for pay and conditions – for a fourth week of paid holiday and for the wage rises that ended the 1968 strikes. When Jean-Paul Sartre launched a revolutionary newspaper, he sold it at the factory gates. A line from one of his plays – 'We mustn't make Billancourt lose hope' – became a catch-phrase for the need to cater to the workers of France. When the left finally won power in 1981, a former chairman of the motor firm became the Minister for Industry. The company symbolised a society in which more than a quarter of the workforce looked to the state for employment. It was as solid as the nation itself.

With car ownership booming in the 1960s, Renault and other motor companies expanded production beyond their urban citadels, setting up new plants on green-field sites in Normandy and importing cheap labour from Africa. Many of the immigrants moved to dormitory tower-block estates on the outskirts of neighbouring towns. One such place was Dreux, a market town west of Paris which had once been a key frontier post between the Kingdom of France and the Duchy of Normandy. In the town itself, there are brick buildings with stucco façades, a Renaissance bell-tower, a bridge over a slow-flowing river and an arrow-straight avenue which points up the hill to the railway station and the ride to the Gare Saint-Lazare. Drive ten minutes out of the middle of Dreux and you land in a very different environment, where the local give-away newspaper carries advertisements for witch-doctors and the lifts in the tower-block are covered with Arabic graffiti. The flats are occupied by immigrants who came to work at the car plants and other factories in the area in the boom years. In the 1980s, robotisation and downsizing threw many of them out of jobs, but they had no wish to go back to Africa. The town's left-wing mayor devoted much money and effort to catering for the new arrivals. The French natives of Dreux resented this, and grew fearful of unemployed Arabs from the car plants and their teenage children. They wanted nothing to do with multi-cultural experiments. And so Dreux became the unexpected testing-ground for France's National Front extremists whose anti-immigrant, law-and-order programme made such an impact that, in 1983, the orthodox conservatives in the town forged a pact with the devil. In return for his support, they appointed the local Front leader to the town council. After his death in a car accident, his wife went on to win the parliamentary seat for Dreux with 61.3 per cent of the vote.

Just as the National Front was exploiting the explosive seeds of unemployment, industrial mutation and racism unwittingly sown by the motor industry in Normandy, Renault was reflecting other changes in France as well. Amid an upsurge in extreme left-wing terrorism, the chairman was murdered in the street as an evil paragon of capitalism. A quarter of Renault's capital was opened to investors in France's privatisation programme. Volvo took a stake in an ill-fated attempt at European co-operation. The management even summoned up the nerve to defy a 22-day strike at one of its factories. And *dégraissage* hit Billancourt with a vengeance. When its workers had led the charge for more pay in 1968, the plant employed 24,000. By 1991, it had 1,230. At 2:30 P.M. on 27 March 1992, France's most famous assembly-line came to a halt. Four days later, the Billancourt plant closed for good. The men went home, and the management looked for buyers for the land. It used to be said that 'when Billancourt sneezes, France catches a cold'. By 1992, France was already ill.

Three and a half months after its Paris plant closed, Renault got a new chairman, a former senior government official called Louis Schweitzer. His first year in office saw another 7,000 jobs cut. Renault had lost 37 per cent of its labour force in the dozen years since the left won power in 1981. Back then, Schweitzer had been the principal aide to the Socialist Budget Minister, and reacted with cold irritation if one dared suggest that the government's plans for reflation and nationalisation might be just a little unrealistic. As for France itself, the experience of the 1980s had been a steep learning curve for him. An Énarque who was distantly related to Jean-Paul Sartre, he had dealt with ministerial problems over HIV-contaminated blood supplies and the blowing-up of the anti-nuclear Greenpeace ship *Rainbow Warrior* by French secret service agents. In the early 1980s, Schweitzer wore shoes with unusually thick soles; by the time he took over the partially privatised Renault, his footwear was a good deal more elegant. Once he was settled into the job, Renault announced that it was going to shed another couple of thousand workers in what the chairman described by the fashionable euphemism of a 'social plan'.

Like a number of his colleagues from the Socialist glory days, Schweitzer has gone through the 1990s with a deeply different ideology. As a member of the elite band of *Inspecteurs des Finances*, his prime loyalty must be to the state rather than to any political faction. But in his new incarnation, he faced the same question which hangs over his colleagues in boardrooms throughout the country. Whether renegades from the left or lifelong true believers of the right, France's business leaders have shown themselves as adept as anybody at sacking people. Now they have to prove that their slimmed-down companies can compete in a positive manner, selling as many cars as Fiat or Ford, prospering across the world in an open business economy, staying abreast of the changes bred by hardware and software, finding French equivalents to McDonald's and Coca-Cola, and mastering the byways of modern finance.

For all the cuts that closed Billancourt, cars remained a key industry – and a major employer. As sales stagnated in the 1990s, the government introduced schemes to give owners a financial incentive to sell their existing vehicles and buy new ones. This brought some temporary relief to the French manufacturers, but the overall trend was for sales of foreign models to rise more than those of domestic marques. Then the government-induced recovery faded away. In 1997, while sales were rising overall in Europe, France suffered a 20 per cent decline in registrations as they fell to their lowest level for twenty-two years: it had been, said the manufacturers' association, an *annus horribilis*.

Despite one particularly successful model, Renault had seen its share of the European market fall steadily. Neither it nor the other big

French manufacturer, Peugeot–Citroën, had expanded sufficiently outside Western Europe. Their prices were higher than most of their competitors – Renault's chairman once even asked rhetorically if customers could afford to buy the cars his firm made. His workforce was older and less flexible than some rivals, and its productivity lower. One new model had to be modified after critical safety reports in motoring magazines, and 160,000 cars were recalled after static electricity triggered off their airbags. Investors who had bought into the firm's first share offering in 1994 watched the value of their stock decline by nearly a third in eighteen months. When Schweitzer moved in, Renault was making a profit of 8 billion francs. By 1996, this had turned into a loss of 5 billion francs, which almost made Peugeot's 57 per cent slump look good. 'Renault is developing a device to stop drivers falling asleep at the wheel,' remarked the *Financial Times*. 'Shareholders could be forgiven for hoping the company's top brass have it installed in their offices.'

The Industry Minister suggested that the very survival of the company might be at stake. There were only three years to go before quotas limiting Japanese imports ran out; the Koreans were moving in and other Asian rivals could not be far behind. Renault had to become more competitive. So plans were laid for night shifts and new plants outside Europe – and there, inevitably, more cuts, including the closure of a factory at Villevorde near Brussels with the loss of 3,000 jobs.

The contrast between the old and new Renault was striking: it had taken years to wind down Fortress Billancourt, but the Belgian decision came out of the blue. The King of Belgium protested; President Chirac made his disquiet known. Others saw the decision as a sign that Renault was serious about getting to grips with its problems, even if its public relations left much to be desired. The new Socialist government hummed and hawed, and eventually acknowledged the industrial logic of what the company was doing. The share price lifted. A big American investment fund bought into Renault. 'Renault has chosen the stock market over jobs,' the Communist-led CGT union federation remarked. Exactly. Within a month, Renault announced a sharp improvement in its performance, which it attributed in part to having got a handle on its costs at last. But, soon afterwards, it was the turn of the maker of Peugeots to dive into the red, and take the long-overdue step of streamlining manufacture of its two previously sacrosanct marques. The question remained as to whether France could continue to maintain two separate car-makers, poised awkwardly between the bigger-volume producers and the smaller, more specialised brands. At least, the case for Renault and Peugeot to pool purchasing of components seemed overwhelming. In the past, there would have been no thought of two such fiercely proud firms admitting that they needed one another, but now another of those old national totems was due for a serious shake-up.

Renault's profits in 1997 were boosted by sales of holdings in the Elf oil company and in Volvo, plus a sizeable tax credit. But the progress of the newly focussed firm really became evident the following year when it moved ahead of Volkswagen and Ford to become the best-selling brand in Europe. Its shares boomed and American analysts spoke glowingly of its upbeat profile. Confidence was so high that talk surfaced of a possible takeover of Nissan. It was all a long way from Sartre and the Île Séguin. Another working-class icon had been overtaken by end-of-century realities.

No political movement has caught the chill that emanated from Billancourt more than the Parti Communiste Français. Since its split with the Socialists in 1920, the PCF had seen itself as the true champion of the working class. Once it had terrified the bourgeoisie and frightened the CIA as it brought hundreds of thousands of supporters out on to the streets. Under the charismatic leadership of Maurice Thorez, it had played a leading role in promoting the Popular Front, and, after initial hesitations during the Hitler–Stalin pact, had been as important as the Gaullists in the internal Resistance. During the Fourth Republic, the party routinely outpolled the Socialists. In the strikes of 1968, it made the rest of the left look like dilettantes; the world might watch images of students occupying the Sorbonne, but what really mattered was how the PCF played its hand. If De Gaulle was to be overthrown, that task could not be accomplished without its solid battalions. But the Communists did not want the General to go – and, above all, they did not want their troops infected by the springtime elixir of young people who declared themselves 'Marxists – Groucho wing'. At the presidential election of 1969, less than twelve months after the crushing of the Prague spring, the Moscow-loyal Communist candidate took four times as many votes as the Socialist. If Georges Pompidou was the major winner of the battles of the late 1960s, the PCF counted itself a close second. But it was in grave danger of losing the war.

Two decades later, the electoral relationship between the two main parties of the left was more than reversed, as the still highly orthodox Communists got just under a fifth of François Mitterrand's score in the 1988 election. In return for its support in the run-off ballot, Mitterrand gave the PCF four places in his first government. They were very much on the second rung of power; their most important post was the Transport Ministry. Still, the chance of participating in the left's first administration of the Fifth Republic could not be resisted. Before long, it proved a poisoned chalice.

The party had lost its way. This was not simply a matter of the diminishing appeal of Communism. On the one hand, there was Mitterrand's superbly orchestrated long-term campaign to build up the Socialists as the major party of the left, taking the Communists into a one-way alliance which sapped their strength. Reformers might talk of forging a new brand of Marxism: a senior Communist civil servant spoke to me at length over a slab of pink calf's liver in a smart Left Bank restaurant of how the Communists could use the Socialists to broaden their appeal. But the party had been so dragooned into Moscow-directed orthodoxy over the decades that it could not get the worm out of its bud, and establish itself as a real working-class party for modern times which would think for itself and stand apart from both the temporising Socialists and the rampant forces of the far right. More than any other political group in this retrospective nation, the PCF is a prisoner of its past, to a degree which the vast majority of its members are unaware. For proof, meet one of the more shadowy figures of French political history, Eugen Fried.

It was not until 1997 that two tireless chroniclers of French communism, Annie Kriegel and Stéphane Courtois, uncovered the extent of Fried's role in ensuring that the supposed white knight of France's workers had been the slave of Moscow. As a young man, he had proved his worth to the Kremlin by organising a campaign against Social Democrats in Czechoslovakia in the 1920s. Fluent in Slovak, Hungarian, Yiddish, Czech, German, English and French, Fried was sent clandestinely by Moscow to France in around 1930. Once installed, he promoted Maurice Thorez and other trusted figures in the trade unions and politics – and blocked the rise of a popular tribune, Jacques Doriot, who switched to the far right and ended up being executed as a Nazi collaborator. Fried made each senior party official fill up a 74-part questionnaire covering everything from his education to his private life; the forms were immediately dispatched to Moscow. Fried himself regularly travelled to the USSR to report to the Kremlin, returning with Stalin's latest commands.

In 1934, Fried came back to France from one of these trips with an order that the PCF should set aside the rancours of the 1920 split and work with the Socialists again. The left was on a major upswing at the time, buttressed by the economic slump, fear of what was happening across the Rhine in Nazi Germany and the activities of fascist groups in France. But when the Popular Front won power two years later, there was another order from Moscow – the Communists were not to join the new government.

Instead, they must put bourgeois politics on one side and concentrate on building up industrial muscle through their labour federation, the Confédération Générale du Travail (CGT). The instruction was loyally followed by Thorez and the party's labour boss, Benoît Franchon, and a future presidential candidate, Jacques Duclos. The loyalty to Moscow was not confined to politicians and unionists; a fair number of French intellectuals also made fools of themselves. 'Death to the saboteurs of the Five-year Plan,' ran a line by the much-honoured poet, Louis Aragon, who also confided later that his pain at Stalin's death was only equalled by the sense of sorrow and personal loss he had felt when his mother passed away.

Rewriting history is a futile exercise, but all the same: what if the PCF had been more independent of its puppet-master answering to Moscow, what if Thorez had grabbed the destiny which seemed to have been his to take at national level in 1936, what if the anti-fascist parties had formed a united bloc in government in the late 1930s? Would France have acted differently at Munich? Would Paris and London have been able to check Hitler sooner? And, if so, would Charles de Gaulle have retired to his country home as an obscure prophet of tank warfare? So much for speculation; the reality was that, after the Nazi invasion of 1940, Fried told the French Communists to collaborate with the occupying power. He himself moved to Belgium, but kept in touch over a clandestine radio linked with Moscow and with Jacques Duclos in Paris. He instructed Thorez to desert from his regiment, and Duclos to open political negotiations with the Germans. Hitler's invasion of Russia finally freed the Communists to join the Resistance, but Fried did not live to resume on-the-spot control after the Liberation: in 1943, the Gestapo killed him during a raid in Brussels. They had no idea who he was. Nor did any but a handful of the French.

After the Liberation, the control from Moscow continued, reinforced by the emotional strength which at least some of the resisters had drawn from news from the Eastern Front as they fought their lonely battle in the west. The first post-war elections gave it a quarter of the vote, but it remained aloof from the twisted manoeuvres of Fourth Republic Cabinet-making, and so could claim a certain purity. It reacted with a famous court case when a former Resistance fighter revealed the nature of the Soviet Gulags in 1950 and, though it lost, could still count on the allegiance of Jean-Paul Sartre and the intellectual left. But the true nature of communism in the East gradually seeped home, and the PCF's devotedly Stalinist leadership became increasingly isolated though it, again, won credit for its opposition to the colonial war in Algeria. The advent of the Fifth Republic did the party no harm, since the Socialists were humbled and De Gaulle's independent foreign policy created a certain warmth with Moscow. But the sands began to shift more decisively in the 1970s, when the Communists became epitomised by a man who hit a political nadir on their behalf.

Georges Marchais, Secretary-General of the PCF from 1972 to 1993, was a scary remnant from the caverns of Stalinism whose outbursts provided regular occasions for national mirth. Under his long rule, the survival of the least fittest became the be-all and end-all of leadership. A bushy-eyebrowed, potato-headed thug whose lack of style could make him almost endearing on occasion, Marchais supported the crackdown on Solidarity in Poland and the Soviet invasions of Czechoslovakia and Afghanistan (the latter in a television interview direct from Moscow). Earning his nickname of 'Jojo' for his admiration for Stalin, he developed ties with Leonid Brezhnev and Nicolae Ceauşescu, and viewed Mikhail Gorbachev's reforms with trepidation.

'What's a Gulag? he once asked. 'What we call a prison, they call a Gulag.' When deportations and executions in the Soviet Union under Communist rule were mentioned, he retorted: 'I tell you, they didn't arrest enough! They didn't imprison enough! If they had been tougher and more vigilant, they wouldn't have got into this situation they're in now.' After pulling back from a tilt at Euro-Communist liberalism in the 1970s, he proclaimed the glories of 'democratic centralism' and muzzled anything approaching *glasnost* in his party. Famously dogmatic, he once told a television interviewer who had cornered him that the man was asking the wrong questions. Such braggadocio behaviour earned him high ratings on the box – higher, it was said, than football matches – but party membership fell by around 70 per cent under his leadership.

Following the lines originally laid down by Eugen Fried, the PCF had always been an outsider. Marchais's leadership ensured that, more than ever, it would not evolve into being seen as a natural party of government, in the way that the Socialists were from 1981 onwards. But then, contradictorily, Marchais allowed himself to be drawn into Mitterrand's web, ensuring that the PCF got the worst of all worlds. Most woundingly, the party found itself losing votes to the extreme right, which emerged as a powerful rival for protest votes in the south and in the old 'red belt' around Paris, where the turncoat tribune Jacques Doriot had set the rabble-rousing tradition in the late 1930s.

Revelations about financing from the KGB and the siphoning off of cash by Communist-run local councils further tarnished the image. Marchais himself could never explain away the fact that he had signed on as a wartime worker at a Messerschmidt plant before the Nazis introduced compulsory labour for young Frenchmen. But all this paled into insignificance beside the huge political failure of the would-be party of the masses to capitalise on the growing discontent with successive governments among its natural supporters. The 1980s should have been the moment the PCF had been waiting for, with soaring unemployment showing up the harsh side of capitalism as administrations of left and right took ever more unpopular measures, and voters searched for new panaceas. Instead, the PCF's woes mounted, as did those of the nation. In the first round of the 1981 presidential election, Georges Marchais, for all his faults, had won 15 per cent of the vote to Mitterrand's 26 per cent. Seven years later,

Mitterrand got about the same level of support but the Communist candidate managed to muster only 5.4 per cent.

In 1993, the party eventually got a new leader, Robert Hue, a bearded, friendly-looking former nurse with an unusual wit who resembled a large garden gnome. At the National Assembly elections of that year, the Communists did so badly that the minimum requirement for a parliamentary group had to be changed to enable their deputies to sit together. In the 1995 presidential poll, Hue took 8.6 per cent of the first-round vote. Georges Marchais, who was to die at the end of 1997, said nothing in public, but sniped at his successor. Undeterred, Hue set out to bring the party into the modern world. Internal discipline remained tight, but reformers were no longer banished. Jacques Chirac's gamble in calling legislative elections in 1997 gave fresh reason for hope. United by pledges to slash unemployment and by scepticism about the demands of the Maastricht Treaty, the Communists and Socialists reached a broad policy agreement that, despite some decidedly grey areas, enabled them to campaign in the name of a united left.

Hue set a target of 10 per cent of the first-round vote; in the event, the PCF got 9.9 per cent, and boosted its representation in the National Assembly from twenty-four to thirty-eight seats. The election result meant the Socialists needed Communist support to achieve a parliamentary majority. Hue overcame opposition from some old hard-liners, including Marchais, and agreed to join the new government; the central committee celebrated with a 1992 *grand cru* claret, cheese and strawberries. A member of the party's national secretariat followed the 1981 example to become Minister of Transport. He lost no time in getting 20 billion francs written off the debts of the state railway system and freezing a job-reduction plan. Flying down to the south-west for the weekend, he told his fellow passengers he was confident that France was facing a new start, with the PCF up there in the driving cab. Not that his new responsibilities had gone to his head: standing behind him at the counter in Rodez airport, I noticed that his hire-car was in the cheapest category, like mine.

The party might be back in government, but it was very much a junior partner alongside ecologists and left-wing Socialists. There was no doubting the decline of the once-mighty Communist machine. The mutations through which France had gone had profoundly altered the nature of its one-time supporters. The collapse of communism in Eastern Europe dealt it a heavy blow. Its past associations could not be easily shaken off – an 846-page account of the crimes of communism around the world went to the top of the French bestseller list in the winter of 1997. The PCF won substantially fewer votes than the National Front, and its score was regularly less than one-third of the non-Communist left. Even the party's annual fête outside Paris began to lose money. On election night, Hue asked a persistent American reporter if he really looked like a frightening person; but that was not the point. When the PCF had been frightening, it was because of its disciplined mass following rather than its ideology. Now, the marchers in the street were a far more disparate lot, following different drums; Georges Marchais was heading for his grave; and it was the extreme right which inspired fear. The old certainties had ebbed even for the party which had once been sure that history was on its side. Appropriately, a guide taking visitors round the PCF's new headquarters remarked on how the building contained no angles, only curves. The party newspaper, *L'Humanité*, dropped the hammer and sickle from its masthead, relaunching its Sunday edition as a glossy magazine with advertisements from privatised companies. And, all the while, Robert Hue proved to be Lionel Jospin's flexible friend: while the party remained sternly hostile to the European common currency, and asked for a referendum on the subject, it kept its ministers in a government which was committed to a goal it opposed. Doctrinal certainty had been replaced by the basic need to survive.

Worse, Jospin faced the PCF with the nightmare possibility of a re-run of the 1980s. If the Socialists did a good job, Communist voters would be tempted to back them next time round – after all, there was precious little to distinguish Hue and his men from the left wing of the Socialist Party. But if the government of the left fared badly, the party would be tarred with failure. At the same time, the domain in which the Communists had depended for their muscle since the 1930s was no longer a garden of militancy. Competition to the CGT from France's two other main labour federations was growing sharper by the strike. The battalions of union members whom the PCF used to be able to call out at the wave of a red flag were growing thinner – only 9 per cent of French workers now belong to a labour federation, and even that figure is an overstatement since it includes pensioners.

French bosses say they are the most fearful of strikes among employers in Western Europe, but union membership has dropped by more
than a third in a decade while employment in the largely unorganised
service industries is the second highest in the continent. Despite the
temporary relief offered to the PCF by getting a couple of ministries
in the Jospin government, and the showy strikes by lorry-drivers, the
decline of union power added to the serious question of how – or
whether – the one-time party of the workers is going to be able to
remain relevant to the France of the twenty-first century, a question
which both illuminates and springs from the decline of the old working class in a country where the unemployed outnumber trade union
members, and where business rules the roost.

6

BUSINESS MATTERS

One French company, L'Oréal, is the world's biggest cosmetics firm, and Michelin leads the way in tyres. French construction firms span the globe, and Danone provides yoghurts and biscuits across the planet. AXA, which swallowed a rival at the end of 1996 to become the world's second biggest insurance company, reaps 70 per cent of its turnover abroad, more than half of it in the USA, and has prospered by following its chairman's very un-French maxim of 'think global, act local'. The LVMH group prospers by selling the world a range of luxury goods from Dior and Givenchy to Hennessy and Louis Vuitton, and has made its chairman, Bernard Arnault, a 20-billion-franc fortune. Hachette is one of the world's major magazine publishers; French utilities have had a field day with British water; and the country's major steel group, once a chronic loss-maker, has turned in annual profits of up to 4.5 billion francs.

Still, few French firms figure among world leaders in absolute size, or revenue. Many successful enterprises tend to be niche players. A list of top European companies by sector in 1996 contained half as many from France as from Britain. Danone, Elf Aquitaine and L'Air Liquide edge into the ranks of the top food producers, oil companies and chemical groups, but only in eighth or ninth position.

With notable exceptions such as those mentioned above and thrusting public works and infrastructure firms like Vivendi, the challenge of innovation and international competition is not something most French enterprises have traditionally relished, particularly when it

means opening up home markets to foreigners. It may be no coinci-
dence that a survey of European business people published in 1999 put
French executives top of the league of those with whom their peers
thought it hardest to do business. In world ranking of competitiveness,
France usually ends up around twentieth, and does badly on the liberal scale when it comes to government interference and the openness
of the economy. There may be more adepts of free trade than there
were in Paris, but protectionism and state regulation lie deep in the
French soul. It was Louis XIV's mighty minister, Jean-Baptiste
Colbert, who gave his name to the doctrine of the state ring-fencing
the economy from foreign depredations – and his spirit lives on.
Chauvinism lurks just below the surface. General de Gaulle dismissed
a visiting Japanese Prime Minister as a 'transistor salesman', and an
offer by a South Korean company to bail out a loss-making arm of the
Thomson group was rejected in 1996 amid horror stories about how
hard Asian bosses make their employees work. But 'globalisation is
imposing itself upon us', the Finance Minister said with a heavy heart
as Moulinex announced it was moving some of its production to
Mexico.

One reason why international competition is so scary for French
companies is that they are handicapped by a series of factors outside
their control. Wages in manufacturing industries may be only twelfth
highest among European nations, but employers' social security contributions are far higher than in Germany or Britain, and thus send
the overall bill soaring. AXA pays more to the state in welfare charges
than it does to its French workers in wages. Effective corporate tax
rates rank below Germany, but ahead of Britain. A growing number
of small businesses moved their operations across the Channel,
attracted by the level of social security contributions and employment
flexibility at the other end of the Eurostar line. 'Explain to me why it
is better to be unemployed in France than a worker in England,' asked
one businessman, who reckoned that his profit potential quadrupled
by moving his electronics firm from Paris to Kent. Such was the
influx that the *Daily Mail* reported concern among Conservative MPs
at the number of young French job-seekers crossing the Channel. A
hairdresser from Valence in the Rhône Valley went a step further,
using her European rights to register her business in Wales while
keeping her operation in France and saving more than 100,000 francs

a year in the process. Such people earned a furious rebuke from the French Labour Minister who insisted, 'If you want to cut French hair, then you have to be in the French tax regime.' Indeed, the hairdresser and others like her will, no doubt, go on availing themselves of public services funded by those who pay French taxes to the full. But the lure of a different fiscal system is undeniable at a time when, whatever excuses it may put up, France's business establishment finds itself on trial.

In the 1980s, a well-connected banker called Jean-Maxime Levêque was something of a political weathercock for French business. Close to leading Gaullist politicians, the sharply-suited Énarque served as an economic adviser at the Élysée before joining the Crédit Commercial de France bank, of which he became chairman in 1976. He lost that job when it was nationalised by the Socialists. Between warnings of the disaster awaiting France under left-wing rule, Levêque did what any dispossessed financier would do. He set up a merchant bank of his own with its headquarters safely insulated from French taxes in the Dutch Antilles, and with an array of shareholders that included a couple of major Middle Eastern arms-dealers and the rogue bull Robert Maxwell.

When the Gaullists and their allies won the 1986 legislative election and Jacques Chirac became Prime Minister, Levêque returned in glory to become chairman of one of France's top banks, the Crédit Lyonnais. He was photographed flashing a shark-like grin as he posed behind a life-sized model of the bank's symbol of a cuddly lion. That ended when the Socialists regained power two years later. Levêque returned to his own bank, which was called Ibsa. But things only went from bad to worse: Ibsa made disastrous property investments, extended huge and dubious lines of credit and paid large commissions to its associates. A former employee told how 30 million francs in cash had been taken out of the bank's tills in Paris over a two-year period. In 1992, it lost its banking license and came under the control of the Crédit Lyonnais, whose chairman described it a couple of years later as 'rotten'. While controversy swirled around some of its property deals, Levêque was taken in for questioning, during which he was held for four months in a Paris prison. Still elegant and tough at the age of seventy-three, he proclaimed his innocence of any wrong-doing, and insisted that his bank had, in fact, been praised by inspectors from the Crédit Lyonnais after it had been purchased.

It was not as if Ibsa was alone in its travails. By the 1990s, France's banks were in what the Gaullist leader in the National Assembly described as their worst crisis since the Second World War. Although the number of finance and credit institutions fell by a third between 1985 and 1995, France is, by international standards, 'overbanked', with too many competitors vying for domestic business. In public, the bankers have welcomed the pressures of the market, deregulation and the increasing internationalisation of their business. In fact, many seemed much more anxious to cling to the old ways: a report by a group of leading accountancy firms found that financial institutions remained overly secretive, providing inadequate information to shareholders on credit risks or doubtful loans. Behind their protective curtain, they were all too easily seduced by flashy schemes and fast-talking hustlers. Their bosses worked under lax controls – as a parliamentary commission put it, in a refrain which will be familiar by now, 'the controllers and the controlled' were often members of the same group of top civil servants. In the late 1980s and early 1990s, the big banks poured 200 billion francs into the increasingly sick property market and other poor investments, often failing to get proper collateral and overestimating rental incomes. They soon paid a huge price, and yet some remained dilatory about taking the kind of decisive action needed to put things right. By 1998, most of the big banks seemed to have put their houses in order, and were reporting good profits, fuelled by a soaring stock market – although concerns remained about bad loans to Asia, the effect on costs of the 35-hour working week and the ever-growing dominance of the City of London in an increasingly integrated European financial system.

One institution, however, seemed to be under a curse. Nowhere had the shortcomings of French finance been more evident, and the end result more painful, than at the big bank which Jean-Maxime Levêque had run while his political friends had been in power. Few combinations are more lethal in business than that of overweening ambition and sheer incompetence. And few testaments to the cost of that combination are more eloquent than the affairs done from the stately white building covering a city block beside the Paris Opéra, which houses the headquarters of the Crédit Lyonnais.

Buoyed by the confidence of their Grandes Écoles backgrounds, Levêque's successors at the Crédit Lyonnais set out in the late 1980s to build their establishment into the equivalent of Germany's all-powerful Deutsche Bank. With the enthusiastic support of the Socialist government, they sought growth by lending money left, right and centre in what the European Commission later called a 'bulimia of investments and acquisitions'. They plunged into the property market, and opened their coffers to a string of crooks at home and abroad. The bank's largesse was extended to Robert Maxwell to keep his empire afloat. It loaned $1.3 billion to an Italian waiter turned financial buc-caneer, Giancarlo Parretti, to buy the MGM studio in Hollywood – a subsequent investigation by *Fortune* magazine produced an allegation that the loan had been tied to a bid to sell high-speed trains to Italy, with a senior Italian minister acting as broker. Control was sadly lack-ing as the bank threw good money after bad. Starting with a single investment outside Paris, one of its subsidiaries ended up owning thirty-six loss-making golf courses, and plunged 1.5 billion francs into a retailing investment which rewarded it with a loss of 700 million francs. There were juicy commissions for go-betweens, a 600,000-franc payment through a Swiss subsidiary to an adviser to a Socialist minister in Paris, and a 2-million-franc deposit in a Swiss bank to an editor on the main French state television channel for his help in keeping the press sweet. By the end of 1997, more than forty separate judicial inquiries were being conducted into the bank's past affairs, and it appeared to have been taken to the cleaners by fraudsters to the tune of several billion francs.

To give its figures an upward tweak, the bank was not averse to revaluing its assets. That made the gap between the figures on paper and the reality outside all the greater when the final reckoning came. In 1994, the government had no alternative but to step in with an injection of 4.9 billion francs. At that point, losses were estimated at 14 billion francs. A year later, they were put at ten times that figure.

The catastrophe was so great that figures no longer had any real meaning to the average person. But what was plain was that nothing on the same scale had been seen before. *The Economist* dubbed it 'banking's biggest disaster'. The head of another major French bank

publicly blamed it on the 'megalomania' of Jean-Yves Haberer, the
Crédit Lyonnais boss in its go-go days who was taken into custody in
1998 for questioning over the bank's role in the bankruptcy of a food
transport firm. One question which was rarely put was how the
board, including some leading names, had allowed the bank to race
out of control. But then how could a group of mere directors be
expected to handle the combination of elite arrogance and political
backing which underwrote the débâcle? After all, Haberer was an
Inspecteur des Finances, and had headed the French Treasury. And
which body was charged with supervising France's banks? Why, the
Treasury. So that must be all right.

Even the rescue effort aroused controversy, and not just for its cost
to the taxpayers. There was serious discord between Paris and the
European Commission, which wondered why a state bank in France
should be propped up to such a huge degree when its competitors in
the private sector were subject to the rigours of market competition.
The Socialist Finance Minister accused his predecessors of political
interference in the sale of assets stripped out of the bad bank. Though
he named no names, it seemed pretty clear what he was talking about.
Assets had been shuffled off to a new company to be sold off. The fact
that a time limit was set on these sales gave buyers a clear edge. One
troubled subsidiary was cleaned up, injected with new capital – and
then sold back to the bank without others being able to put in a bid.
Another transaction involved a stake which Crédit Lyonnais had
bought in a holding company controlled by a close friend of Jacques
Chirac, François Pinault. Pinault made it plain that he refused to
work with a minority shareholder, which greatly reduced the attraction of the stake to other potential purchasers. The Finance Minister
in the Juppé government ordered the stake to be sold to Pinault for
1.5 billion francs. Since Pinault's holding company is not public, the
value of the stake is not known, but estimates put it between 4.5 and
6 billion francs. On top of which, the President's friend got bonds
with a face value of 1.5 billion as part of the deal.

With the taxpayers paying off its debts, Crédit Lyonnais duly
returned to profit, and aimed towards privatisation. Its plans included
cutting staff to only half of its numbers in the heady days of the late
1980s. Naturally, it was all too anxious to put the past behind it, but
fate seemed to have it in for the bank. It found itself with a $12

billion loan exposure in Asia as the region crashed in late 1997. Fire, apparently deliberately started in two separate places, ravaged its headquarters in Paris, causing major damage but sparing the boardroom where so many awful decisions had been made by financiers who thought they enjoyed a special state-protected place in the world. At least the bank's chairman had the grace to remark that Crédit Lyonnais had to 'learn to be modest'.

Even at the nadir of its fortunes, Crédit Lyonnais never gave up the aim of getting itself privatised. Since the right formed its first *cohabitation* government with François Mitterrand in 1986, putting state firms on the market has been a consistent buzzword. But, a decade after the state was supposed to have begun to relax its grip, the evidence is that the public interest – as defined by the state and its servants – remains strong. The privatisation drive launched when Jacques Chirac was Prime Minister between 1986 and 1988 has been a carefully controlled affair, with the state's interests well protected. The original approach was clubbishly cautious: the government put together a 'hard core' of reliable investors to maintain control of the companies. At the top, chairmen often come from the small circle that binds the public and the private sector. As such, they are properly mindful of the continuing role of the state as the source of big contracts and a safety net of succour if they run into difficulties. This may help to account for the finding by the Organisation for Economic Co-operation and Development (OECD) that public enterprises privatised since 1986 show the lowest rates of return on their equity of any group of French companies. Despite having turned in a profit of 4.5 billion francs in the year of its privatisation, the Usinor steel group saw its share price drop below the issue price at the end of 1997. Opinion polls report wide support for privatisation, but the job cuts which might follow would be decidedly unpopular. The bid to sell off some major companies has been bedevilled by nationalism and politics, and by a running dispute over how much power the state should yield – a dispute which the Finance Minister, Dominique Strauss-Kahn, describes as a 'war of religion'.

Letting foreigners take on state assets is not a popular notion for the French, particularly when less comfortable working practices might be imported from abroad. A banker involved in privatisation discussions recalls how the politicians spent more time worrying about the reaction of the public-sector unions than they did about the best offer price for the market – and that was before the Socialists won the legislative elections on a platform which included the slogan 'No to privatisations'. Once in office, the left took a more nuanced approach. Five months after denouncing privatisations at the hustings, the Socialists presided over the successful part-privatisation of the state telecommunications enterprise, France Telecom. France's biggest stock-market flotation, it hit record trading volumes as shares were launched on Wall Street to the accompaniment of cancan dancers, accordion-players and croissants. Shortly afterwards, it became known that the government had decided to sell off nearly all the state's minority holding in Usinor, and that the state-controlled Franco-Italian semiconductor firm, SGS-Thomson, was considering a public offering of its stock. The general approach was to sell off a quarter or so of shares, but to retain a 'strategic stake' or a 'decisive voice'. That meant the state kept the position of principal shareholder and thus was able to direct the management. Within a few months, the government and its Communist Transport Minister had got rid of the highly successful head of Air France, who insisted on a greater measure of privatisation than the rather timid limits set by ministers. It was, a senior government figure insisted to me at the time, just like any board sacking its chief executive – except that most boards leave ideology at home when they make such key decisions. Some international investors saw the administration trying to have its cake and eat it – raising money from the market but retaining state control. When 20 per cent of France Telecom was floated in 1997, the government laid down that the new shareholders were to have a say in the appointment of only three of the twenty-one directors. And when the government sold the CIC bank, the country's fifth largest, in 1998, the majority stake went to a mutual trust, not to a commercial buyer. No wonder one analyst called such partial privatisations an opportunity to buy 'a share in the French civil service'.

That civil service naturally pays great attention to maintaining the place of the public sector, and nobody can doubt how large the public sector still looms. It employs a quarter of the country's workforce, many of them assured jobs for life. Nationalised companies account for 15 per cent of the gross national product – four times as much as in Britain. At the huge state electricity firm, EDF, one expert forecasts that privatisation might cost 30 per cent of the workers their jobs – a sign of how insulated the company had been when run as a branch of government before facing the shock of being forced by European rules to open up its market to foreign competition. The French Post Office employs half as many people again as its British equivalent, and has built up a debt of 31 billion francs. The nationalised railway system gets an annual subsidy of 50 billion francs, but still lost between 15 and 16 billion francs in the mid-1990s; however, an energetic programme of cost-cutting and fare reductions to attract passengers slashed this to 1 billion in 1997, in a sign of what a businesslike management could achieve in the public sector if it had the will.

Far from worrying the French, the scale of activities which helps to produce such a sea of red ink is a subject of national pride. We, the French say, have not gone the British way; our public services really serve the public; the trains run on time between little country towns and you do not have to drive dozens of miles to find a post office. Alain Juppé's threats to such serenity in 1995–97 were seen as an assault on national values. Whether politicians will ever really dare to pull the plug on state spending in a major way is doubtful. At a time of continuing high unemployment, the jobless regard the public sector as their last refuge. The ratio of applicants to jobs in teaching and central state posts has doubled in a decade. A single opening at Toulouse University brought in 1,200 letters. Applications to join the police have jumped by a third since the start of the 1990s. No wonder so many of the French feel personally threatened when they hear talk of reducing the role of the state or cutting the money poured into the public sector.

But then they have to count the cost of paying for that statist comfort blanket. The headline rates make France appear as a nation where killer margins of income tax destroy enterprise. The image is useful at election time. 'Too much tax kills tax,' Jacques Chirac proclaimed in his presidential campaign. The truth is that marginal personal tax rates on the lower and middle income band are lower in France than in Britain, the United States, Italy, Germany or Japan; they only shoot up to the top of the league on annual incomes of 750,000 francs or more. The authorities are so bad at gathering taxes, and the French so good at evading them, that only between a third and half the adult population pays income tax at all – one of France's richest business-men, a close friend of President Chirac, cheerfully admitted that he had taken out a 140-million-franc loan to buy shares in his companies in order to avoid paying any wealth tax at all. For decades, journalists, fashion models, airline pilots, musicians and dozens of other professions benefited from sometimes outrageous loopholes. Historic legacies protect certain regions, such as 'home weavers using equipment powered by electricity at their own expense in the departments of the Aisne, Nord and Somme'. Many of those who pay tax stump up very little. The ratio of income-tax revenue to gross domestic product in France is among the lowest in the industrialised world.

Where the French tax system is deadly is in the array of indirect taxes, in the form of social security contributions, levies on employment, property fees and, above all, valued added taxes on goods and services. According to a calculation by the OECD, it takes the earnings of the average French worker from 1 January to 12 June to cover all the taxes he will pay during a year: in the USA, the end date is 11 April, in Britain 9 May. Since 1965, the period needed to cover all taxes has gone up by thirty-six working days in France, but by only twelve days in the United States and seventeen in Britain. The bias towards indirect taxes is socially regressive, even more so at a time of high unemployment. It makes it expensive to give people jobs, and penalises the poor who have to pay VAT on the essentials of life. Successive governments come to power pledged to reform the tax structure, but the cost of the state holds them back. In one of its first acts, the Jospin government added a fresh weapon to its tax armoury by increasing taxation on companies from 36.6 to 41.6 per cent. That might help to bring the budget deficit into line with the Maastricht criteria, but it was hard to see what it would do to encourage firms to expand. In a world in which reducing taxation is seen as a spur to economic activity, France finds itself talking about the need to grow in order to create jobs while applying the old nostrums of grabbing money from business to try to balance the state books.

Like their peers elsewhere in French society, the nation's business leaders have long seemed indifferent to how deeply their self-protective aloofness jars. Whatever the performance of their companies, they have been used to conducting themselves as a class apart, born to rule, often shielded by political connections and mutually interlocking shareholdings. Too many business chieftains still rely on the comfortable cocoon of corporatism, state contracts and protected markets. Until very recently, they pursued empire-building as an end in itself with little regard for the results. Not content with having become the world's biggest water-distribution company, the Compagnie Générale des Eaux also built up a web of 2,700 subsidiaries, ranging from health care, laundry services and casinos to media, property and restaurants. It paid bribes to win public-works contracts, and got caught in the downturn of the real-estate market. By 1995, the company's debts amounted to 125 per cent of its equity, and it reported the first loss of its 140-year history. Examples like that led the *Financial Times* to argue that French business badly needs some Darwinian progress. In the end, the 76-year-old CGE chairman was replaced by an investment banker who rationalised the group, outlawed bribery and set his sights on the deregulated telephone market. But at many other firms, the tradition of old men clinging to power will be hard to dismantle, if only because some of them come with the landscape.

Take, for example, the case of the grandest old man of French business, Ambroise Roux. A firm believer in para-psychology, said to read a book a day and to take eleven weeks' holiday a year, Roux became managing director of an important engineering company, the Compagnie Générale d'Électricité, in 1963. Over the next two decades, he built it into a huge conglomerate – only to see the firm nationalised by the Socialists before it evolved under a more friendly government of the right into the privatised Alcatel–Alsthom group. Roux had resigned on nationalisation, but he returned as honorary chairman of Alcatel–Alsthom. He sat on seventeen corporate boards, stretching from banking to retailing. He offered advice and guidance on takeovers and appointments, and was a key figure in France's most powerful business lobbying association. Over the decades, he built up his relationships with Presidents and Premiers across the political spectrum. His group employed a former Finance Minister and Premier-in-waiting to run one of its subsidiaries. Despite the nationalisation of CGE, Roux maintained his relationship with François Mitterrand through the decades. State contracts helped to shelter his companies against international competition. If the business–political club had a father figure, it was Ambroise Roux. Naturally, not all his peers were enchanted at his disinclination to retire from the scene, but, as Roux searched for a new boss for Alcatel at the age of seventy-three, the magazine *Le Point* could only note that they had better bite their impatient tongues because the old para-psychologist might outlast them all.

Traditionally, boardrooms are secretive places — except when personal or political rivalries seep into public view. Companies take their time issuing their annual accounts, and too many obfuscate behind accounting rules which allow them to juggle figures behind allowances for special provisions. Most maintain a strictly male atmosphere at the top. Although a survey by a business magazine has found that firms run by women were twice as profitable and grew twice as fast as those run by men, there are only a tiny number of female bosses — other surveys in 1996 reported that while a quarter of all boards had a female member, the vast majority were related to the owners. Only two of the top two hundred companies had a woman as an executive director.

The establishment club looks after its own, and makes sure that there is plenty of room for former political grandees and top civil servants. As they move between their different but connected roles, the graduates of the Grandes Écoles may join companies with whose affairs they dealt in their former official functions. Not many eyebrows are raised, or not very far, anyway. As we have heard George Soros say, they end up by constituting a clique, putting forward their own relations and tolerating incestuous inefficiency.

There are signs that some of this is changing. Symbolically, the employers' federation has altered its name from the paternalist National Council of the French Patronat to the more dynamic-sounding Movement of Enterprises of France. There have been big hostile takeover bids among supermarkets and finance houses — though they have generally ended in cosy compromises. The Compagnie Générale des Eaux not only spent a small fortune giving itself the zippier name of 'Vivendi' but also carried out a major restructuring and linked up with the Havas advertising, television and publishing group to provide France with a potential world-sized media player. But the creation of a new defence industry grouping also showed the strength of tradition. To begin with it was organised and announced by the government, and the state held the biggest single stake in the new enterprise. Any idea of using privatisation was discarded. So was the notion of remodelling France's defence firms to fit into a European context through co-operation with British and German companies. The Defence Ministry spoke of 'industrial logic' – French industrial logic, that is. Defence is, admittedly, a sensitive matter for any administration, but it is also a matter of major international economic rivalry. By ensuring the primacy of the state and turning its back on European link-ups to bolster competition with the United States, the government made it crystal-clear where its priorities lay, and the firms concerned rejoiced at finding themselves in the cocoon of a 'Franco-French solution' to an international challenge.

Life at the summit of the business club has been all the easier for decades because of the quiescent role of shareholders who, when they bothered to turn up for annual general meetings, generally had to make do with a few platitudes from the platform. (The Suez conglomerate used to go one better and distribute tins of a brand of *foie gras* it owned.) Individuals and companies account for 55 per cent of French shareholdings. Most of the individuals never raise their voices; many of the corporate holdings form part of an inter-locking pattern which big companies use to protect themselves from raiders. In contrast, only 18 per cent of stocks are with the kind of financial institutions capable of giving poor managements a hard time – and, until recently, many French fund managers tended to work by instinct and personal preference rather than by using the analytical tools common in the United States and Britain. Some defenders of *capitalisme à la française* say the absence of shareholder pressure means companies have been able to concentrate on long-range planning free from the short-termism of the stock market, in which case one would have expected a rather more impressive stance from them in major international industries. The truth is that, too often, the lack of outside pressure has simply been a passport to inertia. Shareholders certainly didn't benefit; a study of the shares of twenty companies with cross-shareholdings in other big stock-market firms found that they underperformed the index by 29 per cent over three years.

However, the corporate undergrowth is stirring. Consultants have started to advertise their services to tell shareholders how to exercise their rights. In one dramatic departure from the tradition of deference, small investors who lost a lot of money on their shares in the Eurotunnel project showed the board what they thought at a meeting in Paris, tearing up copies of the annual report, hammering their fists on tables and attacking the company's bankers as greedy monsters. 'We are the victims of a scam!' shouted the president of the Association for the Respect of Individuals and Their Patrimony. 'This is immoral. We gave them our money but we are not allowed a say in our destiny!'

A more substantial threat to the Olympian status of company boards is the growing presence of big foreign investment funds on the French market, and of foreign non-executive directors. American, British and Swiss funds have built up holdings of many tens of billions of francs in French companies. By the end of 1997, foreign investors held more than half the capital of the Total and Elf oil firms, and had between 30 and 50 per cent of nineteen other big groups. An American director was instrumental in getting the boss of the big Alcatel group removed as the group's losses soared and scandal allegations swirled. After Swiss, Dutch and German banks bought into Renault, the company appointed a Swiss banker to its board and had also to take note of the opinions of a big US fund which took a substantial stake of its capital. Foreign investors will not sit by quietly and let the business establishment decide what happens to their money. When it suffered from a state bank's misjudgement, a big American fund threatened to pull out of several other major holdings in France unless something was done to correct the situation. In another case, pressure from a Swiss–British merchant bank and French fund managers forced the Banque Nationale de Paris to buy out investors who had been faring badly in a subsidiary. French advisory companies have been set up to tell shareholders how to defend themselves against corporate boards. Threats and pressure are nothing new in French business – some of the biggest groups were built up in the 1960s and 1970s on the basis of boardroom muscle – but now pressure is coming from outside the walls of the establishment, from financiers who play by non-French rules.

Inevitably, in the nation of Colbertist protectionism, this process has begun to raise some concern. French companies have not been slow in expanding by takeovers abroad, but still the President of the National Assembly and former Socialist Prime Minister, Laurent Fabius, felt moved to sound a warning about the 'significant threat' from foreign firms buying into France. Another former Premier, Édouard Balladur, who as Finance Minister from 1986 to 1988 had presided over the first round of French privatisations, wrote in *Le Monde* that: 'If France wants French companies to remain so – and that is a legitimate aim – it is about time it gave them the means to do so.' He seemed to have in mind changes to the tax system to help corporate profits, and the creation of private-sector pension funds which would invest French money in French companies. But some of the state companies which had been taken into the private sector since the 1980s looked relatively weak, had limited equity and seemed like sitting targets for predatory foreign investors anxious to expand their pan-European base as the continental market barriers came down.

When they move into France, the foreigners may also wish to do something about another old-fashioned aspect of its business – the extreme difficulty shareholders have in finding out what top executives are paid. On the whole, it seems that French managers don't do too badly by international standards. A survey of the pre-tax pay of company chairmen in eight countries ranked the French second only to the Americans. Another report by a consultancy group put the average buying power of French senior executives seventh in the world – some way below Switzerland, Germany and the United States but ahead of Japan, Britain and Italy. In keeping with the risk-averse nature of French business, chairmen get a relatively large amount of their total pay in fixed salary and a smaller proportion in performance-linked rewards than in other leading industrial nations.

Such findings make it no easier to discover what the top people make. How much you earn or what you are worth are areas which fall into the national taste for secrecy or, as the French would prefer to put it, *discrétion*. Asked if he would reveal his earnings, the head of a leading bank said he was all for public disclosure, but he wasn't going to be the first to put his head on the block. Corporate information about pay and benefits fall far short of those in America or Britain; the only requirement is for companies to give a figure for the combined pay of their top ten employees. So when a chairman was questioned about his earnings at the firm's annual general meeting, he was able to reply that the top salaries were all included in the annual report. Indeed they were – amalgamated into a total of 51 million francs with no breakdown. The subject of pay disclosure was notably absent in a report by a high-level committee on corporate governance. When the chairman of one bank broke ranks by revealing his pay, it was only to deny a press report that he made much more. The edge of the curtain occasionally lifts a little, sometimes by accident – the 13-million-franc salary of the outgoing chairman of Alcatel–Alsthom only came out when he was forced to step down amid huge losses and allegations of scandal. The boss of the AXA insurance group, Claude Bébéar, stands out from the mass of French executives not only because of his international success, but also because he discloses his personal dealings in company shares as well as his salary: might there be some link between his conquering path abroad and his openness? If so, it looks like a bad omen for French business: the more general attitude was summed up by the head of a large group who told his company's annual meeting that, as regards his earnings, he was not going to give in to 'a form of voyeurism, an unhealthy curiosity'.

Discretion also helps to mask dodgy dealing in a country which the anti-corruption organisation Transparency International ranks only fourteenth on the world cleanliness scale. By the end of 1998, close to fifty chairmen and chief executives of big firms had been fined, gone to prison or were under investigation for illegal behaviour of one kind or another. Among them:

The managing director of one of France's biggest construction firms was charged with the misuse of company funds, and the head of a large retail group was had up for fraud and corruption over alleged bribes to get planning permission for stores from Socialist local government officials.

A major developer was charged with insider dealing, and thirty-six companies were fined for rigging public-works contracts.

The chairman of a leading industrial group was thrown into jail in Belgium for alleged breach of confidence, and then became the target of an international warrant. The boss of one of France's main aircraft manufacturers was the object of another international warrant from Belgium, issued to try to get him to answer questions about alleged bribery. As a result, neither man could travel outside France without risking being arrested.

The head of a large investment bank was charged with falsifying accounts.

The boss of Alcatel–Alsthom – once described as the most powerful private-sector businessman in the country – was given a three-year suspended jail sentence and fined 2 million francs for having had security work at his six-storey home in the Paris suburb of Neuilly paid for from company funds. He was also ordered to pay the money back. Several other big bosses were being investigated for allegedly having used company funds for work on their private homes.

Even such totems of modern French life as television and the national lottery are not sacred: a prominent executive was held in connection with an affair involving rights to screen the weekly lottery draw. Then there are the cases in which the state or its representatives appear to have been remarkably indulgent. The national audit court put at 1.5 billion francs the value of a contract between a state television station and production companies linked to its star presenters which had 'contributed to enriching the companies concerned' but had produced doubtful benefit to the channel. Another report from court, which warned of heavy cost overruns at the main stadium for the 1998 World Cup, noted that the building contract had been signed by the Prime Minister between the two rounds of the 1995 presidential election with a consortium that included a company which also owned the country's main television channel. As it happened, the Prime Minister had just been eliminated from the presidential election, and would soon lose his job, meaning that he would no longer be in a position to sign anything. And, as it also happened, the television channel in question was widely viewed as having been most supportive of him in his bid for the Élysée.

And then there was the case of the public transport system so close to French hearts.

On 18 May 1993, President Mitterrand and his former Prime Minister, Pierre Mauroy, ceremonially rode on France's latest high-speed train link, between Paris and the northern city of Lille, which had been Mauroy's political barony as mayor and boss of the Socialist Party for decades. Since the old industrial belt around Lille was suffering economically, Mauroy had been an ardent proponent of building the line as a means of bringing new vigour to the north-east and providing plenty of construction jobs in the process. One of his successors as Prime Minister, Michel Rocard, had given the go-ahead to build the line in 1988 on the basis of a dossier from the SNCF railway board. Rocard said later that he thought the dossier might have been 30–40 per cent accurate in its forecast that rail traffic between Paris and Lille would double once the TGV was in service. In fact, it increased by only 2 per cent.

A senior civil servant wrote in a confidential note that some fifty or sixty kilometres of track was not needed, ending a missive on the subject to a colleague with the salutation '*Bon courage*'. One station built in the middle of the countryside had just one stopping train a day – except for weekends and public holidays, when it had none at all. The SNCF noted with satisfaction in 1997 that the station's passenger traffic had risen by more than 25 per cent during the year – to 480 people.

It took years for the truth to come out. When it did, the audit court concluded that the SNCF had shown the TGV line's profitability at up to twice what could reasonably be expected on the basis of revenue projections overstated by up to 13 billion francs. If the politicians and the SNCF were pleased at the building of the line, the public-works companies were ecstatic. There is no more juicy prospect for construction firms than a massive state contract, and here was a 40-billion-franc monster, a major new railway line to be built to the most modern and demanding specifications. And that was not all: a subsidiary link was to be laid between the northern TGV and networks serving the south and west of France. Why spoil things by competing for contracts? Much simpler to sort things out in private. An internal note found at one firm put it quite plainly: what was needed was 'an overall strategy with the other major public-works companies instead of classic competition'. When an Italian company refused to join in the price-fixing, it was offered a 'non-participation fee' of 5 million francs to withdraw. The Italians persisted, only to find that a tender from a French rival had been mysteriously changed in handwriting – after being submitted to the SNCF – to undercut its offer.

In many cases, it was evident that there was only one serious tender, and that the others had been thrown together without proper research. Apart from the actual construction of the track, there was plenty of ancillary jam to be shared around. For some stations, the Audit Court found that the SNCF had over-estimated costs by 75 per cent. At the Lille terminus, it contracted for a dozen escalators to be built; only two eventually saw the light of day, but the railway still paid for all twelve, and only discovered the mistake four years later. Officials scrawled out acknowledgement of the tenders on pads that looked for all the world like casual café bills. Some of these notes lacked dates; others did not mention the company concerned. Some, according to the magazine which broke the story, *L'Express*, were duly dated and signed in advance, but were otherwise left blank. The supposedly secret tenders were kept in a cupboard whose key hung on a nail nearby – an indication, perhaps, of how the handwritten last-minute amendment had been made to beat out the unco-operative Italians. That was the degree of care which a hugely loss-making state enterprise showed over how it spent 20 billion francs of tax-payers' money. But carelessness was not the whole story. The Competition Council spoke of SNCF officials participating in 'various practices, including understandings', while the Audit Court uncovered internal memos which showed that the involvement had been known to senior railway management, who had done nothing about it. Worse was to come.

After being hauled in by the police and an examining magistrate for a routine check on his tax affairs, a sub-contractor from Lorraine who had acted as a bagman blew the gaff. Quizzed about some unusual items in his accounts, he admitted that he had passed SNCF executives such inducements as Porsche, Ferrari and Mercedes cars, jewels worth a million francs, and up to twice as much in cash. One man, alone, had received five cars to keep him sweet. Others had had their rents paid, or received salaries for fictitious jobs invented for their wives. In all, the sub-contractor drew up a list of around sixty SNCF managers who had taken bribes. Since the amount he had paid out exceeded his company's turnover, the assumption was that he had acted as a conduit for other firms anxious to buy work from the railway.

Four years after Mitterrand and Mauroy walked down the flag-decked platform of the Gare du Nord to board the first TGV-Nord train, the Competition Council levied fines on thirty of the country's major public-works firms for having rigged tenders for the construction contracts. The penalties totalled 388 million francs. It was an embarrassment, but the size of the fines was only half what *L'Express* estimated the corruption had cost the SNCF directly. Lawyers for the

SNCF reckoned that forty-six separate contracts were involved. Some estimates put the total extra cost to the taxpayer in the billions. Not that being hauled up for punishment seemed to have much effect: handwritten notes seized by police from public-works firms showed that they were already carving up tenders on the next route proposed for the TGV, in eastern France.

Once again, the scandal raised questions which went to the heart of the French way of running things. First, there were the politicians. Nobody accused them of doing anything wrong, but the enthusiasm of senior figures in the ruling party gave the project a following wind which made it virtually unstoppable. Then there was the relationship between politicians and the men in charge of the business involved. Before being given the go-ahead, the project was examined by a section of the Council of State to decide if it was in the public interest. The section's chairwoman had held a senior post in Mauroy's government, and had written a book jointly with the chairman of the SNCF; he, in turn, had been a senior official at the presidency when she had been a Cabinet minister. One senior figure involved on the railway side had been put in charge of a presidential inquiry into the future of the high-speed train. Another top SNCF man had previously been the civil servant responsible for the government's financial control of the railways, and had been involved in the decision about funding the TGV project. All denied any impropriety.

This was happening at one of France's biggest enterprises, which was meant to be under state control but gave every impression of resembling a fortress in which the flower of French chivalry held sway with the complaisance of powerful friends in positions of authority. After briefly breaking even, the SNCF racked up the second biggest loss of any company in the world in 1996, with debts reaching 203 billion francs. But the French showed little concern at how their tax money was being spent. An attempt to reduce staff and increase productivity sparked off a strike in which the railway workers enjoyed widespread public sympathy and the government and management backed off. With its strong unions, its working-class tradition and the sentimental images of the sooty train-driver who gets the express through on time against all obstacles, there has always been a strong link between public transport and the political left. In the Socialist governments of 1981 and 1997, Cabinet responsibility for the SNCF was given to a Communist. In 1995, coming from the other side of the political spectrum, Jacques Chirac had tried a rather similar tactic by appointing a former Socialist senior civil servant and state industry boss called Loïk Le Floch-Pringent as chairman of the railway board.

It had been a bold move, which some of the new President's advisers had opposed. Chirac overruled them. In his rush for change, he believed that 'Pink Le Floch', as he had been known in the 1980s, had the right mixture of business acumen and links with the unions to pull the SNCF back from the brink. Asked what it was like to be a left-wing boss, the former Elf chairman replied that he knew how to keep his business activities and his personal feelings apart. To set Le Floch off on the right tracks, the government announced a plan to take over 125 billion francs of the railway's debt. Le Floch followed this up by opening negotiations with the unions to cut the 180,000 workforce. Then disaster struck as one of the biggest of all French business scandals broke.

The presidential advisers who had urged Chirac against appointing Le Floch had not been motivated by his politics or his business ability, but by his past. In particular, by a friendship which went back fourteen years.

The neat, bearded Breton civil servant had been working for the Industry Ministry in the first Socialist government when he first met a portly textile magnate, Maurice Bidermann, known as the King of the Sentier after the rabbit-warren rag-trade district in the middle of Paris where he made his fortune. Joining the ranks of functionaries of the left who graduated to running state industries, Le Floch moved in as chairman of the chemicals group, Rhône-Poulenc, after it was nationalised. He held the job for four years before the right's victory in legislative elections in 1986 deprived him of his post. By then, Bidermann was expanding far from his origins in the Sentier. One lunchtime, I was among a group of journalists invited to a smart Paris restaurant to eat *langoustines au beurre blanc* and be lectured on how his company had found a new international vocation as it set out to conquer America. Nearer home, there were some hiccups. In one tricky case, a bank claimed that Bidermann owed it millions of francs after a stock-market punt had gone wrong. The matter went to arbitration by a distinguished and impartial outsider. To general surprise, Bidermann won. The arbitrator was Loïk Le Floch-Pringent.

When the Socialists regained power, Le Floch moved in at another major state concern – the Elf oil company. The only French enterprise to figure in *Fortune* magazine's ranking of the top forty firms in the world, Elf has always been a peculiar animal. From its foundation in 1965, it was an arm of government, its boss as powerful as a member of the Cabinet. The first chairman was a former Gaullist intelligence chief. As France's colonies became nominally independent, what better channel than Elf to retain the old imperial links? Elf might have fields in the North Sea and the Middle East and the Americas. It might seek new opportunities in Central Asia, and offer the services of one of its Far Eastern intermediaries to smooth over the sale of French frigates to Taiwan. But the company's core is in Francophone Africa, from where it draws 60 per cent of its oil. Oil and Elf had been France's twin ambassadors in Africa, as Le Floch remarked in a private note.

Alongside its conventional energy activities, Elf has always maintained very special top-level connections. Le Floch's note named Jacques Chirac and the Gaullist former Interior Minister, Charles Pasqua, as the bridgeheads between politics and the company. The firm's operations in former colonies provide a convenient cover for French spies and political agents. Through a banking subsidiary in Switzerland, it was in the habit of paying 'royalties' of up to 150 million francs a year each to various African leaders. The dangers of falling out of favour were shown vividly in the Republic of the Congo, where Elf produces 70 per cent of the national oil output. Revenues from Elf account for around 40 per cent of the Congo's budget. For the oil company, the country's geographical position is important because it sits on the eastern shores of the Gulf of Guinea where Elf pumps most of its oil. No matter that the President professed to be a doctrinaire Communist: he was a friend of France and of its oil company. But, when he lost power in elections in 1993, his successor ended the monopoly and, horror of horrors, brought in an American firm which paid a higher royalty. Four years later, an invasion by the former President, with guns and men supplied by an array of African states, turned the clock back. Two months after returning to power, the restored ruler conferred with the chairman of Elf in Paris before seeing Jacques Chirac – the man he had overthrown was also in the French capital, where he launched unsuccessful legal proceedings against Elf for complicity in 'acts of terrorism, destruction and homicide', and accused it of having backed his rival to the tune of $250 million. To the south, Elf had also invested time and money in both sides of the game in the key regional power of Angola, sending a member of the National Assembly to talk to rebels on its behalf and then celebrating the discovery of a huge offshore oil field which analysts said could increase its reserves by 10 per cent.

But it is in Gabon, to the Congo's north, that Elf really came into its own as a state within a state, blending business, *raison d'état* and politics. Its relationship has been particularly close with Gabon's long-time dictator, Omar Bongo, the unpleasant figure picked as his country's ruler in 1967 by Jacques Foccart. During Bongo's decades in power, his country's oil riches have not saved it from piling up a mountain of debt, while the President himself has become a byword for his repression of dissent. He also hit the headlines briefly for his use of 'models' flown out from the metropole who reported that he does not use a condom: a flurry of speculation that he might have AIDS set off a diplomatic incident in 1995. Bongo belongs very firmly to the ranks of dictators for whom France acted as a protective godfather over the decades, using his land, in return, as a base for military and intelligence operations in Africa. He makes no bones about his debt to the Hexagon: his remark about Africa without France being like a car without a driver was much quoted by Parisian defenders of the old way of doing things in the former colonies. France accounts for three-quarters of foreign investment in his country, and, until he began to express some doubts recently, Bongo has ruled secure in the knowledge that he has been as useful to Paris as it has been to him.

Power is important, but it is money which makes the wheels go round. French political parties, especially the Gaullists, have long found its ironically named capital of Libreville a handy transit point for illicit funding: the 'black chests' of Elf provide a useful conduit. As for the company, in some years Gabon has provided more than three-quarters of its profit. 'Here in Paris, we don't need to know too much of what goes on in Gabon,' a top Elf executive once told me. 'But what we do know is that it is very good for us as a company.'

Under Le Floch-Pringent, Elf made creative use of Gabon as a conveniently distant channel for activities that were best handled with maximum discretion as far away from Paris as possible. Among these was its growing link with Maurice Bidermann, who was running into some problems in his international expansion plans. America was not proving quite the gold mine he had expected it to be. Luckily, he could count on some heavy support back home. Given its track record, it was not surprising that the Crédit Lyonnais lined up to lend him money. Elf's involvement was more surprising. What bailing out a rag-trade firm had to do with the oil business was none too clear. Elf's finance director duly opposed the investment. No matter, the oil firm plunged in to the tune of 787 million francs.

The grateful Bidermann paid for Le Floch to spend luxurious holidays in the United States, including one pleasant sojourn in the chic retreat of the Hamptons. His generosity extended to buying Le Floch's wife a flat in London said to be worth half a million pounds, and granting her a monthly allowance of 30,000 francs for two years. As well as putting money into the textile business, Elf was also spreading its favours elsewhere. It bought a fine white country house outside Paris from one of President Mitterrand's golfing partners, and let him stay on virtually rent-free. It plunged into a round of property purchases in Tokyo, Brussels, Lisbon and Barcelona so that travelling executives wouldn't have to put up with the inconvenience of staying in hotels. There was a report that, during the acquisition activity, 100 million francs had somehow got lost in offshore accounts in the Channel Islands, the Isle of Man and the Caribbean. As for Le Floch, he made liberal use of his company credit card, once allegedly charging it with 68,000 francs' worth of compact discs in a single day. The chairman also got the company to buy 80,000 francs' worth of garden furniture for his country home in Normandy.

In the boardroom merry-go-round after the victory of the right in the 1993 parliamentary elections, Le Floch lost his job, and a judicial-cum-business rollercoaster was unleashed. His successor, an *Inspecteur des Finances* close to the new Gaullist Prime Minister, began civil proceedings. After looking into the investments in Bidermann by Elf and Crédit Lyonnais, the stock exchange control commission concluded that they might give rise to criminal action as well. A tough examining magistrate, Eva Joly, took on the case. The Audit Court produced a damning report on Le Floch's management.

By then, Chirac had brought back Le Floch to sort out the SNCF. No sooner had he moved into his new job than Eva Joly raided the office and home of his friend, Maurice Bidermann. Three months later, she called Bidermann in for questioning, followed by Le Floch's ex-wife. Next came two top managers at Elf. After some beating around the bush, they told the judge that it was Le Floch himself who had given the order to invest in Bidermann. A lawyer who had stood surety for agreements between Bidermann and Elf fled the country rather than face interrogation. On their first meeting, the one-time King of the Sentier complimented Joly on her dress sense. Second time around, he gave her a book inscribed 'to my magistrate'. Such gestures did him no good. At their third encounter, Joly locked Bidermann up, accusing him of having taken out a backdated insurance policy on a factory which had burnt down. The policy, written by an offshore Caribbean company, was allegedly obtained with the backing of Elf.

While Bidermann was held in jail, the judiciary and the police delved into Elf's international connections and, in particular, its African subsidiaries. Ten executives were hauled in – a couple of others either skipped the country or refused to come across the border from Switzerland to be interrogated. The head of Elf Gabon was questioned by police throughout a June afternoon. Omar Bongo and the President of former French Congo sent emissaries to Paris to find out what was going on. Then the magistrate called in Le Floch himself – just after he had announced his restructuring plan for the railways.

At the end of twelve hours of questioning, Le Floch was taken to one of the single-occupancy cells in the Santé prison in Paris kept for special inmates and the mentally ill. There, he was allowed to retain his own clothes, but was forbidden scarves, ties, belts, paper handkerchiefs or a bath towel larger than 1.2 metres square. The Appeal Court refused to free him. Joly said she feared he might try to intimidate witnesses or arrange for the disposal of embarrassing documents. Le Floch was accused of having abused his position as chairman and chief executive to seek 'enrichment of himself, his family and friends' through Elf's Swiss and African subsidiaries. He was forced to resign from the SNCF, and occupied his time teaching bridge to a fellow inmate of La Santé.

While Le Floch languished behind the twenty-foot prison walls for six months before being let out on bail, other intriguing aspects of the case peeped out from the shadowlands surrounding the company. There was, for instance, the tale of Anna Rose 'Lise' Thiam, the daughter of a former Ivory Coast ambassador to Paris. A confidence trickster who passed herself off as the daughter of the former President of her country, she boasted of having easy access to Elf's headquarters, and of knowing Le Floch well. 'Lise told me one day that . . . when she needed money, she would go and see him,' a witness informed Eva Joly. When they inquired further, police were told that Le Floch had a meeting with 'a young coloured woman who said she was the daughter of the Ivoirian president'. An Elf security adviser was ordered to find out more about her, and then told to keep her at a safe distance. In 1993, Lise was arrested in Germany for fraud, and taken back to prison in France. There, she reportedly told Joly that she had received cash from Le Floch which she was meant to pass to others. French police found her car parked near the Swiss frontier. Inside, *Le Monde* reported, was a handwritten note signed 'Loïk'. On it was written: 'Here are 53. The reckoning is $100 + 3$ in the car $+ 53 = 156$. What do you do with all this money?'

A former refinery manager accused one of Le Floch's closest associates of having threatened to have him killed when they disagreed over an investment in the North Sea. There was talk of Masonic links at the top of the company. Le Floch's former wife told of being followed by a mysterious white car. A computer containing details of payments made by a company foundation she had once headed was stolen. There were rumours that it might contain evidence of half a million francs paid to a prominent politician. One witness told of a secret fund used to buy off labour trouble. Other sources spoke of forty people being paid for non-existent jobs and being given company credit cards, including Mitterrand's former golf partner, whose benefits were put at 2 million francs. There was also the matter of a commission of more than $100 million claimed on behalf of a Chinese–American fixer who had worked for Elf in the Far East, and who was lined up by Le Floch's number two to help on a French arms deal with Taiwan. The arms company said it knew nothing about any such agreement, and refused to pay up. But, after a secret document had been retrieved from a bank strong box, an arbitration panel in Paris awarded the intermediary $45 million. By then, the Elf executive in question had joined the ranks of those who felt it prudent to leave France and put themselves beyond the reach of the judiciary which got a 'red notice' warrant for his arrest put out to 177 countries at the beginning of 1999.

Still, the frigates affair provided the ever-persistent judge with another occasion to investigate Le Floch's management practices. Early in 1998, Joly had the former boss up on a new charge of abuse of corporate funds, this time over the way in which Elf had looked after a woman employee who had been close to the Foreign Minister when France's embargo on arms sales to Taiwan was lifted. The woman, who was detained for questioning for six months, had earned around 50,000 francs a month but had still been able to buy a 17-million-franc apartment in one of the smartest streets on the Left Bank, conveniently close for visits from her friend in charge of France's diplomacy at the Quai d'Orsay. Investigations unearthed allegations that the money for the flat came out of a commission of 59 million francs paid by Elf for unspecified services. Elf had also provided her with a monthly credit of 200,000 francs. As the scandal grew, she wrote a book entitled 'The Whore of the Republic' in which she reflected on the nature of love. She needed Elf's money, she explained, because her job required her to be elegant and to spend heavily on clothes. On one occasion, she also helped her friend at the Quai to keep up appearances: a pair of shoes costing 11,000 francs for the Foreign Minister was charged to her company credit card.

In January 1998 the judge raided the home and office of the former minister, Roland Dumas. In the last days of the Mitterrand administration, Dumas had been given a nine-year term as President of the Constitutional Council, to see him into a comfortable and respected old age. Now, the spectacle of the fifth-highest-ranking figure in the state being driven away for questioning in the back of a car with the stern-faced judge beside him was a front-page item. Naturally, Dumas denied any wrong-doing, and said that the shoe payment had been a mistake which he had not even been aware of. He explained the high price as being due to the orthopaedic nature of the footwear. While this episode was just another element in the bulging Elf dossier, it was to take on wider ramifications among the scandals that swirled around the very summit of power under the first Socialist President of the Fifth Republic. From Gabon to the Constitutional Court, the inner workings of the world's eighth-biggest oil company were providing France with a world-class scandal.

As for Elf, the scale of its home-grown scandals widened in a different direction after two police raids on company headquarters. The documents that were uncovered included some pertaining to a commission of 256 million francs paid into the account of a Liechtenstein company in connection with an investment in Germany by Elf in 1991. The transaction, involving two companies called Show Fast and Stand By, was typically opaque. When Joly tried to get to the bottom of who was responsible, she was given contradictory accounts. One allegation was that the money had gone to the ruling German party, Helmut Kohl's CDU; another suggestion was that at least some of the cash had found its way back to the treasury of a French party. In the office of the oil firm's chief security officer, a former intelligence agent, police found notes referring to the funding of political parties and to the private papers of President Mitterrand's oldest friend.

Through it all, the Africa connection kept surfacing. A company came to light run by the chairman of Elf Gabon, André Tarallo, which seemed to serve no purpose except to pass large sums of money through obscure financial channels. Tarallo, an Énarque who had known President Chirac for decades, was investigated for misusing corporate funds, and had to put up 10 million francs in bail. Among other things, he was reported to have bought a luxury villa in Corsica for 90 million francs and to have spent 45 million on improving three of his homes: there was immediate speculation that he was acting as a front for Elf-friendly politicians in Africa. The documents relating to the home improvements provided their own mystery: after being seized in a raid in Marseille, they were taken to Paris where they promptly disappeared from police offices. Then there was the matter of a $2.5 million payment into a Swiss bank account called 'Collette' – the name of Tarallo's wife. According to an international wheeler-dealer known as 'Dédé the Sardine', who talked after five weeks in preventive detention, the payment was part of the proceeds of a $20 million commission paid by Elf for a deal in Venezuela. Cheques drawn on the account by Tarallo were among the papers that had gone missing in Paris.

As the revelations dripped out, the spotlight edged towards the President of Gabon. Acting on a request from Eva Joly, a Geneva magistrate blocked an account in the British Virgin Islands where Bongo had deposited funds. The Elf Gabon chairman broke his silence to say that he had opened the Collette account at the request of a personal adviser to the President, and that the money had gone to buy a plane for a private airline in Gabon. Bongo put in a long telephone conversation to Jacques Chirac to threaten economic sanctions in retaliation to what he saw as attacks on his country's sovereignty. Taking up his pen, under his habitual pseudonym of 'Makaya', Bongo hit back at his French tormentors in the columns of Gabon's main newspaper, sparing neither Le Floch nor his successor, Philippe Jaffré. French politicians and the press, caught up in their own scandals, were 'desperately trying to pick the nits in the President's head', he wrote. Bongo was having none of it. 'The tales of Elf-Loïk the bumpkin-Tarallo-Jaffré and their Norwegian bird, Eva Joly, who smells of salt cod, I, Makaya, find this beginning to get on my nerves,' he explained. After dismissing France as a medium-sized power which owed its place to its relationship with Germany, he warned that Le Floch's successor at the head of Elf was not as white as snow, and that the former Gaullist Prime Minister, Édouard Balladur, and his Interior Minister, Charles Pasqua, were 'the true actors of this badly put-together thriller'.

With Bongo on the warpath, not only Elf but many others in France would, indeed, have cause to tremble. The oil firm had always lived a charmed life, protected from investigation by its special nature and its political links. Now, justice was turning over stones which had laid undisturbed for so long: it was ironic that this was happening just after the state had sold its last shares in Elf and as the new chairman was charting a resolutely international course which was proving highly popular with foreign investors. The question was whether the company whose past impunity had been emblematic of a rotten political, financial and post-colonial system would now become a symbol of a sea-change in France, both in its business dealings and in the relationship between the centres of political and business power. This raised a tricky point: unlike most of the other sleaze coming to light, the Elf scandal involved the state – and at a high level. As such, what the 'Norwegian bird' uncovered went to the heart of the way France was run.

Naturally, this brought Joly and her like vilification around the tables of three-star restaurants and at corporate hunting estates. The chairman of one big company told me that they were all the children of the 1968 student revolt out to destroy French society. Another businessman noted that Eva Joly, who was investigating the Crédit Lyonnais as well as Elf, was not of French origin (she came to France as an au pair from Norway) and that one of the earliest judicial diggers, Renaud van Ruymbeke, did not sound very French. The chairman of the giant Alcatel group blamed his problems with the law on a 'cultural gap' between him and the examining magistrate. But the legal lions showed no signs of relaxing the pressure.

In one sense, though for the wrong reasons, the concerns which the business establishment felt about Joly and her colleagues were justified. They were, indeed, chipping away at the pillars of the temple. One of the former inhabitants of the inner sanctum took time at the end of 1998 to reflect on the vicissitudes of life. Le Floch-Pringent recalled the glory days after the Socialist victory of 1991 when 'I spoke to ministers as an equal. I was in a state of levitation'. His constancy business brings him one fifth of his salary at Elf. On the wall of his office hang photographs of him with Mitterrand, Chirac, and the monarchs of Britain, Spain and Norway. 'Now, I have become a pariah,' he told the magazine *L'Express*. 'I am not invited anywhere. People avoid me. They wish I were dead.'

The embarrassment of the great and less good could only be a source of pleasure to those they had sacked. What worker made redundant by the Schneider industrial group could not relish the vision of the firm's silky chairman having to bed down in a Belgian jail? Former employees of Félix Potin and a hundred other small groceries could only have chuckled when the evening news showed a hypermarket magnate being paraded in handcuffs outside a courtroom. The understandable pleasure in the discomfiture of the *dégraisseurs* was another indication of the fissure in national life, deepened by the moral rift between managers and the masses, between those who considered that their business made them invulnerable and those whose vulnerability was being steadily increased by the way that very business was conducted.

★

In this gallery of tycoons with feet of clay, nobody cut more of a figure than a one-time car salesman turned asset-stripper and wannabe pop singer who rose to sit in the Cabinet as an anointed favourite of a Socialist President. In his way, Bernard Tapie was a legend in his own lifetime; he also came to represent in sharp fashion one aspect of what was wrong with France.

As a wheeler-dealer in the early 1980s, the swaggering, dark-haired Tapie swept through a swathe of ailing companies, buying them for knockdown prices, selling off the pieces he didn't need and posing as a crusader for modern, efficient industry. The sheer momentum and bombast of the man kept his house of cards standing; though two of his early enterprises went bust, the Crédit Lyonnais inevitably fell under his spell and loaned him francs by the billion. Tapie moved up a notch by acquiring companies which were not in great trouble, but which had funds he could usefully juggle with. He was here, there and everywhere. His firms made batteries and scales, jeans and perfume. He bought the sports goods firm Adidas and backed a Tour de France team led by the best French and American cyclists. In 1986, he took over a leading football club, Olympique de Marseille (OM), and bathed in its reflected glory as the team triumphed at home and in Europe with four successive league championships and two European Cup Final appearances. In Paris, Tapie treated himself to a pre-Revolutionary mansion behind high walls in Saint-Germain-des-Prés. A huge yacht with a fourteen-metre-long drawing-room, a dining table for twenty and ten bedrooms awaited him in the Mediterranean. In 1987, he floated a holding company on the Paris stock exchange called simply 'Bernard Tapie Finances'. With all this going on, he still found time to record sub-Julio Iglesias records, put his name to a book of advice for aspiring tycoons, give endless magazine interviews and appear in television and radio shows where he dispensed his wit and wisdom to the nation.

To say that Bernard Tapie had an eye for the main chance would have been like saying François Mitterrand was a political player. As the President's regime staggered into a swamp of unpopularity, the old man in the Élysée fastened on to the brash businessman as a rejuvenating force. Self-assured as ever, Tapie had no hesitation about plunging into politics at the head of a small party allied with the Socialists. For him, it made a perfect fit. With the President behind him, which state-owned bank would dare to query his loans and which minister would feel bold enough to investigate his myriad affairs?

There were, indeed, people Tapie needed to keep quiet. In the 1970s, he had received a suspended prison sentence for issuing misleading advertising, and had undergone a special examination of his personal tax situation. In 1984, the authorities came back. A senior official drew up a report which showed how fragile Tapie's enterprises were – his three main companies were deep in legal suits and, if any one of them crashed, the whole edifice would come tumbling down. There were personal tax problems, too. The report proposed a thorough check of the Tapie group, the chairman's personal revenues and those of the woman referred to by the legal term of his 'concubine'. The Budget Ministry spent a week considering the report. Its decision was to do nothing for a few years, though the ministry covered its own back by making sure that the Prime Minister's office was informed. By then, Bernard Tapie was off and running on his new career.

He was a populist, a bruiser, flash all the way through. That only impressed the salon Socialists even more. He was their bit of rough trade to set against the growing appeal of Jean-Marie Le Pen's National Front. So Tapie went south, to the Front's heartland, to reclaim the heritage of the non-Communist left in Marseille.

The port's long-time mayor died in 1986, leaving a great vacuum in the politics of France's most folkloric city. Tapie's ownership of the football team, OM, eased his entry into local affairs. After an initial defeat, he won a parliamentary seat and bested the far right in regional elections. He renamed his luxury yacht the *Phocéa*, after the port's Latin name, and moored it opposite the city hall as if threatening to storm ashore and take the building. But, important as Marseille might be, there were greater prizes up north. The President of the Republic had noticed him, and had been impressed. When Tapie won a takeover battle in 1990, François Mitterrand had remarked: 'What a success. That man's a winner. We've got to have him with us.' Less than two years later, Bernard Tapie was appointed to the Cabinet as the Minister for Towns.

Within two months, he had to resign when an examining magistrate threatened to charge him with misuse of company policy and receiving stolen goods. Tapie got out of that when a former business partner suddenly changed his mind about testifying against him. He was promptly restored to his government position, though news of his return was sneaked out on Christmas Eve in the knowledge that no newspapers would be published the following day. Even Mitterrand loyalists were unhappy: one of the President's friends publicly called Tapie 'a lout'. Another judged the appointment an act of contempt to the nation; the President of the National Assembly also issued a critical statement. Moves quickly began to strip Tapie of his parliamentary immunity from prosecution – and his real problems began.

Given the range of his activities, his positions in Marseille and Paris, the luxury of his yacht and the fine furnishings of his Paris establishment, there was something pathetic about the fact that Bernard Tapie's greatest disgrace came from a hole in a garden in the drab northern town of Valenciennes. The garden belonged to a member of the local football team which had played Tapie's side in a key match in Olympique's glory season of 1993. Some time after Marseille beat Valenciennes by a single goal, it emerged that the northern team had been bribed to throw the match, and that Tapie had been part of the conspiracy. An OM player admitted to having handed over the money, which a Valenciennes team member hid in the hole in his back garden. The newly-reinstated minister denied everything, and demonstrated his popular appeal by winning a place in the European Parliament. His performance showed the calculations about his drawing power to be well founded: his small party took 12 per cent of the vote – two points above the National Front and only two points less than the Socialists. It was another indication of the volatility of politics, and the search for anybody who could offer something different from the established order. But it did Tapie little good in his running fight with justice. In March 1995, he finally came to trial.

It was not a pretty case. A woman employee of another Socialist minister and northern mayor was hounded out of town when she revealed that her boss had lied to give Tapie an alibi. There were sexist jokes about women's figures. The accused snapped his fingers as though he were in charge of the courtroom, and gestured to witnesses to shut up. At one point, the judge felt obliged to ask him: 'Who is running this trial, you or me?' Outside the courtroom, Tapie held vainglorious press conferences. At one hearing, he was asked if he had tried to interfere with witnesses. Yes, he cheerfully replied. But, he explained, he was acting from the best of motives. He was just trying to get his pals off, like 'what people did to help the Jews during the Occupation'.

Tapie was sentenced to two years in prison. He immediately appealed, and so was freed for the time being. But he was dropped by the French *Who's Who*, and the bank which had loved him, the Crédit Lyonnais, tried to seize the belongings from his Paris palace – only to find that most of them had already been moved out; what remained was worth far less than their mortgage valuation. There then followed a marathon run of cases involving personal bankruptcy, handling stolen goods, misuse of corporate property, the million spent on the annual upkeep of his yacht, tax fraud – and another involving funds taken from the OM club treasury. His wife spoke movingly of the strain of seeing the man she loved in tears, and told a sob story of how their eight-year-old daughter had thrown her arms around her father as a policeman walked towards them at an airport, crying, 'Don't take my daddy to prison.' In true Tapie style, the tale ended with the self-regarding twist that the policeman had only been after an autograph from her dad.

The courts were not impressed. Tapie got three more sentences, and was banned from business activities for years to come. At the end of 1996, the one-time minister who had been privy to Cabinet secrets was stripped of both his national and European parliamentary mandates. A magistrate who investigated his ownership of the Marseille football team found that 100 million francs had been spent on seeking to reduce 'the hazards which inevitably exist in a football match' by rigging games and under-the-counter payments to players to join OM.

By then, Tapie had found a fresh vocation – acting. 'I have paid too dearly for the mix of roles,' he said as he announced his withdrawal from politics. Tapie's first film role was as a high-priced lawyer in a film by the director Claude Lelouch, entitled *Men, Women and How to Use Them*. He made the most of his notoriety to negotiate a contract which a magazine reckoned could earn him up to 8 million francs. For his next trick, he said, he fancied playing the role of Che Guevara. To fill in the time, he turned his hand to television commentating for the 1996 Olympic Games where, it was said, he enjoyed covering the women's gymnastics. Reflecting on his new career in a cover interview with *Paris-Match*, he hit the cliché buttons about all the world being a stage in which one had to know how to act to survive. 'The scenarios of life are often more cynical and cruel than those of films,' he reflected. As for the prosecutors, 'they're not interested in justice, they're just interested in getting me'.

On 3 February 1997, Bernard Tapie telephoned Loïk Le Floch-Pringent to ask what life was like in prison. Next, he made inquiries about whether mobile telephones were allowed in jail (the answer was no), and how often convicts could take a shower. Then, described by his lawyer as being 'ready to meet his fate, resigned and courageous', the one-time political and business whiz-kid was driven to the Santé prison. There the second Cabinet minister of the Mitterrand era to be locked up for criminal behaviour became convict number 265 449G.

The Santé was getting used to housing one-time business celebrities who had fallen from grace. Le Floch-Pringent had just been released on bail. Jean-Maxime Levêque was about to spend four months there while being questioned by Eva Joly and her colleagues. Another inmate was Pierre Botton, the son-in-law of Michel Noir, the disgraced former Mayor of Lyon. Tapie and Botton had fallen out over a business deal some years earlier, and their enmity quickly flared up behind prison walls, with each man striking an appropriately macho pose. Tapie warned that he might give Botton a punch on the nose if their paths crossed: Botton banged on the walls of his cell, accused Tapie of running scared of him, and complained to the warders that they were giving the former minister favourable treatment, including solo use of the gymnasium. Tapie, meanwhile, whined that he was feeling lonely and wanted to mix with the other prisoners. His self-esteem was hit when a sale of paintings from his collection attracted only one buyer – 'his name is no longer a draw', the auctioneer explained. At least he consented to send in his formal resignation from the European Parliament, but still found the bombast to express his desire to 'resume my responsibilities in the great movement of European integration'. Before long, Tapie was moved from Paris to Marseille, where he faced questioning on an alleged 10-million-franc bribe to the former head of the national lottery. To keep him occupied, he was let out of jail one day a week to work for a firm that had once renovated his yacht, and he also recorded a rap single declaring that he had been 'struck but not sunk' by the law.

In one sense, the Tapie affair had all been a wonderful pantomime. However, the man's panache all too easily diverted attention from some troubling questions that went deeper than the hole in the back garden. The public might chuckle at his bravado, but he had, in the end, simply made a fool of the establishment. One of France's most venerable banks had lost more than a billion francs backing a shyster whom nobody in their right mind would have trusted with their first centime. A supposedly wise and austere President had chosen a charlatan to join his Cabinet. If Bernard Tapie was the best the ruling class could find, that said more about them than it did about him. The government job which François Mitterrand entrusted to his protégé was highly symbolic. Picking a man like Tapie to take charge of improving life in France's towns and cities underlined just how great the gulf had grown between the governing elite and the realities of urban life. The appointment of a con-man to improve France's urban condition can stand as a metaphor for the more general failure of successive administrations to get to grips with parts of the country which most visitors don't ever reach.

7

ANOTHER FRANCE

The French city has played a key role in the development of the modern metropolis. The *bourg* gave its name to the middle class; a score of conurbations from Lille to Montpellier, Rennes to Nice are regional powerhouses in business, politics, culture and social life. Many of the greatest works of French literature, art, cinema and song – not to mention the evocations of photography – have been set in the city streets and apartments, particularly those of the greatest metropolis of all.

Each big city has its story – Paris as the capital, the City of Light and the seedbed of successive revolutions; Marseille as the colourful capital of Provence and gateway to the old Empire; Toulouse in the south-west, once a great bastion of regional power now reborn as an aerospace centre; Lille in the north and Nancy and Metz in the east, struggling to free themselves from the decline of their nineteenth-century industrial base; Lyon projecting itself beyond its reputation as the capital of gastronomy to become a home for new technologies and pharmaceuticals; Bordeaux trying to move away from a legacy of elegant complacency.

Smaller cities and large provincial towns have lives of their own, too, a tradition of links with the surrounding countryside, a specific character which sets a town in Brittany apart from one in the Pyrenees, which distinguishes Toulon from Brest, Arles from Dijon. It is not just a matter of geography and climate; though the effect of television and mass food distribution is breaking down old regional

particularisms, the distinctions of attitudes, accents and ways of life
remain sharp, as we will see in a later chapter. But, between these
towns and cities which jump off the map as symbols of the multi-
faceted nature of France, there has also grown up an entirely different
urban culture. Half-submerged, a source of concern and outright
fear, this world is growing in ways that the orthodox society neither
understands nor is able to cope with. As such, it presents one of the
biggest challenges to confront the nation today. Britain or the United
States have inner cities; France has the *banlieue*, and the people who
live there.

Though it has become the accepted term, the word is, in fact, a mis-
nomer for what we are going to be talking about here. *Banlieue*
means, literally, the suburb. When a couple at a dinner party in Paris
say they live '*en banlieue*', they probably mean that they are the proud
owners of a trim house surrounded by a garden in a place with a genteel name like Fontenay-aux-Roses or Saint-Germain-en-Laye, the
neat town which gave its name to the main Paris football team but is
now well separated from the roar of the crowd in the Parc des Princes
stadium. However, when newspapers run headlines about the problems of '*les banlieues*', they do not mean the suburbs to which many
inner-city inhabitants have moved in recent decades. What they are
talking about are places like the Tartarets estate on a hill in the
Essonne department south of Paris.

Down below lies the nineteenth-century heart of the town of
Corbeil-Essonne, dominated by a huge red-brick flour mill. For
decades, this town of 40,000 people was run by the Communists, but
then the voters swung to the right and elected Serge Dassault, a
Gaullist from the aircraft-manufacturing family which has long been
close to Jacques Chirac. His town hall stands on a tidy, tree-lined
square. Faded lettering above a row of shops opposite proclaims '*Hôtel
de la Mairie – Déjeuners, Dîners*'. Another old sign offers '*Graines en tous
genres*'. There are trompe-l'oeil paintings on some of the walls. Up the
road by the railway station, past a shop offering '*Produits Cosmétiques
Afro-Américains*', the atmosphere becomes less relaxed. The main café
sports a notice informing clients that they are under permanent video
surveillance. The barman shouts at an African who has asked for a

sandwich as though he is an idiot. I ask a swarthy man with chains on his chest for directions to Les Tartarets. He grunts and lies: 'Don't know it.' Another man, wearing a black Guns N' Roses T-shirt, comes out of the café after me and points to a bus stop. 'Be careful,' he calls out as he ambles off. 'It's another world up there.' In a nearby telephone box, an Arab yells into the receiver while two teenagers play with an Alsatian in the road.

The estate of Les Tartarets consists of twenty-eight buildings, most of them reaching up fifteen floors. The streets have the names of French artists like Cézanne and Gauguin. The bus stops on the way up from Corbeil station are called Gustave Courbet, Charles de Gaulle, Auguste Renoir, Léon Blum and Henri Matisse. The concierge's room at the foot of each block has a sign offering 'Accueil'. There is an adventure playground and a large open green space in the middle of the estate where a few elderly men sit talking at wooden picnic tables. The municipality has also erected a number of 'free expression' boards for people to inscribe their thoughts.

Though nobody seems quite sure of the exact figures, unemployment here is reckoned to be well over 20 per cent, and for all the street signs, this is a foreign place for the French. Groups of young black men sit on the pavement chatting the day away. A Mercedes car suddenly appears, its black driver stopping to talk for a couple of minutes before roaring away, giving a clenched fist salute as he goes. Arab music blares from the open window of a ground-floor flat, and the names on the letter boxes are from the other side of the Mediterranean or the Sahara. While the free-expression board is blank, the walls and bus shelters are covered with graffiti – 'Fuck la police', 'La Zone Rouge', 'Tartarets fuck la Police'. One local road is known as 'la Rue de la Mort' (the Road of Death) – more graffiti proclaims 'Fuck la Rue de la Mort'. Alarms sprout from doors, garages, cars. Under a bridge, somebody has inscribed a familiar *banlieue* mantra: 'A man falls from the fiftieth floor. As he passes each storey on his way down, he says, "It's not falling that matters, but how you land." '

On the side of one tower-block, somebody has written counter-graffiti with a felt pen. The wording is not entirely coherent, but the message is plain: 'I have friends of all races and colours but not the scum of the Tartarets who screw in front of the television to produce children to get social security and put them outside even late at night – this scum breaks and steals, burns cars, drops its trousers – I owe 1,400 francs in rent and I can't afford to buy an aerosol to tag this wall, I haven't got enough to live on to the end of the month.'

Mayor Dassault says he'd like to provide the young people with a place to meet and socialise and have a non-alcoholic drink. He comes from the establishment which runs France. His photograph appears in the national press chatting to the President of the Republic. His father, a concentration-camp survivor, built the famous Mirage military jets. Inevitably, his life and his language are a million miles from the young Arabs and Africans of Les Tartarets. Graffiti on a big back door to one block on the estate brands him a 'whore's son'. When a government minister paid a visit with the mayor, the young men at the local community centre told them: 'We're not asking for the moon, just get us out of the shit. As for the moon, we'll see about that.'

There are a hundred Tartarets in France, many of them in worse shape than the estate in Corbeil. Though the streets of Paris, Marseille or Lyon are not always the safest of places at night, France's key urban problem is the outer rather than the inner city. These estates are part of a bad dream constructed from high unemployment, social and racial tension, brutalist architecture and decades of neglect. Once they were proud examples of modernity: 'Here, there was a field of beetroots; now I have planted a flag; thousands of flats will sprout,' as one of the first masters of urban development put it in the 1960s. They replaced the shanty towns – the *bidonvilles* – where immigrants once huddled. Now they have become known as rabbit-hutches, symbols for the plight of French people who have been left behind by the economy, and for dark-skinned foreigners who were imported by the million and then abandoned. One former Socialist minister calls them places of despair; another urges 'an effort of solidarity from the nation equal to the one that set up the social security system after the war'. The former Premier, Michel Rocard, has spoken of their crime-forming architecture, but when his government decided to paint such blocks in bright colours to cheer up the residents, only the outside walls got the treatment and the insides remained as drab as ever.

Rocard's initiative was one of a string of official schemes over the years to breathe fresh life into the *banlieues*. In 1996, the Prime Minister, Alain Juppé, unveiled a 68-part plan to grapple with the problem, but he had to admit that the real issue lay in unemployment. However many ideas the government's planners may dream up, the basic question is whether people can earn a living or are relegated to the margins where work no longer figures on the agenda. Estimates put the number of people living on the edge of society at 3 million: before his election in 1995, Jacques Chirac talked of almost double that number. Some beg in city streets; some hustle for francs in the Métro; some are the rural poor; many live in the *banlieues*. In a sign of its priorities, France devotes much more money and attention to its farmers than it does to those in need in the suburbs, but still expects them to feel solidarity with the Republic. At the last presidential election, the reply was clear: the abstention rate on some estates reached 60 per cent.

The *banlieues* have become the nexus of a new form of society which rejects the traditional integrationist dynamic of the French state – and which frightens the hell out of those who would like everybody to live by the same rules in orderly fashion and to respect traditional European social norms. The world of the suburban estate is a universe which the average French person likes to steer clear of. But the more France passes by on the other side, the greater the challenge will be to the settled way of life. Take a series of snapshots from north to south to plumb the depth of alienation.

Start in the northern city of Amiens, capital of Picardy. In distant sight of the cathedral, there are districts where nearly half the children aged under six live in families with no source of income other than welfare. A year after his election, Jacques Chirac visited a huge, sprawling complex housing 25,000 people on the edge of the city. The President spoke of the need for a 'pragmatic' urban policy; he threw his arms around a group of young Africans; he climbed down to a basement to listen to a band called Bestial Overdrive. When he embraced a six-year-old daughter of immigrants, her brother shouted, 'Chirac, don't touch my sister!' From behind the barriers, another child noted the redness of the President's face as he glimpsed the underside of his country. Unemployment varied between 17 and 33 per cent from tower-block to tower-block. Among the residents were

Arabs who had fought for France in colonial wars: half of them were out of work. One-third of residents were behind with the rent. The President's visit was punctuated by cries of 'Work! Work!' as police sharpshooters kept watch from the rooftops.

Turn southwards, to the Yvelines department west of Paris. This is, for the most part, an area of quiet villages and commuter towns. But in the town of Trappes, one-third of the 9,000 families living in the Merisiers estate receive help from social workers, and half are below the poverty line. Many of the local employers have closed down or cut their workforce. Unemployment is so high that people no longer bother to go to the labour exchange. Year by year, they slip down the social scale, from decent-sized flats to homes where four people sleep in a room. Most work that is going is in the black economy, where employers do not pay welfare contributions. 'At the moment, I'm at a dry-cleaners,' an Arab woman said. 'When I went for the job, the manager told me he wouldn't declare me: if I refused, he wouldn't give me work.' Charities distribute food parcels. Street markets sell clothes that have fallen off the back of a lorry. Poor parents keep the money given to them by the state to pay for school meals, and their children go hungry: a magazine reported that, in the town of Mantes-la-Jolie, just ten pupils were having their lunch in a school canteen built for four hundred.

A couple of hours' drive to the south, the Loire Valley is one of France's great tourist attractions, with its châteaux, green, undulating countryside and its fine food and wine. The twenty-two buildings that make up the Croix-Chevalier estate in Blois are a long way from the picture-postcard image of the region. 'They've pissed by the letter boxes,' one of the caretakers told a reporter. 'They say it's the dogs, but . . .' She remembers the estate in the 1970s. 'You'd go out without bothering to lock up. We had parties. Now people call the police if they hear a drill in the afternoon . . . the kids hang about outside from morning to night . . . they break the lighting in the staircases . . . they steal bicycles and never get punished because they deny the evidence and take refuge in the protection of the law.' It goes without saying that she is referring to the young immigrants. For her, the place started going downhill when the foreigners were brought in. 'Some of them are fine, but one bad family's enough to make trouble.' She has had stones thrown at her kitchen window. 'The trouble is that people are cowards. They don't dare to say anything for fear of having their car taken apart. As for the kids, if you ask them not to pull up the flowers, you're treated as a racist.'

In the centre of France, Saint-Étienne was once a symbol of French heavy industry, with big factories and a triumphant football team. This was a region like the Black Country, the Ruhr or Pittsburgh in their prime. Now great regional firms have either closed their gates or reduced their workforce from several thousands to a few hundred. On the Montchovet estate, with its 971 flats, more than half the adults are out of work. Seventy per cent of the population are immigrants. 'We're in a ghetto situation,' a teacher said. 'Eighty-six per cent of pupils are foreigners.'

Another of Jacques Chirac's early presidential forays into the provinces took him to the town of Vaulx-en-Velin, outside Lyon, scene of repeated outbreaks of violence and the dramatic killing in the street of a young Arab, Khaled Kelkal, whose fingerprints had been found on a device used in an unsuccessful attempt to blow up the TGV high-speed train. His death at the hands of uniformed security forces was filmed by a television crew who accompanied them. The drama made Khaled a martyr among the youths of the *banlieues*. Dying 'in combat', he became an icon of their exclusion from society, as well as a reminder of the thousands of young Algerians slain by the colonial army during France's last big war. In the two days after Khaled's death, fifty cars were set on fire in the sprawl of France's second biggest urban area. Telephone kiosks and bus shelters were smashed, and shops set alight. The Mayor of Vaulx blames the media for stressing the problems of his town, turning its 45,500 inhabitants into symbols of the despair of the *banlieues* and depriving them of their dignity and identity. Touchingly, he argues that if a quarter of the adults are out of work, that means three-quarters are 'producing wealth and contributing to the development of the Lyon region'. He laments how the *banlieues* are seen as another world, watched by the rest of France on television as though they were in a different country.

Down on the Mediterranean, in a housing estate in the suburbs of Marseille, three-quarters of families get by on less than the official minimum wage. Two walls topped with barbed-wire separate the crumbling estate from a smart development of individual houses.

Seventy thousand people live here. A third of the adults are unemployed. In another suburb of the port city, what is claimed to be France's biggest shopping centre was opened by the mayor, Jean-Claude Gaudin, in the autumn of 1996. Before the inauguration, local youths attacked the site. The project had been due to create 3,000 jobs; in fact, it produced 1,200. In the north of the city, unemployment reached as high as 50 per cent.

Head east along the coast to the Ariane estate in Nice, which houses 20,000 people – old immigrants from Italy and French people returning from Algeria as well as more recent Arab arrivals. In one area of the estate, Spanish gypsies live beside an incineration plant. A passing reporter watched a woman grilling fish on a fire made out of plastic bags. Neither she nor her husband has a job. Their sons drove a turbo-charged car for which they did not have the registration documents. The nursery school nearby has been closed down: the municipal authorities refused to pay the teacher's salary. A priest tries to help people find work. 'I went with one of them to the job centre,' he says. 'We waited two hours, and then we were told to look at the notices on the wall.' But many of those he tries to help cannot read French. A local councillor set up a scheme for young people to earn some money cleaning up the estate. 'After three days, none of them came any more,' he recalls. 'The desocialisation here is so great that it's difficult to get anything done.'

A family which beds down in an empty flat on the estate simply forced the door open and moved in. 'Everybody takes what they fancy,' a young Arab says. 'It's the same on the buses. Nobody's in charge. We young people would like some order. In summer, we dealt with the drug situation. When we caught a dealer, we gave him a hard time. We have to handle it because nobody else does.' Another group of youths took to holding up motorists at traffic lights and stealing their cash. 'We're the law,' they shouted as they ran off. A café was ram-raided, cars stolen. The mayor's office has asked Paris to deploy a squad of riot police on the estate, and wants the army to station troops on the frontier with Italy to stop illegal immigrants. As the priest from the estate remarks: 'Little by little, everybody feels caught up in this return to a savage state.'

One night, fighting flared between rival gangs on the estate. A Renault car drove up out of the darkness with four men inside. One of the gangs thought they were reinforcements for its opponents. As the occupants of the car got out, they were shot at. One man died with a bullet in the head; another was seriously wounded. They were policemen who had been called to stop the fighting.

The pattern of trouble from Les Tartarets to Nice has become all too familiar. A small incident between local youths and the police escalates into burning and looting which sometimes spreads to neighbouring towns in a chain reaction. A gang society has emerged which naturally nurtures violence. 'If you go to a party now, you need your crew,' says a young man in the Parisian suburb of Chanteloupe-les-Vignes, where the raw ghetto film, *La Haine*, was shot. 'They come in a group of ten, somebody disrespects your girl, all of a sudden your ten have to fight their ten.' Casual violence has become commonplace. In a Marseille suburb, three youths who had been tormenting a handicapped boy stabbed his elder brother to death for daring to object: in Lyon, an eighteen-year-old died after four days in a coma from injuries inflicted by a gang after he refused to hand over his chain necklace.

The violence has spread well beyond the familiar areas of urban tension in France's biggest cities. Almost a thousand cars were set alight in the Seine-Maritime department of Normandy during 1997, and some 550 were burned in the Strasbourg area. Elsewhere in eastern France, buses and municipal buildings were torched and public transport employees shot at. Increasingly, the police and fire crews are targets of stones, bottles and fire-bombs when they arrive to deal with trouble. There are often racial elements in the violence. In the normally peaceful town of Laval, between Normandy and Brittany, shops were smashed and a cafeteria set on fire after police shot dead a young Arab who, they said, had grabbed one of their guns and tried to escape. At a village party in Aimargues, between Montpellier and Nîmes, a group of some thirty locals attacked five North Africans with broken bottles. Two of the Africans were badly injured. Four policemen tried to stop the attack. A couple of young men, one armed with a shotgun, drove them back. When the youths were arrested, a 200-strong mob marched on the police station in protest – around fifty of them appeared drunk. The crowd threw stones and firecrackers, and destroyed a police van parked outside with metal bars. Reinforcements hurried in from Nîmes and stopped the violence. Another day, another incident in a divided, fearful society.

'We have to beat this absurd, idiotic violence across the country, in which you kill to steal a chain or a jacket,' an Education Minister proclaims. The omens are hardly promising.

In the Paris suburb of Grigny, a rumour spreads that a local man has killed an Algerian. A dozen youths try to break into the flat of the man's parents, thinking that he is hiding inside. The police are called, and meet a hail of stones. The youths burn a police car and spread out through the neighbouring estate, pillaging shops and trying to attack a petrol station. The next day, fifty youths, some carrying baseball bats, march on the town hall, shops and public buildings. For four hours, they play cat and mouse with the police, but nobody is arrested and the trouble evaporates as suddenly as it had started. In another Paris suburb, police run a gauntlet of Molotov cocktails and stones when they raid a council apartment block, and get similar treatment after a suspected drug-dealer is found beaten to death on an estate in the Val-d'Oise department. At Neuilly-sur-Marne, police have to be deployed to protect the filming of a popular television cop show on a housing estate; when the television crew leaves, youths who had watched the filming and congregated around the star for her autograph see the police off with a volley of stones and smash one of their cars. North of the city, the normally quiet town of Montataire is rocked by five days and nights of rioting after a 27-year-old immigrant was shot dead by an irascible and xenophobic neighbour in a housing estate.

South of Paris, half a dozen youths walk up to a building on the Cité d'Orgemont estate in Épinay-sur-Seine. They are from a similar estate in another suburb. After a row with some youths from Orgemont, they are out for revenge. One carries a rifle, another a sawn-off shotgun. One has fair hair; one is black; the others are Arabs. They fire an aimless shot at the window of a shoe repairer. Another bullet wounds a five-year-old who came running up to see what was going on. A third round hits a pregnant 25-year-old woman who was visiting her brother. She dies in his arms. Where did they get the guns? 'If you want a weapon, boys of between twelve and thirteen will find you one within a quarter of an hour,' the Mayor of Épinay explains.

The violence is a year-round affair. Take Christmas-time in 1997.

In a Lyon suburb, rioters set fire to thirty vehicles and a supermarket after a fatal shooting in a police station: witnesses said that, after arresting a local man, a police officer confiscated his shotgun, pointed it at his face and pulled the trigger, not realising it was loaded. On a housing estate outside Paris, the fatal police shooting of a sixteen-year-old Arab who crashed through a roadblock sets off nights of mayhem in which youths fling petrol bombs from rooftops and riot squads fire tear-gas grenades that smash through apartment windows and force residents to flee into the streets. In a dozen towns and cities from Rouen to Marseille, bus-drivers go on strike to protest at gunshot and fire-bomb attacks, and assaults by youths wielding baseball bats and throwing stones. At the end of 1998, Toulouse was hit by three days of rioting after police shot dead a seventeen-year-old immigrant in a stolen car. Forty cars were torched in Strasbourg over the New Year, and twenty more in Givors, south of Lyons, in mid-January. A report by a senior police officer identified nearly two-thirds of 700 'sensitive' districts as scenes of gang violence. Many are in housing estates. In eighteen, the report found 'collective rebellion and premeditated attacks against police, ambushes, throwing of paving stones and metal balls, Molotov cocktails, shots from firearms'. At the start of 1999, the Interior Minister set 'the republican reconquest of our suburbs' as a target for the year.

More than 60,000 youths are involved in crime each year – the total rose by 7 per cent in 1997 when people under eighteen accounted for one-third of street crime and 20 per cent of all delinquency. Many come from the *banlieues*. At the funeral of the immigrant killed in Montataire, the priest spoke of 'a generation of young people who have no chance, without work, without housing, without money, facing a world of adults who judge, condemn and exclude them without understanding'. Younger and younger children are involved. Some gangs are made up of eight- to ten-year-olds. In schools, thefts, rackets and drugs are increasingly common. According to the Education Ministry, between 34 and 57 per cent of secondary schools report that they have experienced violence from pupils. In four towns in the Paris suburbs, schools shut down in early 1998 because of violence. Some teachers have launched imaginative schemes to deal with unruly pupils, but, given the scale of the problem in the *banlieues*, they are but well-intentioned pinpricks.

A mother living on the housing estate where *La Haine* was filmed begs her elder child, in his twenties, not to act as a monitor on school buses. She has good reason. Another of her sons, a chubby seventeen-year-old called Imed Amri, had won a moment of fame when he appeared in the background in some scenes in the film. One night, Imed went to a rap evening organised by a local Franco-Algerian sol- idarity organisation to raise funds to pay for a skiing holiday for immigrant children. The youths from his estate and visitors from the nearby *banlieue* of Argenteuil got into an argument. Going outside the hall, they began to trade punches. Knives came out. The boys from Argenteuil went off to get a gun. When they returned, they shot Imed in the head. He died in hospital five hours later. No wonder his mother, knowing how many boys might carry weapons on the school bus, fears for her other son.

Or go back to Les Tartarets. In the spring of 1998, a fifteen-year-old boy from the estate was shot dead in broad daylight by an equally young member of another gang. For ageist reasons it had been diffi- cult for me to do any more than observe the local teenagers on a summer's day. But an enterprising – and younger – reporter, Darius Sanai, got closer to give a vivid picture of the alienation of youth in such places. Sanai joined a mission of revenge for a seventeen-year-old called Karim, who had been beaten to a bloody mess by youths from an adjoining estate after he had dated one of their girls:

> Hisham dropped back from the rest of the gang, whispering as we marched along the deathly grey of the housing estate. 'Sir,' he said, addressing me formally, 'when we go in you should keep your dis- tance. They will have knives and, you know, worse things. It could become very dangerous. Okay?'
>
> I nodded and Hisham jogged up to join the rest of the comrades, around forty young men. The group looked menacing enough: most were dressed in a uniform – blue jeans, blue tops, blue baseball caps, faces half-covered with the blue of Palestinian-style checked scarves. The few local residents on the streets scuttled away, often dragging massive, jet-black pitbull–Labrador crosses. There were no policemen in sight.
>
> Earlier, when they had been gathering in an abandoned car-park, the gang's leader had beckoned me over. Rocco, a stringy 21-year-

old with a worn, scarred face and a slight goatee, told me: 'You'd better see we are serious about this; we mean business.' He opened his jacket and yanked a gun from inside his belt. 'Brazilian Rossi snub-nose .22 LR,' he said.

Now Rocco was at the front of the pack, along with Fabien, a tall, good-looking sixteen-year-old with a baby face who was another of the gang's 'packers' – meaning he always carried a gun. We reached the bottom of a spiral staircase leading to the heart of the estate. Above, somewhere in the half-light, was the enemy: anything between 60 and 300 kids carrying a similar assortment of weaponry. If the other side had received a tip-off, they would be waiting for us on one of the concrete walkways or gathered on the roofs of the high-rises holding concrete blocks and paving stones to rain down on us.

'Let's go.' With that, the band of teenagers poured into the narrow staircase leading upwards, many of them visibly nervous, determination and pride etched together with fear on their young faces. The whole estate was swathed in deathly silence; nobody looked through the few windows where lights shone. I heard snippets of harsh whispers from the group. They walked all the way to the smashed glass door at one of the main entrances; from deep inside the building came the sounds of slamming doors, then silence; the enemy was retreating, not wanting to fight today. Like a shoal of fish, they turned around as one, marched back and funnelled down the stairs.

'We came, we saw, there's nothing there,' joked Fabien as we walked back home. The mood was relaxed and upbeat. But surely they had failed in their mission? No, replied Fabien: they had walked through the heart of enemy territory, it was a victory of sorts.

Afterwards, we are sitting in a bar near the heart of Paris. 'I never wanted to be doing this when I was seventeen,' said Fabien, who is lucid and calm, the son of immigrants from the Ivory Coast. 'But you have to understand where we live, it's a state of war. We are fighting for our territory, we have to protect ourselves from the police and from other gangs and we have to have respect. That's the most important thing. It's very clever. They put us all in these desolate places and we fight each other.' When, he added, they weren't fighting the police.

'This is misery and hell,' he went on as we walked back on the estate. 'Nine out of ten young people here are unemployed. The police are racists who are out to get us. The only thing we have is our pride, our culture.' Later, he admitted he was still at school. 'We have a trip to Edinburgh this spring,' he confided. 'Is it a beautiful place? Are the people racist like here?' Suddenly he sounded like a child.

The next day, a Sunday, a section of the gang had a rendezvous at 4 P.M. at their local Métro station. They gathered amid the coming and going of ordinary suburban life. When an elderly man peered over a faded railway map on the wall, trying to work out his connections, Rocco and Hisham, with perfect politeness, showed him the quickest way to get where he was going, addressing him with respect.

On the estate, drugs are, inevitably, a recurrent and growing problem. A young French narcotics runner recalls his trips to estates south of Paris. 'You made sure you only went to places where you were known. Otherwise, as a white kid, you could be in trouble. And when you got there one of you stayed in the car: otherwise it might be stolen within five minutes. The outsides of the blocks of flats had been repainted, but inside it was just the same – dirt, graffiti, human and dog excrement on the landings. And inside the flats, you had this Ali Baba cave of hi-fi equipment, videos, all the latest gear. And any drugs you wanted. The law didn't exist; they didn't give a shit. It was their world, and they were going to make the most of it.'

Small deals are conducted in the street, with boys as young as eight or nine keeping watch from the nearby rooftops. Any patrolling police are spotted long before they arrive on the scene. But the real drug transactions take place inside flats. Nathalie knows that better than anybody. She came to Paris from the Mediterranean in the 1980s and has spent a dozen years as a policewoman in the suburbs of the capital. She patrols an estate in the Seine-Saint-Denis department outside Paris, checking cellars and lift-shafts and the concrete alleyways between the tower-blocks. When she joined the force, she thought her blue uniform would win her respect. Instead, 'the young people treat us like shit . . . the insults rain down on us'. Two of her colleagues have killed themselves in despair.

Nathalie dreams of being posted back to her home region on the southern coast. Instead, the local hoods sidle up to her and tell her she could make much more money as a prostitute. Others set fire to a car and call the police; when they drive up, a dozen youths run out into the street and bombard their vehicle with stones and metal bolts. Her windscreen has been smashed several times; once it was broken by a flower pot dropped from ten floors up. 'You just have to hope that the doors are well locked and the reverse gear doesn't jam.' Her bus-driver husband finds her growing more bossy at home. 'I've lost all my sensibility as a woman,' she says. 'Seeing only the bad side of society means I trust nobody any more. I feel as if the whole world reproaches me for being a cop. My only friends are in the police. At least they understand me.' Early on, she was shocked by the bad language of the streets, the petty crimes, the drug trafficking; then she absorbed the ultimate survival technique of the *banlieue* cops – the shrug of the shoulders. Just as her husband no longer reacts when youths get on his bus without paying, kick the doors and horse around. But, still, there are moments which even a dozen years on the beat cannot deaden. One evening, Nathalie was called out on an emergency. A man had fired his rifle by mistake while cleaning it. The bullet went through the floor into the flat below and hit a two-year-old baby in its cot. It died in her arms. When she got home at two in the morning, her uniform was still stained with blood.

These are the parts of France where councils propose a night-time curfew for children. The mayor of the town where Imed Amri died wants welfare withheld from parents of delinquents. Reflecting on a suggestion that youth crime might be reduced by more civil education in schools, he shrugs and says: 'Imagine a child who has been break-ing into cars and stealing radios with impunity for years because he's under thirteen. Do you think he'll stop it because he gets a civil edu-cation class once a week at school?' A cartoon in *Le Monde* showed a schoolmistress teaching her pupils to decline their verbs: written on the blackboard was 'I want to burn a car; you want to burn a car; he, or she, wants to burn a car' and the teacher is warning the class not to forget the circumflex accent on *brûler*.

In such suburbs, dogs are kept for protection or attack, not to be patted. A supermarket in the Paris suburb of Stains sells rottweilers in its pet department, and the authorities in the Hauts-de-Seine depart-ment had to ban pitbull terriers in public housing estates because there were so many. Among non-immigrants, the depressed suburbs are a natural breeding-ground for support for the political extremes – once it was the Communists; now, the alienated voters seek another vehicle for their fears and concerns. The Socialist mayor of one *banlieue* town south of Paris compares the way members of the far right have targeted French residents in tower-blocks to the tactics of the Nazis in the tenements of Weimar Germany. 'Every day,' she writes, 'the precariousness of life gathers ground, public services wither, the Welfare State retreats . . . and when these words take shape in the faces of men and women, the unbearable leaps to your eyes and touches your heart.' For many immigrants caught in the vice of the *banlieue* and rundown city areas, it is not surprising that France's second biggest religion offers an increasingly attractive means of escape from the rejection so many feel in their daily lives.

France is home to between four and five million Muslims. It is probably true to say that the majority are not strongly religious – only between 10 and 15 per cent are reckoned to worship on a regular basis (about the same proportion of Catholics who go to mass each Sunday). For most Arabs and some Africans, Islam is above all a social and community glue in a foreign land, an assertion of their identity rather than any threat to those around them. A poll for *Le Nouvel Observateur* magazine in 1998 reported that only 24 per cent of them felt any affinity with fundamentalism. But, for many of the French, the imams, mosques, veiled women and Halal butchers have become a symbol of the separateness of the immigrants. Muslims and Arabs are seen as being pretty much the same. One poll showed that nearly two-thirds of the French thought the country had 'too many Arabs' and 'too many Muslims'.

There are regular rows over whether Muslim girls should be allowed to wear religious scarves to state schools. The number of mosques has grown to more than a thousand. Muslim religious schools have been set up in back rooms. The Arabic graffiti on city walls shouts for itself. In prisons, warders keep watch on fundamentalist terrorists to prevent them making converts. An imam who was subsequently expelled from France spoke openly of imposing Islam on the country. A police association has warned of the religion's potent appeal to 'young delinquents who are seeking their identity and are ready to wage a struggle against the country's institutions which is presented to them as legitimate'. One of the nation's most politically correct newspapers ran a headline about 'Islamic gangrene'. In a Lyon suburb, *Le Monde* reported, militants of a Koranic teaching association warned immigrant parents in the street: 'If you don't send your son to the class, we know your family in Algeria and we'll deal with them.' Nearby, a nun who has spent her life working with young people in the housing estate told how a young man walked into a neighbour- hood fair and spoke a few words in Arabic. 'Immediately, all the *Maghrébins* left; outside, bearded men in djellaba robes were waiting for them.'

For the resentful youth of the *banlieues*, Islam meets a psychologi- cal need which all the anti-racist, integrationist movements of the 1980s never touched. 'Better to count yourself as a Muslim than as one of the unemployed,' as a saying goes. To which one of Bernard Tapie's successors as minister responsible for towns and social integra- tion responded: 'They do not want mosques but jobs. They may not have the same roots, but they want the same pay-slips.' The trouble is that the jobs simply aren't there. A growing number of *banlieue* fam- ilies have two generations without work. Islam, whether actively practised or not, is a counter to what they see as the indifference of French society to their plight. The evident suspicion that officialdom shows towards the religion only increases its appeal to those who already regard mainstream society as hostile to them.

Behind this lies the colonial legacy in North Africa and the support Paris gave to the repressive, anti-fundamentalist regime in Algiers. Militant Islamists proclaim that their holy war will continue until the whole world is conquered – and France is their first foreign target. In Algeria itself, five people died in an attack on French diplomatic quarters, a French bishop was blown up and seven French Trappist monks had their throats slit after being kidnapped by the main fun- damentalist group. A French airliner was hijacked across the Mediterranean. France itself was hit with a series of bomb attacks, one of which killed seven people in a Paris station – and Khaled Kelkal tried to blow up the TGV train track. The combination of terrorist bombs, the threatening cloud of violence in the suburban housing estates at home and the horrific bloodletting in France's former colony makes it easy for the far right to warn of France being swept by a murderous horde from the Maghreb, poised to cross the

Mediterranean and join up with their brothers in Corbeil, Vaulx-en-Velin or Marseille. One of France's most famous names thinks they have already landed. Brigitte Bardot, who married a National Front supporter as her fourth husband, said she might have to emigrate because of the overpopulation of foreigners, especially 'manic throat-cutter' Muslims, with their ritual slaughter of sheep. 'We have to submit against our will to this overflow,' the actress turned animal-rights fanatic declared. 'Year by year, we see mosques flourish across France while our church bells fall silent because of the lack of priests.' Such language earned her a 10,000-franc fine for inciting racial hatred, by which time she had publicly pledged support for the National Front in an election in southern France and, against the background of horrifying massacres in Algeria, was ratcheting the rhetoric up a gear with a vision of how the fundamentalists would 'slit our throats one day – and we'll deserve it'.

The perceived Islamic threat has been given a new edge by an emerging link with organised crime. Since 1994, police report having broken up a web of Islamic groups involved in hold-ups, explosions, gun-running and forged documents in Paris, Toulouse, in the east and on the Mediterranean coast. The network was said to have ties not only with North Africa but also with Bosnia, Chechnya and Afghanistan. One gang, based west of Paris, raised millions of francs for Algerian fundamentalists by selling forged documents to immigrants. In the capital itself, a front company specialised in shipping stolen cars to the brothers across the Mediterranean. There have also been cases of native Frenchmen who converted to Islam, underwent military training in Afghanistan and returned to France to join the fundamentalist movement at home. And then there was Christophe Caze.

The son of a cleaning woman and a unemployed worker, Caze became a Muslim while a medical student in the northern city of Lille. He changed his first name to Walid, grew a beard and began to attend a fundamentalist mosque. In 1993, he abandoned his studies and went to Bosnia, where he worked in a medical outfit, fought on the Muslim side, and married a seventeen-year-old nurse. Two years later he returned to France and was called up for national service. Within two weeks, he had deserted. Christophe-Walid had brought weapons back with him from Bosnia. He also acquired a police scanner radio. With a band of sympathisers, including another French convert to Islam, he established a headquarters in a brick house in a suburb of the depressed northern town of Roubaix.

Ten days after he deserted, Caze and his gang held up a supermarket, killing a motorist. Six weeks later, they attacked a Brinks security truck with a rocket launcher. The money they stole was dispatched to Muslims in Bosnia. Next, Caze left a car with three bottles of gas in the boot outside the main police station in Lille, where the leaders of major industrial nations were due to meet three days later. Only the detonator went off. The following day, heavily armed police moved in on the brick hide-out house at dawn. If they thought they would catch the gang asleep, they had got their religion wrong. The four people inside 59 rue Henri-Carrette were already at their morning prayers. The police opened fire on the house. According to an eyewitness, one of the attackers went to the back of the house with a rocket launcher, lay down in the street and fired. 'The roof went up like the lid from a saucepan. It fell back in flames and set the whole building alight. It was like a house of cards that had caught fire.' From inside, a man engulfed in flames went on shooting with a Kalashnikov rifle. When four bodies were pulled from the ruins, they were so shrunken by the heat that some locals thought they were children.

Caze was not among the dead. He had been out of the house for the night, and picked up news of the attack on his scanner radio. With another member of the gang, he drove towards the Belgian frontier. Police were waiting for him. Their fusillade killed Caze outright. His companion, wounded, took two women hostage before giving himself up.

Roubaix, a forgotten part of France's industrial decline, suddenly came under the national spotlight. One-third of the town's population are immigrants, and few Arab women do not cover up in the streets. An English journalist, Mary Dejevsky of the *Independent*, reported seeing teenage boys with Arafat-style headgear in the streets a few days after the shooting. There is a raging drugs problem in the largely immigrant southern suburbs. The porous border with Belgium up the road makes it simple for illegal immigrants to slip into France, and for drugs to be brought from the Netherlands. Unemployment stays stubbornly high in the shadow of the old spinning mills and the factories that once provided work for all in the great northern urban sprawl around Lille. Five months after Caze and his companions died, journalist Sara Daniel visited the Alma-Gare district where the gang had established itself:

> In summer here, nobody goes on holiday. But round rue Henri-Carrette, the silence of the dead reigns. A silence of mourning. Approaching Number 59, a woman draws the edge of her veil across to cover her face. So as not to see the little charred house with its windows covered with planks. Between the Alma district and Christophe Caze, a kind of love affair has come to life. A strange alchemy. Here the problems of living bring people closer. Everybody knows each other. Here, the young man who had converted to Islam found a new family. Christophe was something of the favourite son of the district. The kids in the street speak of him with respect. 'He tried to persuade us to go to the mosque. He was intelligent, educated, but not haughty. We talked about football, anything and everything. He was tolerant. As for religion, he said it was up to us to make the decision, nobody could force us.'

In the once bustling textile centre of Tourcoing to the west of Roubaix, a different tone is to be heard. Tourcoing has also fallen on hard times. Racism, fear, unemployment and extremist politics meld into a sour brew on a run-down estate. 'My father told me: Arabs are worse than mice,' a 31-year-old mother of five told a visiting reporter from *Le Monde*, pointing at a little Arab boy. 'What we need is a boat to put them in, or a good bomb.' Another woman sounded a softer note. Her neighbour, Fatima, is nice – during Ramadan she hands out her couscous and cakes. That did not stop the second woman referring to the Arabs as 'wogs'. The first woman's husband had never had a job; their evening meal was bread and cheese. 'And to think that my mother and father changed jobs in the cotton mills whenever they wanted to.'

People in places like this tell of young Arabs attacking old French people in the cemetery, of police who either turn a blind eye or suggest that they take the law into their own hands. A municipal basketball court was built just for Arabs, they say: a Frenchman who went there to play was turned away. A 28-year-old woman has had to put up wire fencing around her garden to keep out the Arabs who used to shoot up with drugs and leave the syringes behind on her grass. Racism and unemployment feed off one another. A former trade union official recalls how, in the old days, you could break off from work to have a cigarette; now, there will always be an Arab standing in line to grab work, while an army of illegal immigrants is pouring into the country in search of jobs and the shopfloor manager will remind you that there were two thousand people waiting to take your place. A retired Frenchman with a Socialist Party card who keeps several guns in his flat says he votes for the far right in local elections 'to stop the wogs getting above themselves'. It was hardly surprising that one-third of the voters on that estate backed the anti-immigrant candidate in the first round of the 1995 presidential election, or that the far right came close to the Gaullists in Tourcoing in the legislative poll two years later.

What fuels French racism is the changing face and colour of those who come from abroad. Throughout the century, France has attracted a large flow of immigrants, starting with Polish mineworkers and Jews from Eastern Europe. Immigration accounts for 40 per cent of the national population growth since the Second World War, and a quarter of the population has immigrant family links. In the 1960s, 75 per cent of those who came to live in France were from Europe, most of them Catholic Spaniards and Portuguese. Generally, they looked like the natives and fitted into a comfortable pattern; the men worked in factories while their wives were concierges or cleaning women. They kept to the rules, and their children grew up in the French system. A Portuguese concierge in our street on the Left Bank told my wife proudly that her daughter had voted for the National Front in 1995, as if that was proof of belonging.

Today, half the immigrants are from Africa. When the French talk of the foreigners in their midst, they do not think of Portuguese concierges or Spanish waiters but of the brown- and black-skinned people living in run-down sections of major cities or in the suburban housing estates – the substantial Turkish population usually manages to avoid notice, though it has been at the centre of some incidents in northern industrial cities. Whenever possible, the French put immigrants out of their minds, and pay little attention to the conditions in which they exist. In the mid-1990s, a member of the National Assembly investigated how one group of immigrants lived. He found over-crowding, black markets, drugs, prostitution, health problems, the growth of AIDS and tuberculosis. One place he visited contained three times as many people as its legal entitlement; another had four people or more sleeping in the same room; a third served 3,000 meals a day with no health controls. Was the deputy, Henri Cuq, writing about a hide-out for illegal immigrants? No, these were some of France's 710 official hostels for foreign workers.

Cuq's report emphasised not only how the nation had given up on its immigrants, but why men from Mali or the Maghreb were so intent on coming to France. If they could find work, the economics are simple. The minimum wage was 4,900 francs. In an immigrant hostel, meals cost 7.50 francs, and the monthly price of a bed was 450 francs. So there was no problem in saving 3,000 francs a month to be sent home to a country where that was a great deal of money. 'This can only encourage a flow of illegal immigrants,' as Cuq concluded. Soon after his report was published, a fifteen-year-old Moroccan travelled 1,200 miles from Tangiers to France hidden in the luggage compartment of a bus, and a group of Chinese was found making shoes in a garage in western France in conditions of virtual slavery. Others died locked up in containers, or were thrown overboard from ships after they had paid to be smuggled to France.

How such people are received once they arrive in France has become a touchstone of the tension between the humanism on which the country has always prided itself and the more visceral reactions encouraged by unemployment, social discord and national uncertainties. After a highly publicised incident in the summer of 1996, in which 220 Africans without residence papers were hauled from sanctuary in a Paris church to be expelled, the editor of Le Monde described immigration as 'that moment of truth in which an age is plainly revealed and generations radically divide'. The immigration laws were rewritten three times in five years in a left–right tussle over how tight controls should be. But legislation only scrapes the surface of a deep social divide. The inevitable gulf between a North African family in a *banlieue* tower-block and an orthodox French family has become immeasurably deeper because the feeling of non-acceptance is mutual. Increasingly, immigrants are asking what France is going to do for them. The jobs that brought them north are drying up, but they do not want to leave. Religion is the only rallying-point in which they can have confidence but, by its nature, it sets them even further apart. When a right-wing Interior Minister spoke of developing 'a French Islam', an imam from northern Paris countered: 'What is being asked of us is not integration but assimilation, which requires us to leave our identity behind. Individuals can be assimilated, a community cannot . . . the arrival in France of Protestants and Jews required changes in French society; now it is the time of the Muslims.'

Before he embarked on his brief career as a terrorist, the would-be bomber of the TGV train, Khaled Kelkal, spoke of what being a Muslim meant to him. 'I am neither Arab nor French, I am Muslim,' he said. 'When I go into a mosque, I'm at ease. People shake my hand, treat me as a friend. When I see another Muslim in the street, he smiles, we stop, we chat. We recognise one another as brothers.' The contrast between his words, published after his death, and the television image of a policeman turning the young man's body over with his boot summed up the cleavage between the world of the *banlieues* and mainstream French society. Fundamentalist terrorism had become a home-grown threat to society. The terrorists were no longer wild figures from the Middle East or North Africa, but young men who had been brought up in France itself. Some, like Christophe Caze, were even Frenchmen who rejected the ways of their homeland. In their desperate way, they had come to be an archetype of the submerged world of the other France.

That frightens a lot of people. They see the Arabs and Africans as outsiders who can only be a threat to the cohesion of their country and their own lives. Racism against black and brown people thus takes on a wider resonance than simple 'wog-bashing', and draws on the image which France has had of its own social fabric for two centuries. The French do not see themselves as living in a land of separate ethnic communities: Islamists, as the Gaullist Interior Minister said, should be French. The country may receive people from different nations and cultures, but it requires them to conform to the unity of the Republic. The education system and the authority of the state are meant to impose a uniformity which ensures that the melting-pot produces a single national stew. There are exceptions – in the immigrant communities of Marseille or the Jewish traditionalists of the Marais district in Paris – but, as a general rule, multi-culturalism and the right of different ethnic groups to be treated on an equal plane with the native French are new, and often uncomfortable, concepts. 'If immigrants, no matter where they are from, settle in our country, then they must adopt our civilisation and bend to our rules, habits and lifestyles' – the formulation from the Comte de Paris, the Pretender to the French throne, is an unequivocal expression of an attitude widely shared across the nation. Or, as an adviser on immigration to Alain Juppé's government said: 'When somebody emigrates, he changes not only his country, but also his history. Foreigners arriving in France must understand that henceforth their ancestors are the Gauls.'

Such a message takes no account of places like Vaulx-en-Velin, with its thirty-eight different nationalities; or the tower-block suburbs outside Paris in La Courneuve, Aubervilliers and Saint-Denis; or the tower-block estate of Les Bosquets, north of Paris, where the 9,000 people come from scores of ethnic backgrounds and the youth centre is the only public building not to have been attacked during recent troubles. As well as Arabs, many *banlieues* are home to substantial numbers from black Africa who bring their cultures and traditions with them. In the suburb of Montreuil, where 5,000 immigrants from Mali live, the mayor fights an uphill battle against their polygamy. More than a hundred African religious sects have set up in the hinterland of France's cities. Each weekend, a bare, neon-lit hall in La Plaine-Saint-Denis north of Paris resounds to a *Zaïrois*-style band of electric guitarists and singers laying down the path to salvation. At a Sunday service of the Cherubin Christians of Drancy, black immigrant girls parade in immaculate white dresses and bonnets. A woman in African costume slumps to the floor in a trance while a young man is taken through an exorcism ceremony. In another suburb, a pastor from Madagascar preaches to the faithful in an annexe to a fast-food restaurant. The quest is for roots as much as for religion. At the end of one service, the mighty brass of the Kimbanguiste Fanfare band blares out. However drab and cold their suburban world may be, however threatening the shadows of xenophobia, the faithful can almost feel at home for the space of a Sunday morning.

Sarcelles, the suburb in which the pastor from Madagascar exhorts his flock each weekend, counts sixty different nationalities among its 58,000 people. Its bus stops strike a high French cultural note, being named after César Franck, Camille Saint-Saëns, André Gide and

Albert Camus. But the walls of the bus station are covered with posters advertising concerts by Le Sénégal en Musique, Le Afro-Jazz and Le Turbo de l'Afrique, or offering the services of Le Plus Grand Coiffeur Afrique-Antillais. In the big square housing blocks by the train tracks, the vast majority of faces are black. In the sprawling street market, each immigrant community is represented in the food stalls – mint and North African spices, sweet potatoes, soja and kosher meat. Nobody can pretend that Sarcelles is French in the way that the Comte de Paris or most traditionalists would define the word. But it has become home to the immigrants, many of them of the second generation, and they refuse to conform to a straitjacket forged by France's past. As an imam in the 19th *arrondissement* of Paris pointed out to the American writer Milton Viorst, his flock was part of the French family, and accepted their responsibilities towards it, but it could not be alone in making accommodations. If such mutual understandings remain as elusive as they are at present, or are actively rejected, the *de facto* distance between communities can only grow. After a lengthy study of the Paris *banlieue*, the publisher and author François Maspero was led to observe that, if a plan for ethnic separation was regarded as viable for the former Yugoslavia, 'one day, we must expect such a plan, in the name of the same logic, to be set out for a just ethnic division of the people of Aubervilliers and La Courneuve'.

France's difficulty in coming to terms with the dysfunction between the old, all-encompassing idea of the nation and the ethnic separations which it cannot ignore is heightened by the high profile of Arabs born in France – known as *beurs*, from the reverse *verlan* slang for *Arabes*. The first generation of immigrants were overwhelmingly single men recruited from North Africa to work in factories and mines. According to a recent compiler of an oral history of the immigrants, Yamina Benguigui, their minds were set on returning home one day; at first, they kept their belongings packed, ready to make the journey back. But the longer they stayed in France and the more their families joined them, the further that prospect receded. 'If you go to Algeria, you will see the houses the immigrants had built for them,' Benguigui notes. 'Often there is no more than the first storey: the building stopped at that.' For their children, the process went a step further. The idea of returning to North Africa became a non-starter, but, at the same time, France was not a real home. 'We were neither from here nor from there,' as Benguigui puts it. For teenage *beurs*, the process is complete. No question of crossing the Mediterranean, but little question of adopting traditional French ways either. They see themselves as a community – the second most numerous in France – which has the right to live in its fashion by its own rules. They want to have their cake and eat it; but their cake can be pretty thin and explosively discriminatory – an official report at the end of 1998 showed that 42 per cent of 20–30 year-old children of Algerians who had moved to France were out of work compared to 11 per cent of offsprings of native French parents.

Amid such dark shadows of apartheid *à la française,* one outcome of *beur* pride is a vibrant alternative street culture, expressed mainly in rap music which has bred a true international star in the singer MC Solaar and claims brotherhood with the Bronx, Watts or Brixton – a self-conscious lexicon of *banlieue* language lists terms like 'gangsta' and 'homeboy' (no *Académie Française* gurus here). But, despite sometimes high record sales to a wider public, this is essentially an outsider culture which loses its edge if it allows itself to be embraced by the mainstream. Its base in the youth of the *banlieue* lives resentfully and with a clannish pride on the edge of society. There may have been cause for national pride when the formidable black athlete Marie-José Pérec notched up an Olympic double in the 200- and 400-metre races at the Atlanta Olympics and a *beur* won a gold medal for judo, but, for many white French people, the young blacks and Arabs are a threatening force. Inevitably, the separateness reaches into that sacred area of French unity, the language.

The *banlieues* have a slang which can be virtually impenetrable and can act as a wall in both directions. 'We are not like them, the words we use are not the same as them because they speak old French, we talk our slang,' as a twelve-year-old from the suburbs said about white children from inside Paris. 'Traditional French language finds itself in a foreign land,' remarked a film-maker after finishing a documentary on the housing estates. In a further twist away from the universal language spread across France by the centralisers of the nineteenth century, this new tongue can vary from estate to estate, from race to race. In Noisy-Le-Grand, outside Paris, Africans call white French people '*babtou*' while Arabs call them '*gaori*' or '*gouère*' and gypsies call them '*roum*'; elsewhere one popular term is '*from*' – from *fromage*. There is nothing inherently menacing in young immigrants calling a condom a '*passe-port*' or talking about '*dunk*' to mean hitting somebody. But, to those not in tune with ghetto life, it is a considerable step further when the slang for 'leave me alone' becomes 'fuck your mother'. And when the rap band of that name – Nique Ta Mère – performs a song urging 'kill the cops', the liberal establishment is in a quandary. Condemnation means lining up with the racists who wax indignant when the band is booked for subsidised music festivals. But to shut one's eyes and ears in the name of racial harmony is, as the journalist Élisabeth Schemla points out, to renounce moral values needed to stand up to the extremism which threatens civil society. If NTM can get away with it, how about a band that sings a ditty entitled 'Kill the Jews'?

The law eventually stepped in: two members of NTM – one from white Portuguese parents, the other a West Indian black, both of them French citizens – were given suspended prison sentences for singing a song which declared: 'I piss on the courts. The police are fascists and murderers. It's those motherfuckers in blue and the courts who break our balls all the year. Our enemies are the men in blue and we piss on them.' Soon afterwards, two other rap singers were fined for another cop-baiting song entitled 'Sacrifice de Poulets' – *poulet*, or chicken, being the slang term for the police. The fear is that it is not all a matter of words. As the sentence was being handed down to NTM, two teenagers were arrested and accused of dropping a block of cement on a policeman from a tower-block on a suburban Paris estate, breaking his skull. And on the Paris Métro, four Arab youths and one black slashed a woman officer's face while shouting: 'Filthy cop! We're going to kill you!' as they repeatedly raped her.

The tension that surrounds the presence of native-born children of immigrants has given rise to recurrent suggestions that French nationality should be defined by blood rather than by simply having been born on French soil. The questioning of a hallowed element in France's tradition as a land that welcomes foreigners has gone as high as a former President of the Republic. At a less elevated but more pertinent level, an immigrant living close to Valéry Giscard d'Estaing's Auvergnat homeland in Clermont-Ferrand issued a striking appeal entitled 'To My Brothers':

In this land of welcome, we meet two attitudes. One regards us as the source of all the country's social ills – that's the extremism of hatred, demagogy, of people closing in on themselves, sometimes the result of ignorance and naïveté. The other imagines us to be angels, simple victims of the economic crisis and its 'natural' corollary, racism. That's angelic racism, smart, romantic and sometimes condescending. Come what may, the results are the same: we are disliked more and more; we irritate; we are always on display.

Unfortunately, it is not simply a matter of racism. People speak about us for good or ill without really knowing us. They think for us. Really, it's time to realise that we upset them. Nobody can talk about us without passion, and we can't talk about ourselves without emotion.

The presence of foreigners in the West in general, and in France in particular, is the direct result of colonialism and the demands of the flourishing industry of the 1960s and 1970s. You have to take the consequences of history. To justify violence in the suburbs by blaming unemployment and people's feelings of helplessness is easy. But how many French farmers work sixteen hours a day for less than 3,000 francs a month? How many unemployed French people who no longer get benefits live in destitution without drawing attention to themselves?

And where would you be in a similar situation back home? You'd be without work, without benefits, without rights and subject to totally arbitrary regulations. You couldn't even smash up the lifts because, when there are any, most are already broken. You couldn't tag the walls because, back home, there aren't any aerosol canisters. Even less could you hassle the police – you'd be risking your life.

So why do you feel this contempt for the country that welcomes you? For its laws, for its leaders. All they ask of you is not to impose your culture on those who don't want it. I listen to African singers and to French singers. I read French and North African writers with the same admiration. I watch a European or an African football match with the same passion. I watch *Cyrano de Bergerac* and *Omar Gatlato* with the same emotion. All that without my neighbours knowing it. That's what integration is all about.

Such voices are rare in France today on either side of the racial divide. A lot of French people find street gangs of Arab or African teenagers genuinely threatening, while immigrant youths who rioted in Strasbourg at the New Year of 1998 clipped out newspaper stories mentioning them as a badge of honour. The nation's growing sense of insecurity leaves little room for strangers from another culture. With its finger on the pulse as ever, the National Front hammers on about the 'exclusion' of native French people from housing and benefits which should, by rights, be theirs – to the advantage of invasive immigrants sucking up welfare, homes and jobs and getting away scot-free with breaking the law. The gang rape of a Dutch tourist on an Atlantic beach and the fatal stabbing of a young man during a gang fight outside a discotheque by the Mediterranean became *causes célèbres* when it emerged that, in each case, the attackers were youths on subsidised holidays from the ghettos. Each *banlieue* riot involving young immigrants sends more votes to the far right.

The exact degree of racism in France is impossible to define, but there is clearly a lot of it about. A report to the United Nations Human Rights Commission depicted a country being shaken by 'a wave of xenophobia and racism'. Nearly two-thirds of those questioned in another survey acknowledged that they harboured racist attitudes. Anti-Arab jokes arouse chuckles rather than indignation around the dinner table of a resolutely left-wing middle-class family. When a passing motorist from Montpellier came into a village café in the middle of France with the news that a leader of former settlers in Algeria had been murdered down south, the universal reaction was: 'Must have been the niggers.' (In fact, it was the work of three other right-wingers). There are few prominent immigrants in French national life – the National Assembly has just one black or brown member from metropolitan France – he is also the country's only mayor of African stock.

Some people react with denial. A prominent university professor banned the use of the word 'immigration' among his students because it might encourage racism. A Christian group called on all public organisations to remove the word 'race' from official texts. Others try to walk a fine line but fall from the tightrope. Though no racist, and a firm opponent of the National Front, Jacques Chirac has spoken of his understanding of what ordinary French people feel about the noise and smells of their immigrant neighbours. Just before the 1997 legislative election, his minister responsible for urban affairs went on the radio to talk about immigrants. The President regarded the bluff, supposedly streetwise Éric Raoult as one of his trump cards in the fight against the Front, a kind of Bernard Tapie of the right without the sleaze. Using a patronising collective term derived from the African name 'Amadou', Raoult said that, to be integrated, 'Mamadou, if he is here legally, must wear a suit and tie.' The correct attitude for immigrants should be to behave as children do at school. That was a bit like a Cabinet-level official responsible for urban affairs going on television in Washington and telling 'Sambo' to get his hair cut if he wanted a job. It must have gone down a treat with the *beurs*.

A survey carried out with the brave help of the CFDT trade union federation revealed a devastating account of racism at the workplace: a wife coming to meet her African husband for lunch hears his colleagues calling for 'the monkey'; two firms in a high immigrant area of the south employ six dark-skinned people among their 1,000 staff. Hearing that an Arab employee of the railway system has prayed on the platform of a station, one of his colleagues explodes that: 'If I'd been there, I'd have kicked his ass till he left.' Or the reaction of a watchman at a housing estate: 'We'll go in with machine-guns and bury them.' Not surprising, then, that a survey by a human rights commission showed that 61 per cent thought there were too many Arabs in the country – and that the behaviour of some immigrants justified racist reactions.

'We're not at home here,' said one of the women on the estate in Tourcoing. 'They spit in our faces.' On the other side of the divide, a North African community worker in Khaled Kelkal's home town of Vaulx-en-Velin recalled that ten years ago, young Arabs wanted to become French. 'Today, it is exactly the opposite. Whatever we do to adapt, it will never be enough to get us accepted. White people can get out of the *banlieues* if they make the effort. We'd have to move the whole Earth to do that. We are the slaves of the year 2000.' And, so often, slaves without work: a study of 360 big companies shows that in the last ten years they have laid off 41 per cent of their immigrant workers compared to 12 per cant of native, French staff. Has the land of the enlightenment come to this? Tragically, yes – and there is only one winner.

SPECTRE AT THE FEAST

The lights go out. The recording of Verdi's 'Chorus of the Slaves' (from Egypt, not Vaulx-en-Velin) rises to a deafening pitch. Two thousand people jump up on the rows of red plastic chairs set across the exhibition hall, craning their necks to catch a sight of the conquering hero. Outside the big utilitarian building, they had been a collection of individual groups – farmers slapping one another on the back, shopkeepers joshing with their customers, a white-haired priest darting through the throng to pay his respects to an elderly woman in pearls. The smell of grilling meat and sizzling chips was heavy in the spring air. Men drank beer from the bottle and chewed spicy *merguez* sausages stuffed inside chunks of bread; some bought their companions *cuvée spéciale* champagne at 10 francs per plastic goblet. Once inside the hall, having paid a 40-franc entrance fee, they milled around, picked their seats, waved to acquaintances and chatted through the warm-up speeches. Stalls were selling reprints of newspaper front pages detailing great colonial humiliations – Indochina, the Suez expedition, Algeria – as if the organisers wanted to remind the audience of what France had lost. A small bar of soap with an evocative label lay on each chair.

As the star of the evening bursts through the back door of the hall, the individuals become a single, cheering mass. Surrounded by television cameras, Jean-Marie Le Pen marches towards the platform. The cheering drowns the Verdi choir. Placards bob in the air – 'Vas-y Jean-Marie' and one held aloft by a touchingly solitary young woman,

'Jean-Marie, our only friend'. The priest stands in front of his chair, his eyes staring straight ahead. The elderly lady beside him holds her hands to her mouth, like a reincarnation of a bobby-soxer seeing Frank Sinatra for the first time. In a side aisle, three young men with shaved skulls punch one another playfully on the shoulder. As the leader reaches the platform, the roar from the hall grows even louder. Plump and sleek in a dark-blue double-breasted suit, his one good eye glistening in the spotlight, his chest stuck out like a pigeon, the boss of France's National Front punches the air with both fists and waits for the din to subside. Then he tells a story.

He had arrived late that evening in Toulouse, and he apologises for keeping the good people of the south-west waiting. But it had not been his fault. On the way down from Paris the good French pilot had told him why the Airbus – made in the great city of Toulouse – was running behind schedule. It was all because control of French skies was now based – guess where? The crowd didn't have the faintest idea. So their friend Jean-Marie told them: French air-space was con-trolled from Maastricht. That's right, Maastricht – he draws out the long first double vowel with a grimace and snarls the final '*icht*'. Yes, Maastricht, the Dutch town where that terrible European Union treaty was signed which would wrench away national sovereignty and reduce the good people of the Hexagon of France to vassals of face-less bureaucrats of Brussels. And what had happened when the air control centre at Maastricht had been given authority over the skies above our country? Why, the French air-traffic controllers who worked there had been sacked. Their places had been taken by the Dutch, the Germans and the British who were delaying French air-craft on purpose in order to give their own national lines an unfair advantage. This was why Jean-Marie Le Pen's Airbus had been delayed on its way down to Toulouse that April evening.

Before the crowd can quite digest this revelation, the man who speaks for all that is irrational, extremist and xenophobic in the nation of liberty, equality and fraternity is off and running. If the national madeleines are crumbling around them, the man on the platform tells his audience why. For two hours, he paces from side to side of the wide stage, pausing occasionally to grin at one of his own jokes, halting to stand to attention when he invokes the memory of those who died to preserve France over the centuries. In a horribly great stand-up act, he plumbs every depth of national insecurity. Immigration and law and order flow like poisoned streams, sometimes apart, sometimes intertwined. He tells of Arab families living on welfare who bring in their second and third cousins to squat in municipal housing estates: the bailiffs dare not evict them because they would be found later with their severed heads tucked under their arms. Ministries in Paris are trying to create a mongrel nation by making it easier to adopt an African or South American baby than a French child. And, as always, the mantra: three million immigrants sent home – three million jobs for the French – the social security system saved – public order restored – pensions safeguarded.

The mood of the crowd swings as violently as the orator's words: these farmers and townspeople are alternately moved to indignation at the perils facing them and to elation at Le Pen's evocation of France's greatness. 'France is beautiful!' he cries. 'Let us show ourselves worthy of her. Defend her! Rebuild her!' Joan of Arc and the heroic defence of Verdun crop up in almost every Le Pen speech; so do the traitors and enemies conspiring to bring the nation to its knees. After four decades in politics, his persona is set in rancid aspic – but he still aspires to be the great patriotic leader who will tear down the temple in order to rebuild it. He is waiting for the ultimate big bang which will open the gates of power.

The next morning, his audience will wake up in a more humdrum world. They will not go out on an anti-Arab pogrom or be mugged by drug-smoking children of immigrants when they travel home from work in Montauban, Albi or Castres. But they may read in their morning newspaper that the photofit of a serial-killer in the Bastille area of Paris is of a 'North African type' and, as they cast their minds back to the previous night, they will recall the clues offered by the portly man in the double-breasted suit as to why they feel a lot less happy than they should be about being French.

Every country has its dark side. It is, however, difficult to imagine a politician in another major Western democracy spouting quite the same degree of wild hogwash as does Jean–Marie Le Pen, and surviving as a significant national figure for more than a decade. This former paratrooper epitomises much of the problem France faces at the end of the twentieth century. Seventy per cent of the French recognise him as a danger to democracy, but the nation cannot shake itself free of his influence. An opinion poll reported that approval for his ideas had jumped by 50 per cent in just two years to 28 per cent of those questioned, and that backing rose to one-third when it came to immigration and law and order. In the end, it was internal bickering, not electoral rejection, that threatened the position of his National Front movement as France's fourth most popular party.

Mainstream politicians have been unable to deal with the phenomenon. Some thought that when the left lost power in the mid-1990s, the Front would wither. But nearly half those polled in 1996 felt that its influence had grown in the year since the election of Jacques Chirac to the presidency. And nearly half of those who classed themselves as belonging to the right expressed support for Le Pen's policies.

Finding it impossible to accept that the Front has a place in late-twentieth-century France, apostles of political correctness would wish it away, like children hiding their heads beneath the pillow until the wicked witch flies out of the window. After the Front won control of three big towns in municipal elections in 1995, and a former member had been installed as mayor of the nation's fifth biggest city, the political editor of *Le Monde* declared that the party only prospered in conditions of backstairs intrigues and was rejected whenever the full light of day was shone upon it. Others played with words. For years, many French commentators preferred to call the Front a movement rather than grace it with recognition as a political party. Some of its opponents simply count the days until Le Pen quits the scene, believing that the Front will wither after he goes. A leading Socialist put forward a simple solution – ban the Front. The idea that the only way of stopping the rise of a perfectly legal political group was to declare it illegal speaks volumes about the fear it arouses.

Jean-Marie Le Pen feeds off such reactions. He is incorrigible, the eternal bad boy who claims to be telling home truths and could not give a damn what anybody thinks. When he sets off a storm by declaring that he believes the races are unequal, he quickly adds that he is only saying in public what most French people think in private. When he inveighs against the corruption and self-interest of the political class, he tills fertile soil after the tide of scandals that has swept the country. The slogan on the wrappers on the bars of soap placed on each chair at his presidential rallies in 1995 went straight to the point: 'Head up high and hands clean: Le Pen the great washer.' No matter that most of his personal fortune was inherited from an eccentric alcoholic and psychiatric patient who died of liver failure at the age of forty-two. Though the Front ran into trouble over election financing in a couple of constituencies in the south, its mainstream opponents have provided it with more than ample ammunition for outbursts of righteous indignation, and enabled Le Pen to deflect questions about the doubtful past of some of his followers by declaring that his party welcomes Vichy collaborators and Resistance fighters alike, so long as they have not been corrupt.

His position is further strengthened by the evident appeal that part of the Front's rhetoric has for some orthodox conservatives, especially when they face a strong electoral challenge from extremists. A conservative deputy from a southern constituency where Le Pen won a third of the vote in 1995 proposed banning immigrants from his department. A Gaullist member of parliament from the Paris suburbs called for mayors to be allowed to refuse municipal housing to foreigners. Another spoke of an invasion by 'ten million Muslims'.

The repeated proposals on immigration from governments and parliamentarians which are clearly designed to meet the grass-roots pressure they feel is being whipped up by the National Front only serve to reinforce the party's perceived influence. Sometimes such measures stick; sometimes they are dropped in the face of protests from those who fear France is slipping on to a racist path. During the period of *cohabitation* between the Socialists and the right in 1993–95, harsh immigration legislation was introduced by the tough Interior Minister, Charles Pasqua. Three years later, a parliamentary committee brought forward an even more draconian set of regulations against immigrants without valid papers, suggesting that they be deprived of health care, that they could be detained for questioning for forty-five days pending deportation, and that people who had put them up should be listed by the police. The government stepped back from such steps, but the legislators felt they were reflecting what their native-born voters wanted. Alain Juppé's government introduced legislation requiring non-Europeans to hand in a 'departure tab' when they leave France, to ensure that they do not overstay their welcome – a more severe measure requiring their French hosts to report to the authorities when visitors left was abandoned after protests led by artists and intellectuals. One of the early acts of the new Socialist government was to commission a report on immigration which, tellingly, left many of the measures introduced by its predecessors in place.

There is no doubt that public attitudes are shifting, with the Front both propelling the movement and profiting from it. By legitimising the fear and resentment aroused by dark-skinned youths on street corners or late-night Métro platforms, the upstanding members of the National Assembly's committee of inquiry bestowed a fresh lick of respectability on Jean-Marie Le Pen. They also handed him a major argument. Why be satisfied with their half-measures when the real medicine was waiting in his cabinet?

It is not that the Front's rhetoric is confined to immigration. The party makes much of the need for stronger law-and-order measures often, naturally, in conjunction with references to the criminality of immigrants. Le Pen blasts Socialism as 'political AIDS'. He flies to Moscow to express his support for Russia's most extreme nationalists, to Belgrade to meet Serbian ethnic-cleansers, and to the Slovak Republic at the invitation of the far-right party there. He lambasts mainstream politicians as a bunch of like-minded Social Democrats who have sold out the nation in the name of personal ambition. He woundingly described a former Head of State attempting a political comeback as being like a woman in her fifties trying to seduce young lovers. He earned himself a symbolic one-franc fine for producing a cut-out cardboard head of the Mayor of Strasbourg, one of his pet hates, on a plate at a rally in her city. He inveighs against a media plot which prevents the Front's message from reaching the people, and against lazy, left-wing teachers who pervert the minds of youth.

Le Pen invokes the era of France's empire, with particular reference to the way in which the nation was sold out by conniving politicians over Indochina and Algeria. One of the Front's candidates in the 1997 legislative election was a founder of the OAS terrorist group which was involved in an attempt to assassinate General de Gaulle. Le Pen once attacked France's national football team for containing too many immigrants, but even he could not find fault with the black and brown players who won the World Cup – instead he simply claimed double goal scorer Zizou Zidane as an example of an Arab who had learned to be a good Frenchman.

And then there is the matter of the foreign plot, and of the Jews. As a Gaullist deputy, Patrick Devedjian, remarks tartly: 'There is a general consensus that our problems always spring from elsewhere – Europe, the United States, foreigners, globalisation.' That consensus is made for Le Pen, who constantly warns that *la patrie* is the target of a foul international conspiracy. He fulminates about foreign finance, international organisations and, above all, 'cosmopolitans'.

Between the wars, this was a far-right codeword for Jews. The term dropped out of currency after the Liberation, but has come back with a vengeance fifty years later. Not that such code is always necessary. Le Pen can be quite open about identifying the 'risk' international Jewry represents for France. This might be put down as yet another one-dimensional piece of hatred were it not given awful resonance by what happened in France between 1940 and 1944, and by the nation's reluctance to come to terms with this shameful episode of its modern history. How any politician can flirt with the ignominy of that time and get 15 per cent of the national vote raises another question which, until recently, France preferred not to address.

The plaque at the Gare d'Austerlitz in Paris is unobtrusive, set along a wall from a souvenir shop, a car rental office and a left-luggage office. Few of the train passengers hurrying by give even a glance to the only memorial to more than 11,000 Jews deported by French police from the station during the Nazi Occupation. The plaque was not put up by a post-war government or by the city authorities to atone for France's role in the deaths of so many innocents. It was placed there many years later by a Jewish students' association.

There is a phrase that some people like to bandy around when people talk about what happened in France between 1940 and 1944 – 'the right to forget'. It is a phrase which applies to many who would never vote for Le Pen, but who would prefer not to remember the Nazi Occupation – in particular the deportations of tens of thousands of Jews to their deaths from French soil. There is a good reason for this.

In the northern Paris suburb of Drancy, a drab housing estate was used as the main transit camp to which Jews were taken before being sent to their deaths in Eastern Europe. There were twenty water taps for up to 5,000 inmates. Many slept on the concrete floors. Meals sometimes consisted of bowls of warm water, with a daily ration of two lumps of sugar. The deportations started in March 1942 and speeded up to three convoys a week that summer. On arrival at the camp, mothers and children were forcibly separated. Some of the mothers went mad with despair, and some threw themselves to their deaths from the tops of buildings. A witness told of seeing one convoy which consisted entirely of children.

Today, an inscription on a marble plaque at Drancy reads:

IN THIS PLACE
which was a concentration camp
from 1941 to 1944
100,000 men, women and children
of Jewish religion or descendence
were interned by the Hitlerian occupiers
then
deported to Nazi extermination camps
where the immense majority
met their deaths

There is a nagging problem in those words 'interned by the Hitlerian occupiers'. True, Drancy came under the overall command of the SS officer who supervised all Jewish affairs in France. But for most of its existence as a transit camp for Auschwitz, only a few of its staff were German. The day-by-day running of the camp was the responsibility of the Paris police, following a decree signed by the Head of State of occupied France. French officers framed the rules governing the camp. For two years, all the guards were French. The files for the 2,000 children who passed through the camp were drawn up by French bureaucrats. Even after SS men moved in at Drancy during the summer of 1943, many local police remained. French gendarmes loaded Jews into the wagons on the 'sheep platform' at the nearby station. The French remained responsible for them until the trains crossed the frontier in the East, and the guards showed no compunction for those who passed through their hands.

Consider the case of a woman known to history as 'Mlle B.', who arrived at Drancy on 20 June 1944. She was twenty-two years old. The French police told her to bring her valuables with her when they arrested her. On arrival, the camp staff noted her possessions in their ledger – three gold bracelets, diamond rings, a strand of pearls, two watches, two diamond brooches, stock certificates, bonds, cash and a collection of seventy-five English books. Mlle B. died in Birkenau concentration camp on 27 January 1945. By then, her jewels had been stolen by the French staff at Drancy, and her stocks and bonds had been lodged with the French state in the official Caisse des Dépôts et Consignations.

Such matters were not mentioned in official memorials even half a century later. How could they be? The mythology of the Liberation needed to believe that, with a few wild exceptions, the French people had been anti-German during the Occupation. To say anything else until fairly recently was close to treason.

France has its tiny group of obdurate Second World War revisionists. A handful of would-be historians insist that the Holocaust never took place. A magazine editor was fined 30,000 francs for publishing articles denying that the only concentration camp on French territory, at Struthof in Alsace, was used to kill Jews. Putting aside such people, what is still striking, given the tragedy that gripped the nation between 1940 and 1944, is the proportions which more innocent insensitivity can reach. It took a storm of last-minute protests to get France's synchronised-swimming team to drop a water ballet based on the concentration camps from its programme for the Atlanta Olympics. In 1996, a physics teacher in a town outside Paris gave her teenage pupils a test to calculate the volume of carbon gas required to kill Jews in a death chamber: when a scandal broke, she said she was trying to show the children the evils of the Holocaust. The following year, a maths teacher in Normandy set a problem involving counting the number of people killed in the Dachau concentration camp. At around the same time, it emerged that millions of dollars' worth of jewels, gold, stocks, bonds and cash confiscated from Jews like Mlle B. had ended up in a state-run financial institution. The newspaper *Libération* found that banks had still been selling plundered Jewish stocks two weeks after the Allied invasion of 1944. *Le Monde* reported that French banks had held on to the contents of Jewish accounts now worth a billion francs which had been blocked on Nazi orders, while nearly 2,000 works of art stolen from Jews during the Second World War were still housed in national museums, most of them in the Louvre.

For decades, what had happened to the Jews during the Occupation was swept under the carpet. The concentration-camp survivor and future minister, Simone Veil, recalls how wounded she was by the way in which nobody wanted to know what had happened to those who survived and returned to France in 1945: 'Resistance fighters who came back from imprisonment in Germany were, quite legitimately, honoured, while Jewish deportees had the feeling of being rejected, that their return bothered people.' In the immediate post-war years, mention of anti-Semitism was virtually taboo – the historian Léon Poliakov had to wait until 1951 before publishing the first of his seminal works on the subject. Police archives were among official papers that were sealed for sixty years. The state television service sat on a groundbreaking documentary, *Le Chagrin et la Pitié*, that showed the extent of collaboration, and it took an American historian, Robert Paxton, to reveal how Vichy had done the Nazis' job for them. When the leading French historian of the Holocaust, Serge Klarsfeld, calculated that some 80,000 Jews had been deported from France, he was met with a mixture of indignation and disbelief. The feeling was that the French could not have participated in such an atrocity, and, if it turned out that they had, the less said the better. So Klarsfeld produced the names and birthplaces of 75,721 of the dead.

Symbolic of the ambivalence of the past half-century towards this substantial period of history were the stories of the only two Frenchmen to have been convicted of crimes against humanity for their wartime activities. Brought up in an extreme right-wing Catholic family, where it was taken for granted that twentieth-century Jews bore the responsibility for the death of Christ, Paul Touvier became head of the wartime collaborationist militia, the Milice, in Lyon. He may have been primarily a leg-man for Klaus Barbie, the Gestapo chief in the region, but he also undertook some freelance activities – kidnapping and killing an elderly Jewish couple; flinging grenades at Jews as they left a synagogue; murdering seven Jews on Nazi orders in retaliation for the Resistance's killing of a Vichy official (the eighth of his captives was allowed to escape because he was gentile).

So far, so bad. But the Touvier story becomes more than the story of an evil man making the most of his wartime opportunities because of what happened to him after the Nazis were driven from France. Summary execution as the Allied tanks rolled into Lyon? Arrest, trial and sentencing? None of it. By the time Touvier was sentenced to death *in absentia*, he had disappeared into the inner sanctums of a Catholic order which hid him from his pursuers. In 1947, Touvier ventured out, and was arrested – for armed robbery. He escaped before being tried, and went back into his high church refuge. Twenty years later the statute of limitations expired, and Touvier was able to move about more easily, portrayed by his supporters as an old man who deserved charity. In 1971, the President of the Republic granted him a pardon, declaring that 'the time has come to throw a veil over the period when the French people were caught up in hatred, civil strife and even murder'. As more evidence surfaced of Touvier's crimes, he fled back to his Catholic friends, but pressure rose to deal with him. In 1989, he was finally arrested at a Benedictine priory in the south-east, echoing Édith Piaf to tell the police: '*Je ne regrette rien.*' He was duly sentenced and died in a Paris prison in 1996, after going through a civil wedding to a woman he had married in church while in hiding half a century earlier. A Gaullist member of parliament raised eyebrows by attending his funeral.

The trial of Touvier was the trial of the Milice, of the Frenchmen who had actively co-operated in the attempt to liquidate democracy, Gaullists and Jews for ever. The trial of Barbie, in 1987, had been the trial of the Nazi occupiers. Ten years later, after interminable delays, the third aspect of the Occupation years finally came to court, and it raised questions which reached beyond those evoked by Touvier or Barbie.

From 1942 to 1944, Maurice Papon had been a senior civil servant at the regional prefecture in Bordeaux. Later, he became chief of the Paris police under De Gaulle and a Cabinet minister under Giscard d'Estaing. For six months through the winter and spring of 1997–98, at the age of eighty-seven, he sat behind a protective screen in a courtroom in Bordeaux accused of complicity in the deportation to Drancy of more than 1,500 Jews, including 200 children, in his official functions between 1942 and 1944. As a stream of witnesses, some even older than him, told how relatives had been rounded up and sent to their deaths, Papon remained unrepentant, insisting that he had tried to save Jews and portraying himself as a scapegoat for a nation's guilt. His arrogance was astounding: in the apt description of Robert Graham of the *Financial Times*, he exuded 'the irritation of a self-important man interrupting a weekend in the country to attend an unwelcome business meeting'. Still, his cause was bolstered by the rambling proceedings with 764 separate charges, and by the counter-productive histrionics of a showy young lawyer representing the families of the dead. But, little by little, the truth emerged. Appropriately for the trial of a consummate bureaucrat like Papon, it was often the documents which delivered the most chilling evidence: when a round-up at a hospital ran into problems because one victim was too ill to move, a handwritten annotation on the order simply instructed: 'Must be dragged'.

On 2 April 1998, after deliberating for eighteen hours through the night, the jury found Maurice Papon guilty. The old man in the dock cupped his ear to hear the verdict better, and then covered his face with his hands. He looked totally alone: his wife of sixty-six years had died a few days earlier – Papon blamed her death on the prosecution. The sentence was ten years' imprisonment and payment of 4.6 million francs in damages and costs. Naturally, Papon appealed. Given his age, nobody expected him to spend any time in jail. The defence denounced the verdict as 'neither fish nor fowl' and Robert Paxton judged that, though the French had expected a black or white outcome, 'they've gotten shades of grey'. Instead of a racist monster, France had put a pedantic old civil servant in the dock. Clearly, Papon had done grievous wrong, and deserved punishment. But when he turned on his accusers to remind them of the time 'when we had bayonets in our backs', many people might reflect on how easy it was to be courageous fifty years on and wonder what they would have done in Papon's place.

The litany of revelations in the media that accompanied the trial was such that there seemed a danger of swinging from the old Gaullist fiction that all the French had been resistants to the belief that they had all collaborated with the Nazis. There were apologies from the Catholic Church and from associations of lawyers, the police and doctors for the discrimination against Jews by their professions between 1940 and 1944. A plan to put a portrait of the inventors of the cinema on the last 100-franc note was scuppered when it was pointed out that the Lumière brothers had sympathised with Vichy.

Despite all that had been written on the Occupation, an opinion poll carried out during the trial showed that 42 per cent of people still regarded Vichy as a period like any other in the nation's history. This was not, in fact, so surprising. Had not the towering figure of Charles de Gaulle declared the Vichy episode to be null and void? Some prominent wartime officials, including one who would become the General's Foreign Minister and Prime Minister, had pursued zigzag wartime careers. Having been among the 569 deputies who voted power to Pétain in 1940 (with only 80 voting against) did not stop René Coty becoming President of the Fourth Republic in 1954. Successive Presidents sent wreaths to the tomb of Marshal Pétain on the anniversary of his death, as though his leadership in the First World War blotted out his record as head of the Vichy collaborationist administration. France's first President of the left, François Mitterrand, insisted half a century later that the state bore no responsibility for what happened to the Jews in France during the war. 'If the French nation had been involved in the unfortunate Vichy undertaking, then an apology would be due,' he said. 'But the French nation was never involved in that matter; nor was the French Republic.' It was not until 1995 that his successor acknowledged the debt that could never be repaid. Had the French been, in the title of a history of the period, *40 Millions de Pétainistes*, or was it simply, as Papon himself put it, that 'history is a fluid matter, and difficult to apprehend'?

But what happened to tens of thousands of people during the Occupation was, in reality, all too easy to understand. Take, for instance, the story of Sarah Yalibez. She grew up in the Marais district of Paris, a strange mixture of streets from the Middle Ages, pre-Revolutionary mansions and the place where the Jews from Central Europe settled. For Sarah Yalibez, it was the *pletzl* – the village square. Her parents had arrived there in 1922 from Poland. Her father ran an antiques shop. Twenty years later, under the Occupation, the Marais was classified as Zone 16. Marshal Pétain planned to raze it to the ground and build a new district for his senior bureaucrats. Jews were banned from owning property there. Sarah's father joined the Resistance, and was caught in 1944. He was deported to Auschwitz with his three sons. All died there. Two of the sons were teenager twins; they died in the wing where medical experiments were conducted at the camp. Sarah was also deported, but she survived. And she campaigned for fifty years to get a memorial put up to her father. 'I wrote to presidents, prime ministers, prefects and all the mayors of Paris. And I just kept doing it, even though no one replied.' Then, in 1995, she attended a ceremony at the memorial to the Unknown Jewish Martyr in Paris. Jacques Chirac was also there. 'I decided to stare at him,' she recalled. 'He asked what was wrong.' She told him. A couple of months later Chirac became the first President to admit the 'inescapable guilt' of the leaders of Vichy France. More personally, Sarah received an official letter which authorised her to put up a memorial plaque to her father and brothers. She has fastened it to the wall in the garden of her father's old antiques shop in the Marais. It says: 'Here lived Mr Elias Zajdner, who died for France at the age of 41. A resistance fighter, he was deported to Auschwitz by the Nazis in May 1944 with his three sons, Albert aged 21, and Salomon and Bernard aged 15 who died in the experiments wing. We shall never forget.'

In the chronicles of the persecution of the Jews in France, no event stirs more shame than the great round-up of 12,884 men, women and children on 16 July 1942. Some 4,000 of the children and 3,000 adults were held in stifling summer heat under the glass roof of a Paris cycling stadium, the Vélodrome d'Hiver, generally known as the Vél d'Hiv, which gave the round-up its name for posterity. On that day, a French gentile from western France who was on holiday in Paris happened to go to pay a visit to the parents of a Jewish friend called Jacques at their home in the north of Paris. That night, Roger Galéron wrote in his diary:

Go to the home of Jacques' parents, 38 rue Arthur-Rozier. Nobody there. Go opposite, 2B passage des Annelets, second floor. Knock at the door for five to ten minutes. No reply. However, I hear the sound of gas. Go up to the third floor. The neighbour questions me, and then takes me into the Schpeisers' place.

I had realised that they dared not open the door because of the round-ups going on since morning. Plain-clothes police inspectors arrive, give the unfortunates half an hour to put together their little bundles of possessions, and then cram them into a bus. Their destination? Forced labour in Germany or a concentration camp.

I will long remember the little drama that played itself out in front of me. Monsieur and Madame Schpeiser are there, with their daughter Fanny and the two little ones: a boy of nine and a girl of four – both very good-looking. They gave me tea and delicious cakes cooked by Madame Schpeiser. I had trouble eating. Fanny and her mother were crying.

Five times, there were knocks at the door. Minutes of anxiety. We had to keep quiet. The police? A friend? They checked, looking through the half-closed shutters, when the unknown person left. A stroke of luck in their unhappiness – the neighbour living below is humane and helps them as much as possible. For fear of being caught, they do not dare go outside, even to get milk for the little ones. Can this really be happening in our century and in France, blessed land of free spirits?

In any case, the reprobation is general, even among a number of anti-Semites. Children of a certain age are separated from their parents. Jacques' sister, Sarah, and her son of 11 were taken this morning. Only Fanny knows. Happily, Jacques is not aware of this drama.

I leave after embracing them and wishing them the strength to put up with their trials which, it must be hoped, will be halted one day by the victory of reason and humanity. The poor folk are convinced that they are victims of a new inquisition and that the extermination of the Jewish race is being planned. Fanny talks about suicide by gas. Facing this extreme ill fortune, I feel shameful, I who can move about freely and without fear.

I leave, upset, my heart full of sadness and bitterness. In the street, a new warning (Bekanntmachung). Any person who harms the German army will be shot, as well as his brothers, brothers-in-law, cousins etc. (all the male members of the family over 17 or 18 years of age). I have to read it twice to believe it.

There were many instances of French people saving Jews at the risk of their lives. More Jews survived the Occupation than died. Luck could play its part; one concierge might keep quiet while another tipped off the police or the Germans in the hope of stealing the family silver as the Jews were led away. The deputy Director of France's Institute of International Relations tells how his mother was taken into hiding in a convent in the south-west on the very day that his father, who had been decorated with the military cross in 1940, was arrested by the Germans after having been denounced as a Jew by a Frenchman. A boy cousin of the family whom Roger Galéron visited was picked out of the line at Auschwitz because he was carrying his violin, and musicians were needed for a camp orchestra: he died four decades later as a featured soloist in Hawaii.

The tragedy was all the greater because many of the adults who were deported to their deaths had fled to France from Central and Eastern Europe in the 1920s and 1930s; some had been specifically encouraged to come west to help make up for France's population losses during and after the First World War. There is no doubt that they aroused the kind of racial prejudice which new immigrants often suffer, with their foreign ways, their difficulty in speaking French and their clannishness born from generations of persecution. But they shared a general feeling of trust in the Republic, and could be re-assured by the knowledge that many of their children were French citizens by dint of having been born on French soil. But, in the great 1942 round-up in Paris, it was French police who took thousands of those same children from their parents and sent them off in cattle trucks to die alone in the east.

Some of those involved in such oppression complained about the job they were given to do, and they may have exercised their duty with less than full rigour. As one eyewitness of the raids in Paris noted of the French police, 'some did not push it; others kicked down the doors'. A few families were tipped off by friends at police headquarters. But there was only a handful of resignations in the Paris police: at a similar round-up in Lyon, a local commander did refuse to let his forces be used to round up Jews, and was obliged to retire by his French superiors, not by the Nazis. At war-crimes trials, Germans noted that the whole of the French police were at their disposal. The occupying forces drew up the plans; as loyal lackeys, the French executed them virtually without question. 'The French police have so far carried out a task worthy of praise,' a German security chief advised his masters one week after the Vél d'Hiv round-up.

Sometimes, indeed, the Pétain administration in Vichy went further than the Germans demanded. Even veterans who had been decorated in the First World War fighting for France were not spared. The French produced a definition of Jewishness which was wider than the one the Nazis proposed, and it was the Vichy Prime Minister, Pierre Laval, who decided that children should be deported with adults. If he could not quite deliver Jews like goods in a shop, he declared, he would do his best.

Tens of thousands of Parisians visited an anti-Jewish exhibition which equalled anything staged in Germany. Frenchmen who signed up with the collaborationist militia, the Milice, swore to fight against Jewish leprosy as well as combating democracy and Gaullist insurrection. Associations of lawyers and doctors purged Jewish members. French people took 100 francs from the Germans for each Jew they denounced. Bishops and priests kept their silence when not actively celebrating the values of Vichy. Members of the French SS division 'Charlemagne' were among the last defenders of the Reichstag before the Russians took Berlin.

Though historians have found that bureaucrats who resigned rather than carry out German orders were not punished by the occupiers, many officials preferred to fall under what the historian Marc-Olivier Baruch has dubbed 'the anaesthesia of the conscience of civil servants'. Jewish goods and assets were painstakingly listed. At the Prefecture of Police in Paris, an archive of 600,000 record cards was put together, listing Jews by name, nationality, address and profession. There were censuses of Jewish ex-servicemen, of Jews who owned wireless sets, of Jews with bicycles. In 1942, a Prefect in Normandy forbade Jews to travel more than five kilometres from their home, and the Vichy regime then banned them from leaving their commune of residence. In Bordeaux, the prefecture paid a taxi firm 350 francs to drive two Jewish girls to a railway yard to make sure they did not miss the train to Drancy. Even after the Allied landings in Normandy in 1944, some Prefects were drawing up new lists of Jews in their areas, and one official was planning a ration card which would enable him to keep track of where Jews shopped.

And as a *post scriptum* to the fate of tens of thousands who were deported to their deaths between 1940 and 1944, there was the simple observation from Sarah Yalibez as she told her story fifty years later: 'I never saw a single German uniform when they took us away.'

Humans forget. Life moves on. Two generations have passed since the
Occupation. And yet what is still striking about France is that a nation
with so much on its conscience should, in the 1990s, give a sixth of its
votes to a party on the wilder shores of racial extremism. Or perhaps
the two are linked more closely than proper-thinking French people
would like to believe.

Le Pen denies that he harbours anti-Semitic feelings, and tells you
that Jews vote for him. (Indeed, had he been of age during the Second
World War, the ex-paratrooper might well have led a Resistance
group of the patriotic right, putting aside that his father had died
when his trawler hit an English mine in 1942; of De Gaulle, he
observed simply but woundingly that it was easier to resist in London
than in Paris.) Still, by its nature, part of the appeal of the National
Front harks back to the collaboration of the Second World War. The
forces of order which did their duty at Drancy, the militiamen who
worked with Touvier, the ordinary people who thought that natu-
ralised Jewish immigrants were not 'true' Frenchmen – the
descendants of such people and the attitudes they held are major
sources of support for Le Pen's party.

France has the largest Jewish community in Western Europe, but
this does not make relationships as easy as they should be. Anti-
Semitism has a long and often virulent history here, and still crops up
in casual conversation in a way that would be rare in England or
America. In the 1970s, my son was once warned by a hotel-owner in
deepest France that he should not admit to being half-Jewish for fear
of what might befall him. A Jewish dentist who has practised in the
west of France for many years still does not mention his race for fear
of losing patients. Brown and black immigrants are the main target for
the far right today, but Jews represent a more deeply-rooted source of
fear and loathing which draws on old wells of hatred stretching
through the 'better Hitler than Blum' motto of the 1930s and the
abuse of the great Jewish politician Pierre Mendès-France when he
led decolonisation in the 1950s to the demonology of nineteenth-
century anti-Semitism and the Dreyfus Affair – apart from the
abominable treatment of the Captain himself, and the unbelievable
back-covering of the French establishment, there were anti-Semitic

riots in Bordeaux, Rennes, Saint-Malo, Grenoble and towns and cities from Alsace to the Mediterranean. While Lionel Jospin tried to put all the anti-Dreyfus blame on the right, and claim that the left was for the wronged man, the truth is that some prominent Socialists were initially all for condemning the Captain – the great tribune of the left, Jean Jaurès, even thought he should have been executed rather than being sent to Devil's Island, while a less illustrious Socialist deputy hailed a fist-fight on the matter in the National Assembly as being the beginning of revolution. The 1998 centenary of the publication of the most famous French headline – 'J'ACCUSE' – over Émile Zola's article on the Dreyfus affair showed how alive the issue of anti-Semitism is today. The President of the Republic declared that it was a reminder that 'forces of darkness, intolerance and injustice can penetrate the highest levels of the state'. Clearly, nearly a century after the rehabilitation of Dreyfus, there is still a question about the rights of the individual as against the *raison d'État* invoked to maintain his condemnation long after the forgeries on which it had been based had been exposed for what they were. But, in this context at least, it is not so much the top of the state that one should be worrying about. Rather, it is the defiling of the statue of Dreyfus in Paris with anti-Semitic slogans, or the way in which a descendant of the family still gets racist digs simply because of her family name.

Le Pen has repeatedly called the gas chambers 'a detail' in the history of the Second World War, a judgement which led to him being sentenced to fines and damages, and becoming the target of a judicial investigation by a German court at the end of 1998. He again hit the headlines with an awful pun in which he elided the last syllable of the name of a Jewish minister, Michel Durafour, which means 'oven' in French, with the word for a crematorium. On another occasion, he observed of Simone Veil that 'when I speak of genocide, I always say that, in any case, they missed old woman Veil'. Beside such remarks, he seemed almost benign when he dubbed France's best television interviewer 'a kosher butcher' or dismissed the Papon trial as being an example of 'Judeo-centrism' by which 'history must compulsorily order itself by events which affect the Jewish community'.

The Front once adopted a declared neo-Nazi as an election candidate. One of its representatives in the European Parliament referred to the 'invented' Holocaust. A Front figure in the south wore a swastika necklace and liked to sing Third Reich anthems. After one of Le Pen's long-standing companions-in-arms became mayor of the port city of Toulon, the authorities threatened to shut down the synagogue because its fire extinguishers were held to be below safety standards, and tried to stop Jewish students attending a Holocaust anniversary ceremony. A Jewish boy was suspended from a Toulon school for having punched another boy who praised the gas chambers, and a bookshop opened in the city centre specialising in works commemorating Nazi Germany. Another National Front mayor evoked an unfortunate historical echo when she told an interviewer from across the Rhine: 'You're German, so you must understand us.' Le Pen himself noted that 'big international groups, such as the Jewish International, play a not-negligible role in creating an anti-national spirit'.

The 'Israelite conspiracy' always lurks around the corner. After a Jewish cemetery at Carpentras in the south was profaned in 1990, the natural reaction was to view it as the act of members of the far right. Le Pen reacted angrily, seeing an attempt to smear him. Six years later, the perpetrators were finally identified as members of a neo-Nazi group, some of whose members had had links with the Front. Le Pen grew even more indignant, and insisted that it was nothing to do with his followers. And how did he phrase his counter-attack? It was, he insisted, all a matter of insinuations against him by 'Jewish extremists' like the former Education Minister, Jack Lang.

It might be argued that Le Pen had scented that anti-Semitism was a paying political proposition again, and was simply playing any evil tune that came his way. But his history argued for a longer approach. Take just one speech, made a decade earlier, on the campaign trail. One balmy night in Corsica, Le Pen had fallen to musing in the masterly way in which he feints and dodges around a subject like a champion boxer. His target was Simone Veil, France's most popular minister of the time. Veil later became the first Frenchwoman to be awarded an honorary British damehood as 'one of the great figures of France and of Europe'. Le Pen took a very different view. Wasn't it unfair, he wondered, that he came in for criticism every time he attacked her. 'If I'm not allowed to criticise her because she's a woman [pause], or because she's [another pause] ugly, or because she's [after a longer and more pregnant pause] a Jew, where's our freedom of speech?' he asked in mock indignation. Those words might stand as a monument to the baseness of the man. The audience laughed and clapped.

Or listen to another remark, made in 1982 when Le Pen's career was at a nadir. Sitting in the salon of his smart villa in Saint-Cloud outside Paris, I asked him if he had a dream of how he and his party could recover from a series of electoral humiliations. He stroked his chin with his index finger as he reflected. Imagine, he replied, a fight between a group of Frenchmen and Algerian immigrants in which 'one of our compatriots' was killed. Then imagine that Algerian immigrants stage a protest march down the Champs-Élysées. Things get out of hand. Shop windows are broken, stores looted and policemen injured. That, said Le Pen, would give him the fuel he needed for electoral ascent, even to as much as 10 per cent of the vote.

He grinned, downed a Chivas Regal and drove off to a fund-raising dinner. Saying goodbye to his first wife, who later sought to embarrass him by posing semi-nude for *Playboy* in a skimpy maid's pinafore, I wondered what inner resilience kept Le Pen going. In the 1981 presidential election, he had not even been able to muster the 500 signatures of local officials needed to qualify to run. Parliamentary and local polls were proving disastrous. Perhaps not surprisingly, the British newspaper for which I wrote up the interview spiked it on the grounds that Le Pen was a never-had-been who was not worth reporting.

A dozen years later, in the evening of 23 April 1995, the leader of the National Front was entertaining a small circle of friends and political associates in his white villa on a hill. At noon that day, he had been in ebullient form as he voted in the first round of the presidential election and then glad-handed his way around a café in the shadow of the Eiffel Tower. He pumped hands, gave bear-hugs, drank a quick coffee and stepped out into the sunshine flanked by watchful bodyguards.

Wherever Le Pen goes, there is an element of menace. It comes partly from his bruising presence; he is no stranger to fights and lost one eye in an electoral brawl on his way to becoming France's youngest member of parliament in the 1950s. There is also the inescapable feeling that if any French politician is an assassination target, it must be him. His staff say that he does not travel by train because he would require extra security protection. The skinheads patrolling the aisles at his meetings are tensed for trouble. His followers are regularly involved in election punch-ups. In 1995, they shot an immigrant dead in one incident; others threw a North African to his death off a Paris bridge during a Front rally. Even on this sunny spring day under the Eiffel Tower, there is something slightly sinister in the air as Le Pen steps into his car, black and with tinted windows. The two bodyguards look up and down the road and then get in with him. The car roars off through the narrow streets and jumps a red light. It is like a scene out of an Italian political thriller of the 1970s involving plots by financiers, neo-fascists and generals bent on setting up a new regime. And why not? The leader of France's National Front makes no bones about his desire to replace the system which Charles de Gaulle established in 1958.

As he drove to Saint-Cloud that Sunday lunchtime, Le Pen could look back on a fruitful decade. After the low point of 1981–82, his tenacity was rewarded. Austerity had nipped at the coat-tails of ordinary people, and the orthodox right descended into an unedifying fight between its rival chieftains. While the Communists lost ground, their working-class followers looked for another populist, anti-establishment movement to support. After the breakthrough by his followers in the Norman beach-head of Dreux, Le Pen took 11 per cent in a local election in a poor, melting-pot *arrondissement* in the north of Paris. Then, European Parliament elections provided an ideal ground for the Front's brand of bad-tempered revolt – the equivalent of a nationwide by-election at which a danger-free protest vote would not affect the way France was actually run. The party's score shot up to 11.2 per cent, and it got 8.8 per cent in the more responsible local elections in 1985. Then François Mitterrand handed Jean-Marie Le Pen a great gift. Seeking to save his Socialist Party from disaster, the President introduced proportional representation. As a man who put short-term tactics above any morality, he may also have wished to embarrass his opponents on the right by boosting the Front's chances.

The result was horrible for those who believe in France as a decent nation: the National Front won thirty-five seats in the National Assembly. Two and a half million men and women – nearly 10 per cent of those who cast a valid ballot – voted for Le Pen's party. As always, there were predictions that it was a flash in the pan. Indeed, some deputies elected under the Front's banner in 1986 did soon revert to the more orthodox formations from which they had come.

But at the 1988 presidential election, Le Pen, who had been unable to gather enough support to run seven years earlier, confounded the predictions once again to take 14.4 per cent. It was not long before the Front's imminent decline and fall was again forecast when new National Assembly elections held under the traditional constituency system cut its parliamentary representation to a single deputy. Those who greeted its impending eclipse might have noted that Le Pen's party still took nearly 10 per cent of the overall vote.

Once a primitive conspiratorial band of colonial die-hards and fascist sympathisers, the far right was developing into a real political party. Unlike the fascistic groups which sought to undermine the Third Republic in the 1930s, the Front was careful to stay within the law. A significant slice of its voters lived in areas where there were few immigrants and little crime. Its highest electoral scores might be won amid racial tension and high unemployment, but the Front has also been able to muster 16–17 per cent of the vote in the smart Parisian suburb of Neuilly and the even smarter 16th *arrondissement* of the capital. As a presidential candidate, Le Pen polled strongly in law-abiding regions of eastern France, where there are few Arab or African faces to be seen, as well as in his home region of Brittany, far from the crowded, crime-ridden urban housing estates. Fear of what might be around the corner was enough, particularly if it has a dark face. One of the Front's greatest coups has been to make law and order such an issue at a time when crime is actually falling. But this, after all, is a country where only 25 per cent of people questioned in a European poll said they would describe themselves as not at all racist.

Call it a movement or a party, the Front has a network of organisations to cater for young people, women, pensioners, ex-servicemen and farmers. There is a National Front union for prison officers and, in professional elections in the Paris police, it took 13 per cent of the vote: in six police units charged with preserving order in the capital, its score shot up to 48 per cent. The party holds well-attended summer teach-ins. It has a 'Blue, White and Red' festival on the outskirts of Paris each year, which reaches its climax with a rant from the leader (at one event, effigies of Chirac and Juppé were put up as targets at the shooting gallery). Two ÉNA graduates run a network of think-tanks. The Front has the support of a clutch of magazines whose virulence is in inverse proportion to their limited circulations, and links with reactionary Catholics: Le Pen heads an annual march on Joan of Arc Day. After the defeat of the orthodox right in 1997, he announced that he was constituting a shadow Cabinet capable of taking over the government of the country in a national emergency.

Preparing its future, the party trains its leaders of tomorrow in public speaking and handling the media as well as in the finer points of the ideology of extremism. At the first round of the 1995 presidential election, the Front won 18 per cent support among voters aged under twenty-five. For young people in search of a cause, the Front has its obvious attractions compared to more orthodox political movements, with its pugnacity, its nationalism, its anti-Americanism and its array of quick solutions to problems. The members of its youth wing are as one in defending France's soil and blood, and denouncing globalisation. Some joined the party for precise reasons: 'The day two Arabs harassed me, I decided to take a party card right away,' says one adolescent. Others see the Front as transcending orthodox politics in an echo of a wartime collaborationist slogan: 'Neither right nor left, but French!' They speak with veneration of their leader, and pose with him in front of a huge banner proclaiming 'Decontaminate the mind'. At the end of their course, the thirty best students get a trip to a meeting of Front leaders, held in a friendly town in the south, where they can absorb the wisdom of their elders and betters on the path to a Sixth Republic.

The early news about voting in the first round of the election on the night of 23 April 1995 threw the National Front's boss into a foul temper. Ah, the paradoxes of politics. Le Pen never had his riot on the Champs-Élysées which he had once thought might get him 10 per cent at the polls. But thirteen years of patient work, of rhetorical excess and of unscrupulous exploitation of the nation's insecurities had served him even better. The eternal outsider of French politics had turned in a tremendous performance. With 15 per cent, he finished only three points behind the Gaullist Prime Minister and five behind the strong favourite, Jacques Chirac.

But there was a lead lining to his success. Another candidate of the far right, a viscount from western France with an earnest, gawky manner, had won 4.74 per cent. If Philippe de Villiers had heeded Le Pen's calls for him to withdraw, the Front leader reasoned that he might have scooped up 20 per cent of the vote to finish third, ahead of Prime Minister Édouard Balladur. That would have put him hard on Chirac's heels, able to dictate terms in return for support in the decisive second round against the Socialist candidate. The Gaullists would have been utterly embarrassed and deeply split over whether to make a deal with the National Front, allowing Le Pen to play the situation for all it was worth. That would have been his apotheosis, a vital step on the march towards bringing a new brand of politics to France. Whatever Le Pen's dreams, things probably couldn't have worked that way even if De Villiers had pulled out. Many of the Viscount's supporters were rural conservatives uncomfortable with the Front's populism. But the mere possibility that this political snake-oil salesman might have held the balance in deciding who became the next Head of State was enough to confirm the depths of France's problems.

The breakdown of the vote underlined what Le Pen had achieved. While some regions remained indifferent to his message, he took 23 per cent in Marseille, 27 per cent in Mulhouse and between 20 and 25 per cent in working-class suburbs around Lyon. The Mitterrand era had impoverished and disenchanted millions of workers from the traditional left, while the right had fumbled with the electoral prize which had fallen in its path. As creatures of the French establishment, both sides were too much a part of the system to profit from the social changes occurring far from their seats of power. To seize the day took an outsider whose appeal catered to the spreading disillusionment as old barriers came tumbling down. 'At last, we can say what we really think,' said a man leaving the rally in Toulouse, 'and at last we have somebody who says it for us.'

The flirtation is made all the easier by Le Pen's skill at playing on two strings at the same time: he appeals to base racism and fear, but remains the jovial chap at the bar who doesn't take himself too seriously, and so needn't be a source of revulsion. He scatters speeches with references to criticism of him, and then spreads out his arms and begs the audience to judge whether he is really the terrible fellow others make him out to be. His mastery at dodging and weaving was played out in prime-time for the whole nation, when a television comedian performed a sketch in which he impersonated Le Pen singing a number entitled 'Beat Up Blacks'. There was an outcry. To try to retrieve the situation, the television station showed Le Pen watching a recording of the programme, roaring with laughter at the depiction of himself. Once again, he came out the double winner. The image was clear: clever Paris newspapers might depict him as a stormtrooper bully-boy, but, really, he's one of us, a bloke who can take a joke against himself – but who still believes in beating up niggers. Whatever the original intention of the comedian (an ardent Chirac supporter), the net result was to have got the anti-black message peak viewing prominence. The comedian and the station boss were subsequently fined for provoking racial hatred. Jean-Marie Le Pen could grin all over his florid face. Chalk up another hit for the Front.

Did voters react with fear and loathing to the extremists' score in the presidential poll, or to televised satire? Not a bit of it. Editorialists might fulminate, but soon after Chirac moved into the Élysée, the Front won the mayor's office in the Mediterranean port city of Toulon and three southern towns. In the festival town of Orange, with its Roman amphitheatre, the National Front mayor talked of establishing electronic 'draw-bridges' to protect citizens from what he stigmatised as the increasingly medieval conditions outside. To shield them from subversive literature, one of his associates undertook a 'rebalancing' of books available in municipal libraries: in the interests of diversity, works of which the Front disapproved were removed and replaced with books on the international Jewish–Masonic conspiracy and Jewish finance. Distribution of anti-Front pamphlets in the street was prohibited for a while before the order was overturned in the courts. Politically undesirable civil servants were driven out. When a dance troupe of whom the mayor disapproved performed in a municipal building, the town council ordered those who wanted to attend to submit photocopies of their identity card with their address, their rent payment, plus documents showing they had paid local tax and two photographs. Critics spoke of ideological cleansing. 'Orange under the reign of hatred,' read a headline in Le Monde.

In another Front-run town in the south, the mayor marked Christmas by slashing spending on feeding the poor. Subsidies to pay for special food for Muslim and Jewish children were cancelled in the name of the lay Republic. In Toulon, where rivalries on the mainstream right gave the Front its first city of more than 100,000 inhabitants to run, the new mayor began in folksy mode, showing his concern for law and order by bringing back bicycle police patrols. Although the law prevented him from implementing the Front's policy of giving preference to native French people over immigrants in paying out social service benefits, Jean-Marie Le Chevalier boasted that he had refused all requests to allow immigrants to settle in Toulon. Hitting out on another front, he engaged in a running battle with an experimental dance theatre in the city which had been given the status of a national institution in 1987: Parisian left-wingers who denounced him for cultural barbarity conveniently ignored the way in which local tax-payers were contributing large subsidies to make up for its unpopularity at the box office. The Front was not fazed in the least by the outrage it aroused among intellectuals up north. On the contrary, this was just the kind of opposition which Le Pen and his followers had always relished. When a troupe of eminent film-makers, artists and writers took the train to Toulon to march in protest through the streets, the mayor's wife stood on a balcony at city hall blowing them mock kisses, with a glass of champagne in her hand.

It was in Toulon that a court sentenced the two rap singers from NTM to three months in jail for having performed their anti-police anthem at a local concert. As signs of anti-Semitism surfaced, Le Chevalier told reporters that support for the Front was rising among local police. Soon afterwards, he hit the national headlines by quashing a literary award at a local book fair to an author descended from Polish Jews, arguing that the writer, Marek Halter, 'has an internationalist vision whereas we are for family and nation'. As a result, all France's main publishers boycotted the occasion. Unabashed, the mayor set up the 'Fair of the Freedom of the Book' and denounced Halter's supporters for backing 'France's cultural Gulag'.

There is nothing the National Front likes more than to cast itself as the wronged outsider, the voice of truth outlawed by the leftist establishment, the target of an elite which is opening France's borders to a mongrel horde. The Halter affair gave it an ideal opportunity. In a masterly exposition of prejudice that switched in half a dozen sentences from Halter's Jewishness to the genetic threat of polygamous immigrants, the mayor put his case: 'I do not care that Mr Halter is

Jewish. Jews are rarely unemployed and they come broadly from the same cultural framework. But in France we risk being overwhelmed by an Islamic invasion from North Africa. In France, bigamy is against the law. Yet we are importing bigamous, or even polygamous, unemployed foreigners and their children. The risk is that our country, a product of its heritage and its combined genes, will be transformed.'

Such activity might shock, but, in some respects, it undoubtedly struck a popular chord. Concern about subsidising little-watched dance troupes or the protection of France's identity is not confined to the extremes of the right. The growing appeal of the Front received its ultimate recognition in elections when Socialists and the moderate right sunk their political differences to run a joint candidate as the only way of repelling the Front. That only seemed to prove Le Pen's argument that all politicians to the left of him were basically in league to retain their positions at any cost. Orthodox parties appeared more afraid of his followers than they were of one another. As one of the organisers of demonstrations against tougher immigration laws, film director Arnaud Desplechin, put it: 'The problem with this country is that all the politicians, left as well as right, have been spending their time trying to win over the 15 per cent who vote National Front; no one has been making laws for the 85 per cent who don't vote NF. The politicians keep claiming it is the people who are being Le Pen-ised, when it is in fact they who are Le Pen-ised.'

The 'republican front' was not always effective. At the beginning of 1997, the orthodox conservatives withdrew from an election in the southern town of Vitrolles to enable the incumbent Socialist mayor to wage a straight fight against the extreme right. The Front still took 52.5 per cent of the vote to bring another municipality under its control. The new mayor was the wife of Le Pen's lieutenant, Bruno Mégret, who had been ineligible to stand himself because of problems over his election spending, and was aiming to get to parliament from the nearby constituency of Marignane. On the day after the election, Bruno Mégret arrived to claim possession of the town hall. His wife had no bones about how she saw her place: a woman's role, she said during the campaign, was 'to bring up her children, run the house and support her husband'. Not that she was any shrinking violet when it came to her own views: soon after being elected she characterised immigrants as 'colonialists' and backed the notion of racial inequality – sentiments which earned her a fine and suspended prison sentence for racism, and which naturally provoked accusations from her husband that France was like a police state where judges decided what politicians were allowed to say.

As always, there were special factors at work in Vitrolles – Madame Mégret's opponent, as one visiting journalist put it, summed up much of what went wrong with the supposed Socialist revolution of the 1980s, with his 'blow-dried greying hair, the casually worn white designer scarf, the naming of unswept streets after leftist saints (Avenue Nelson Mandela, Place Olof Palme), and the multiple charges of embezzlement of municipal funds'. Vitrolles had both a large immigrant population and 19 per cent unemployment. It was just the place for Le Pen's men and women. And so commentators were, once again, able to write off the result as a flash in the pan. As in Toulon and Orange, the Front showed that it meant business: one of Madame Mégret's first decisions was to double the number of municipal police and to station them on immigrant housing estates. Nobody missed the significance of the move – unlike the national police in the town, the municipal force was directly responsible to her office. A popular cultural centre which featured rock and rap bands was closed down for encouraging what the new powers at the town hall called 'uncivic behaviour'. Avenue Salvador Allende was renamed after the National Front pioneer in Dreux, Jean-Pierre Stirbois, while Place Nelson Mandela became simply Place de Provence.

With the exception of the time François Mitterrand changed the rules, legislative elections have not been kind to the Front in terms of the number of seats it has won. For most of its recent history, it has been lucky to have a single representative in the National Assembly. That is the lot of parties which fall just below the threshold needed to win through the two-round, geographical constituency system in which the candidate who polls best at the second round takes the constituency. But there was no mistaking the Front's achievement at the Assembly election of 1997. Although it only ended up with one seat, won by the Mayor of Toulon – who was later barred from parliament for funding irregularities and whose wife was narrowly beaten in the subsequent by-election a year later – the party kept its 15 per cent slice of the vote. Not only was this an improvement over its 12.7 per cent score at the previous legislative election, but the Front showed that its

roots were spreading. There were the expected high scores on the
Mediterranean coast, but in the north, once a solid bedrock for the
left, it chalked up between 16 and 20 per cent in a string of constituencies, rising to 25 per cent in the town of Tourcoing, which we
visited in the last chapter. Seven of its ten candidates in the coal and
steel lands of the Moselle department in Lorraine topped 20 per cent.
The voters of Saint-Étienne, for decades a symbol of manufacturing
in the centre of France, gave the two Front candidates 23 per cent
backing. In Khaled Kelkal's town of Vaulx-en-Velin, the party's man
finished in second place, only 1,500 votes behind the Socialist.

The long-held belief that once Le Pen disappears from the scene
the Front will crumble into insignificance is contradicted by findings
that only one-fifth of Front supporters say they back the movement
just because of the personality of its chief, while nearly two-thirds
invoke their general agreement with the party's policies. If support for
the anti-immigrant message appears to have peaked, concern for law
and order and the defence of traditional values earn increasing backing. Above all, as Europe comes to be seen as a threat and the idea of
the all-embracing Republic loses its sanctity, the Front offers the
vision of the old nation-state secure within its borders, a homoge-
neous population and a settled social order which would protect
French greatness and the French people from the perils that surround
them. International capital, big-brother organisations, lobbies and
rootless cosmopolitans are all working, Le Pen warns, to 'destroy
nations by promoting supranational structures, doing away with frontiers, following anti-life policies, and massive immigration and
naturalisation'. The President of the Republic is their accomplice. He
is asking the French people to be a partner in national suicide, having
sold out to the Jews, to the Communists in China and to pro-
Europeans who were about to 'achieve the dream of Adolf Hitler'.

Clearly, in Le Pen's eyes, only one man can save the nation of Joan
of Arc from the multiple threats confronting it. That view, however,
is shared less and less in the Front's increasingly fractious ranks thanks
to the emergence of a slight, dark-haired challenger who has dared to
stand up to the movement's historic chieftain.

By definition, leading figures of the National Front see themselves
as exceptions to the rules of mainstream French politics. As he
approaches his fiftieth birthday in 1999, Bruno Mégret conforms to

another convention – the power of rejection in propelling ambitious young men towards political extremism. After graduating from the École Polytechnique and spending a year in California at Berkeley, where he is said to have smoked marijuana once, Mégret became a civil servant and a moving force in hard-right political discussion groups which put the accent on the preservation of the European way of life. By the time he was thirty, he was a member of the central committee of the RPR party. Self-contained and confident of his own intellectual powers, he sought to make a mark in the 1981 legislative elections by asking for an unwinnable constituency. He was granted his wish, running against the Socialist star, Michel Rocard, in his long-time fief west of Paris. In the first round of voting, Mégret took 26 per cent, forcing Rocard into a run-off ballot. At a time when the left was running rampant, the young man had scored an undoubted success. But the RPR apparatus rejected him as a loser. He might have been at one of the leading colleges, but it was not quite leading enough. His problem, Mégret later reflected, was that he was not an Énarque. That was why he had not been given due recognition for having grappled with Rocard. Although it took him five years to line up with the National Front, he had evidently already developed the persecution complex which any genuine extremist needs.

Quitting the RPR, Mégret set up a group of his own, and, in 1986, was elected to the National Assembly in alliance with Le Pen's party. Two years later, he ran the National Front's highly successful presidential campaign. In 1989, he became a member of the European Parliament and, then, piloted his wife to become Mayor of Vitrolles. By the beginning of 1998, he was the undoubted number two in the party – in the headline of *L'Express* magazine, quite simply 'a dangerous man'. The paradox is that, in such a personalised movement as the Front, the *dauphin* should be so different from the king.

One, a veteran of street battles in 1956, is visceral; the other, twenty-one years younger, is all calculation. One fires from the hip; the other is an ideological intellectual. One embarrasses even his own followers; the other is self-effacing. One lives for the day when he will march to power; the other promotes a gradualist strategy. One looks increasingly like a man of the past; the other appears as the face of the future which the unsettled right may not be able to resist. One, when all is said and done, is a hustler, an Elmer Gantry who found his snake oil in Algeria, Indochina and the failure of the political establishment since 1983. The other is something more worrying – a man who believes in racial supremacy and health checks for foreigners, in the biological and genetic separation of human beings and in dressing the police in Vitrolles in black commando uniforms.

As Mégret moved out of the shadows the relationship became ever more strained between the loming, bulky figure of Le Pen and his five-foot-something dauphin. In the spring of 1998, 10 per cent of those questioned in a poll for *Le Figaro* saw a future for the younger man as a political player, only three points behind the leader. While Le Pen grew increasingly violent and authoritarian, the younger man offered a new path, and the success of his entryism in regional politics emboldened him to mount an outright challenge at the end of the year.

The old bull was in a spot of legal trouble – his conviction for assault after attacking a Socialist woman politician meant he might be disbarred from leading the Front's list in the 1999 European elections. Logically enough, Mégret argued that, as number two in the party, he should step in. But Le Pen wanted to keep it in the family, proposing his wife for the job, though she was no politician. The row led to Le Pen expelling Mégret and his close aides from the party. The rebels promptly set up a faction of their own, called National Front-National Movement, at the beginning of 1999. The Front might be split in half, but its rhetoric remained as robust as ever. Thundering against a 'putsch' by 'perfidious lieutenants and quartermasters', Le Pen denounced Mégret as a racist and a small-time diva who dreamed of becoming a star, while the younger man's camp hit back with a picture of an egotistical absolute monarch 'drowning in messianic ridicule'. Parallels were drawn with Caesar and Brutus, except that Le Pen insisted he would stab first.

While the insults flew and the rival camps went to court over the party's emblem and the allocation of its funds, the mainstream right heaved a great sigh of relief as it spied the imminent break-up of the distinct bloc which the National Front electorate had become. In the 1988 and 1995 presidential elections, as many of its voters said they felt close to the traditional right as they did to the Front. Two years later, a big change had occurred: nearly 60 per cent of its supporters expressed their prime loyalty to the Front, and only 13 per cent said they felt close to the mainstream right. The way in which the party has put down local roots was underlined in regional elections in March 1998, when, while taking its usual 15 per cent of the vote nationally, it came first in Alsace and scored 27 per cent in the south-east. Even more significantly, the elections gave the Front the balance of power in more than half the regional assemblies, once again under-lying its position as the malign arbiter of French politics – and, as we shall see, provoking an implosion among orthodox non-Gaullist con-servatives split between those who were ready to sup with the devil and those who still regarded the Front as an anathema.

That made the split between Le Pen and Mégret manna from heaven for the Gaullists and the loose centre-right UDF coalition. The very public nature of the feud was an anathema to a movement which had always prided itself on its unity behind its chief. The prospect was that voters who had come to the Front during the pre-vious decade would drift back to their previous allegiances, or simply join the army of abstainers. Had the Front not split the right-wing vote so effectively in the 1997 legislative election, the left would prob-ably not have won. 'Hold on, we're coming,' the party's posters proclaimed as Le Pen boasted that 'between us and the socialo-com-munists, there is only a backwater which we have to dry out'. Now he was the one on the defensive. The Mégretists might lag behind the Le Penists among the party's rank-and-file, but the younger man had taken the Front's brightest minds with him – and, significantly, its boiler-suited security service. Worst of all, the man who had promised to wash away scandals in high places was now buffeted by references to him as a colossus with feet of clay who put his family's interests above those of his party.

The outlook for the RPR and the UDF – not to mention Chirac's reelection – was suddenly much brighter. It hardly seemed a coinci-dence, either, that the Socialist government talked more firmly of law and order and that Lionel Jospin stressed the importance of the nation; after all quite a few of the Front's voters had come from the old left. But the implosion of Le Pen's movement made it all too easy to ignore the lesson which he had brought with him in the previous fifteen years. The decline of his party as an electoral force would not mean that the problems on which it had fed had diminished. Unemployment, racial tension, crime and concern about the nation state in an era of globalisation were as real in 1999 as they had been when the Front won thirty-five parliamentary seats thirteen years earlier.

Extreme right-wing movements can draw on a long tradition, from reactionary royalists and anti-Dreyfusards through the fascist leagues of the 1930s, Vichy and the Milice, the Poujadist small shopkeepers of the Fourth Republic, and on to the OAS desperados of the last days of empire in Algeria. Le Pen's achievement was to have taken this inheritance and to have built a movement which was truly populist, and which stayed the course for so long. As the Socialists became a middle class, civil service establishment party and the Communists were pushed back to the fringe, the Front had taken up the banner of protest with gusto. Now that it was fading, there was an urgent need for mainstream politicians to step into the vacuum not just electorally but with real policies – or to risk an even more incoherent extremism emerging.

Many of those on the margins of society, or afraid of finding themselves there, had had enough of being lectured to by the proper-thinking left and had lost faith in the fractious, self-absorbed right. The prospect of playing truant from the real world with Le Pen was quite appealing when you saw unemployment rising and worried about your daughter walking home at night. Nearly half the Front's voters said they considered themselves to belong to the industrial or office-working class, well above the proportion among Socialist and Communist supporters. By 1998, it was calculated that almost one-third of French voters had cast a ballot for the Front at one time or another, and a poll showed that 48 per cent of those questioned said they felt close to the Front and its ideas. Tempting though it was to write off the party as a passing phase which had at last met its self-inflicted Valhalla, the reality is that Le Pen headed a vehicle for a deeper discontent. Shocking as that may be, it is really not so surprising given the way France's powers-that-be have provided so many reasons to join in the paranoia propagated by the man whose Airbus was late arriving in Toulouse.

9

'FOG OVER CHANNEL'

But what if Jean-Marie Le Pen has hit on a truth? Not in his overblown racist rhetoric, but in detecting deep reserves of Francophobia on this cosmopolitan planet. At first sight, such a proposition seems ridiculous, given the appeal France enjoys around the globe. But there is fuel enough for at least mild paranoia. At times, the world and France become caught in an irrational minuet of bad temper that brings out the worst on both sides. Take, as a prime example, the flare-up provoked by Jacques Chirac's decision to resume nuclear testing in 1995, an episode which tells much about France, its search for national glory and its vision of its place in the late-twentieth-century world – and the reaction which that provokes.

Nuclear weapons are special, and nowhere more so than in France. To a far greater degree than in Britain, possession of nuclear arms is a source of national pride. The nuclear force was closely associated with the revival of national prestige after Charles de Gaulle returned to save his country for the second time (though its development had, in fact, been decided under the Fourth Republic that preceded him). The name given to the nuclear arm is revealing. Elsewhere, governments speak of nuclear defence or deterrence as if these are weapons only to be used against offensive enemies. France, on the other hand, has a *force de frappe* – a means of hitting out. While other countries targeted their missiles at their opponents, the French reserved the right to point theirs anywhere they wished, and disdained any thought of graduated use of nuclear weapons in favour of an immediate, all-out big bang. In all this there is a strong historical strand. Defending his decision to resume testing, Jacques Chirac conjured up the country's lack of combativity in the face of Nazi Germany: 'You only have to look back at 1935. There were people then who were against France arming itself, and look what happened.'

Since Waterloo ended their most sweeping military expansion, the French have generally depended on outside help to bring wars to a satisfactory conclusion, and in the case of the two German wars of the twentieth century, to drive the invaders from their very soil. However great the heroism of the massed ranks of ordinary soldiers of the Flanders trenches and the Resistance fighters risking their lives against the Nazi occupiers, it was the force of American and British arms – plus the mighty pressure from the Eastern Front in the Second World War – which put France among the eventual victors. Counting on others is, however, not a palatable recipe for a nation which thinks as much of itself as France does.

So, as a supreme realist in the nuclear age, De Gaulle determined that France needed its own arms of mass destruction if it was to enjoy the independence in which he so ardently believed. When it came to the crunch, he reasoned, Washington would not actually get into a planet-destroying missile duel with Moscow to stop the Red Army crossing the Rhine. Would a government in Paris risk the nuclear ruin of Lyon to save Iowa? Of course not. So why should one expect Washington to go to war for Alsace? Had it done so in 1940? Had the British answered French pleas to send in more aircraft to stem the Nazi invasion? In the end, a nation had to look after itself, and the man who disposed of the ultimate weapon had always been a visceral nationalist; as a boy De Gaulle had always insisted on having the French troops when playing toy soldiers with his brothers. So the Gallic nuclear warriors had to be ready to fight on their own from submarines under the ocean or in bunkers and silos dug deep into some of the most beautiful scenery of south-eastern France. Who their missiles would hit they did not know. Their potential role in setting off Armageddon as Soviet troops rolled across Germany did not seem to faze them. When I visited two of the main units of the *force de frappe* in the 1980s, the men in uniform seemed entirely relaxed. On the flower-strewn Plateau d'Albion, there was a modest Côtes du Rhône to sample, and on a nuclear submarine in Brest, the commander told jokes about the British navy.

Nuclear disarmers might march in Britain; opponents of missile deployment might demonstrate in Germany. In France, to oppose the nuclear force is tantamount to denying greatness to the nation. 'There are subjects, among them national defence and deterrence, which should receive the united support of the French political class,' declared one of Chirac's foreign affairs advisers. Spending on the nuclear force rose under the left as well as under the right. Sitting in an elegant eighteenth-century ministerial salon behind the Boulevard Saint-Germain one morning during the Cold War era, I asked the official opposite me who was in France's nuclear sights. The Russians? Yes, of course, came the reply. And the Americans? He smirked and batted back a 'why not?' that was meant to amount to a confirmation. This was no rampant anti-American Docteur Folamour, but a highly intelligent and cultivated senior aide to a Socialist minister. 'Yes,' he said, 'France remains a good Western ally, but we have to be completely free when it comes to deciding how we use our military forces. Especially when this involves setting off . . .' – he paused, if only for effect because the phrase was clearly one he had massaged in his mind for some time – '. . . the nuclear orgasm.'

No matter that the policy has never made much sense or that the *force de frappe* has never been quite as powerful as the publicity would suggest. Embarrassingly, it was revealed in the 1980s that missiles housed in the east of the country could only reach as far as Frankfurt, and so could only be used to devastate the ally France was meant to protect. Still, Gaullists could swell with pride, generals could plan strategy and the Socialists could touch the forbidden fruit; it took François Mitterrand a decade to suspend testing, and then only after the world had moved on from the Cold War. As the man who had set out to reclaim General de Gaulle's heritage after a twenty-one-year gap, it was natural enough that Jacques Chirac should resume testing. The adrenaline rush was irresistible to a politician who has been spotted using a ball-point pen decorated in the national colours. So the blasts resumed at the bottom of a bore-hole below the South Seas atoll of Mururoa, and protest erupted around the world.

That summer was not an innocent time. Russian soldiers burned Chechens alive in their cellars, and reduced their capital to a second

Stalingrad. Serbs slaughtered Bosnians. Algerian fundamentalists murdered at will – and were massacred in turn. Mass killings continued in
Rwanda. Authoritarian regimes around the world went on jailing and
persecuting opponents. But there were very few demonstrations about
any of this. If international anger can only cope with one major issue
at a time, the target that year was clear.

Nobody was killed in Mururoa, no human rights were abused; of
the 2,038 nuclear tests conducted over the years, only 204 had been by
France, first in colonial Algeria and then in Polynesia. Nearly half had
been carried out under Mitterrand to scant international notice.
China let off a nuclear device of its own in 1995, and received only
passing criticism. When France did the same, it instantly became a
nation on which every shortcoming could be dumped and for which
no reproach was too trite.

There were unprecedented demonstrations throughout Asia and
the Pacific. In Polynesia, Tahiti airport was set on fire and squads of
riot police had to be flown in to handle the protests. Boycotts of
French goods sprouted, and business slumped at the Club Méditerranée holiday villages in the Pacific. Share prices of manufacturers of
French luxury goods wobbled amid worries about sales in the Far
East. Restaurants struck French dishes and wines from their menus. In
Bangkok's huge weekend market, a bar gave pride of place to a wine-
bottle labelled 'Château Nuke – Appellation Atomic Superieur
Contrôlée'; in Japan, a store invited customers to come in and smash
bottles of Beaujolais Nouveau. Visiting Bali, my French wife earned
some peace and quiet by pretending she was Swiss.

As if its nuclear arrogance was not enough, Paris was quickly
accused of being a latter-day colonialist. Its insistence that the
Mururoa test site was as French as the Côte d'Azur seemed ridiculous
to those who lived a lot closer to Polynesia than any French minister
ever had. Paris would not be swayed. France, one member of the government declared, is a Pacific nation and so can do what it likes there.
In an echo of the attitude that led France to blow up the environ-
mental boat *Rainbow Warrior* in New Zealand in 1985, one minister
called the test lagoon a private place – sailing in a protest vessel would
be 'like me walking into your bathroom'.

If the tests were so safe, critics asked, why not conduct them in an
isolated corner of metropolitan France? A Japanese minister suggested

the Massif Central mountain range. What also became evident was that, for all the rhetoric about the togetherness of being part of the worldwide French network, the authorities in Paris did not demonstrate quite the same concern for the well-being of the local population as it did for its Bretons or Burgundians. A report by the medical organisation Médecins Sans Frontières showed that, despite its relatively young and generally healthy population, French Polynesia had cancer rates 20 per cent above those in metropolitan France. Blood and bone-marrow cancers, which are associated with radioactivity, appeared high. The report broke new ground for one simple reason: the French authorities had never bothered to study the possible effects of the 137 tests carried out at Mururoa on the local population, or even on the 10,000 manual workers employed at the atoll. This seemed all too typical of what boiled down to a faraway administration presiding over a colonial economy where the gap between rich and poor widens by the year, as the locals go unemployed and civil servants count the 'hardship allowances' paid to them for the pain of living in Gauguin-land.

There was another problem which does not seem to have been taken into account in Paris. It showed blind arrogance, or arrogant blindness. French generals wanted to get the tests over before Paris signed up to a general test-ban treaty. Mitterrand had procrastinated, but the military made the most of Chirac's gung-ho attitude. That meant the first explosion came hard on the heels of celebrations of the fiftieth anniversary of the defeat of Japan in 1945, and that brought with it two historical echoes which would have been picked up in advance by a country better attuned to sensitivities on the other side of the world.

The end of Japan's imperial adventure could have led to the independence of large swathes of East Asia; in fact, it only turned the clock back to the return of European imperialism in Indonesia, Malaysia and Indochina. In France's main Asian colony of Vietnam, the Japanese defeat brought a brief flowering of independence. The military soon blasted that away, and thus set off an epochal anti-colonial military struggle that would kill 35,000 French troops and perhaps half a million Vietnamese over the following nine years. For a European power to carry out a nuclear test just at the moment when Asia was remembering what might have been in 1945 was particularly ill-timed. But that was not all, since 1995 also marked the fiftieth anniversary of the dropping of atom bombs on Hiroshima and Nagasaki, with all the commemorations of devastation which that brought.

But France remained unmoved, and the anger moved closer to home. After the second test, officials at the European Commission joined in the protest. The Nobel Committee awarded its peace prize to an anti-nuclear activist and urged France to think again. In Vienna, an artist flung 180 litres of pigs' blood at a giant canvas outside the French embassy. A Spaniard hijacked a French airliner in protest. The British naturalist Dr David Bellamy urged an assembly of travel agents to 'boycott everything French you possibly can'. An opinion poll showed that 85 per cent of the British opposed the testing, though the nuclear-tipped British government remained one of Chirac's few friends. Even the normally discreet Swiss rebuked France, while the Danish Prime Minister replaced the cognac with grappa, sambucca and metaxa at official dinners. Norway cancelled the dispatch of its traditional Christmas tree to Paris, and a delegation from the National Union of Santa Clauses demonstrated in full costume outside France's embassy in Oslo. A video game in Britain put Chirac up there with Saddam Hussein in a gallery of world villains. At an international awards ceremony in Paris, the Irish singer Bono denounced France's Head of State from the platform and called him a 'wanker'.

Nowhere was the anti-French mantra more virulent than in Australia. Schoolgirls in Adelaide came up with a new version of the 'Frère Jacques' nursery rhyme, which began: 'President Jacques, President Jacques, Vous êtes fou, Vous êtes fou.' An Australian mayor urged his fellow citizens to post stuffed cane toads to Paris; a senator wondered whether the French might be 'murdering their children, mincing them up and turning them into pet food'; and the press, never known for donning kid gloves, went into overdrive.

'Slaughter a horse. Torment a goose. Press a duck. Amputate a frog. If you burn something, add water and call it *jus*,' the *Bulletin* magazine advised readers who wanted to show their disapproval of the nuclear tests by boycotting French restaurants but who still fancied some cuisine at home. 'Remember that French etiquette obliges the French to leave the table to fart. It also requires them to fart in the faces of a distant table.' That led directly to an Australian newspaper's verdict:

'They pong. I'm serious. The French smell of those filthy cigarettes they smoke all day, Gitanes and Gauloises . . . Women. If French women are so gorgeous, how come French blokes keep leaving to join the French Foreign Legion? Cowardice. Remember Agincourt? England's Hundred Years' War with the French only lasted that long because the French army couldn't stop fleeing long enough to be destroyed. Cultural wankery. The line of French masturbators is too long to list here. But let's start: Marcel Marceau, Charles Aznavour, Plastique Bertrand, Michel Foucault . . .'

It would have been a waste of time to note that, as its name suggests, French nationals make up fewer than 50 per cent of the Foreign Legion, or to recall that France emerged as the eventual winner of the Hundred Years' War, or to point out that Plastique Bertrand is Belgian and Charles Aznavour of Armenian extraction. Australians were not to be put off by such niceties. Their prostitutes boycotted French sex equipment, and doubled charges for French clients. There were some snags in all this ire down under – a stripper in Canberra found that appearing as an Italian maid didn't get quite the same rise from her audience as portraying a French *soubrette*. Drinkers of Jacob's Creek had to order another bottle to make themselves forget that the wine firm was owned by Pernod Ricard of France. And, for all its sound and fury, Australia went on exporting 300 tons of uranium to France a year, with no guarantee that it was not being used in the explosive charges being tested at Mururoa.

The French reaction to all this was as inept as Chirac's timing. The Minister of Agriculture banned kiwi fruit from his home, and a Gaullist waved 'this unhappy little green fruit' in the National Assembly as he called on patriots to buy home-grown produce instead. The government threatened to sue a French newspaper for suggesting that the explosions might damage the surrounding atoll. Within a week, another newspaper printed a photograph showing a three-metre crack which it said ran for several kilometres in the coral. The gala opening of a James Bond film in Paris was cancelled because the star made his opposition to the tests known after visiting Polynesia. The President put off summit meetings with Italy and Belgium after they dared to vote at the UN against nuclear testing. When the Secretary-General of Nato resigned, Paris employed all its diplomatic firepower to block the appointment of a Danish successor because of Copenhagen's opposition to the Mururoa explosions. Ignoring international criticism, a parliamentary report concluded that 'by its determination, France appears as a strong country and this image is undeniably positive'. Two and a half years later, France ratified the international treaty banning all forms of nuclear weapons testing.

Occasionally, the diplomats got it right. The ambassador to Australia complained that the impression had been spread that France was just a criminal country run by a criminal President and inhabited by criminal people. As the Consul-General in Hong Kong said, criticism of the tests was one thing, but it was quite another matter when the French were attacked simply for being French. A member of the Dutch government wrote that France was 'really great, but what a pity it's full of French people'. It reminded one of the old joke: on the first day God created the coastline, on the second the mountains, on the third the rivers, on the fourth the fertile plains, on the fifth the vineyards and on the sixth the forests – and on the seventh day, He reflected that He had given too many good things to a single country, so he made up for it by creating the French. Just as Jean-Marie Le Pen gets quick laughs as he pretends to stumble over Arab names, so, around the world, a jab at the French is as simple as falling off a log.

No people is more critically concerned with the French than the British. The distrust that flows south across the Channel ranges from serious politicians who believe Paris is fundamentally untrustworthy in international dealings to popular commentators who know the easiest way to knock off a quick column or headline is to bash the Frogs. MI6 had no compunction about bugging the French ambassador's residence in London or stealing top-secret technology for tracking nuclear submarines from its Nato ally, but it is France which is always seen as devious and slippery. 'HOW MUCH DO YOU DISLIKE THE FRENCH?' asked a capitalised classified advertisement in *The Times* back in the 1980s. 'With a book in view, Arthur Marshall would welcome accounts of unfortunate experiences or anything else you have to say about our closest neighbours.' Eleven years later, a survey by the French polling organisation Sofres reported that only 35 per cent of the British had a 'largely favourable' view of the French, and 20 per cent expressed outright antipathy. Seven per cent saw honesty as a

French characteristic and just 4 per cent thought the French were brave. As the historian of the Channel Tunnel put it: 'The British propensity for wading rivers, and the French for seeking out bridges, has long been scrutinised.'

The clichés are set in stone. The French are rude, dirty, shifty and obsessed with sex, preferably outside marriage. Start with hygiene. 'The otherwise sophisticated French have long had a reputation for a certain blithe disregard for personal cleanliness,' *The Economist* observed in 1998, with figures to back up its claim. But later that year, an annual survey of social trends in France reported the astounding news that the French bought almost exactly the same amount of soap each year as the British, and showered or bathed more often. They also purchased more deodorants than any other people in Europe.

The Economist also managed to establish a link between cleanliness and sex by asking: 'Does the disappearance of the bidet, used by philanderers for at least 250 years, mean that the French nation is abandoning its passion for *l'amour*?' Apparently not in the case of a ski instructor who appeared in court in Britain after he touched a woman's bottom in the street and gave it all away when he confessed that, being French, he had 'slightly different standards so far as these things are concerned'. François Mitterrand's varied love-life was never much of a secret, but the French may have been more surprised when a magazine reacted to Monica Lewinsky's allegations about Bill Clinton by disclosing a string of other presidential affairs, linking Giscard d'Estaing with the soft-porn actress Sylvia Kristel, and Jacques Chirac with Claudia Cardinale and a Soviet air hostess – and attributing an illegitimate son to Georges Pompidou. There was no puritanical shock, however, and the French reaction to the White House scandal appeared best summed-up by a woman in the street who told an American news agency reporter: 'So what? It was only about sex.' Some might see that as an eminently sensible point of view, but it didn't stop the French media going to town on '*l'affaire Monica*'.

As for rudeness, the *Daily Telegraph* left its readers in no doubt with an eight-column headline proclaiming that 'BEING HOSTILE AND RUDE IS LIKE BOULES TO THE FRENCH'. The accompanying article quoted a Japanese psychiatrist in Paris as defining a condition among foreigners caused in part from 'an impression of persecution by the French'. Nagging, as a columnist in a Sunday newspaper put it, is the only time a French wife will deign to speak to her English husband in his native tongue. A contribution to a debate in the letters column of the *Independent* on how offensive the French were to foreigners brought forth the observation that, 'During the summer, large numbers of French students obtain jobs as waiters in restaurants, with the intention of cheating customers out of as much money as possible, while amusing themselves by being as rude as possible.'

The distribution of tickets for the 1998 World Cup goaded the *Star* to remind its readers of France's 'slimy ways' and to thunder: 'As we proved at Agincourt and Waterloo, a good kicking on their Gallic *derrières* is the only language the greedy frogs understand.' What do you call Frenchmen who have an IQ of 180, asked the *Sun*. Answer: A village. And why are there so many tree-lined streets in France? So that the German army can march in the shade. Oh yes, and what do you call a pretty girl in France? A tourist, of course. Or relish this observation from a star writer in the *Sunday Times*, using that mock-humour the English are so fond of when having a dig at other races: 'French women are the opposite of English ones. With us the mystery is all on the inside; with them, it's plastered all over the outside. What's inside is rather dull and spiteful. But, if you're into appearances, then a French woman is for you. And if you like to spend a long time in the bath, she'll be perfect. They rarely go near water.'

The writer John Mortimer finds French taxi-drivers the nastiest people in the world and the French difficult to get to know. As for the country they inhabit, 'Northern France is terribly boring and I think the south of France is one of the worst places in the world.' British tourists polled by the Paris Chamber of Commerce said they found the French hostile, aggressive and utterly disorganised. (Americans complained that they made no effort whatsoever to speak English – just try striking up a conversation in French in a New Jersey shopping mall.) When the Cotswold town of Stow-in-the-Wold rejected a proposal to twin itself with a town in the west of France, the local council chairman reflected that the inhabitants would rather have twinned with any other country – one suggested concreting up the Channel Tunnel, and an old soldier was wheeled in to say that the Germans had behaved better than the French when he fought there in 1944.

Margaret Thatcher never trusted the politicians in Paris; when the President tried to talk to her about cultural matters, she sensibly turned the conversation to the weather. As an admirer of Edmund Burke, she refused to join the celebrations of the 200th anniversary of the Revolution in 1989. The rulers of France, according to the commentator Paul Johnson, 'hate the British, and our freedom-loving ways, because they consider us, and our example, as an insidious threat to their grip on the French masses'. As the unscrupulous Prime Minister Francis Urquhart of the *House of Cards* series remarked of a colleague, in words of fiction that have the ring of fact, 'He just can't stand Frenchmen, and who can blame him for that?' Not that there was anything new in all this. For Sir Philip Sidney in Tudor times, France was 'that sweet enemy', while George III wandered around the grounds of Windsor Castle urging boys from Eton to hate the French.

Mrs Thatcher's adviser, Sir Charles Powell, has remarked on the way in which the British are far more obsessed with the French than vice-versa. He recounts the story of a young British diplomat seconded for a spell to the French Foreign Ministry. 'On her return to London, Foreign Office colleagues eagerly quizzed her as to where Britain figured in the master plan of French diplomacy. The answer was: nowhere. It seemed that the French simply did not spend time worrying about us.' The author Pierre Daninos produced a best-selling stereotypical Englishman, Major Marmaduke Thompson, but the portrait was affectionate satire at most. The French press can be roused to indignation by the way the English went on exporting animal feed suspected of causing BSE across the Channel long after its use was banned in Britain. In one outburst of press hostilities, a French writer described the slaughter of the French at the battle of Agincourt as a crime against humanity, and took the British to task for their obsession with 'knitting jumpers and breeding pet rabbits'. But, as a rule, the xenophobia so easily mined in Britain is not reflected in France. The Sofrès polling organisation found in 1997 that half the French had a favourable opinion of the British, while the number of French people registering at the consulate in London has risen by 70 per cent since 1990. And when it comes to political models, the 1997 election saw French right-wingers, as well as born-again Socialists, proclaiming their ideological kinship with Tony Blair.

In a sense, the lack of French antipathy towards *les rosbifs* is surprising: there are plenty of historical reasons for the French to entertain a hearty dislike of the English, if not their auld allies in Scotland. For almost four centuries, the English either ruled large tracts of France, or simply claimed to be kings of the country across the water. Mercenary bands from the north raped and pillaged their way through the country – one can still find tunnels dug in the Middle Ages for local people to hide at their approach. South-west France is dotted with ruined castles where minor nobles from the Midlands held ruthless sway. One Anglo-Norman crusader chief had a simple recipe for dealing with heretical natives – 'kill them all, God will know his own'. The Burgundians sold Joan of Arc for £10,000, but it was the English who burned her. After the Reformation, the Channel gave a physical manifestation to Europe's great religious divide. England stood in defiant opposition to the Catholic kingdoms to the south, and the distinction was not only political and military. It is hard to imagine France producing a Shakespeare; he was far too unbuttoned a character, his freebooting genius and independence of mind lying light-years from the order of Corneille or Racine.

After some royal alliances across the Channel under the two Kings Charles, France and Britain fought seven major wars against one another between 1689 and 1815. It was not that they hated each other as such, just that the monarchs of Versailles and the Louvre could not give up the idea of ruling the continent while the politicians in London were intent on preventing any one power from dominating Europe. Britain usually came out best. The Duke of Marlborough established the island's military credentials on the battlefield, and is remembered to this day in a French children's song but, given the usual outcome, there are not many other mementos of eighteenth-century Anglo-French conflicts around in France.

The British, on the other hand, anticipated Bonaparte's faithful soldier with their triumphalist chauvinism. Predating the mad-cow controversy by a couple of centuries, the French philosopher La Mettrie believed that the British contempt for other nations sprang from their excessive fondness for rare beef. As if to confirm his thesis, William Hogarth produced a striking depiction of the humbling of the French before a great side of beef from across the Channel in his painting *The Gate of Calais, or, The Roast Beef of Old England*. Being French, he declared, amounted to 'a farcical pomp of war, parade of religion and Bustle with very little business. In short, poverty, slavery and insolence with an affectation of politeness.' Or, as demonstrating artisans were reported to have shouted in the streets of Bristol in 1754: 'No French . . . No lowering of wages of labouring men to four pence a day and garlic.'

The last military landing on mainland Britain – by the Jacobites – was backed by the court of Versailles. Half a century later, Napoléon represented the greatest threat of invasion between the Armada and Hitler. But the cross-Channel antipathy went deeper once the Revolution had overthrown the old order. From 1789 on, the example of France stood in counterpoint to the essence of the English political system. Even after the first flush of revolution had passed, the jumped-up marshals and imperial parvenus of Napoleonic France posed a meritocratic menace to the Tory and Whig aristocracy. 'The prolonged success of French arms in Continental Europe did more than threaten British territorial autonomy,' observes the historian Linda Colley. 'It was also politically subversive, casting doubt on the belief that men of land and birth were inherently more suited to the exercise of authority than any other social group.' On top of which, the idea of a mass army headed by generals who had won their way to the top by merit rather than birth was truly disturbing, as was their leader's use of symbols – flags, decorations, recognition of individual regiments – to rally his men behind him and induce them to go the extra kilometre for his own greater glory.

The American ambassador to London might be astonished at the way in which English guests at an official dinner spoke to one another in French three years after Napoléon's final defeat, and Edmund Burke might note that France had 'always more or less influenced manners in England'. But British prejudices against the French were becoming ever more deeply rooted, with more than a tinge of sexual suspicion. As Ms Colley puts it: 'The British conceived of themselves as an essentially "masculine" culture – bluff, forthright, rational, down-to-earth to the extent of being Philistine – caught up in an eternal rivalry with an essentially "effeminate" France – subtle, intellectually devious, preoccupied with high fashion, fine cuisine and etiquette, and so obsessed with sex that boudoir politics were bound to direct it.' That contrast referred to the late eighteenth century: it could just as well apply to John Major and François Mitterrand, or to the Euro-sceptics' view from Westminster of the Euro-Énarques of Paris.

Perhaps Great Britain made a great mistake, as the West German

Chancellor Konrad Adenauer once reflected, in so fearing the emergence of a new Napoléon that it extended Prussian power to the Rhine to block any future French expansion. In retrospect, France had less harmful potential for Europe than Germany. So try a what-if of history: if Britain had lined up militarily with the French in 1870, would Bismarck's Prussia have been contained, and the world spared two great wars? Maybe. But the French were continental, the British insular (Jane Austen managed to omit any mention of the Napoleonic Wars in her novels). France was a continental nation which felt a need to be among the top dogs on too many fronts – on land, at sea, in the Atlantic and the Mediterranean, and in the far-flung colonies. Having opted for the world maritime role, Britain was content to leave mainland Europe to its own devices, so long as no one power dominated. In each case, geography dictated the national destiny; in the historian Paul Kennedy's phrase, the two nations were like a whale and an elephant, each the largest creature in its own domain but neither able to master the other.

National differences grew as the nineteenth century progressed. Looking northwards, Balzac observed that, for his compatriots, 'Britain is either the Machiavellian Albion or the model we must all imitate. It is the Machiavellian Albion when French interests are at stake or when it comes to Napoléon. It is the model country when the opposition wants to lambaste the government.' For the British, London was serious, industrious, the master of the industrial revolution. Paris was the capital of an unreliable race weakened by sexual license and over-eating. The French emperor might have had his brief moment in the sun after the Crimean War, but he had to be daubed with rouge to hide his pallor as his troops were routed by the Prussians at Sedan in 1870, and ended up seeking refuge at a Benedictine abbey built by his wife in Hampshire. As the century ended, a British flotilla steamed down the Nile to the outpost of Fashoda to force France to give up its colonial ambitions in East Africa with a mixture of whisky and brute force – a slight which entered the French language as an example of duplicitous behaviour. Britain's Crown Prince and some of his more sexually adventurous subjects-to-be slipped across the Channel to enjoy *fin de siècle* fruits in Paris, but the Third Republic's politics were the object of scorn: 'French ministries are as ephemeral house-flies,' wrote the *Financial*

Times in 1886. As a contemporary joke went, the rise of Germany over France meant that Europe had lost a mistress and found a master.

It took the British rather too long to wake up to what Berlin's vision of mastery entailed, but all the Allied bloodletting in the trenches did not lay the ground for the deeper confidence between London and Paris needed to combat the rise of Hitler and the tricky matter of dealing with Mussolini. At times, Britain still seemed ready to prefer Berlin, even if this meant putting a distance between itself and Paris. In war and peace, cross-Channel relations continued on a switch-back course. The old view of France as a flighty female lay deep in the masculine British psyche. 'As a nation, France is like a pretty woman, who expects to be flattered, and is not always above being spiteful,' wrote one apparently typical English author, Philip Carr, in 1930. French schemes for alliances with Eastern Europe to contain Germany were dismissed as will-o'-the-wisps by insular officials in London, while governments in Paris grew alarmed by British cosying up to Hitler. When they returned from signing away Czechoslovakia at Munich, the British and French Prime Ministers were both acclaimed for having prevented war; the vital difference was in their minds. Neville Chamberlain had a clear conscience; Édouard Daladier feared he might be lynched when he got home, and the French took to pronouncing the British Prime Minister's name as *J'aime Berlin*.

Within two years, attitudes had swung round. In 1940, it was the British War Cabinet which took the extraordinary step of offering France a Union between the two countries, and the French Cabinet which set its heart on suing for peace with Hitler instead. Soon afterwards, Churchill welcomed De Gaulle to Britain as the embodiment of France's involvement in the continuing fight, but, before long, he was describing the leader of the Free French as 'the cross I bear'. By the time of eventual victory, this had hardened to describing De Gaulle as 'this menacing and hostile man in our midst'. Not surprisingly, when De Gaulle took a leaf out of Churchill's 1940 book and offered an exclusive Franco-British alliance, London responded negatively for the sake of the warmer relationship across the Atlantic. If Britain was absolutely right to stage the Dunkirk evacuation and to refuse to throw more of its aircraft into fighting the Luftwaffe over France, the French could only see this as an act of desertion by *perfide Albion*. And when, sixteen years later, Britain was forced by the reaction of Washington to recognise the futility of the joint expedition to Suez, France saw itself as having been let down by an untrustworthy ally who was no better than an American vassal.

De Gaulle once told an aide: 'We're going to take back from the English all they stole from us: Quebec, which is in hand, then Mauritius, and then the Anglo-Norman islands.' By which he meant the Channel Isles. The idea of a Gaullist-led invasion of Guernsey and Sark would have spooked even the British tabloids – perhaps setting off page-one demands for a landing to seize back Henry II's kingdom in Aquitaine or William the Conqueror's Norman domains. But, with military conflict a matter of history, this touchy relationship and its attendant antipathies are now being played out on a different stage.

The French have become the main villains in Little England's disenchantment with the construction of Europe while, in Paris, as *The Times* put it, 'wise' British policies were seen as 'emasculating measures from perfidious Albion'. Hence, the glee with which British Eurosceptics greeted disagreements between Paris and Bonn about the single currency – though they may have been less delighted to find that logic forced them to side with the more easy-going French view that domestic politics should be allowed to hold central bankers in check. It is a conflict which reaches deeper than headline-grabbing clashes over the shape of cheese or dodgy French schemes to gerrymander their budget to meet the Maastricht criteria.

France epitomises state power, Britain the rule of the market. The pragmatic British have never felt much empathy with France's long-term state planners. France signs up to agreements and then breaches them; the British see themselves as men of their word. Paris is stickily nationalistic in business, but Britain wakes up to find that its *laissez-faire* ways have enabled a French company to own fifty of its utility firms. The British spy a Franco-German plot behind the rhetoric of European union; French ministers shake their heads at London's lack of vision or European spirit. France does not need a tunnel to be physically connected with the rest of Europe, while the proverbial *Times* headline – 'FOG OVER CHANNEL, CONTINENT CUT OFF' – has always said more than it knew about Anglocentric attitudes, and, for most people in Britain, the Continent means France.

No matter that London dismissively refused to join the founding Common Market nations; when De Gaulle turned down Harold

Macmillan's belated attempt to get into the club, the offence was deeply wounding to post-imperial Britain. By his own logic, De Gaulle was correct – the British would have been a disruptive pro-American force, and their economy was too weak to stand the pace The Six set themselves. But the General's way of going about it grated. He was grandeur personified, and the British found that rather ridiculous, and then downright insulting when he likened the suppli-cant Prime Minister to the man in the Édith Piaf song whom she urges: 'Go and have a cry, Milord.' In private, the Milord's reaction was equally forthright: Macmillan told John F. Kennedy that De Gaulle simply wanted 'to be the cock on a small dunghill instead of having two cocks on a larger one'. For his part, De Gaulle replied to a venerable French politician who objected to his treatment of Britain by sending him an empty envelope on the back of which he wrote, in his own hand: 'In case of absence, please forward to Agincourt (Somme) or to Waterloo (Belgium).'

Britain's entry into the Common Market in 1973 agreed by Edward Heath and De Gaulle's sensible successor, Georges Pompidou, might have put relations on track, but the next Labour government across the water threw everything into doubt with its referendum on Europe, and then the strident years of Margaret Thatcher descended on the European Community. Mrs Thatcher had a good point in wanting her just dues, but the way the campaign was fought and the desire to play to the gallery back home took its inevitable toll, and there was no easier target in all this than the French. 'We have by-elections to win, bugger France, bugger Europe,' as one of her principal aides told me at a European summit. He could have reflected that, had it not been for French help with information about the Exocet missiles sold to Argentina, the Falklands War might not have been such a vote-winner. When Jacques Delors moved from the Finance Ministry in Paris to the Presidency of the European Commission, Eurosceptics were presented with their perfect devil figure. Not only was he a former trade union official and a member of that strange (to the British) breed of Catholic Socialists – he was also a Frog, and could be told to hop off.

The French could usually find aspects of Britain to admire – and some of them found it a handy refuge, from the Huguenots fleeing the wars of religion and émigrés escaping the Terror to the Free

French of 1940. But the mutual ambiguities were rarely far from the surface. The two peoples simply seemed to be set apart. 'The French,' wrote De Tocqueville after journeying through Britain and Ireland in the 1830s, 'want no one to be their superior. The English want inferiors. The Frenchman constantly raises his eyes above him with anxiety. The Englishman lowers his beneath him with satisfaction.' Through the centuries, some of the French may have wished that their fellow citizens had more of the commercial spirit that went with the Protestant work ethic, that their country was less influenced by its southern roots. Others were less impressed. Asked if God loved the English, Joan of Arc replied the He loved them best when they stayed at home. Later, they were linked in the French mind with the power of money. An eighteenth-century Foreign Minister concluded that they thought of nothing but money. Napoléon dubbed them a nation of shopkeepers and railed against the 'cowardly oligarchs of London' who bankrolled his enemies. Alexandre Dumas denounced 'impious England' as the 'executioner of all that France held divine'. More recently, a former adviser to President Mitterrand declared that the land across the Channel was on its way to becoming an underdeveloped nation, while a school textbook judged Britain to be so divided socially that it could not move forward economically. Fundamentally, General de Gaulle observed, France and Britain have always been at war. Or, as Hogarth put it in a template for tabloid leader-writers:

> Let France grow proud, beneath the tyrant's lust
> While the rack'd people crawl, and lick the dust:
> The manly genius of this isle disdains
> All tinsel slavery, or golden chains.

★

The extraordinary thing in all this is that no country engages the British more than France, be it as a holiday destination, a source of food and fashion, the home of their most frequently studied foreign language or the land which has produced as many great works of art and literature as any other place on Earth. The cross-Channel currents reach from pre-history (did Bretons build Stonehenge?) through legend (did King Arthur die in a forest in Normandy, or in Brittany

or in Cornwall?) to the National Anthem (adapted from a tune originally written by the French composer Lully for Louis XV's mistress)
and sport (not just Éric Cantona and *les rugbymen* but also even a
French silver medal for cricket at the 1900 Olympics). And so on to
the final building of the most logical tunnel in the world nearly two
centuries after Bonaparte first proposed it. The French owe the name
of their currency to the ransom paid to the English for a captured
medieval king whose payment made him *franc des Anglais,* while a
gastronome insisted at dinner one night that the quintessentially
French dish of *confit de canard* originated in the potting of poultry left
naked by the Black Prince's soldiers after they had ripped out their
feathers to use on their arrows as they marauded through the south-
west. Six centuries later, the most popular Prime Minister of Britain
remarked that, 'If you've ever lived in Paris, it's hard not to love
France.'

Soon after Tony Blair recalled his nights working in a French café,
Paris discovered British theatre and films — as a headline in the
International Herald Tribune early in 1998 put it, 'BRITAIN'S CREATIVE
BOOM FINDS A HOME AWAY FROM HOME: FRANCE'. A flock of British
designers, led by John Galliano, Alexander McQueen and Stella
McCartney, moved into some of the most august fashion houses, and
English plays and films packed in audiences. The Jeu de Paume gallery
in the Tuileries showed British sculpture from Jacob Epstein to
Damien Hirst, and young British artists won recognition with a show
of their own at the Paris Museum of Modern Art.

It was the nineteenth-century English who made the Riviera into
a holiday resort for the rich and distinguished, and Queen Victoria
who gave it the royal stamp of approval. As Prince of Wales, her son
regularly took his mistress to Biarritz in the spring, while a friend of
a more recent princely mistress says that the peak of ambition for
Charles and Camilla Parker Bowles would be to go painting in
Provence. The 198 inhabitants of the southern village of Saint-
Martin-d'Oydes were reported to have been thrilled to have Tony
Blair and family staying with them in the summer of 1997, as New
Labour sensibly showed that Tuscany was not the only suitable holi-
day destination. A local pensioner noted approvingly that Mr Blair
even spoke decent French.

In which case, he would have come to see, as we have remarked earlier, how the two languages refract off one another. While the British take French leave, the French *filent à l'anglaise*. Males in Paris or Mulhouse don *capotes anglaises* while their counterparts in London or Doncaster slip on French letters (from 'let' in the sense of hinder rather than pertaining to mail). The House of Lords still uses old French when it amends a bill, and when the Queen gives her assent, the official notation is '*La reyne le veult*'. (On a different but significant royal note, the Queen Mother decided to send one of her horses to be trained in France for the first time – and by a French trainer, to boot.) So is all this talk of an Anglo-French divide just *une tempête dans un verre d'eau* or a storm in a teacup? *Honni soit qui mal y pense* – except that it says *honi* in my British passport.

Regretfully, the answer remains in the negative, and a new form of cross-Channel difference opened up when Tony Blair addressed the National Assembly in March 1998. He may speak better French than any Prime Minister since Anthony Eden, but Blair's message was more of a hit with the beleaguered right than with his Socialist hosts. He recalled his days as a young man working in a Paris bar, and remembered how after a few weeks he had noticed that he was the only member of staff putting his tips into the communal kitty – the Labour leader's subsequent joke about it being 'his first lesson in applied socialism' met with delight from the RPR and UDF benches. When asked about his reception, the visitor simply observed: 'If you get applause from both sides, that's just good politics.' Not exactly the approach of the still ideological French left.

Blairmanie might sweep the boulevards, but there is no denying the fratricidal sentiments which flow southwards across the Channel. As the critic Anthony Lane remarked, 'The English fondness for France is normally a sort of neutron love: take away the people and leave the buildings standing.' And, along the way, Francophobia has found a fresh twist: don't just accuse the French of being dirty and undemo- cratic – hit them in what are generally taken to be their strong suits, and do so in such a way that any objections can be dismissed as symp- tomatic of the absence of a sense of humour. (This is, remember, the country that regards Jerry Lewis as a comic genius.)

Food is a favourite field. British food writers can try to make a case that London has become a better place to eat than Paris, particularly after it became known that Jacques Chirac was so impressed by a pigeon served to him when lunching in London with Tony Blair that he asked for the chef's telephone number. Some people who know what they are talking about strike a different note – 'Anybody who believes that English cooking is better than French cooking can't be taken seriously,' as the British chef Marco Pierre White puts it. 'The French are the greatest cooks in the world.' But the jibes go on. 'I'm just back from a week in France,' a British journalist announces. 'Naturally, I took a case of non-French wine over on the ferry so as to have something decent to drink.' More subtly, the food writer Digby Anderson gets to the heart of the way the world likes to have its French cake and eat it. Every year, observes Mr Anderson, the culture across the Channel slips another notch, both in manners and food – but from such a high level that, whatever the decline, the level of its food is still way above that of England. And that is exactly what makes things so perfect. 'The upshot of this mixture – the mixture of the good and bad food – is that now is possibly the best point in the decline for eating in France. You can sit and eat the best food in the world while still being able to denounce the decadence evident immediately about you.'

So that's clear, then. Enjoy France, but criticise it and its people – if possible, for one and the same thing. As a Balzac character reflects of conduct she cannot understand: 'It's like an Englishman on holiday; you have to expect some strange behaviour, but there are limits!' Buy your house in the Dordogne and lament the lack of the delicacies you find in the boutique grocer in Islington; snap up a bargain holiday home in Gascony and complain that you can't understand the local accent. If the farmers shake your hand, they are too forward, if they don't, they are stand-offish. If they have video-cassette players in their homes, they have betrayed their roots at the altar of consumerism; if they don't, they are backward peasants who don't deserve their huge subsidies from Brussels. Contemplating the combined effect of France's popularity and of the large numbers of the French who like to vacation at home, even *The Economist* slumped into tabloid-speak to write of 'the hell of French holidays', while the Irish novelist Josephine Hart complained of how holidays at their Riviera villa were marred for her and her husband, Lord Saatchi, by the number of friends from London they bumped into when they went out for a walk.

Inevitably, one reaches the ultimate put-down – the French are lousy lovers. Take Napoléon: we all know about not tonight, Joséphine, and his remark on their honeymoon that they would have time to make love when the war was over, but he is now revealed as a premature ejaculator who liked to pour coffee over the clothes of the countless women he bedded, and who may have seen his first wife as an Oedipal reflection of his mother. Jabbing at French sexual performance in bed is even more rewarding than spitting in their soup. After all, as we have seen, the French and sex are synonymous – a British newspaper headline about one of the greatest writers of the century was content to describe André Malraux simply as 'PHILANDERING FRENCH MINISTER'. We all know that their men are actually one-minute wonders with hairy bodies who rarely wash and smoke while making love. Their women dream of lesbian affairs with film stars, or have to resort to perfumed bras to turn their menfolk on. Alternatively, they are, as one male British columnist put it, like French trains – 'the bodywork's great, they're comfortable, but, when you want to get on board, they're always on strike'. A poll in 1997 seemed to back up the charge as it reported that 44 per cent of men and 53 per cent of women in France acknowledged a flagging sex drive. But that was soon overtaken by an international survey by a maker of condoms which put France at the top of the sexual activity league. Twenty per cent of the French are reckoned to have regular affairs (though unfaithfulness is reported to be far less than in the US). Even the elderly keep up the national reputation: nearly half France's pensioners consider themselves sexually active, and 17.5 per cent of over-60s say they have at least weekly sex.

So why are the British so anti-French, the former Prime Minister, Édouard Balladur, asked a lunch party in London after he had left office. He might have drawn his answer from a volume of reflections by the writer and journalist André Frossard, entitled *Pardon Me for Being French*. It was, Frossard noted, a bad habit he got into when he was born and 'had never succeeded in correcting'. Reading British commentaries and reports on France made it plain that he was 'egotistical, vain, servile, jingoistic, uncivil, hopeless in big business, peevish, undisciplined, garrulous, intemperate. I never go out except to chase glory which always escapes me . . . I devour frogs and I belong to the most beaten-up and oft-defeated people in the world. Forgive me, please.'

The question is not so much whether the attacks on France and the French which ebb and flow around the world are justified. Any country and its people can be attacked on a variety of scores. But the natural reflex to all this may be for France to draw closer to those nations where Francophobia does not find fertile soil – to mainland European neighbours rather than to the island to the north and all those places where Jacques Chirac was portrayed as something close to a war criminal for ordering the Mururoa tests. Despite three wars in the space of a century and the four-year Nazi Occupation, it is not surprising that the embrace across the Rhine holds such appeal, since the Germans generally accept the French for what they are (they even go so far as to have a saying that happiness is like being 'God in France'). The extraordinary act of reconciliation and recognition of mutual self-interest which underlies the Franco-German relationship has led the two countries to see one another as natural partners, not just at government level but in the tens of thousands of young people who move between the two countries on exchange programmes each year. The importance of this, and of the progress of Western Europe from a theatre of persistent wars to a region of peace, is not something which much interests or impresses the British, with their inability to shake off memories of the Battle of Britain and the years of standing alone against Hitler in the last national glory days. Crude baiting of the Germans and the French reflects an attachment to a national comfort blanket which is bound to set the island apart. The very use of the word 'Europe' to mean the mainland part of a continent to which Britain belongs speaks volumes.

The problem for those who drop so easily into Francophobia is that the French insist on remaining themselves. Their national personality is so clearly marked, so evidently stamped on them, that it unhinges many critics. At the same time, the British find the French so intriguing precisely because they are so different from them, because they resolutely refuse to listen to the plea of Professor Higgins and be more like us. What is certain is that France will remain France and the French will not stop behaving in a French manner, however many McDonald's outlets open and however many anglicisms creep into the language. While they must be central to the process of European unity, France's people are intent on remaining a proud nation-state of an old-fashioned kind, whatever the rest of the world thinks. That presents them with a difficult trick to pull off, but theirs is a country which has long been used to juggling with paradoxes. For a century or more, it has kept the balls in the air despite military defeat and occupation, the loss of empire and the rebirth of the mighty neighbour to the east. But now some of those balls are falling to the earth in another threat to the France we know and love, or hate.

10

Divided We Stand

It may be no accident that France was the Western country where the Manichaean heresy took deepest root, positing an absolute division between light and darkness, between the spirit and base matter, between an ultimate paradise for perfect followers of God and the irredeemably sinful world where the rest are damned. This is a people which lives on its divisions. A tradition of dualism courses through French life and history: the extended social structure of the south against the nuclear family of the north; the linguistic dichotomy between the *pays d'oïl* in the north and the *pays d'Oc* in the south; the old nutritional division between the dark bread and red plonk of the masses and the white bread and wine of the elite – peasants consumed food that came from the earth, while their lords feasted on the winged treasures of the air.

The land was torn by violent wars of competing faiths, by the St Bartholomew's Day massacre of the Protestants and Louis XIV's revocation of the Edict of Nantes which had granted toleration to the Huguenot dissenters, by the bloody eight-year war that ripped through the Cévennes at the beginning of the eighteenth century and the emigration of some 400,000 fleeing persecution – many of them artisans and businessmen whom France would sadly miss during its industrial revolution. Naturally, there were accommodations. Henri de Navarre thought Paris worth a mass and converted to Catholicism to become Henri IV. At the height of religious strife, Protestants and Catholics shared the nave of the fine sandstone church in Collonges-la-Rouge in the Corrèze, Protestants in the southern half, Catholics in the northern half. But it was not until 1764 that Protestants gained their religious freedom, and only during the Revolution that they became full citizens of France. Though religion is hardly a hot topic any more, the old divisions peep through at the summit of politics – if he had had a religious role, François Mitterrand would surely have been a calculating Cardinal of the Ancien Régime (didn't he call his illegitimate daughter after one?), whereas his chief rival in the Socialist Party, Michel Rocard, was the epitome of Protestant reason; equally, Jacques Chirac characterises cavalier Catholicism whereas Lionel Jospin radiates earnest Calvinism.

Then came the struggle of enlightenment against obscurantism, Revolution against monarchy, Republic against reaction, state against church, anti-Semitism and the Dreyfus Affair, the divorce of Communists and Socialists in 1920, right-wing extremism of the 1930s against the Popular Front, the bitter splits over the Spanish Civil War, and the traumatic divisions of the Occupation: resistants against collaborators, the General in London against the Marshal in Vichy who had once been his protector, partisans against fascist militiamen – and the difference between those who deplored the wartime splits as a national tragedy and those who saw them as the chance to end the sickness of pre-war society. Each camp had its internal divisions. The court around the First World War hero in Vichy was rent with jockeying for power and official favours, while the rivalries in the Resistance were accentuated by the inevitable paranoia that dogs any clandestine movement. Half a century later, unresolved arguments hang over allegations that the first head of the internal Resistance, Jean Moulin, was betrayed to Klaus Barbie's Gestapo by a colleague – though a French historian now claims that the Germans got their lead from a captured American agent. Much later, one man who had been deeply involved in the shifting patterns of the times laid a blunt charge: 'De Gaulle did all he could to eliminate the leading figures in the internal Resistance, either by covering them with honours in London or perhaps, even, in some cases, by letting them be physically eliminated,' François Mitterrand alleged. 'He fought the internal Resistance more than he did the Germans.'

At a grass-roots level, take Saint-Amand in the middle of France as an illustration of the starkness of the Franco-French enmities of the war.

The town contained both Resistance and fascist militia groups. Hearing of the Allied landings in Normandy, the Resistance partisans took control. They held some of their opponents hostage, together with the wife of a national leader of the militia. He responded by taking hostages of his own, threatening to kill them if his wife was not set free. As German troops moved in to re-establish control, the Resistance fighters killed thirteen of their captives. In retaliation, the militiamen turned on the local Jews. Thirty-eight were thrown down a well, and then had bags of cement and rocks dropped on them until they perished.

The Liberation of 1944 naturally brought a righteous settling of scores which perpetuated the divisions of wartime. Some 4,000 collaborators were sentenced to death, and 767 were executed. The Vichy Prime Minister, Pierre Laval, was shot after trying to poison himself while awaiting execution. There were less official revenge killings – some estimates put the number of those who perished in the settling of scores in the tens of thousands. Another 25,000 went to jail, and Marshal Pétain ended his days in lifelong detention on an island off the Atlantic coast. Sometimes the punishment of those who had been too close to the occupiers was ideological, but often the cause was more human. When accused of collaboration for her affair with a German officer, the actress Arletty could be bold enough to tell the court: 'My heart is French but my cunt is international' and get away with it. Many other less fortunate women who were never more than sexual collaborators had their heads shaved by kangaroo courts before being paraded in the streets in shame. As Vichyites tried to keep their heads down till the storm passed, the Liberation brought with it a regiment of latter-day converts to Resistance – one French literary historian remarked acidly of the country's most famous post-war couple: 'On 11 August 1944, Jean-Paul Sartre and Simone de Beauvoir entered the Resistance, at the same moment as the Paris police.'

The Fourth Republic brought new cleavages that went deeper than the everyday jockeying for positions by parties involved in the merry-go-round of Cabinet-making. Despite their electoral support, the Communists preached revolution from political purdah. The decolonisation in the 1950s and 1960s produced bitter divisions, exacerbated at a crucial phase by virulent anti-Semitism directed at the great Prime Minister, Pierre Mendès-France. The traumatic defeat by the Vietnamese at Dien Bien Phu now belongs to the history books,

but the end of France's colonisation of Algeria is still a living memory
to anybody over fifty-five: Jacques Chirac served there as a sub-
lieutenant. As national traumas go, the withdrawal from France's last
major possession was about as searing as you could get for a modern
European nation. Apart from the bloodshed, the repression and the
violent demonstrations in Algeria itself, it is easy for foreigners to
forget that, as comparatively recently as 1958, France faced the very
real prospect of an army coup. At a time when Dwight Eisenhower
was presiding over bland Republican prosperity and Harold Macmillan
was telling the British they'd never had it so good, generals in French
Algeria were drawing up plans for Operation Resurrection, complete with the mobilisation of paratroopers and tanks in Paris to
surround the National Assembly, City Hall, police headquarters,
broadcasting stations and the Eiffel Tower. A detachment of paratroopers actually landed in Corsica on a self-proclaimed mission of
revolt against the elected leaders of the nation. The President of the
Republic and the Prime Minister held all-night crisis meetings, and,
within two weeks, De Gaulle was back in power, using the menace
of army action to carry out a political coup that incommoded only
the resentful politicians of the old regime. The men who dreamed
up Operation Resurrection insisted that their only aim was to bring
the General to power, but there would have been all the world of
difference between a new republic born out of a military coup, and
the one which evolved through De Gaulle's masterly and ruthless
handling of the situation. Outside the ranks of the displaced *pied noir*
settlers and some revanchist National Front supporters, it would be
hard to find even a handful of people today who think that military
action in 1958 would have achieved anything positive. But, in considering the condition of modern-day France, it would be
short-sighted to overlook the place in the national memory occupied
by the events of 1958 – and the assassination attempts against De
Gaulle by the ultras of Algérie Française that lasted until 1962.

For all his rhetoric about rallying the French into a single historic
mass, De Gaulle's style was hardly calculated to avoid dispute. Having
returned to power in the most dramatic circumstances of any post-war
West European leader, he invited controversy from the start with
France's politicians, its allies and the Algerian settlers who soon realised
that he was no providential saviour. The Gaullist process injected France

with the new life it so badly needed, but, once the threat of military action had been lifted, nobody could pretend that the President acted as a balm to the country's divisions. A decade after the barricades of Algiers, the nation was again split beyond the realms of orthodox politics by the biggest combination of urban strikes and street revolt of the century. That opened the way to thirteen years of rule by the centre-right, but, as we will see in detail in the next chapters, it was also a time for a different kind of political in-fighting to emerge, with long-running civil war among the once-impregnable conservatives and the phenomenon of Presidents of the Republic of one political camp having to appoint Prime Ministers from among their opponents.

Underscoring politics, old geographical traditions constantly assert themselves as regions stand aside from the mainstream. The medieval home of the Manichaean heresy in the south-west became a hotbed for Protestants and then for the left. The plateau around Chambon-sur-Lignon in the rugged Haute-Loire department, which sheltered Jews and others fleeing from the occupiers in the early 1940s, had been a Huguenot bastion in the wars of religion. The Resistance stronghold of the Limousin remained one of the last bulwarks of the Communist Party fifty years after the Liberation, and one of only two areas which resisted the triumphal sweep of the right in regional elections in 1992. On the other side of the political spectrum, the anti-Revolutionary lands of the Vendée in the west gave birth to a family-values, anti-European party two hundred years after the republican army massacred its Chouan rebels in the 1790s, and the progenitors of the new age in Paris proclaimed that 'the Republic consists of the extermination of all that oppose it'.

Take any element of French life and it will almost certainly contain rival factions. There are two national honours systems, for example: the Légion d'Honneur and the Ordre National du Mérite. The *cassoulet* stew may be the quintessential dish of the south-west, but don't expect regional solidarity as you sit down at the table. In the town of Castelnaudary it comes with pork, in Carcassonne with roast shoulder of mutton, and in Toulouse with the local sausage; and each version has its fervent disciples. To avoid becoming entangled in the gastronomic civil war, the writer Anatole France opted for an all-round spiritual benediction which hardly fits the temporal solidity of the dish – the *cassoulet* of Castelnaudary was God the Father, that of

Carcassonne the Son and the Toulouse version the Holy Spirit.

There are competing associations of chess-players and authors, film-makers and anglers. The number of concierges may be falling by the year, but they still have no fewer than five unions to represent them. Even criminals might be said to be divided by the moral demarcation drawn between *crimes crapuleux* and *crimes passionnels*. Two centuries after the execution of Louis XVI, the old royal family is badly split: the pretender to the throne, the Comte de Paris, disinherited his eldest son and denounced four other children for trying to stop him selling off family treasures. Not to be outdone, the Bonaparte clan has recurrent rows about who is the rightful claimant to the imperial succession.

We have seen how Muslim immigrants are divided from mainstream society in counterpoint to the Catholicism which the French profess but practise little. Religious persecution may be long gone, but the 900,000 Protestants still remain, in many ways, a group apart, characterised by their seriousness and their perceived absence of social graces. Within the seemingly solid ranks of the middle class, a strain of anti-bourgeois thinking has been kept alive and kicking by critics from Gustave Flaubert to Claude Chabrol. In the country's top kitchens, civil war has broken out between defenders of traditional French gastronomy and those whom they branded as being guilty of 'globalisation'. There is always a good pretext to set up a new organisation whose chairman will revel in the title of 'Monsieur le Président' until his dying day. Thus, the National Union of Restaurant, Café and Hotel Owners might seem a pretty all-inclusive body to represent the catering trade. But no; it has a competitor, the French Confederation of Hotel, Restaurant, Café and Discotheque Owners. Ah yes, the disco owners must not be left without a voice.

Politics provides handy labels for divisions that reflect human differences and ambitions as much as real ideological divides. The main Islamic and Masonic organisations have each been upset by internal political rifts which overlie more basic battles for influence. There are rival organisations of hunters which put up competing lists at regional elections. Feelings in the world of former French settlers from Algeria grew so heated that the head of the main *pied noir* organisation was murdered in 1993 by three members of another group. In some places, one café is frequented by Socialists, another by conservatives, perpetuating an old tradition – in the mid-nineteenth century, Balzac noted that 'in the provinces, tradesmen had to profess a political opinion in order to attract customers'. Sometimes it pays to cover both sides of the field: in the 1980s the powerful newspaper-owning Baylet family of Toulouse had a son in the Socialist government in Paris while a daughter sat on the city council among the supporters of the centre-right mayor. Even family feuds can take on a political gloss: a long tussle for a very large provincial inheritance was recounted to me by one of the old lady protagonists in terms of 'my son is true to our radical tradition, but my sister's son has sold out to the right'; in fact, the only issue at stake was how to carve up the fortune.

The three main trade union federations carry on doctrinal disputes alongside the fight for members; each labour conflict is likely to produce a different line-up between them as they balance tactics and strategy. In the name of equality of the sexes, the normally sensible former Prime Minister, Michel Rocard, once proposed twin-track constituency elections, one with women candidates and one with men, since 'humanity is made up of two different sexes – and our institutions ought to be changed to reflect that'. The main political parties of left and right have long been rent with internal feuding, and there is no real bi-partisan or independent centre between them: as a rule, politicians who call themselves centrists either forge timid alliances with the moderate left or, more often, find themselves prisoners of an alliance with conservatives. In the Gaullist ranks, left-wing followers of the General fought waspish battles with the movement's mainstream through the 1960s, and ultra-orthodox disciples banded together to try to block the ascension of his successor on the grounds that he lacked sufficient devotion to the historic tablets of the faith. The extreme right was stridently divided for years. The once-monolithic Communists fell prey to splits which led to a champion of *glasnost* running against the official candidate in the 1988 presidential election. Even before Jacques Chirac moved in to the Élysée, a group of his followers had geared up to challenge his chosen Prime Minister. The Socialist Party is famously fractious – at one point, its nineteen-member national secretariat contained ten different groupings, one of which was generally believed to have gone out of existence. The *Quid* reference book lists 150 parties, movements and political clubs.

In this galaxy, each side believes that it, and it alone, is right. That makes the kind of reasoned compromises which are commonplace elsewhere difficult to achieve in France. Mutual antagonism has a macho value that can be infantile. Consensus has not figured prominently in the political lexicon, which is why the long period of joint rule by Jacques Chirac and Lionel Jospin arouses such interest as a possible pointer to a new and less presidential form of government – though deepening cracks began to appear after eighteen months of the new regime. For far too long, the French system has worked through petty political rivalries, directives and demonstrations which put a premium on divisiveness for its own sake.

Though this was not his intention, the constitution which Charles de Gaulle introduced in 1958 enshrined a different kind of division at the summit of French politics. By separating the functions of the executive President-Head of State and those of the Prime Minister-Head of Government, he provided for two power-centres, unequal to be sure but each with its separate mandate and source of legitimacy. The President in the Élysée is directly elected by the nation once every seven years; the Prime Minister in the Hôtel Matignon across the Seine depends on the President for his appointment, but is usually the man or woman who can command a majority in the National Assembly, which is elected on a different timetable and basis to the Head of State. Under the first two Presidents of the Fifth Republic, the presidential and parliamentary majorities coincided. In his love-me-or-leave-me style, De Gaulle would no doubt have resigned the presidency if the opposition had won a parliamentary majority. His successors proved more supple. From 1974 to 1976, the President and Prime Minister came from different parties of the centre-right. More strikingly, from 1986 to 1988 and again from 1993 to 1995, the first President of the left was forced to appoint a Gaullist as his Prime Minister, making concrete the divisiveness at the very top of French life provided for in the constitution. And then, in 1997, it was the turn of Jacques Chirac to call on the Socialist Lionel Jospin to become Prime Minister, eleven years after he, himself, had launched the *cohabitation* process as head of government under François Mitterrand. By then nobody found the idea of such fundamental division at the pinnacle of the nation strange – indeed, the opinion polls showed that it was positively welcomed, so much so that some saw a new form of Republic in the offing.

Indeed, the period since 1981 has seen a significant switch in the balance of politics, with the Socialists holding the presidency until 1995 and forming governments for twice as long as the right. On that score, the left may now appear the dominant force. But, given its crushing rejection in the 1993 legislative elections and its failure to build on its 1997 victory, the jury must remain out before pronouncing the lasting triumph of social democracy – particularly given the unsocialist nature of many aspects of the later Mitterrand years. Naturally, the vision of France as the bearer of the true Socialist flame in the face of rampant Blairism is seductive to true believers. This is, after all, known as a land of revolution. History, with its powerful political role, is seen as belonging to the left, resounding to the memory of the forces of liberal progress and modernity, the eighteenth-century writers who threw their literary darts at royal absolutism and Catholic obscurantism, the rallying slogans of the Revolution and Zola's 'J'Accuse' denunciation of the show trial of Captain Alfred Dreyfus, the euphoria of the Popular Front governments, the questioning of shibboleths by post-war existentialists and the free-thinkers of the 1960s. Recognising the thread, De Gaulle responded to a suggestion that Jean-Paul Sartre might be arrested for sedition with a historical put-down: 'One does not put Voltaire in prison.'

In fact, modern France has hardly been a triumph of the forces of enlightenment. Most governments of the last two hundred years have come from the conservative side. The first Revolution ended in a dictatorship led by a man who advised his brother that there was 'only one thing to do in this world, and that is to acquire money and more money, power and more power'. The Revolution of 1830 installed a bourgeois monarchy, and that of 1848 led to a second Bonapartist autocracy. The Paris Commune was followed by the Third Republic, with its wheeler-dealer politics in which personal position took precedence over principle. The Popular Front was followed within five years by Vichy. The student revolt and general strike of 1968 ended with an election which routed the left. The Mitterrand years turned from nationalisation to privatisation within half a decade. The old Socialist monarch spent his last two years in the Élysée with a huge right-wing majority in the National Assembly.

If conservatives keep their heads, they can usually be confident of returning to power and wealth. 'French society dreams of revolution but, in fact, is repelled by change,' as the former minister and historian

Michel Poniatowski put it. It can well be argued that, behind the
political slogans, the revolution which the left promised in 1981 was
really the last manifestation of post-war economic and social conservatism, promising to keep life as it was through massive intervention
of the state just at the moment when computers, the decline of
Communism and the economic rise of East Asia were changing the
balance of the world: rather than putting itself in shape to meet such
fundamental international shifts, supposedly radical France reacted
with outdated nostrums and flirted with isolationism. Even the
nationalisations of 1981 can be seen as part of a tradition of state
power which was espoused by the right as well as the left. Reaction
beneath the cloak of revolution – a lesson which France may meditate
upon as it votes to slow down the clock of change and conjure hundreds of thousands of jobs from the air. Equally, the supposedly
left-wing governments from the mid-1980s onwards implemented
economic policies which would not have brought a blush to the
cheeks of the right. After Jacques Chirac's second failure to become
President in 1988, the right was out of power for five years, but its
ideas ruled in many respects. The left had become a party of management, far from the euphoria of 1981. For all its domination of
government, it no longer had any big ideas to offer on the social and
economic front that had always been its *raison d'être*. Mitterrand
devoted his energies to Europe and came back with the Maastricht
Treaty, which was more unpopular among the working class than
among conservatives.

Naturally, influences from each lurch to the left have not vanished
completely. But, in terms of real power, the progressives get the write-
ups and the realists govern. France needs to be able to think of itself
as the cradle of revolution, a place of daring ideological innovation, a
powerhouse of ideas – and, until very recently, those were seen as the
property of the left. The notion of progress stemming from the right
was, for the French, an oxymoron. Now that has changed. More
important, the French have always felt a need to reassure themselves
that they are a people which knows that there are limits. After the fun
and games, common sense will prevail.

Hence, the respect for the solid values of the countryside. Hence,
the outcome of the 1968 strikes and riots – while the uprising on the
streets would live in history, liberate culture and affect the way French

universities were run, the victor was the Prime Minister with 'one eye of a vicar, the other of a rascal' who brought it to a conclusion that pleased both the big battalions of business and the Communist Party. The French, in the old truism, wear their hearts on the left, their wallets on the right. They like to think of themselves as individualists who believe in the power of independent ideas, but they put great store on order and conformity as well. Which leads to another paradox surrounding the French – the obeisance which this divisive people pays to the state.

L'État is sacrosanct, the glue which holds the nation together and which must receive its utter loyalty in return. *L'État* is *la France*; *la France* is *l'État*. While Britain and the United States embarked on free trade and economic liberalism in the nineteenth century, France opted for the protection of the state. Building on the Ancien Régime base of Colbertist protectionism, and buttressed by the centralisation of both the revolutionaries and top-down Catholicism, the state became established as the guarantor of national order, providing a framework which could contain the occasional lurches to the left. The accidental course of history which played such a role in other countries was to be eliminated by the all-seeing authority on high. France, in the process, became a unique mixture of conservatism and socialism, whatever the political colouring of the government in power. De Gaulle, who launched France on a post-war version of this mixture in 1944, had no doubt that, as he once put it, 'there can be no security, no freedom, no efficiency without the acceptance of great discipline under the guidance of a strong state and with the enthusiastic support of a people rallied in unity'. Asked for the keys to France's national identity, the historian Emmanuel Le Roy-Ladurie put the state in first place. One of Mitterrand's chiefs of staff at the Élysée defined it to me as the guarantor of France's identity against the law of the jungle, while Jacques Chirac makes no bones about it: 'For a Frenchman, the notion of the public good is inseparable from that of the state.'

The state, for its part, has drawn on this lay faith to buttress its own position. In so doing, it has been powerfully helped by the relative weakness of organisations that act as counterbalancing forces in other countries. The Revolution abolished intermediate associations which stood between the state and the citizen. The First Emperor laid down his legal code to impose the values of the state as he perceived them on the nation. With it came the drive for linguistic unity, a uniform currency, a single system of weights and measures and the same educational process for all – as the historian Alistair Horne has observed, roads and bureaucracy radiated in tandem outward from the single centre of Paris to exert physical control over the furthest-flung regions of France. Later in the nineteenth century, the weakness of French capitalism and finance left a far greater economic role for the state than was the case in Britain or the United States, and its influence, in turn, dampened down the growth of financial and industrial enterprise. *L'État providence*, which ensures the well-being of citizens whether they want it or not, was a French concept long before the welfare state came into being.

So the state survives through thick and thin, and its servants exist to do its bidding without question, from the highest-placed Énarque to the gendarme on the beat. The tradition was set long ago, epitomised by the ever-adaptable Charles-Maurice de Talleyrand, successively Catholic Bishop of Autun in Burgundy, servant of the revolutionary church, Foreign Minister for Bonaparte and then for the restored Bourbon monarchy, and finally ambassador to London for their Orleanist successor. For those liable to pose moral questions about such survival shifts, this might cause some problems – Bonaparte called Talleyrand a 'shit in silk stockings'. So it is much easier all round if blind obedience to the state's commands is the order of the day. Marianne, or rather her living representatives, knows best. For two centuries, civil servants and lawyers have grown used to the ethical somersaults involved, from the religious school in the town of Vendôme which quickly slipped a fawning mention of Napoléon into its catechism when it saw the way the wind was blowing, to the judge at the trial of Philippe Pétain in 1945 who had sworn allegiance to the Marshal a few years earlier. Politicians get in the way; without them the functionary can exploit his personal identification with the state to the full. For some French civil servants, at least, the Occupation years were an unanticipated delight, in which they could erect a new model state free of politics in which a law professor became Minister for Justice, a leading academic ran the civil service and a well-trained official took over the Finance Ministry. It was just the kind of set-up to suit Maurice Papon, the civil servant who was eventually brought to trial over the deportation of Jews from Bordeaux and who, as much as any man, can be taken as a symbol of devoted service to the state – and, thus, to himself.

As a young man, Papon belonged to the moderate Radical Socialist party, the main political grouping of the declining Third Republic. In 1931, at the age of twenty, he joined the staff of the Air Minister, a senior member of the party. Five years later, he took a bigger job with another Radical Socialist member of the Popular Front government. At the end of 1940, he joined the Vichy administration, rising to become Secretary-General of the Prefecture of the Gironde department, based in Bordeaux. There were plenty of prefectorial jobs going since Vichy had sacked half the old staff to ensure loyalty to its order. In his new post, Papon was given responsibility for activities linked with the war and the Occupation, including Jewish affairs. Convoys of Jews left Bordeaux at regular intervals, and Papon earned high marks from the Germans for his 'quick and trustworthy' work. In May 1943, there was a disagreeable episode in which Gaullist graffiti was found scrawled in the toilets of the Prefecture; Papon had the toilets watched and a twenty-year-old employee was duly caught and sent off to forced labour in Germany.

At the end of 1943, as the Allies were landing in North Africa, Papon agreed to shelter a civil servant who had joined the Resistance after being sacked because he was Jewish. In January 1944, he turned down the offer of a prefecture of his own: at the same time he signed a warrant for 228 Jews which even told the police how to deal with the pets of those arrested – the servants of the state are sticklers for detail even in the worst of times. That spring, he made contact with a local Resistance leader and, when Bordeaux was liberated in August, became his chief of staff. After a post-war career as a prefect in France and its colonies, he worked as a senior official for the Socialist Interior Minister and was then appointed chief of the Paris police. Holding on to the job under the Fifth Republic, he was in charge of the force of order who killed hundreds of Algerians in the capital in 1961. Elected to the National Assembly in 1968, he headed the parliamentary finance commission and became Minister for the Budget under Giscard d'Estaing. It was only in 1981 that, as a result of an electoral manoeuvre which we will hear more about later, the truth about his wartime career came into the spotlight.

Setting aside questions of morality, what is so striking about
Maurice Papon's career is how he worked for whoever was in power
whatever their creed. It is one thing for a civil servant to regard himself as being above politics, but still quite a feat to have laboured for
the Radical Socialists in the 1930s, Vichy in the 1940s, the Socialists
in the 1950s, De Gaulle in the 1960s and Giscard in the 1970s. And it
is equally amazing that his successive bosses did not seem to care
about his past affiliations, so long as he did the job. For sixty years,
Papon was the embodiment of the administrative continuity which
that state prizes so highly. As he himself wrote: 'There are no crises of
conscience when one obeys the orders of the government.' Or, as the
war criminal Paul Touvier pleaded when he was finally brought to
trial: 'All I ever did was to serve the French state.'

Article two of the 1958 constitution proclaims France to be an indi-
visible Republic. 'When the French are arguing with one another, one
has to talk to them of France,' De Gaulle advised. The triumph of the
Jacobin revolutionaries after 1789 imposed the idea of the nation on a
heterogeneous people. To believe in the Revolution was to believe in
the all-powerful unitary state, and vice-versa. Apart from scattered proponents of le libéralisme avancé who would entrust all to the market, the
French are uncomfortable with any idea of the state withering away.
Despite the continual grumbling about bureaucracy and taxes, there is
not much indication that they seriously want it to re-think its role. 'The
dominant political culture is to worship the cult of the nation state,' as
the Gaullist deputy Patrick Devedjian puts it. 'We are an old country
which has astonished the world by our influence, but we continue to
doubt ourselves to the point at which we imagine that our future
depends on the power of the state. A state to which we confide our soul
and which we prefer to the rule of law.' Asked by pollsters what they
most desired in the spring of 1995, the number-one answer of respon-
dents was 'a strong state'. Only in France could there still be a General
Commissariat of the Plan to chart the nation's path – though the
Commissioner was replaced at the beginning of 1998 after expressing
less than full enthusiasm for government policies. Significantly, the
standard-bearer of market economics and a smaller state, Finance
Minister Alain Madelin, was the first man to resign from the Chirac
administration when his ideas threatened to disturb the status quo.

If the state is to hold the country together, it has to be present everywhere – whether in the extensive public transport network or in the incomprehensible official notices pinned up outside the *mairie* of every commune. It has to coddle teachers and allow them to rule their own roost because it has traditionally depended on them as its representatives to the youth of the nation. 'France is saved from death by education,' wrote Émile Zola in 1898, and there was never any doubt as to the strict republican form which that education should take. Teachers were more than mere educators; they represented the Republic and modernity. That strain in French life lives on a century after Zola's panegyric, or the warning from the Tiger of the Third Republic, Georges Clemenceau, that outlawing non-secular teaching would mean the tyranny of the state. So the idea of introducing more creativity into the classroom is deeply worrying just because of the way in which it could shake old certainties inherited from the nineteenth century. To withdraw the special pension privileges of teachers would be to betray their century-old republican mission on behalf of the state in classrooms throughout the land. Equally, to shut down hugely subsidised rural railway lines would be an abdication of responsibility to its people – even if the state employees at the SNCF account for 20 to 30 per cent of all days lost through strikes. Decentralisation has reduced the authority of prefects, but the existence of these emissaries from Paris has never been questioned. They represent the skein of *l'État* and a great in-bred domain for the graduates of the Grandes Écoles.

This state which cannot accept that any part of national life is beyond its reach is by far the biggest employer in the country. Its civil servants make up a quarter of the workforce – compared to 14 to 15 per cent in Britain and Germany. Their salaries take up almost one-sixth of the national income. As for the general belief that selfless civil servants are less well-paid than their peers in the private sector, an independent study in 1994 showed the reverse to be true in non-executive jobs. Despite the declining number of farmers, the Agriculture Ministry still employs as many functionaries as it did a decade ago. Long after the last big war, the Ex-Servicemen's Ministry costs 26 billion francs a year. Reform of other sectors of national life may be on the agenda, but not the sacred caste of the functionaries of the state. Whereas public-sector companies have been put under the spotlight, readied for privatisation or gone through painful slimming cures, the state has left its great administrative army alone. One investigation suggested that the number of hidden civil service scandals might exceed those that had come to light elsewhere – but no investigating magistrates have stuck their noses into the inner workings of the nation's administrative machinery. A list of white elephants spawned by bureaucratic incompetence drawn up by the magazine *Le Point* contained some of the following gems: the 880-million-franc high-speed train station at Lyon airport that handles only 500 passengers a day; the railway construction in Normandy where a new platform was built 300 metres away from the station; a 70-million-franc museum in Nice which was still empty ten years after being commissioned; a projected road tunnel in Toulon which collapsed and was abandoned after 1.4 billion francs had been spent on it; a planned conference centre in Paris which remained unbuilt despite the expenditure of 800 million francs; and a road bridge in Normandy with no road connected to it. No heads have rolled, or not to the knowledge of the taxpayers who footed the bill in each case. From teachers to mandarins, the civil service is unaccountable to anybody except itself. A damning report by an *Inspecteur des Finances* who had been close to the Socialists spoke of a looming disaster caused by the failure of successive governments of left and right to get to grips with the size and cost of the public-service sector.

In the nineteenth century, the state was at the vanguard of modernity, the guardian of the legacy of 1789. 'The English have William Shakespeare,' wrote the historian Jules Michelet, 'we have the French Revolution.' Having despatched their royal family, the French bowed the knee before the Nation and its representative on Earth. By the end of the twentieth century, however, the state has become a bulwark of conservative paternalism which the French find too comfortable to be questioned. Envious as they may be of Tony Blair's success, few politicians in Paris would dare to proclaim the New Labour doctrine that the issue is not what the state can do for you, but what it can enable you to do for yourself. For the French, what the state can do for them is a central plank of existence, and one which they will not readily give up.

That is not to say that they do not complain about its tentacles, particularly when this involves endless form-filling. In his 1995 presidential campaign, Jacques Chirac spoke stirringly about the need to make the state less grand and more impartial. But, while they may sometimes resent its encroachment on their individual lives, the French do not necessarily want any less pomp and circumstance, or any less of a buffer against the cold world outside. They would probably like the state to be more impartial, less political – at least, when their own interests are not being advanced. But they know that the chances are slim of any President loosening the grip of his men and women on the levers of power in the official apparatus, the state banks and companies, public utilities and a hundred other domains. In the republican ideal, the state should be not only the national glue, but also above reproach. In practice, it is the supreme power machine. No politician to date has shown any sign of taking a self-denying ordinance on pulling its levers, and the people whom *l'État* is meant to serve are caught in its vice, lacking the will or the nerve to free themselves and without leaders who would take them down such an adventurous path.

National unity has, in some ways, been bolstered by the standardisation of life. Local dialects and customs have been swamped by a television culture and by the mobility of modern transport. If regional media flourish, they are increasingly uniform: one group controls 36 per cent of the press with chains of local newspapers that share services and pages. More than a third of France's population live in suburban houses. The nuclear family of northern France has definitively won out over the extended family of the south. The nationwide Minitel computer service has made local telephone directories a thing of the past.

Despite this, France remains a country of many parts, and its regions prove a balance for the state to which they belong. The split dates back for more than 2,000 years – Julius Caesar famously found Gaul divided into three parts. In a highly imaginative declaration, François Mitterrand spoke of the Gauls as having forged the first manifestation of French unity. Sheer rubbish: the Gauls were split into dozens of warring tribes which made them effective guerrilla fighters, and it was only when they made the error of banding together into large armies that the Romans defeated them. But the conquerors still failed to impose unity on the land and then, under Charlemagne's empire, France itself was divided along the Loire. The Vikings found the country so permeable that they sailed three times down rivers to Clermont-Ferrand in the heart of the Massif Central. The dynastic conflicts of the Hundred Years' War tore the land on lines of variable geography.

It is not surprising, therefore, that, since the unifying genius of Louis XI brought the modern nation together at the end of the fifteenth century, France has been obsessed by the idea of itself as a single entity bounded on three sides by the sea and on three others by its neighbours. It couldn't do anything about the sea, but, as the historian Fernand Braudel observed: 'Europe, by surrounding France, both traced and limited its destiny.' The search for patriotic balm after the loss of Alsace-Lorraine to Germany in 1870 led all the way back to the baptism of the late fifth-century Frankish king, Clovis, in the eastern city of Reims. This event, it was argued, marked the birth of France under the umbrella of the Church. The reality is that it took six more centuries for monarchs to call themselves kings of France, and historians date the first cries of '*Vive la France*' to 1580. But, though the date given for the baptism is probably wrong, the myth remains as strong as ever, and 1996 saw a succession of 1,500-year anniversary celebrations. The French unitary state, it seems, needs sources of reassurance as much as its people.

But, alongside this mantra, the legacy of regional power-players runs on down the ages. Some were mightier than the king sheltering in his small domain of the Île-de-France. A Duke of Normandy conquered England; and an Aquitainian marriage gave the English a great domain and the pretext for a hundred years of war on French soil. Normans and then the Counts of Anjou reigned over Sicily; other Normans set up as rulers in the Holy Land. Had they possessed greater will-power, the Counts of Toulouse might have established a separate kingdom in the south which, with neighbouring Provence, would have looked west and east along the Mediterranean coast, rather than northwards to Paris.

As France took shape, there was often a complex continental dimension which added an ingredient that the island nation to the north never experienced. Take, as an example, the story of the strikingly beautiful fortress on the hill of the town of Najac in the Aveyron department of the south-west. Probably a Roman oppidium in the first century after Christ, it gravitated into the orbit of the powerful Counts of Toulouse, but then passed to the English after Eléonore d'Aquitaine was repudiated by the King of France and married Henry

II from across the water. The destinies of England, France, Toulouse
and northern Spain collided there when Henry's son, Richard the
Lionheart, met the ruler of Aragon at the castle of Najac to forge a
pact against the Count of Toulouse. But then the Count's son married
one of Henry II's daughters, which put Najac back under the authority of Toulouse. Najac was strategically important because it towered
over a vital river route through a lush and fruitful area where four
powers jockeyed for influence. As the thirteenth century dawned,
Anglo-Norman Crusaders swept down from the north to exterminate
the followers of the Albigensian heresy in one of the most damnable
expeditions of European history. After the Counts of Toulouse bent
the knee to the invaders, the inhabitants of Najac were declared
heretics and sentenced to build a large church atop the hill beside the
castle. But when Count Raymond VII failed to produce a male heir,
the fortress returned to the King of France, only to revert to the control of Toulouse five years later. Half a century after that, the English
regained control of the region, but their rule provoked the people of
Najac into a revolt in which they massacred the occupying garrison.
Other English occupiers returned for a while, but Najac then became
French for good. Such places show the complexities of history behind
the façade of a single French identity. From the Rhine frontier to the
Pyrenees, France is made up of a complex of characteristic regions,
localities and characters which draw on different pasts, and need to be
woven together rather than being taken as given parts of a uniform
whole by the centralising heirs of the revolutionary Jacobins.

To add to the complexity, some regions, and their capital cities,
look beyond France's frontiers to old links that confirm their wider
identities. Thus, Montpellier and Toulouse shared southern roots with
Barcelona and Catalonia; Bordeaux retains links with Britain, some of
its best vineyards being called Montrose, Talbot or Lynch; Nice has a
strong Italian streak; and the towns of Alsace could be Rhineland
German. In the west, an organisation called the Atlantic Arc, with its
headquarters in the Breton capital of Rennes, is trying to stitch
together the old Gaelic world of Ireland, Wales, Cornwall, western
France and northern Spain.

Within France, regional groupings reach into the heart of the capital. Hard-working men and women from the Auvergne and Aveyron
dominate the café trade in Paris: a parish priest who runs a hostel for

young men up from the Cantal department reckons he can find them a job as a waiter within twenty-four hours of their arrival. There has long been a Corsican bond in the Paris police and the civil service – a 'Corsican clan' whose members were called Tiberi, Dominati and Romani helped Jacques Chirac to run the capital for many years. Associations linked to rural communes in far-flung parts of the country attract hundreds of diners to their annual banquets. The area round the Gare Montparnasse, where the trains from the west arrive, is stuffed with Breton restaurants – in one street alongside the station, there are restaurants and cafés named after the towns of Saint-Malo, Nantes and Morlaix, plus L'Atlantique, L'Océan, Au Rendez-Vous des Bretons and a branch of the Banque de Bretagne. Some of the best *choucroute* in town is to be found by the Gare de l'Est at the end of the tracks from Alsace. (In London terms, this would be like finding a collection of haggis restaurants around King's Cross, Yorkshire Pudding joints at Euston and Dover Sole specialists at Victoria.) As wise rulers have understood, the people of France want their regional diversity to be respected: they need to feel that they are Savoyards as they sip their *vin jaune* or Vendéens as they remember their ancestors' resistance to the pagan revolutionaries of 1789.

Long ago, De Tocqueville and Montesquieu admired England as a nation where local government flourished and the edicts of the centre were circumscribed by local power bases. Two centuries later, France had one elected local councillor to every 110 voters, compared to one to 1,800 in Britain. The layers of government enshrine the nation's diversity – the central administration in Paris, 22 regions, 96 departments and the 36,500 communes, each with its own mayor and council. In Paris, the twenty *arrondissements* have a mayor under the city's supreme boss. In the provinces, departments and regions of France, the local rulers have always been anxious to flex their muscles against the power of the capital and the mandarins in the ministries – and against one another, as seen in the long-running political contest between the power-brokers of individual departments and the politicians running the larger regions to which they belong.

When France rises against the central administration's proposed changes to public-sector working conditions, sociologists detect a strong element of revolt against Paris as the place which issues orders. Marches through the streets of the capital may catch the eye of foreign correspondents, but the real action is often in the provinces – in Marseille, in Brest or Nice, where mass demonstrations in 1996 became festive occasions harking back to 1968 and even to the Popular Front. As the old nation looks warily at the modern world, its regions become places where France is still France, the living symbols of freedom from the embrace of the central power, with its technocrats and its unsmiling modern logic. Beneath the unity imposed on the country over the last two centuries, there are still two nations, the old divisions fanned into new life by the social and economic changes of the late twentieth century. For mayors of big towns and cities from the opposition parties, these upsurges of anti-government local feeling can provide a useful means of buttressing their own authority. But, even in the absence of such rallying causes for resentment against the rule of the technocrats in the ministries in Paris, the strength of regionalism provides an essential and enduring counterpoint to the homogenisation of French life and the political power of the centre. Ironically, this applies even to the very seat of that power.

As well as being capital to the nation, Paris is also a great regional city whose people have a historic role in rising up to deliver judgement on the national authorities. The Revolution and the Commune have been succeeded by more peaceful manifestations of the popular will, but Paris was not allowed to have an elected mayor until 1976 because of the central government's fear of the authority he would wield. The surrounding region of the Île-de-France houses one-sixth of France's population. An official survey in 1998 placed it as West Europe's biggest economic region, accounting for 5 per cent of European Union production. It is a truism to note that Paris isn't France, but the way the city was run by Jacques Chirac for eighteen years did much to explain the earlier fears about creating his post. 'What we've done for Paris, we will do tomorrow for France,' he announced as he moved down the right bank of the Seine to the Élysée Palace in 1995. If his country was to be a beacon for the world, he had spent the previous years trying to make sure that its capital would light the way for the nation.

From the City Hall by the Seine, Chirac commanded a system of iron political control, efficient public services, gentrification and expansion helped along by the state. As shown by scandals which oozed out after his departure, the city fathers knew how to cut deals – and corners. But he kept the municipal debt low by the standards of France's expansive city governments, though some experts warned that taxes would have to rise sharply as the true price of Chirac's spending finally came home to roost. Like its mayor, Paris is a proud place which wants to look good. It spends 20 per cent of its budget on keeping itself clean, and employs 4,200 gardeners to tend 6,425 acres of parks and gardens. The public buildings spawned by three Presidents of the Republic have given it a new allure, from the renovated Natural History museum in the Jardin des Plantes to the Science Park in the old slaughterhouse district of La Villette. The renovated Louvre, with its once-controversial glass pyramid in the courtyard, attracts twice as many visitors as it did when you had to search for its treasures through musty rooms and endless corridors. The Prince of the City works in the biggest office in the whole country. His City Hall, rebuilt after being burned during the Commune uprising in 1871, has 1,290 windows and 142 Baccarat crystal chandeliers. For a while after France's first defeat by the Germans, it was the seat of the national government. The index of the great French reference book, *Quid*, has a single entry for Hôtel de Ville: naturally it is for the one in Paris.

In the world's imagination, the city remains unique, a city of style, beauty and love with more familiar monuments and heart-stopping second-hand memories than anywhere else. This is where Americans fall in love, and Ted Hughes and Sylvia Plath honeymooned. But the French themselves say they would rather live in a dozen other cities elsewhere in the country. *Le Figaro* judges the capital to be a joyless, overcrowded metropolis where neighbourhoods have lost their individual character to bargain-basement conformity. Half a million dogs (nearly one for every four inhabitants) deposit 16 tonnes of excrement in the streets each day. Fundamentalist Islamic terrorism hit with murderous attacks on public transport and shops. That led to the lids on street litter-bins being temporarily sealed to prevent bombs being put inside, after which newspapers reported that the feast of rubbish on the pavements had produced a breed of super-rats up to a foot in length.

On the Left Bank of the Seine, the classic intellectual mecca of

Saint-Germain-des-Prés has been declared dead by the intelligentsia as fashion outlets replace bookshops, philosophers vanish, jazz joints close and publishers move to cheaper areas. The district, meanwhile, merchandises itself with a vengeance. 'Limoges pillboxes with Jean-Paul Sartre's glasses on top of them: I mean, who the hell buys them?' wondered the American journalist Stanley Karnow as he recalled the village of Saint-Germain he had known in the late 1940s. 'And here is the Simone de Beauvoir ashtray.' Local residents, including the actress Catherine Deneuve and singers Juliette Gréco and Charles Aznavour, grew so worried that they formed an association called SOS Saint-Germain to save the district's soul. 'Little by little, Saint-Germain has turned into Monaco,' lamented the Goncourt prize-winning novelist and former presidential adviser Éric Arnould. But Ms Gréco was still reported to have found time to help design a four-storey fashion and entertainment emporium for Giorgio Armani in the heart of the *quartier*, beside the venerable political eating-house of the Brasserie Lipp.

The popular spirit that was once an essential element in the city's lifeblood has been swamped in many areas by gentrification. Lightly-clad whores still throng the upper reaches of the Rue Saint-Denis, and bicycling police have been reintroduced to control the straight and transsexual prostitutes of the Bois de Boulogne. More than 10,000 concierges defy the onward march of the entry phone, and there are plenty of old courtyards to rouse nostalgia from one end of the city to the other. But the days of sparrow singers in the street, *bals populaires* and the great food market of Les Halles are long gone. The *petites gens* and the craftsmen who made the reputation of Paris as a bustling, irreverent people's city have moved to the suburbs. The city centre has become an upper-middle-class place; 'the world centre of nostalgia', in the words of the *Times Literary Supplement*. Paris gave France the idea of democracy being exercised in the streets, from the barricades and populist chaos of the nineteenth century to the marches against Alain Juppé in 1996. The boulevards can still be relied on to provide a touch of political psycho-drama for the nation, but for many of its inhabitants – and even more for the workers commuting from the ever-growing suburbs – the capital is becoming 'a decor city', a splendid showplace from which the mass of people grow increasingly alienated.

For their part, not all foreigners are charmed when they reach the

City of Light. A survey carried out by the Paris Chamber of Commerce reported that tourists found the inhabitants rude, aggressive, dirty, idle and disorganised. English visitors down the decades have taken the short manner in which the natives often deal with one another as a deliberate attempt to be obnoxious to visitors. 'Age cannot wither, nor custom stale, her infinite vulgarity,' was the verdict of the writer William Gaddis after living in the city. A KGB agent recalled how, meeting a French contact, he found Montmartre nothing but a 'hell' of exhaust fumes from tourist buses – in 1997 the mayor's office recognised the extent of the problem by banning buses from driving up the hill to the Sacré Coeur.

Many of those who live in the twenty *arrondissements* have been hit where it hurts most, in their pockets: the value of old flats which Parisians bought with enthusiasm as investments in the early 1990s fell by more than a quarter in the following five years while average property values slumped by 62 per cent in the six years to 1996. Nor are Parisians as rich or productive as might appear. A survey by the Swiss bank UBS put Paris ninth among world cities in the cost of living but eighteenth in net wages. Although it is Europe's biggest economic region, the Île-de-France ranks only fifth in productivity.

And when it comes to the sheen of art, the capital is hardly what it was. Zola wrote of the Belly of Paris, Hugo put Quasimodo up on Notre Dame, Proust wended his way through turn-of-the-century salons, the Impressionists immortalised the banks of the Seine, the boulevards and the Gare Saint-Lazare, while a string of entertainers and actors made the most of the *parigot* accent. The city will always have a unique face, with the Champs-Élysées, Eiffel Tower, Arc de Triomphe, Louvre museum, three-rosette restaurants, *bateaux-mouches* on the Seine, cafés under the chestnut trees and an enduring air of cosmopolitan life. But who writes great novels about the city or paints great pictures of it any more? The last moving song about waking up in the capital was written in the 1970s.

Politically, the city offered a model for any statist control freak for two decades after Chirac became master of the Hôtel de Ville. From the start, the mayor drew Giscard's supporters into his tent – and he certainly knew how to look after his citizens. Thirty-six per cent of city spending goes on social services and education, 16 per cent on the environment. Buses for the handicapped, hostels for AIDS sufferers, help for the aged, sumptuous boxes of chocolates for pensioners at Christmas . . . there was no end to the largesse. Chirac operated through a select band of officials and a few trusted councillors with a kitchen Cabinet that was as notorious for its internal rivalries as for its loyalty to the boss. In 1993, the Gaullists and their allies won control of all twenty *arrondissements* of the capital. In Chirac's last year as mayor, his opponents occupied only 22 of the 163 seats on the City Council. They increased that to 61 in municipal elections in 1995, but the Gaullists and their allies still held a comfortable majority as they battened down the hatches against a storm of scandal allegations stretching all the way from the new mayor's family to the financing of the Gaullist machine. In 1997, however, Paris was hit by the national wave of rejection against Chirac and his former lieutenant at the Hôtel de Ville, Alain Juppé. Followers of the mayor-become-President lost seven of their National Assembly seats in the city to the Socialists who, with their allies, now held nine of the twenty-one Parisian parliamentary constituencies. Chirac's successor, Jean Tiberi, held on to his constituency by under 3,000 votes, but the former Minister of Justice and long-time Chirac companion in arms, Jacques Toubon, lost his.

The political change owed something to the wearing effects of almost two decades in power. But it also reflected the sides of the city's evolution which Chirac didn't talk about too much. While the Île-de-France boomed in population and riches, the population of Paris itself has fallen by a fifth since the early 1960s. The city is increasingly dependent on the transitory service sector for employment. There are big problems with homelessness, drugs and AIDS – not to mention unemployment only just below the national level. Crime has risen on the streets and under the ground, where late travellers on the Métro watch over their shoulders and hurry through the corridors. All the cars driving to its multiplying parking garages have sent air pollution to unprecedentedly dangerous levels. Nearly half of all emergency calls by doctors to children in Paris involve respiratory problems. How the pigeons survive in the traffic-clogged square in front of the Opéra or the Place de la Concorde is a miracle. One story about Chirac's pride in his city concerns a drive he made with the Minister of the Interior. Remarking on their uninterrupted progress, he congratulated himself on the success of his administration in getting the traffic moving so smoothly; the minister replied that it was more of a tribute to his own success in getting the police to make sure all the lights on their route went green as they approached.

Among the people of Paris, some paid the price for the Chirac vision of the capital as more and more traditional labouring areas turned into middle-class developments. 'Simple people have been made to leave, the very character of parts of Paris has been destroyed,' lamented one opposition leader. The old pattern of property owner-ship was broken by taxation and inheritance duties. In 1950, 68 per cent of Paris buildings were owned by individuals; now, that has shrunk to around 20 per cent. The gentrification of the city was matched by an office construction spree, which led to a glut of new commercial property and the descent of foreign 'vulture fund' investors out to buy empty buildings for half their original price. On the edges of town, rows of charming two-storey houses have been remorselessly torn down to make way for flats. The developers ruled, and the authorities made sure nobody got in their way. That pained lovers of old Paris, and gave rise to persistent allegations of kickbacks. But the sentimental folklore forgets the decaying dwellings, the shared lavato-ries on the landing, the insalubrious conditions which fuelled cross-Channel jibes about French dirtiness. A walk through the Sentier district off the Grands Boulevards, with its crowded workshops, fire-hazard buildings, dim cobbled courtyards, illegal immigrants, creaking stairways, prostitutes, rats and zinc-bar cafés provides a quick shot of nostalgia. Not many people would like actually to live there.

If Paris is a region of France, it is, by its nature, a rather special kind of region. Local and national interest overlap, and its mayor of two decades was a master at exploiting the situation. Nearly 30 per cent of the city's revenue comes in grants from central government or the sur-rounding Île-de-France. Farmers in the Jura or Languedoc help to keep Paris Métro tickets cheap by subsidies paid with their taxes. They do not complain because, wherever they are, the French regard Paris as a city that represents their land: they may not want to live there, but they wish it to shine. Jacques Chirac knew how to exploit that feeling and the relationship with the sugar-daddy up the road in the Élysée to the full. When François Mitterrand unveiled his plans to renovate the Louvre, including the controversial pyramid in the court-yard designed by the Chinese–American architect I. M. Pei some

Gaullists urged the mayor to denounce the project as a sacrilege. Chirac said nothing. The Louvre became a sparkling marvel, opening on to the restored Tuileries gardens and the spruced-up Place de la Concorde, and then along one of the world's great perspectives of the Champs-Élysées to the Arc de Triomphe. The glory belonged to Paris, and Jacques Chirac was the prince of the city. But, of the whole stretch from the courtyard of the Louvre to the Place de l'Étoile, only the Champs-Élysées was his concern. The rest – like Notre Dame, the Pompidou Centre, Les Invalides or the Seine – belonged to the state. But who cared? The government paid for their upkeep; Chirac smiled and took the credit for his city and himself.

On a rung just below the Mayor of Paris, his peers in other cities are also real power-brokers in a way unknown in Britain since the beginning of this century. This country which has made a religion out of centralisation has also nurtured a multi-layered structure of regional authority whose influence was boosted by the decentralisation of the 1980s. But, in a Gallic twist, the provincial nabobs are not content with their weight back home; they also want a national stage. So they become ministers, run parties, even head governments, and all the while remain mayors of large cities and smaller towns, and preside over regional councils. Some leading politicians remain at the head of local government for an extraordinary length of time – a tradition set under earlier Republics when a figure like Édouard Daladier, the pre-war Prime Minister, held sway as mayor of the southern town of Carpentras from 1912 to 1958. The elder statesman of the post-war right, Antoine Pinay, outdid him in mayoral longevity, reigning in the town of Saint-Chamond in the middle of France from 1928 to 1977. A leading Gaullist of the Fourth and Fifth Republics, Jacques Chaban-Delmas, carried on the tradition as Mayor of Bordeaux for almost half a century, from 1947 to 1995.

There is a term for all this – *cumul des mandats*, or the accumulation of electoral mandates. The practice has diminished from the days when a provincial notable could hold half a dozen posts simultaneously. Members of the National Assembly are now permitted to occupy only one other significant elected post, and their total incomes have been capped. Lionel Jospin is committed to reducing the accumulation further. He is struggling against an entrenched tradition in which some 90 per cent of deputies also held a local government post. More than half were mayors. Eighteen ministers held local posts. Governments in Paris come and go: provincial politics are for life.

Thus, Chaban-Delmas made sure he hung on to his fief in Bordeaux as he moved from the Defence Ministry to the Presidency of the National Assembly and eventually to the Hôtel Matignon for a not particularly happy spell as Prime Minister. Through it all, he never neglected the city, and it never forsook him. Eating the local speciality of oysters and sausages in a restaurant there, I was surprised when the other clients suddenly got to their feet and burst into applause: Chaban-Delmas was passing by, and they wanted to say hello. Another Gaullist, Alain Juppé, succeeded him in wine heaven when he, too, had just become Premier in Paris. In his national role, Juppé earned an unenviable reputation for his lack of anything like the common touch, but he left the Matignon every Friday to devote the weekend to getting to know the capital of Aquitaine, touring the city, opening trade fairs, cheering on the Girondins soccer team, dropping in at bars and jogging in the park. He ran for a parliamentary constituency from the city, and was there when the catastrophe of the 1997 election results began to filter through.

Other towns and cities were put on the national political map by their mayors. A slightly dotty defender of small businesses was emboldened by his record running Tours to mount a quixotic presidential bid. The moderate Mayor of La Rochelle became a symbol of the alliance of environmentalism and orthodox politics after turning his port into a green citadel. The undistinguished towns of Château-Chinon in the west of Burgundy and Conflans-Sainte-Honorine outside Paris acquired unwarranted fame through the presence of François Mitterrand and Michel Rocard as their mayors. In a different mode, Canon Félix Kir, Mayor of Dijon, became one of France's most celebrated names through his taste for mixing blackcurrant liquor and the local white wine.

Despite the media's concentration on national politics as played out in the republican palaces of Paris, political shifts in the regions often pre-figure national movements. One key to the left's victory in 1981 was the way it had expanded its control of electoral bastions across the country in the previous years. A sweep of twenty of France's twenty-two regional councils by the right in 1992 foreshadowed its subsequent parliamentary and presidential victories. The left's recovery in regional polls six years later was a key element in the Socialist strategy of retaining the presidency. A death-knell had sounded for the Communists when they began to lose their local government strongholds in the 1970s and 1980s – and were constrained by economics to close down the regional editions of their daily newspaper. Once they had got over the shock of defeat in 1981, the former President and Prime Minister each began their comeback bids in the middle of the country, not in national politics.

Like Richard Daley in Chicago or Willy Brandt in West Berlin, French big-city mayors can be the epitome of the place they run – Pierre Mauroy the bluff friend of the workers who takes coach trips to Portugal for his holiday; Chaban-Delmas and Juppé the suave representatives of their elegant city on the Gironde; the former Prime Minister Raymond Barre symbolising the sensible conservatism and gastronomic excellence of Lyon; or the disgraced Mayor of Nice, Jacques Médecin, as the raffish, high-living symbol of the Riviera. But, while underpinning the dichotomy between central and regional authority, the combination of powers which they exercise reinforces the closed political society in which the same limited circle of politicians have their hands on the levers in Paris and the provinces, guiding the state in their chosen direction. Ideally, the regional element should provide a countervailing influence to centralism. The snag is that, increasingly, both Parisian and provincial interests have been swallowed up by the same closely-knit group. With their range of social, economic, cultural and geographical differences, France's provinces might have come up with diverse answers to the problems facing the nation. But the system ties them to the centre, not only by the authority of *l'État* but also through the men and women who hang so determinedly to both their ministerial offices and their mayoral sashes. Just as politicians of different stripes swim in the same mainstream, so the interests of the regions end up in the lap of the central power. In the late 1980s, Jacques Chirac was Prime Minister, leader of the RPR party and Mayor of Paris at the same time; ten years on, the only difference for Alain Juppé was that his mayoral office was by the Gironde river rather than the Seine. In each case, whatever their concern for their cities, national destiny was bound to take first place. For an even longer-lived example of how the system works, and the perils it can contain, take a trip to the port city which regards itself as one of a kind.

For four decades, Gaston Defferre *was* Marseille. An afternoon with him at the height of his power was a living illustration of how a big boss operated – a clique of courtiers bowing to his every whim, a ward boss explaining what favours he needed to keep key voters happy, a businessman coming in to talk about planning regulations, a boat-builder submitting plans for the mayor's new yacht, and the editor of the main local newspaper ringing to read out the leading article of the night. Defferre had grabbed the paper at the Liberation in the summer of 1944 by the simple expedient of walking into the building with two pistols stuck in his belt and taking control from its collaborationist proprietors. Four decades later, he tried to convince his friend the President of the Republic that his wartime background would enable him to persuade the terrorist Carlos not to attack French targets if only they could meet and talk as one resistance fighter to another.

Such romanticism goes to the heart of Marseille, the city after which France's revolutionary national anthem is named. Defferre was the only French minister to have risked his life in a duel – not once but twice, with swords and pistols. That was the kind of exploit that his city loved, and that made France love his city. Marseille has a special place in French hearts, with its buccaneering tradition, its flamboyant gangsters, its *bouillabaisse* fish stew, and its equally pungent local accent. More than a century as the gateway to the colonies brought wealth from trade with overseas possessions. It was the door to adventure and fortune-seeking in Africa or the East, for the eventual return from exotic journey – the poet Rimbaud came home to die in a Marseille hospital with his leg amputated after a decade of travels in Africa – and, in the other direction, for deportation of political prisoners to exile in Algeria. The city thrived on melodrama and a belief in its special corner in southern folk wisdom. Its people like to think of themselves as being larger than life, personified by figures like the late *pastis* king, Paul Ricard, whose name appears each year on 90 million bottles of the world's third-biggest-selling brand of spirits, and who, though not a Catholic, took his entire workforce to Rome to be blessed by the Pope. Throughout the twentieth century,

Marseille provided a home for immigrants from all around the Mediterranean – Armenians fleeing Turkish massacres, Greeks from Asia Minor, Spanish Republicans, Jews and Christians expelled from Nasser's Egypt, and then tens of thousands of *pied noir* settlers from former colonies in North Africa. The city was both outward-looking and self-regarding. The port was not unlike a stage. Its theatrical potential was not lost on one of the great dramatic figures of modern France: Charles de Gaulle once addressed a crowd from a boat moored opposite the main quayside to such effect that those standing at the front were pushed into the sea by the pressure of those behind. Music hall, operetta and popular theatre merged into every-day life and politics, epitomised in Marcel Pagnol's immortal fictional characters of Marius, Fanny and César in the Vieux Port. As played by the prodigious actor Raimu, César gave France an iconic father-figure, a dominating presence swinging from pathos to humour, an unschooled fountain of native wit and cunning. As the cinema histo-rian Ginette Vincendeau has noted, the Pagnol trilogy was a paean to archaic values, spreading the notion of a specifically southern culture to the rest of the nation through the cinema. If Marseille already believed itself to be special, Pagnol and millions of cinema-goers con-firmed it in that belief.

It was an amenable place, ready to offer anything the visitor wanted. During the First World War, a British troopship filled with Indian soldiers being sent to die on the Western Front hove into view and sent a request for 1,000 'girls' to be waiting for them; the mayor said he could summon up 300 young women immediately. The message was then corrected to call for 1,000 'goats'. If that's their plea-sure, so be it, said the mayor. Even the underworld was painted in romantic colours, as in the hit film *Borsalino*, which brought Jean-Paul Belmondo and Alain Delon together in a tale of men who did what they had to do under cover of their broad-brimmed hats. The reality was less glamorous: the two gangsters on whom the starring roles were modelled formed a compact with quasi-fascist officials in the 1930s which allowed them to ply their trade unhindered and to get into the drugs business.

During the war, the city became the base for an extraordinary American Scarlet Pimpernel, Varian Fry, who arrived in 1940 with a dress suit bought in his last hours in New York, $3,000 taped to one leg and a list of 200 artists and writers he had come to spirit out of occupied France during what was meant to be a three-week mission. In the end, Fry, the son of a stockbroker with a red carnation in his buttonhole, stayed in Marseille for thirteen months. Working with false passports from the Czechoslovak consul and forged papers, he personally helped Marc Chagall, Hannah Arendt, Max Ernst, Wanda Landowska and 1,200 others to leave France for the safety of America. His wider operation, run from Marseille, is estimated to have saved 4,000 in all. Evidently, the local police were impressionable: when they took Chagall away from his hotel in one of the early round-ups, Fry telephoned to warn them that the arrest of such a famous artist would embarrass Vichy. If Chagall wasn't freed within half an hour, Fry threatened to inform the *New York Times*. Chagall was released, and, after bizarrely assuring himself that there were cows in America, crossed the Atlantic.

After the war, the hoods who had picked the winning side took control of France's biggest port. They helped the CIA by attacking the Communist dockers' union and, in return, got a free hand to export heroin across the Atlantic. Marseille became a major world narcotics centre. The heroin 'cooks' worked in remote houses in the country-side, in cellars, out-houses, garages and tenements. At the pinnacle of production in the mid-1960s, according to a historian of the opium trade, Martin Booth, there were about two dozen laboratories operating around the clock, producing high-grade heroin of a purity usually difficult to attain. The drugs went to America either direct or via France's overseas possessions in the Caribbean, where customs checks were minimal. In time, the American authorities hit back, arresting a top chemist involved and shutting down the main distrib-ution point in New York – known as the Pleasant Avenue Con-nection. *The French Connection* told of the fight against the Marseille traffickers. And, as the exports to the USA became more difficult, some of the narcotics barons began selling heroin in their own country.

Through all this, the nominally Socialist Gaston Defferre held the city in the palm of his weather-beaten yachtsman's hand. He was invulnerable, and did not need to be too scrupulous in his choice of associates. A suppressed photograph showed the mayor at the head of a political procession arm-in-arm with a leading underworld figure. This man helped to organise his campaigns, had an office in the City

Hall, and told police who had the audacity to try to arrest him: 'Let me go or I'll talk.'

Defferre was a fixture in the national parliament and served as a minister under the Fourth Republic. In 1969 he made an ill-advised bid for the presidency, netting just 5 per cent of the vote. That didn't dent his authority, however, for his passport to power was down on the Mediterranean, where he ruled from City Hall behind the Quai du Port or by remote-control from his large yachts. While nobody suggested that he had anything to hide personally, the fact was that Gaston could get away with just about anything he chose. The Socialist Party needed the Marseille electorate, and Defferre always delivered. It was an era when taxis were sent to pick up elderly voters who could be counted on to vote as he wished. This ensured that nobody on the non-Communist left in Paris would raise any questions about how he ran things back home, and would accord him proper deference when he travelled north. Successive governments of the centre-right saw him as a dependable anti-Communist bulwark, and did not object if their local chieftains allied themselves with City Hall. Defferre's system had room for every shade of opinion, so long as it wasn't Communist. He maintained a right-wing newspaper, *Le Méridional*, alongside his pale pink flagship, *Le Provençal*.

After thirty-five years in power, Defferre set off on a fresh crusade against the local Marxists, aiming to hit where it would hurt them most – in their party's pocket. That is to say, in the welfare system of the Bouches-du-Rhône department around his city, which was controlled by the Communist-led union federation, the CGT. The ensuing saga demonstrated the way in which regional and national politics merge into one another. An efficient civil servant from the Paris region, René Lucet, was brought south to do the job on the Communists. Lucet went to work with a will. He discovered how welfare funds had been diverted into party coffers, and began to take steps to put things right. The Communists were up in arms, but Lucet had the backing of both the mayor and the right-wing government up in the capital. So far so good. Then the left won power in 1981, and everything changed. Gaston Defferre became Interior Minister and the second-ranking member of the first Socialist government of the Fifth Republic. It was an honour which brought obligations with it. Some of Defferre's Cabinet colleagues were of a more ideological bent than him: a left-wing Socialist took charge of Social Security, and a Communist became Minister of Health. Defferre saw the way the wind was blowing. The heat had to be taken off the CGT. René Lucet was abruptly sacked. In March 1982, he killed himself.

The outcry was deeply embarrassing for Defferre. It appeared to show him as a man who, in his new national functions, could not – or would not – stand up to the Communists or left-wing Socialists in Paris as he had done in his own city. After four decades in power, clay seemed to be adhering to the feet of the César of City Hall. The right-wing press made sure that story ran and ran, and gave it additional spice by reporting two conflicting autopsy findings: one showed that Lucet had a single bullet in his skull, the other disclosed two. In a city where the police and the underworld traditionally drank at the same table, that went down as *suicide à la Marseillaise*.

The Lucet case symbolised the decline of a city. A string of municipal scandals which once would have been hushed up broke into the open. A local police chief and five members of his family were murdered by three Gaullist toughs. Even the mayor's associate in the underworld with his office in City Hall wound up in jail. With the colonies gone and nothing much to replace it, local commerce slumped into the doldrums. Rising unemployment and a big immigrant population helped to raise social tension. Once a centre for drug traffickers who exported their poison, Marseille increasingly became a home for hard-core addicts, reckoned to number 5,000.

Defferre died in 1986. His successor, a local doctor without a solid political base, ruled in an increasingly solitary manner. The Defferre coalition fell apart in a jungle of feuds: the old man's widow, a distinguished author known for her implacable hatreds, banned any mention of those she considered to have been disloyal to her husband from the pages of *Le Provençal*. With growing tension over the presence of immigrants from across the sea, Marseille and the surrounding area became a breeding-ground for the National Front, while the left could find no better champion than Bernard Tapie, who even managed to tarnish the city's sporting pride and joy. In National Assembly elections in 1993, the Socialists contrived to hold only two seats in the Marseille region, one fewer than the Communists. And, in another change whose symbolism spoke volumes, a national press chain run by Paris businessmen sympathetic to the right bought Defferre's old newspapers, merging *Le Provençal* and *Le Méridional* into a single daily to support the old lion's one-time opponents.

In due course, the mayor's office passed to the mainstream right, and the national connection which had thrived under Defferre re-emerged. The new conservative king of the city, Jean-Claude Gaudin, proved himself adept at melding his power-base on the Mediterranean, his position as a leader of the main non-Gaullist party of the right – the Union pour la Démocratie Française – and his ministerial claims in Paris. He became Mayor of Marseille, Senator or Deputy for the Bouches-du-Rhône department, president of the regional council and leader of the UDF party group in the National Assembly – and also found time to put his name to three books. At the end of 1995, Gaudin gave up his seat in the Senate – but only because he was named as Minister of Regional Development, Towns and Integration. As one of his aides put it: 'A mayor who is a minister is precious, particularly when it comes to getting European funding.' The *cumul des mandats* might be a target of attack from the Socialist government, but if it brought industry and jobs, the people of Marseille were not going to complain – not in the state in which they had found themselves amid the ruins of the Defferre system.

Several chapters have passed without mention of food, so let us get back to that key subject, and look at its contribution to the diversity of the nation. Nothing embodies French regionalism so much as what people consume. 'Tell me what you eat, and I'll tell you what you are,' said the gastronomic writer Brillat-Savarin. He might have added, 'and where you come from'. We have noted the link which food provides to the countryside as a whole. Now focus this on the regions. Yes, sales of mass-processed food rise year by year. Yes, France likes to experiment with exotic fruit. And, yes, chic new restaurants in Paris offer tamales, Caesar salads and even English grub. Still, the essentials of eating are rooted in provincial diversity. Dishes may be available across the country, but each has its home. If you can get a perfectly fine *cassoulet* or *sandre au beurre blanc* in Paris, the dishes should truly be eaten in restaurants in Toulouse or the Loire Valley. Tripe in Normandy is different from tripe in Nice or Lyon. How fish is treated in Brittany sets it apart from the Mediterranean. Wine from different regions not only tastes different; it is also put into differently shaped bottles – from the thin containers of Alsace and the elegance of Champagne to the wine pots of Lyon, with their thick glass bottoms designed to keep them upright in the gravel of boulodromes. Regional cuisine is a serious matter for the swelling ranks of food historians and academics. An ethnologist from the south has written a treatise on 'The Influence of the Sardine on the Mediterranean Imagination', while a conference in the eastern city of Nancy heard papers dealing with subjects such as 'An Unusual Island of Stockfish-Eating in Rouergue-Quercy', 'A Spatial Analysis of the Alimentary Habits in Lozère: Oil, Soup and Pig Meat', and 'Pork as a Cultural Determinant in the North-East of France'.

Less academically, the French simply relish the persistence of old dishes from their region. Take some of them and realise why it is no wonder France loves its provinces: Tourte de la Ville de Munster, Choucroute Alsacienne, Kougelhopf, Galette Charentaise, Cul de Veau à l'Angevine, Oie Farcie de Sègre, Boeuf aux Herbes de Massiac, Potée Auvergnate, Toro de Saint-Jean-de-Luz, Sauce Béarnaise, Homard à la Morbihannaise, Brochet Braisé au Champagne, Cou Farci du Quercy, Pommes Sarladaises, Confit d'Oie du Gers, Tête de Veau à la Parisienne, Poularde Demi-deuil de Lyon – not to mention such world favourites as Boeuf Bourguignon, Gratin Dauphinois or Salade Niçoise.

The next course, cheese, has a whole set of regional and historical culture all of its own. The Emperor Charlemagne developed a taste for the unique ewe's milk cheese of Roquefort and had brie from the town of Meaux sent to his court twice a year. Twelve hundred years later, never confuse the Meaux brie with a rival variety from nearby Melun: the head of a three-rosette restaurant in Paris completely lost his customary cool at a lunch some years ago when he was caught out mixing up the two. In another fading of a French icon, consumption of Camembert is falling by 5 per cent a year, but Normans venerate the memory of Marie Harel, the farmer's wife who gave the world the cheese after learning a secret recipe from a priest she hid during the Revolution – in 1928 the President of the Republic, no less, inaugurated a memorial to her in the village of Vitmoutiers in the Orne department.

For the traditional French, a full meal without cheese is like a kiss without a moustache, to adopt an old phrase. It adds a key element to the gastronomic occasion, which becomes essential within minutes of the main dish being cleared away and a new bottle of wine opened. As the food writer Peter Graham points out in his seminal book, *Classic Cheese Cookery*, its makers are true alchemists given the variables that go into their craft: '. . . the type of pasture where the cows are put to graze, the time of year they are milked, the breed of cow, the type of coagulation induced, the way the curd is cut and pressed, the technique of salting, the shaping of the cheese, the length of curing, and the very specific temperatures required at each stage of manufacture. The end product, not surprisingly, assumes a multitude of guises, sizes, textures and flavours that is quite stagger-ing given that most cheeses have but one ingredient: milk.' And nowhere is that staggering range more apparent than in France, with its 250-plus varieties. Criss-cross the country and taste a cheese that goes by the name of the old smelly man of Lille; delight in the deep pungency of Pont-l'Évêque; savour the depths of a mature Cantal cut from a huge chunk, and swallow a tiny goat's cheese in one mouthful; be bored by the blandness of Port-Salut and wolf down the *aligot* and *truffade* of the Auvergne, which mixes local cheese with potatoes in a manner that can only induce *gourmandise*. And pick the right regional wine to go with it – not always the traditional reds, either: those who can afford it hold that a glass of fine Sauternes or two is the perfect accompaniment for Roquefort as well as for *foie gras* and desserts, while the chef's wife at a highly-rated restaurant in Tours insisted that we accompany our goat's cheese with a Loire white, and she wasn't wrong.

For, like food, wine is a reflection of France's regional riches. In the restaurant of the Fagegaltier sisters at Belcastel, which we visited in Chapter 4, one of the delights is to sip the local 80-franc red wine while eating food that elevates the region beyond compare. Meursault is made to go with *suprême de volaille* and Aloxe-Corton with the red-meat dishes of the Côte d'Or; Alsatian wines partner *choucroute*; Muscadet washes down oysters; the rosés of Provence make a sunny fit with Mediterranean fish; and the reds of the south-west stand up to the robust cooking of the area. How could it be otherwise in a country which boasts champagne, the great growths of Bordeaux and Burgundy, Anjou, Sancerre and the wines of the Loire, the ten *crus* of Beaujolais, the riches of the Côtes du Rhône, and the eastern delights of Riesling, Sylvaner and Gewurtztraminer, not to mention Cahors and the flinty wines of Auvergne, or the better products of the Corbières, the Costières de Nîmes and the Minervois, tiny appellations like Bellet on the edge of the southern Alps or Condrieu on the Rhône, or the '-*ac*' vineyards from the south-west – Gaillac, Marcillac, Frontenac, Bergerac? Or take the regional aperitifs, sweet wines and liqueurs: *pastis* from Provence, Vermouth from Chambéry, Salers from the Auvergne, Pineau des Charentes, Banyuls, Rivesaltes and Muscat de Beaume de Venise, Cognac and Armagnac, Marc from Burgundy or Champagne, Calvados from Normandy, Vieille Prune from the Lot or Framboise from Alsace. Each wine, *petit apéro* or *digestif* has a resonance of place, direct proof of the diversity and richness of the land.

For all the frozen pizzas, Dutch pork and German cold cuts on sale in mini-supermarkets throughout rural France, provincial cooking has never been better, and it belongs to the regional wealth of the land from ordinary kitchens to the establishments with three rosettes. France's perennial celebrity chef, Paul Bocuse, is resolutely Lyonnais even if he spends so much of his time trotting the globe; the ascetic star of the wild Aubrac region, Michel Bras, goes running in the morning to find new herbs in the hills around his home town of Laguiole; and to listen to the brothers and sons of the Troisgros restaurant in Roanne talk of the local produce brought to the back door in the morning is to be reminded of the importance of local roots in perhaps the world's greatest eating establishment.

So we have a nation which seeks unity but relishes division, which venerates the strong central state and the fruits it hands out to its people, which is becoming increasingly homogenised on urban, international lines but which craves older values and protection from the rigours of modernity. All this is taking place in a geographical context which appears stable, but which contains some illusions.

The French speak of their country as the Hexagon, clearly defined on all six sides. That has not spared it recurrent invasions – from the migratory movement of pre-history to the last great German attack. The Romans moved up from the south-east, the Arabs from the south-west, the Franks from the east and the English from the north. But today, most of those natural frontiers look pretty solid. Unless you count all those Brits buying up country houses as the heirs of Simon de Montfort, there is no problem with the Channel, while the long Atlantic coast has not seen a hostile force landing since the Duke of Buckingham was repulsed by Richelieu at La Rochelle in 1627. The last conquerors to come ashore in Provence in August 1944 were more than welcome – though Jean-Marie Le Pen would, of course, point to a rather different cross-Mediterranean invasion in recent years.

Internally, regional pride has bred separatist movements in various parts of the country, but, for the most part, their support has been small-scale, connected more to folklore and tradition than to any widespread desire to throw off the yoke of Paris. Brittany has its autonomists, but, apart from setting off a bomb or two, they appear to have been calmed by being given bilingual road-signs and Breton language classes in schools. Along the border with Spain, France's 250,000 Basques proudly guard their identity in far less militant or violent manner than their counterparts across the mountain frontier, and have considerably less say in running their own affairs. In 1996, 63 per cent of mayors in the region voted for the creation of a Basque department, but the central authorities refused to entertain the idea. As the Bordeaux newspaper *Sud-Ouest* noted, France has good reason not to be seen as an encourager of separatism in Quebec: just think of the problems that would be caused if such aspirations were transported to the Basque country. So the Pyrenees can be counted as forming another natural frontier, complete with the duty-free shopping haven of Andorra, whose joint princes are the President of France and the bishop of the nearby Spanish town of Urgel. Then, to the east of the junction of mountains and sea at the Spanish frontier, there stretches the long Mediterranean coast. Here students can learn Provençal, but there is no movement to re-create the great fiefdoms which ruled southern France in the Middle Ages. So the nation seems pretty secure on most sides, but then, 180 kilometres off its southern coast, there lies a cancerous growth on the state of France.

★

On 6 February 1998, the Republic's leading representative in Corsica set out to walk to a classical music concert in the island's capital of Ajaccio. Claude Érignac, a no-nonsense administrator, had been appointed Prefect of Corsica by the government of Alain Juppé in January 1996, and kept in his post by the Socialists the following year. During his two years in the job, the sixty-year-old Érignac had not hesitated to use his authority to block a number of potentially lucrative projects backed by Corsican and Italian entrepreneurs, including a scheme to double the number of slot machines in the Ajaccio casino and another to turn the military barracks in the picturesque port of Bonifacio into a luxury hotel. He had launched probes into alleged fraud in the use of national and European subsidies, and into contracts for waste-disposal and public car-parks. He also had in his files a police report recommending investigations of local banks and racketeering by two well-known gangs – and, most explosive politically, of the island's agriculture which would involve some leading nationalists.

While Claude Érignac was engaged on his prefectoral house-cleaning, life went on as usual on the island justly known as the Île de Beauté. Lying in the Mediterranean between France and Italy, Corsica has a long tradition of violence, clan politics, racketeering, poverty – and a desire to affirm its own identity, if only it knew how. Although it has been under French rule since the eighteenth century, the island and its people are not really French at all.

If the sub-Sicilian gunmen who bomb for independence from the metropolitan government in Paris were not such B-movie hoods, they would have a smidgen of a point. Their homeland is, indeed, a separate place. It is much closer to the Italians who used to rule it than to the mainland. But Corsica faces some major problems in even thinking of divorcing itself from the Hexagon.

After centuries of rule by Genoa, the island did enjoy fourteen years of quasi-independence under Pascal Paoli, the 'father of the nation', in the middle of the eighteenth century. After Paris asserted control, the post-revolutionary wars encouraged Paoli to stage another rising. This ushered in two years of nominal rule by George III, who was proclaimed 'Anglo-Corsican King'. It cannot have been much of a consolation for having lost America. In 1796, Napoléon Bonaparte, who came from one of the island's many feuding clans, reasserted French control. He made no bones about his belief that Corsica should be French once and for all, and that the British-era nonsense about local democracy should be forgotten. He also introduced clan politics to the mainland at the highest levels – the first Bonaparte to become Emperor made sure, disastrously, that he looked after the family, a Godfather before his time. The island is littered with his statues and mementos of his achievements, but his centralising zeal is rarely mentioned – a plaque in the Corsican capital of Ajaccio does, however, recall his role in developing Europe's beet industry. Even his memory is not always greatly respected: the sword on one of the main statues in his honour was bent for many years, and a developer was allowed to pull down his mother's mansion to put up an office block.

More to the current point, the home of the Foreign Legion is an economic basket-case which could not live in its accustomed style without cash from Paris now amounting to 7 billion francs a year. Most of its 250,000 people know that, and the depths of their devotion to their island's separateness is open to considerable doubt. Classes in the island's language have been introduced into the school curriculum, but three-quarters of pupils do not bother to go to them. Only 2 per cent of those sitting the *baccalauréat* take the examination in Corsican. France owes Corsica a blood debt; the island lost huge numbers of men in the trenches of the First World War, and became a land of widows and wounded veterans and sons and daughters without fathers. The dependence on state pensions bred a welfare habit which combined with the outlaw traditions of the maquis brushlands (that gave their name to the Resistance of the Second World War). Together, they created a hopeless culture of life. Today, less than 10 per cent of the population pays income tax, but this is not a poor place – car ownership is above the national average. The island has no industry to speak of and its gross domestic product is 30 per cent below that of France as a whole, but it contains four airports and six harbours built with subsidies. For generations, the young people have gone off in search of fortune elsewhere. Corsicans have long formed the backbone of the civil service on the mainland, and helped to bolster its mainland security forces, often on the edges of legality. The equivocal chief of the Paris police during the fascistic riots in the 1930s, Jean Chiappe, was a Corsican; so too was De Gaulle's faithful bodyguard Pierre Comiti, who, with his sunglasses, deeply bald head and pencil moustache, looked more like a small-time enforcer from a *film noir* than a man charged with protecting the President from assassination. (He had, it must be said, spent time as one of the leading heavies, or *gorilles*, who served the General so faithfully.)

There are a thousand associations of Corsicans in France and two hundred abroad. Corsicans pop up in Venezuela and Indochina, Canada and Hong Kong, in business and in the underworld. Corsicans ran the Marseille 'Connection'. During the wars in Indochina, Bonaventure 'Rock' Francisci headed an airline which flew morphine base from Laos to Saigon on its way to Europe and America. According to one former French anti-narcotics agent, an illiterate Corsican called Barthélémy Césari, who would have been heading for retirement in any other profession when he was nabbed, was one of the best heroin chemists the world has known, making the drug 'the way a French grandmother might make dinner – stirring, sniffing and tasting to perfection'. Another drug kingpin from the island arrived in New York in the guise of a priest from Brittany; the snag was that he had a distinctly Mediterranean complexion and spoke with a thick accent, and so was immediately marked down as somebody for the New York police to keep tabs on.

Keeping another connection on the other side of the world alive, Corsicans smuggled gold, gems, currency and narcotics to Marseille from Indochina long after the last French soldiers had left their former colonies. At one restaurant by the main cemetery of Saigon, which served excellent steak *au poivre*, I was assured in the mid-1960s that one was safe from Viet Cong attacks because '*le patron est Corse*'. Three decades later, Big Joseph Pantalacci sat shuffling a pack of cards at a table in his restaurant in the Laotian capital of Vientiane. He had arrived in Indochina on a troopship in 1937, became a timber trader, went into construction and married a seventeen-year-old French–Vietnamese. As the French empire collapsed around him, he watched his compatriots from Corsica trade in drugs and precious metals: 'They were not the Mafia, but they acted like the Mafia; some of them were wild men, crazy, too much wine and too many women.' Big Joseph went into the restaurant business instead.

Now, unemployment on the mainland and around the world keeps law-abiding young people of Corsica at home, but still jobless. Sixty per cent of the island's income comes from state aid. The national audit commission found that subsidies paid to Corsican agriculture were nearly two and a half times the amount budgeted, were ten times as large as those allocated to the average farm on the mainland, and supported 70 per cent of the island's full-time farmers. 'The practice,' the report added, 'sent many farmers deeper into debt as they seem to have become used to requesting and obtaining fresh subsidies.' Investors from the mainland show little interest in taking generous subsidies to provide jobs: in four years in the mid-1990s, just two companies signed up – and one of them lost its factory on the island to a fire. Apart from wine and agriculture, tourism is the main revenue earner, but the militant separatists do their best to sabotage this lifeline by bombing empty holiday villas. Corsica gave birth to the vendetta tradition of mutual murder; its hoodlums love to pose for the cameras in black masks waving guns. There are far too many hunting rifles that can be used for other purposes. 'Everyone is armed in Corsica,' an Interior Minister observed. The last two decades have seen more than 8,000 attacks on property and people.

The island's politics are riddled with in-fighting between clans defending their territory and income. Fraud at the polls is endemic; regional elections in 1998 were annulled after widespread irregularities. Corsicans are famous for being able to vote from beyond the grave and for the avalanche of postal votes that may land on selected constituencies – a village with 165 registered electors once recorded 5,998 ballots for a favoured candidate. The clans distribute money and jobs to their followers, and help them out of trouble. Their chieftains seem to live for ever, with power being handed from father to son. In southern Corsica, the Rocca-Serra family has held sway since the 1920s. When the father fell into disgrace for wartime collaboration, his son – known as 'the silver fox' for his cunning and his hair colouring – took up the reins. Mayor of the beautiful coastal town of Porto-Vecchio for forty-seven years and a member of the National Assembly for thirty-six until his death in 1998, he paid for funerals, gave free consultations in his medical practice and seemed to know everybody. Once, when a village mayor gambled away the communal funds, Rocca-Serra met the loss from his own pocket and kept the police quiet.

There are compensations for such godfatherly behaviour. Though Rocca-Serra was above such things, public works of the kind which Claude Érignac was busy investigating just happen to facilitate access to restaurants and hotels in which local potentates have an interest. In another case which the Prefect promised to look into, the cost of a water-treatment plant on the coast inexplicably went ten times over budget. Links with Italy, as in the Bonifacio barracks-to-hotel project which he vetoed, have led the President of the Republic to speak of Mafia-like interests on the island, and the nationalists have joined the game with a vengeance. One independence-seeker received a large grant to enable him to get into the pork processing business; in another case, a mayor was murdered by a nationalist gunman after failing to pick the designated firm for a garbage contract. A public prosecutor estimates that three-quarters of the so-called nationalist bomb attacks are in fact staged as part of private disputes.

Some parliamentarians in Paris have had enough. 'If the Corsicans aren't happy, forget about them,' said one conservative. An opinion poll on the mainland showed that no less than 42 per cent of voters would back independence for the island – just to get rid of it. For such a unitary state as France, that is a challenge and a half which the powers in Paris have no idea how to meet. The former Prime Minister, Raymond Barre, went straight to the point: 'If the Corsicans want their independence, let them take it.' But there is little sign that they really do. Polls show support for casting adrift from the mainland at between 7 and 10 per cent. A larger number would like some form of greater autonomy, which would let them feel more Corsican but not threaten the subsidies from across the water. From time to time, the central power tries to come to terms with the island, usually extending a nationalist carrot while waving the stick of a security clampdown. In the mid-1980s, François Mitterrand decided to give greater recognition to the island's language and specific identity. At the same time, he sent one of his top police officers – a tough man with an open mind – to deal with the terrorists. One sunny day, the Head of State, in person, alighted on the island and raced around in a flurry of security. It was all somewhat farcical. A sharp-shooting bodyguard was literally deafened when the bell began to ring in greeting at the top of the church tower where he was standing watch. Despite the worries about terrorist attacks, I had no problem wandering into an official candlelit garden party in Ajaccio through a back door, while, not far away, separatists daubed graffiti on the walls and waved a banner demanding 'decolonisation'. The Constitutional Council turned down the Mitterrand proposals as being counter to the unity of the nation; the bombers planted fresh explosive charges and the mess became even worse.

A dozen years later, the Gaullist Prime Minister flew to Ajaccio and warned that the island could not be allowed to escape from the law of the Republic. 'Corsica is part of the nation,' declared Alain Juppé. 'Corsica is French.' Still, he announced that more attention would be paid to teaching the Corsican language. National solidarity would be demonstrated by establishing a tax-free zone on the island. 'A tax-free zone is designed to resuscitate, not to save something which is already dead,' a local mayor remarked bitterly. The Corsican terrorists showed what they thought by bombing the Prime Minister's mayoral office in Bordeaux. A Magnum-packing anti-terrorist judge was put on the case, but blasts followed at half a dozen official buildings on the mainland as well as fifty in Corsica itself. A couple of months later, more than forty bombs went off in seventeen towns across the island, hitting businesses such as Air France and the telephone and electricity companies. Another series of attacks included the headquarters of ÉNA among its targets, while some historically-minded bombers planted three charges in the town of Vichy during the Maurice Papon trial, to mark 'the true nature of a state which is not well placed to give lessons on democracy'.

Don't look for logic in all this, or else for a logic which is nothing if not self-destructive. Corsica is a land where cash-dispensers are rare because they are routinely ripped open with explosives left over from attacks on tourist villas and official buildings. Or take the tale of 'Gulliver' and the golf club, at Sperone in the south of the island, which gives some idea of how things work in Corsica. One day at the end of 1996, a group of men paid a visit to the club and an adjoining resort village. They left a simple message: the club had been the target of three bomb attacks, and it was time for the owner to call a woman lawyer who was closely associated with the leader of one of the nationalist movements. She asked him to meet a go-between in Paris who would go by the codename of 'Gulliver'. The subterfuge was superfluous since the golf club owner recognised his visitor as the owner of a local restaurant in Corsica. 'Gulliver' asked for several million francs; otherwise, it would be too bad for the golf club. The owner refused to pay. The next day, the guard-house at the club was blown up. The owner went to the police. The woman lawyer was arrested. Her companion, who headed the legal arm of the national-ist movement, gave himself up as a point of honour. Everybody congratulated everybody else. The Prime Minister said that the episode might be a turning-point in the fight against nationalist extor-tion and violence. Within a month, the golf club received a demand that it close, or face reprisals. It promptly shut down. 'We can't take risks with the golfers,' the owner told reporters.

The representatives of the state shelter behind high walls and barbed-wire as the island demands more and more financial aid from them. The deeper danger is that Corsica may introduce the idea that, in one region of France, the law of the whole Republic can be taken for a fool. What, asked the head of government on his visit to the island in 1996, is left of the Republic when the law is flouted openly by armed groups which escape the control of the authorities?

It is always easy to shrug off Corsica as a special place with pecu-liarities which have no relevance to the rest of the nation. But to do that is to chip away at the notion of the unitary state. If separatists and gangsters are allowed to get away with it in one part of France, others may be tempted to try the same game elsewhere – as we have seen, some worry about the creation of an Islamic state-within-a-state on shabby urban housing estates. L'État is not there to be mocked, but the Corsican hoods do not hesitate to cock a snook at it, operating wireless scanners on police wavelengths from their prison cells or attacking the law courts in Ajaccio. When an Interior Minister visited the island, the Corsican Liberation Front stole the headlines by invit-ing journalists to a night-time meeting with 600 armed members in a retreat in the mountains. Gangsters parade themselves as nationalists, and gain legitimacy from the readiness of high officials to talk to them. The penalties they face are hardly intimidating. Conviction for illegal possession of arms got the leader of one militant separatist group a twelve-month jail sentence, two-thirds of it suspended. The verdict was handed down in absentia since he had holed up in the brushlands with his bodyguards.

This was the kind of jungle which the Prefect, Claude Érignac, was trying to come to grips with. In one all-too-familiar incident amid the wave of attacks on the island and against mainland targets in the autumn of 1997, nationalist commandos raided a police barracks in the southern town of Pietrosella. They blew up the building and took two gendarmes hostage, later freeing them in the maquis scrubland. Before letting them go, the raiders took a photograph of his family from the képi cap worn by one of the policemen and sent it to the local press. They also stole a nine-millimetre Beretta automatic pistol, engraved with the policeman's initials and bearing the registration number A00199.

Five weeks later a nationalist group calling itself 'Sampieru' sent a statement to the newspaper *Libération*. In a reminder of how Corsica had been a staging-post for the nascent military coup of 1958, the group proclaimed its fidelity to 'paratrooper and legionnaire ideals' and swore an uncompromising struggle against the French state. Its leader was identified as a former paratrooper whose involvement in the cause stretched back to an incident in the town of Aléria in 1975, when two policemen were killed while dislodging nationalists from a wine cellar they had occupied in one of their early protests. In January 1998, some of the members of Sampieru left the mysterious group after it staged an attack on the leader of another nationalist organisation. In a statement, they denounced in advance 'any action that may be undertaken against certain civil servants and leading representatives of the colonial state'.

A month later, two young men walked up to Claude Érignac as he made his way to the concert in Ajaccio. One was unshaven and fair-haired, the other dark and wearing a T-shirt. One of them shot the Prefect in the back of the head with the Beretta stolen at Pietrosella. He died immediately. The killer dropped the pistol and fled with his companion. Three days afterwards, a statement from Sampieru claimed responsibility for the murder.

Érignac's assassination shocked even the blasé Corsicans. Almost a sixth of the island's population joined in silent protest marches. Jacques Chirac and Lionel Jospin flew south to condemn the deed. The Interior Ministry declared the discovery of the killers to be its number-one priority. However, the first arrests were less than convincing – three Moroccans who had had nothing to do with the killing. Subsequent suspects from nationalist ranks also had to be released for lack of evidence. The leader of Sampieru was arrested after a raid on his home uncovered a cache of arms and explosives: he refused to answer questions except through a Corsican interpreter. But the indications were that he was not directly implicated. Instead, as the National Assembly set up a commission of inquiry, suspicions widened out towards the shadowy nexus between the underworld and the hoodlums of nationalism. Parallels were drawn with the Italian Mafia's readiness to kill officials who stood in their way.

The government in Paris soon swung into action, seizing tonnes of documents from the local Crédit Agricole bank, going through the accounts of Corsica's development fund and looking at doubtful loans amounting to a billion francs. It then emerged that the explosive police report recommending a probe into the island's agricultural affairs had fallen into the hands of hard-line nationalists. As the investigation into the Prefect's death dragged on, the French state remained as exposed as ever in its island in the sun where the Republic could only be shamed by the spectacle of police hiding behind masks when they went to arrest toughs for whom easy money, illegality and nationalism had become inexorably entwined.

One of Louis XIV's ministers may have dreamed of '*Germanis Gallia clausa*' (Gaul closed to the Germans), but the east is where France's identity is most porous, in land and people. Start in the south-east — and where better than Nice, which only became French in 1860 and which briefly reverted to Italian rule during the Second World War? Today, the people of the old port and the flower market and the sardine-codfish-and-tripe restaurants remain as much Italian as French in their way of life. Turn north and things become ever more murky as one moves from Italian-French, to Swiss-French, to German-French and then to Belgian-French. While the proximity to Italy has brought charm in food, architecture and living, and the Swiss border provides Alpine casinos with some of their highest rollers, it is the Rhine which counts for most in history. German possession of Alsace-Lorraine from 1871 to 1918 was the great territorial wound of modern French history. School children were made to conjugate a sentence about looking longingly over the Vosges hills to Alsace. Pledges to regain the 1.4 million hectares of lost lands to the east were a leitmotif of political speeches. The snag was that nobody in their right minds thought that France could actually wage war on

Germany and win on its own – and not all the 1.6 million people of the region seemed too unhappy at finding themselves under Teutonic rule.

Setting aside the three German invasions of 1870, 1914 and 1940, the pressure which France has felt through these regions has not always been a bad thing – from Charlemagne and the commercial influences that flooded into Paris from the Low Countries and Germany in the late Middle Ages to the political refugees who brought new life, art and culture with them in the 1920s and 1930s. Still, understandably given the military history, French officials can sometimes worry about the immediate east in near-apocalyptic terms. In the 1980s, a Foreign Minister sat over breakfast in his office at the Quai d'Orsay and pondered his deepest concern. West (as it then was) Germany was an unstable nation, he said, a child beside France, a state only a century away from a galaxy of feuding princedoms. It could break apart again under the strain of Cold War rivalry, nuclear armaments and the Green movement. France had a historic obligation to hold its neighbour together, to give West Germany the backbone it lacked. So François Mitterrand flew to Bonn and made a speech backing the installation of new American nuclear missiles on German soil. The French, the minister believed, with the supreme assurance that hands France's critics so much ammunition, had saved the Germans from themselves. What he did not mention was that, as part of an unspoken deal, the Germans kept France from financial ruin by supporting the franc.

A decade and a half later, the French fear is different – that Germany may become too powerful as the central power of an increasingly united Europe, with a direct line to Washington and, under its new Chancellor Gerhard Schröder, a closer relationship with Britain. France would then be boxed in. It cannot isolate itself economically. Its north-eastern regions are bound up as closely with Germany as they are with the rest of France: the fortunes of Alsace and Lorraine rise and fall with German prosperity, and the best hope for the old industrial region round Lille is to stitch itself to the Ruhr. Politically, there can be no European vocation separate from Bonn or Berlin; but the relationship risks being that of Greece to Rome, London to Washington. This is a tough fate for any French President to accept after nearly four decades of playing an independent international role. The notion of the Gallic cock flapping along behind the German eagle is deeply unpalatable, particularly given the economic and political troubles afflicting the government in Bonn. But is there any other way?

Jacques Chirac and Helmut Kohl used to meet every six weeks or so. Schröder's first foreign visit was to Paris. Regular intercourse is good for the body, no doubt, but the French soul wants to soar free. The trouble is that it has nowhere to go. There is an in-built contradiction between the geographical position and foreign policies of Paris and Berlin. France, perched on the edge of Europe, has aspired to play a central role between East and West while Germany, though lying in the middle of the continent, has been tightly bound to the trans-Atlantic superpower. Now, seeing the choice that looms for their nation, the more apocalyptic of French observers imagine a renewed conflict between Paris, temple of the enlightened West, and Berlin, champion of the lands where Huns meet Slavs. 'We were happy when Germany meant Bonn,' one French diplomat says. 'Bonn is a Rhineland town, they grow wine there, it's only an hour over the border. But if we have to deal with Berlin, we will be in another world. With Bonn, we could feel equality; with Berlin, we will be ground under foot again.' And Washington, Paris knows, will be behind Berlin, if only to keep the uncertainties of the dismantled Soviet empire in some kind of check.

Does this mean that, inevitably, the border on the east will fade away and that France is destined to become, in fact if not in name, a satellite of united Germany? Despite his attempts to rewrite history in a mendacious book published posthumously, François Mitterrand saw the danger for his country and was lukewarm about German unity. As the writer François Mauriac remarked while the Berlin Wall still stood: 'I like Germany so much that I'm happy there are two of them.' Early in his presidency, Jacques Chirac back-tracked on agreements to open borders made by his predecessor. He cited the need to safeguard France from roaming Euro-criminals; the move could also be seen as a reflection of something much deeper. Kings, presidents and an emperor had built modern France behind these lines. Now, the Chancellor embraces the President in his bear-hugs; the power across the Rhine engulfs the Hexagon; and there is precious little Paris can do about it. Geography and the realities of politics and economics meet: the French can only shiver. They have no hinterland to the east or trusting line to Washington. This may be the ultimate paradox to come: France as second string in a German-led Europe, but still telling herself that nothing has changed, that she can still be her proud old self – even though she is tied to the Bundesbank, the Ruhr and to monetarist constraints so alien to what she would wish to be.

In a world where invasion is more likely to come from currency dealers' terminals than from marching feet, the Hexagon is as vulnerable as any other medium-sized country caught in the globalisation process. Equally, the nation is less united and the centralised state less omnipotent than republican theory imagines, but the people are still required to worship as loyal citizens at the traditional altars. The contrast between France's invigorating taste for individualism and the in-bred subservience to the state, between the diversity of its people and the heavy-handed vision of unity, between an international role that it assumes to be its by right and the clouds that swirl around it: all create a set of paradoxes and puzzles that call for strong but sensitive handling by the national leadership.

Like their ancestors, the Gauls, the French need chieftains who can meld the country together in their own person. Each of the myriad groups, units, associations and factions which make up the mainstream of the nation needs to be able to feel itself reflected in the man in the Élysée. The President should bind this disparate nation together, and incarnate its unity under the state, as Charles de Gaulle largely did in the early years of his presidency once opposition to his seizure of power had evaporated. Instead, France has found itself wounded by politicians who have fallen short of the task, invariably exceeding even the normal egotism of their profession. By exploiting either side of the paradoxes of French life, and failing to achieve the reconciliation they were elected to perform, they have contributed powerfully to the condition in which their country finds itself. For, if there is one divisive burden, from which France has suffered above all in the last quarter of the twentieth century, it has been the way that three men have conducted a combat for power that has no equal in any other major democratic nation.

11

THREE MEN AND A COUNTRY

As political conflicts go, France's Thirty Years' War had its deadly aspects: two spectacular suicides and a lot of personal wounds, sometimes of a terminal nature. Many men and women saw their careers destroyed and their lives diverted to serve the ambitions of François Mitterrand, Valéry Giscard d'Estaing and Jacques Chirac. Between them, these three men have encapsulated France's political history since the decline of Charles de Gaulle. When hostilities opened, Lyndon Johnson was in the White House and Harold Wilson was in Downing Street, American troops were beginning their big build-up in Vietnam and the Soviet invasion of Czechoslovakia was still three years away. Other countries renew their leadership by whatever means. France works in impossibly long cycles as its politicians use the system to cling on to power. Victory is usually frittered away, and defeat is rarely final. The national play may move through fresh acts, but the same actors cling to the stage. Both the last two Presidents of the Republic were beaten twice before finally winning the job, and each of them plummeted to the bottom of the opinion polls within a few years of seizing the ultimate prize. In France, politics is the ultimate game, and the only losers are the people.

In the opening engagement of this war, the oldest of the three protagonists was in the north Burgundian town of which he was mayor when he learned that his first presidential bid had failed on 19 December 1965. With greater difficulty than expected, France's reigning monarch had repulsed the challenge to his throne from a collection of competing forces ranged against him from the far left of the battlefield to the far right. De Gaulle's final victory in France's first presidential election of the twentieth century by universal suffrage was no surprise, however, and François Mitterrand's 45 per cent of the vote was an honourable score which established him as the leader of the left ready to mount a fresh challenge when the ageing patriarch finally stepped down.

That became increasingly likely as the 1960s drew to a close. After a decade of Gaullist pre-eminence, the ground was shifting. The General and his country were growing out of touch with one another – while the king pursued grandeur from his castle, his people were becoming concerned about their standard of living. As a leading political commentator put it, France was getting bored. De Gaulle reflected that he should have ruled from the royal surroundings of the Louvre rather than from a more modest palace in the 8th *arrondissement*: but voters were more interested in inflation and wages than in grandeur. It seemed that Mitterrand had only to wait patiently to claim his ultimate reward after more than twenty years in politics.

Three years later, everything fell to bits for the challenger. The General's hour of greatest danger, during the strikes and student riots of 1968, should have been a time of maximum opportunity for the opposition and its chief. But the upheaval caught the orthodox left as much by surprise as the Gaullist government. Mitterrand resorted to history, imagining himself on the barricades of 1848 or 1870, and proposing a Government of National Salvation. The Gaullists easily turned that into an attempted coup. Spectacular as the unrest was, most of the French soon came to want salvation from disorder. If they entertained doubts about De Gaulle, it was because they wondered if he really was in charge any more. So they rallied behind the reassuring Prime Minister, Georges Pompidou, who bought off the unions, made concessions to the students, and ended the revolt without a life lost on either side.

In the way of such things, the General sacked Pompidou as soon as victory over the strikers was in the bag. That only made De Gaulle's position untenable. At last, France had an alternative Head of State from the Gaullist ranks to whom it could turn; a man who, vitally, was now a free agent. Scheming against him by Gaullist diehards goaded the phlegmatic Pompidou into action. The former Rothschild banker had served the General loyally for years before becoming his Prime Minister, looking after his finances during the time in the wilderness and running a foundation dedicated to the memory of his invalid daughter. But, within months of Pompidou leaving office, Gaullist ultra-loyalists spread rumours that his wife was mixed up in a sex ring with Yugoslav hoodlums and French film stars. The former Premier was an easy-going man, but respect for his tall, ramrod-backed wife, Claude, was something he could not allow to be broached. There was a frosty dinner at the Élysée with the De Gaulles, which did no good. Pompidou went on television to warn that some boundaries should not be crossed. The General seemed unable, or unwilling, to rein in his zealots, who saw the prospect of a Pompidou presidency as the end of everything they believed in. On a visit to Rome, the former Prime Minister made it plain that he would stand for the presidency if De Gaulle left the Élysée. When the Head of State responded by asserting his intention to serve out his seven-year term, his former Premier spoke to a Swiss television interviewer of his own 'national destiny' – a phrase that could have only one meaning. That helped to propel the enfeebled founder of the Fifth Republic into a last bid to regain the initiative and restore the link between himself and the people. He opted for the old Bonapartist device of a plebiscite, but, unlike the first Emperor, he was not the kind of man who would arrange either for a farce in which he got more votes than there were voters, or to get himself elected for life. When he announced a referendum on regional reform and the composition of the Senate early in 1969, De Gaulle must have known in his heart that he was doomed. The subject was not one which excited the voters, the spectre of the May–June events was still alive in people's minds and, above all, the General could no longer play his favourite card of warning France that it faced a choice between him and chaos. Georges Pompidou was an all too solid bulwark against disorder.

After receiving secret polls by the police in the week before the referendum, De Gaulle gave orders for his personal files to be moved from the Élysée Palace. He recorded a broadcast to be transmitted in the event of defeat, and drove to his country home in Colombey-les-Deux-Églises in the Haute-Marne department of eastern France.

On Sunday, 27 April, the General went to mass in the morning, voted in the village and then shut himself away in his austere house. By 10 P.M., he had been told that the referendum had been lost by 47 per cent to 53. At ten minutes past midnight on 28 April 1969, the French news agency put out a terse statement from the Head of State: 'I am ceasing to exercise my functions as President of the Republic. This decision takes effect at noon today.'

Now it was time for treason. François Mitterrand decided not to stand in the 1969 presidential election that followed De Gaulle's departure; nobody asked him to, anyway. Pompidou won an overwhelming victory. Gaston Defferre and Pierre Mendès-France ran in tandem for the Socialists: they got just 5 per cent of the vote.

After the heroic founding epoch of the Fifth Republic, with its reassertion of national glory, the ending of the Algerian war and the development of the nuclear force, the Pompidou presidency ushered in a more businesslike era characterised by the construction of industrial empires rather than great international ambitions. It was one of those lulls which punctuate prolonged conflicts, a respite during which the left licked its wounds while the ambitious men of the centre and right planned their future. Things changed sooner than any of them had expected. Pompidou's face ballooned, and he increasingly had difficulty walking. It was generally believed that he was taking cortisone; was it for cancer and, if so, how bad was the illness? Speculation about his health became the leading subject of gossip, but the secret was well kept.

By the end of March 1974, however, the President was too ill to attend the annual dinner of the diplomatic corps in Paris, and had to cancel a trip to Bonn. On the last day of the month, he left Paris with his wife for a weekend at a country estate. His pain grew even more intense, and he was transported back to his personal apartment on the Quai Bourbon, overlooking the Seine. There, opposite Notre Dame, the second President of the Fifth Republic died of cancer on 2 April at the age of sixty-three. That night, the state television service ran a caption along the bottom of the screen on which a film starring the English actor Alan Bates was showing. It announced baldly: 'The President of the Republic is dead.' That was in keeping

with Pompidou's image. He had been the Head of State France
wanted, but he did not go down as a heroic figure. Sensible people
rarely do.

Pompidou's death precipitated an era of treason, with a vicious
three-cornered battle ensuing which established the pattern of French
politics for a quarter of a century and has its repercussions even today.
The dead ruler left no *dauphin* in the way that Pompidou had been De
Gaulle's obvious heir. There was a leading Gaullist candidate in the
person of Pompidou's Prime Minister, Jacques Chaban-Delmas.
Chaban-Delmas had impeccable credentials and the status of a former
head of government. He had been a hero of the Resistance in his
twenties (and was incarnated by Alain Delon in the film *Is Paris
Burning?*). A lieutenant of De Gaulle since the 1940s and Mayor of
Bordeaux since 1947, Chaban was fit and attractive. An accomplished
golfer and fine tennis-player, he ran up stairs four at a time at the age
of sixty. He should have been a natural winner, but he was distrusted
by many Gaullists on two counts.

The first was that he had swung too far to the left, listening to siren
voices like that of his adviser on social affairs, Jacques Delors, as he
sought to craft what he called a 'new society' for France. While
Pompidou was preaching unadventurous corporatism, Chaban-
Delmas promoted employees' involvement in running the companies
they worked for. His second problem was more personal. He had run
into difficulties over revelations about his tax affairs; he was a lacklustre
campaigner with an unpleasantly metallic voice; and he seemed to
many not to possess a true hunger for the job. In short, for the hard
wing of the Gaullist party, Chaban-Delmas was not nearly tough
enough to hold the most important post in France.

In contrast, meet two people who are virtually unknown outside
France and rarely appeared in public at home. However, their influence on the country's politics was pivotal. Without them, the fortunes
of the Gaullist party over the ensuing two decades would have been
very different, the Socialists might not have come to power in 1981,
and Jacques Chirac might never have been President. If Chaban-
Delmas was judged insufficiently brutal, nobody thought Pierre Juillet
and Marie-France Garaud came from anywhere but the hard Gaullist
right. By the time of Pompidou's death, this duo from the provinces
had achieved near-mythic status in political circles as the forces

behind the throne, driven by an intense desire for the Gaullists to hold on to power at any cost and an equally visceral hatred of the left. Garaud was a lawyer from Poitiers, a Lady Macbeth with a dominating manner that seduced and subjugated the men around her; Juillet was a man of the shadows who walked with a cane and kept a sheep farm in the Limousin. In 1974, their main aim in life was to prevent the Socialists and their allies winning the presidency. To do that, they were convinced, they had to stop Chaban-Delmas being the Gaullist candidate.

There was no doubting the task that the centre-right faced in retaining power. In one of the extraordinary recoveries which marked his political career, François Mitterrand had established himself as the single candidate for the main parties of the opposition as he launched into his decade-long exercise of drawing the powerful Communist Party into his tent in order to strangle it. In 1969, the Communist presidential candidate had won 21 per cent of the vote – four times as much as the Socialist. Now, Mitterrand had got the whole of the left to line up behind him. Parliamentary elections saw big gains for the opposition and the loss of a hundred constituencies for the governing parties. The Gaullist crown was under serious threat. Showing the lack of scruples which marks consummate tacticians in politics or war, the powers behind the vacant throne sought a new alliance.

Valéry Giscard d'Estaing looks and acts like an aristocrat from the great days of the court at Versailles, though his family was actually only authorised to use the *d'* in 1922. Born four years later in Germany, where his father was a civil servant with the occupation forces after the First World War, Giscard was one of those brilliant individuals who shoot through the upper reaches of France's education system to run the country. He joined the Prime Minister's staff at the age of twenty-eight, won election to the National Assembly by the time he was thirty and was a junior member of the government at thirty-three. De Gaulle found the young man too clever by half, and there were doubts about the Algérie Française affiliations of some members of the right-wing political group he led. But nothing could stop Giscard. He became Finance Minister a month before his thirty-sixth birthday.

The post usually ranks just behind that of Prime Minister in terms of power, since its occupant controls so much of what his colleagues can afford to do. Giscard held the post for nine years, during which he and the job became synonymous. When I told a taxi-driver I wanted to go to the Finance Ministry one Saturday morning, he nodded and replied: '*Ah, chez Giscard.*'

The minister had style to spare. He spoke for hours in parliament without notes. Tall and self-assured, he looked perfect in formal dress, but he also met me that Saturday in his ornate office in the Louvre wearing a cardigan and no tie. Touching all the bases, he played the accordion and turned out for football in his native Auvergne – photographs taken in the changing-room showed that he carried not an ounce of surplus fat, in striking contrast to his well-padded Cabinet colleagues. Giscard had ambition by the kilometre. After a dozen years at the top of government, he was ready to make his bid for the summit in 1974, and the time was right. France was ready for a change from Gaullism. Giscard knew he could capture that national mood, without frightening the conservative middle classes. He was the thoroughly modern leader his country needed, a French Kennedy. And, in terms of personal ambition, he was well aware that, if he did not grab the opportunity in 1974, he might never have another chance: either Mitterrand would win, possibly going on to a second term, or a failure by the left would ensure Gaullist rule into the next century.

The snag was that, for all his attributes, the young man lacked one essential element – a mass political movement. However much De Gaulle may have despised parties and aspired to rule above them, the election of the President by universal suffrage which he introduced in 1962 means that the Head of State needed a big political organisation to get out the voters and maintain electoral discipline. Giscard had his followers, organised by a much more truly aristocratic friend, Prince Michel Poniatowski. But there were not enough of them; his Independent Republican party had only fifty-four seats in the National Assembly. Like their centrist allies, Giscard's followers tended to be local bigwigs, the notables who ran French country towns, men and women at home in upper bourgeois houses and small châteaux, where the food was excellent, the service discreet and money not mentioned as deals were made in a quiet corner of the salon after a day's shooting. However highly they might prize themselves, such folk were simply not numerous and well-organised enough to withstand Mitterrand's challenge. Rattling pearls at the peasants wasn't going to repel the populist hordes.

Giscard's problems found their mirror image across the Seine from his office in the Louvre. Pierre Juillet and Marie-France Garaud had no great liking for the Finance Minister: in many ways, he was the antithesis of their idea of a leader. Still, they needed him, as he needed them. Pompidou's death had come two years too early for the backroom pair. They were grooming their presidential candidate; but, like a classic racehorse being trained for the Derby or the Prix de l'Arc de Triomphe, timing was everything. If Pompidou had lived to the end of his term in 1976, it would have been a different matter. But this was 1974, and there was an inescapable symmetry. The anti-Chaban Gaullists had the troops to put into the field but no general to lead them; Giscard had few troops but was the ideal man to head the charge.

So a deal emerged. A breakaway group of Gaullist members of the National Assembly distanced themselves from Chaban-Delmas and lined up behind Giscard. In the first round of the two-stage presidential voting, Mitterrand easily topped the poll with 43 per cent. That had been expected. The vital thing was that he had fallen well short of the outright majority needed for election. The significant figures came next: Giscard took 32.6 per cent and Chaban-Delmas only 15.1. Although the left's man had finished first, the electoral arithmetic was stacked against him. A dozen candidates had run in the first round, and most of the votes for those who were eliminated would go to the right. Mitterrand could count on far smaller reserves of new support than Giscard. Even the Gaullists who had backed Chaban-Delmas reconciled themselves to the treason which had knocked their candidate out of the race.

At fifty-seven, Mitterrand looked decidedly dowdy compared to the cool young intelligence opposite him. He was still identified in many people's minds with the discredited Fourth Republic, in whose governments he had often served. He had been out of power for sixteen years whereas Giscard had run the Finance Ministry for most of the past decade. When his opponent asked him a direct question about international finance in France's first televised presidential debate, Mitterrand couldn't reply. Capitalising on his advantage, the young candidate told his ageing opponent that he did not have a monopoly on feelings of the heart. It was no shock when, on 19 May, Valéry Giscard d'Estaing became the third President of the Fifth Republic with 50.81 per cent of the vote. The only surprise was that the margin had not been larger. Much as Giscard wanted France, the electorate did not seem entirely convinced it wanted him.

Again, Mitterrand had not done badly. He had come much closer than in his first bid for the top job. But the seven-year length of the term in the Élysée Palace and the awesome power of the office make opposition a lonely, ill-defined job: France does not recognise a Leader of the Opposition as Britain does, which is sensible since there are nearly always several oppositions. As a man who knew the value of time, Mitterrand devoted the rest of the 1970s to building up a new Socialist Party and to his long-term campaign to snare the Communists in his web as he prepared for what would be a third tilt at the Élysée. For the moment, the field belonged to the new alliance which had defeated both the left and the old-style Gaullists. Giscard, the presiding general of the victorious forces, moved in to the Élysée on 27 May. His first action was to appoint as Prime Minister the man who had made victory possible.

Jacques Chirac was Georges Pompidou's political son. After a flirtation with the left during his late teens, when he sold the Communist newspaper L'Humanité in the street and signed a Moscow-inspired anti-nuclear petition, he had turned into a dyed-in-the-wool Gaullist. Pompidou had taken the young Énarque on to his staff while he was De Gaulle's Prime Minister. The product of a comfortable upper-middle-class family, Chirac had had a full life already: he had trained as a cavalry officer, had gone to sea and had spent a summer in America, where he studied at Harvard, won a certificate from a Howard Johnson ice-cream parlour for his skill in making banana splits, and gave a southern belle Latin lessons – and her first kiss, which she said she remembered forty years later.

To blood him politically, Pompidou sent the young man off to the Corrèze department in France's agricultural heartland to conquer it for the Gaullists: Chirac and his wife drove through the night from

Paris each Friday or took the train that arrived at 4:10 A.M. to campaign through the weekend in the markets and *charcuteries*. He became a municipal councillor, and, in 1967, went on to win the parliamentary constituency he still held when he became President two decades later. After Pompidou moved into the Élysée in 1969, he had promoted his protégé to be Minister for Relations with Parliament (where he was a disaster), then Agriculture Minister (where he ferociously defended French interests), and finally to the Interior Ministry (where he took office a month before Pompidou died). The President's death was a huge blow. 'I had the feeling of suddenly being an orphan,' he wrote. At the memorial mass for Pompidou on the Île Saint-Louis in Paris, he sobbed uncontrollably.

Had Pompidou lived through his presidential term and then been prevented by bad health from running for re-election, Chirac might well have been the Gaullist candidate in 1976. That was what Pierre Juillet and Marie-France Garaud had planned. They had taken Chirac to their bosom. On his way home in the evening from his various ministries, he would drop in to see them. If Pompidou was his political father, Pierre and Marie-France were his uncle and aunt. An only child, Chirac hides an unexpected need for mentors behind his straight-ahead style. It is as if he requires confirmatory approval from father (or mother) figures, whom he does not always choose with the greatest discrimination.

Since 1974 was too early for a presidential bid, Chirac and his closest advisers decided that if he could not be in the Élysée himself, he should at least become the power in another man's reign. As Interior Minister he organised the election, and Fifth Republic tradition did not require ministerial impartiality. Chirac had access to police polls which showed that Jacques Chaban-Delmas would lose to Mitterrand. With Juillet and Garaud orchestrating every move, forty-three eminent anti-Chaban Gaullists published a joint text saying that there should be just one representative of the governing majority in the coming election. The signatories included four members of the government, headed by the Interior Minister. Their message was clear: they would swing a significant section of Gaullist support away from Chaban-Delmas and behind the Minister of Finance and the Economy. 'Chirac is a falcon placed on the gloved fist of Marie-France,' Chaban-Delmas wrote later. 'From time to

time, Juillet slips the chain so that Chirac flies for an hour. And kills.'
Nine days after being elected President, Valéry Giscard d'Estaing
appointed the leader of the Gaullist *fronde* as the sixth Prime Minister
of the Fifth Republic.

The two men were strikingly young for a country which generally
liked its leaders to show their age. Giscard was forty-eight, Chirac
forty-one. They had first worked together when Chirac held a junior
post at the Finance Ministry. They had been in endless Cabinet meetings since then. They seemed the perfect team to move their country
to the forefront of the modern age. They may even have believed it
themselves: winning battles can provoke dangerous illusions. The
truth was that victory opened up a steadily-widening war between
two men pursuing the same prize.

Valéry Giscard d'Estaing set out to be a great President. He introduced
a flood of social reforms, with particular attention to women's rights.
His administration liberalised the abortion laws. He modernised
France's telecommunications and sought to free up the financial
system. With Helmut Schmidt, Germany's equally brainy Chancellor,
Giscard set up the European Monetary System. He mended fences
with the United States and pressed ahead with the construction of
Europe. But, as his presidency wore on, much of what he did could
be summed up by Marie-France Garaud's dismissive phrase – '*des
gadgets*'. Whether because he was, at heart, more conservative than he
seemed or because he was too removed from the realities of daily life,
Giscard's reforms changed things less than he thought. The President
was like one of those eighteenth-century aristocrats who played with
all the most advanced ideas about changing society, who set up model
farms and chatted with Voltaire and felt good envisaging a new
enlightenment – but who were never really ready to challenge the
society which had bred them.

There was another problem with Giscard. The exorbitant powers
of the presidency were irresistible. The opportunities to put his finger
in every pie could not be passed by. De Gaulle and Pompidou had
known that the President needed to limit the reach of his power, to
leave the Prime Minister room to breathe while the eyes of his boss
rested on loftier horizons: if France had been a business, the Fifth

Republic gave it a Chairman and a Chief Executive Officer. De Gaulle told the Americans to get out of Vietnam; his Prime Minister dealt with public-sector wage negotiations. Pompidou let Britain into the Common Market; his Prime Minister worried about workers' rights. Giscard relished the world horizon, but he also found it impossible to delegate at home. This was partly a personal trait. He wanted to be Chairman of the Board, Company President, CEO, CFO (he kept the Finance Ministry under close watch) and any other O around. He also had ambitions to replace Gaullism with Giscardianism, thus establishing his centre-right followers as France's main political movement. His anti-Gaullism was no new development – in 1967 he had spoken openly about preparing 'France for her future' and his party had discreetly advised its members to vote against the General in the 1969 referendum. Had he seized the moment in 1974 and called legislative elections, Giscard might have taken a big step towards his dream of a dominant centre-conservative party. Instead, with a Gaullist as Prime Minister, he made the mistake of contenting himself with the parliamentary majority bequeathed by Pompidou. Still, he kept a tight hand on the government, paying scant attention to the constitutional nicety that it should have been run by the man who had made his victory possible. Giscard had won the great prize, but would not take the distance necessary for a supreme leader, above the hurly-burly of everyday politics and administration. He telephoned ministers directly, endlessly by-passing Chirac. He appointed his close friend, Michel Poniatowski, as Interior Minister with the job of building up their Independent Republican party and cutting the ground from beneath Chirac's troops. But, as the President's men sought ways to change the face of French politics, the soldiers who had crossed the lines to win him victory in 1974 were preparing to move in a different direction.

For Marie-France Garaud and Pierre Juillet, Giscard's presidency was an unfortunate, if necessary, period whose only virtue was that it had stopped François Mitterrand becoming Head of State. France, they calculated, would tire of this hollow neo-aristocrat, and be ready for the return of dyed-in-the-wool Gaullism. Though Giscard would remain in office until 1981, preparations had to be made for the return of a true believer when the next election eventually came around. In the interim, the President could be reduced to a puppet by draining off his power towards his Prime Minister. So while Giscard sought to undermine the Gaullists, they were out to do exactly the same to him. It was a recipe for disaster, exacerbated by the basic differences of temperament between the men leading the two groups.

The new Head of State was desperately eager to find the common touch. He made regular television appearances to tell the nation what he was doing. He shared a barbecue at his Mediterranean presidential retreat with North African soldiers who had fought for the French, and invited dustmen to breakfast at the Élysée. He ventured out from time to time to dine with ordinary citizens – a lorry-driver, a picture-framer, a gamekeeper and a young couple in Garaud's home city of Poitiers. Sometimes, the President would abandon his official car and walk to official appointments through the streets of Paris. There were stories about him having crashed into the back of a milk delivery van while driving himself back to the Élysée in the early hours after a romantic assignation.

Away from the public-relations machine, Giscard had a strikingly lordly style for a supposedly modern man. He instructed his Prime Minister to walk three paces behind him on official occasions. His wife, Anne-Aymone Sauvage de Brantes, was said to have been flummoxed when a magazine photographer doing a feature on their home life asked her to put a pot on the stove. Even if the story wasn't true, it fitted their personalities so well that everybody believed it. After their initial honeymoon, life with Giscard became steadily less pleasant for Jacques Chirac. If he did not exactly condescend to the younger man, Giscard revelled in his own superiority. The President's broad intellectual approach sat ill with the hyperactive Chirac, who found himself frozen out of decision-making and reduced to jiggling his long legs beneath the Cabinet table in frustration. Their taste in food betrayed the essential gap between the two men. Chirac likes nothing better than large meals of solid country fare; his favourite dish has long been calf's head with a piquant sauce. Giscard prefers truffles – either with scrambled eggs or in a soup under a pastry shell created in his honour by Paul Bocuse. 'Tell me what you eat and I'll tell you what kind of man you are,' as the gastronome Brillat-Savarin observed.

Not that the President's sense of superiority could not be punctured, even if nobody dared to notice it. His reign included a prime example of *farce à la française*. When OPEC sent oil prices soaring, Giscard produced a reassuring phrase. France might not have oil, he intoned, but it had ideas (an alternative was to call French agriculture 'green oil'). All very well, but when he was offered a revolutionary key to oil wealth and military security, the Head of State reacted like a child in a candy shop, and thereby became the most eminent figure in the cast of a farce that also involved two Gaullist bosses of the Elf oil company, the state Audit Court, intelligence agents, a vanishing Italian inventor, a Belgian count and the doyen of French conservatives, Antoine Pinay. Jacques Chirac was kept in the dark. He would have been furious had he known at the time. When the affair came to light seven years later, he must have blessed his stars that he could plead complete ignorance.

The self-styled inventor Aldo Bonassoli claimed to have two electronic devices, codenamed 'Delta' and 'Omega', which could shoot a newly-discovered particle into the earth. This particle would play back images or sound-waves revealing the existence of oil deposits. By mounting the equipment on aircraft known as 'sniffer planes', an oil company could avoid the high costs of exploratory drilling and would be able to buy leases in the precise sites where the miracle boxes housing the devices detected big reserves.

Bonassoli had an associate, a Belgian count who brought the invention to the attention of a well-connected French lawyer who also happened to be a reserve officer in France's counter-espionage service. The lawyer told Pinay, a former Premier who had reformed French finances for De Gaulle and become something of a political father-figure to Giscard. Pinay informed the President and the Chairman of Elf, Pierre Guillaumat, himself a former Gaullist intelligence chief. The President and the chairman leaped at the chance of giving France the jump on its rivals; Giscard also observed that the technique had military significance, since it could be used to detect deep-diving nuclear submarines.

The Head of State insisted that the project be developed in the utmost secrecy. When he gave Elf Aquitaine approval for a first investment in June 1976, the board of the oil group's holding company was not told anything. Nothing appeared in the accounts. Secret official clearance was given for the transfer of funds to the scheme's promoters in Switzerland. Not everybody involved appeared completely convinced: when a prominent Gaullist politician, Albin Chalandon, was appointed Chairman of Elf in 1977, he covered his back by asking for written official approval of the unorthodox way in which the project was being handled.

The Italian inventor and the Belgian count shared the obsession with secrecy. They told the French that they were investing large sums in the project, installing computers in their laboratory and equipping the sniffer planes with the necessary accessories, which included gold-plated ashtrays. Nobody at Elf was allowed to get a proper look at the equipment for safety reasons. The promoters of the scheme warned that the boxes were dangerously radioactive. Tests were held. Giscard attended one. Although the results were poor, Elf decided to buy the process. Soon afterwards, the Industry Ministry, which was on bad terms with the oil company, took an initiative which somebody might have thought of a bit earlier. An independent expert, Professor Jules Horowitz, was called in to sniff out the sniffers.

The professor went to see the Omega device, which was said to be able to show images from the other side of a wall on a screen as proof of the power of the miracle particle. On his first visit to the laboratory, Horowitz placed a test card behind a wall opposite the Omega box. Nothing happened. Then the machine minders gave him a metal ruler and suggested he take it behind the wall. When the professor did so, an image of a straight ruler appeared on Omega's screen. Good enough – except that, on his way to the back of the wall, the Professor had bent the ruler into a V-shape.

On a later visit, Professor Horowitz repeated the test-card experiment. This time two vertical bars came up on the screen. Excellent, except that they appeared before the professor had put his cards in place. When Omega was eventually dismantled, it was found to contain sheets of photocopied images and cheap components. Elf broke off the agreement. The Belgian count and the Italian inventor vanished. The whole affair remained secret. When the Audit Court looked into the oil company's accounts at the end of 1979, it was told that any mention of the oil-sniffing scheme should be kept confidential. Three copies of the report were sent to the government; the head of the Audit Court kept three others in his desk, and destroyed them when he stepped down from his job in 1982.

The story of the sniffer-plane project eventually surfaced the following summer in the whistle-blowing weekly *Le Canard Enchaîné*.

Initially, it produced smiles but little reaction. Then, just before Christmas 1983, the *Canard* reported that the Audit Court copies of the report had been destroyed. An indignant Giscard went on television to show that he had a copy and that it was still intact. He insisted that secrecy had been essential in view of the sensitive nature of the project. Elf's expenditure, estimated at up to 790 million francs, was, he argued, small by the standards of the oil industry.

The affair was soon submerged in the wider political battle, but it had produced the agreeable image of an omniscient Head of State slipping on a banana peel like any ordinary mortal. As Max Gallo, the Socialist writer and politician, observed, it was irresistibly reminiscent of the harebrained inventor of the Tintin comic strip, Professor Calculus. Not the kind of association the superior Giscard would relish.

A few months before he was told of the sniffer scheme, Giscard decided to reshuffle the government, which was nominally under the charge of the Prime Minister. The President drew up the list of new ministers himself; only then did he summon Jacques Chirac back from the country at a moment's notice on a Sunday morning to tell him whom he had chosen. That alone might have been grounds for resignation, but the Prime Minister bit his lip and soldiered on.

The Whitsun holiday of 1976 brought him a ray of hope. He and his wife were invited to spend the weekend at the presidential retreat at Brégançon on the Mediterranean coast. It was meant to be a simple occasion – Le Président and Madame Giscard d'Estaing invite Monsieur et Madame Chirac to a weekend by the sea. The Prime Minister, a man in whom hope springs eternal, thought this might be an opportunity to sort things out. It turned out to be a Weekend From Hell.

Chirac flew south expecting a meaningful *tête-à-tête* with the President. As soon as he arrived, he was disabused. One other guest was present – Giscard's ski instructor. That set the tone. As Chirac later recounted it, the President and his wife sat down for meals in armchairs while their guests were relegated to straight-backed seats. Things went from bad to worse. On a joint visit to review the fleet off

Nice, Chirac became so annoyed with a television interview the President was giving that he grabbed a pair of binoculars and scanned the sea as a diversion, not noticing in his rage that he was holding the glasses the wrong way round.

On 25 August, the Cabinet assembled at the Élysée following the summer holiday. After a ninety-minute trot through the agenda, Giscard regaled his ministers with a lengthy account of his recent trip to Gabon, where he enjoyed the big-game hunting laid on by the friendly dictator, Omar Bongo. Eventually, the President looked across the table at the man who had enabled him to win power two years earlier.

'Prime Minister,' he said, 'I believe you have something to say.'

'Mr President,' Chirac replied, 'I have the honour to present you with the resignation of my government.'

It was a first in the history of the Fifth Republic. Previously, Presidents had thanked Prime Ministers and sent them on their way. Now, Jacques Chirac was declaring his independence. This was the Gaullism of 1940 and 1958: fuck-you, in-your-face politics. Nobody was better suited to that than Jacques Chirac. A new civil war had erupted. Whatever his brilliance, Giscard was condemned to eventual ruin by the Faustian deal he had done in 1974, and by the nature of the partner he had chosen so mistakenly – the squire who ended up destroying his master.

Jacques Chirac's drive can be positively alarming, particularly for those who have crossed him. Four days after leaving government, he travelled to the Creuse department in the centre of France to spend the last Sunday in August at the country home of Pierre Juillet. Also present were Marie-France Garaud and two other Chirac loyalists. At lunch, Mme Juillet placed four-leaf clovers on each plate. By the time night fell on the calm countryside, the quintet had mapped out plans for a new political movement. It would be headed by the recently departed Prime Minister. It would be a mass party, an army of political militants based on the existing Gaullist movement but reaching out more widely with a message of national rebirth and dynamism.

The new party's strengths would be incarnated by its chief, per-

sonifying all that was strong and true about France, safeguarding the
unity of the state and its leading role in the world, bringing together
the disparate threads of the nation in a single great movement. The
setting that day was symbolic: not a château or a Parisian apartment,
but a farmhouse deep in the true heart of the land they would lift to
new heights. The new party was to come from the real France, and
the potency of the rural myth underpinned that day at the farm.
Though its progenitors had actually spun their partisan webs on either
side of the Seine for almost a decade, this was to be a movement
which would stand above and beyond selfish, sectional Parisian concerns. The people around the table simply believed in the recurring
Gaullist mantra: they, and they alone, knew what was best for France.
A fly on the wall might have been a trifle concerned at the quasi-
fascist superman tone that hung in the air.

That autumn, Chirac travelled to Égletons in his electoral home
department of the Corrèze, a town celebrated for the excellence of its
sausages. In a rousing speech in a gymnasium built with funds which
he had arranged to be allocated to the region, the former Premier laid
the groundwork for the new movement, calling on the nation to
rally to its basic values. Such was the Chiracian surge that the existing
Gaullist party agreed to be swallowed up: it helped that most of its
barons were promised important posts in the new enterprise. In
December 1976, at a great meeting in a Paris exhibition hall, the ex-
Premier launched the Rassemblement Pour la République (Rally for
the Republic) to take Gaullism into the next millennium and prove
that ideologically-led populism had a future. The name had a vital historical echo: De Gaulle had called his post-war political movement
the Rassemblement du Peuple Français.

From the start, the RPR had one over-riding aim – the election of
Jacques Chirac as Head of State in 1981. That meant there were now
two competing presidential candidates on the right, for an election
where they would face a candidate of the left who was busy turning
the Socialist Party into a vehicle to get him to power at long last. This
intensely personal pattern, set in the mid-1970s, was to continue for
two decades to the disadvantage of the nation caught in the hammer-
lock of the three contenders.

The long wait until the next presidential election was no problem
for the reigning Head of State. His opponent on the left needed the

years ahead to consolidate and build his strength. For Jacques Chirac, on the other hand, no time could be wasted. Leading a big new party was a necessary platform for his ambitions. But he was also a man who had been in government for almost a decade and who was used to exerting authority: the idea of being bereft of power was unnatural. He did not have to wait long for a chance to get back from the wilderness.

Among the reforms Giscard cherished was the idea of giving Paris an elected mayor in place of the officials who ruled it at the behest of central government. As Prime Minister, Chirac had not been convinced; a real boss of the capital might become a thorn in the side of the national authorities, a countervailing challenge to the Jacobin centralism he had always practised. He was not alone in such thinking: it was why there had been no elected mayor of the city for so long. But Giscard had his way, and the poll was set for March 1977. The Head of State took personal charge. Ensuring that a friendly figure ran Paris would further enhance his own power. So, at a luncheon at the Élysée Palace in November 1976, Giscard picked one of his most faithful lieutenants, the Industry Minister Michel d'Ornano, as the Mayor of Paris to be. Two days later, Pierre Juillet and Marie-France Garaud had an idea: why didn't Chirac run against d'Ornano? Another front opened in the battle between the companions-in-arms of 1974.

Once the RPR leader had announced his candidacy, the idea seemed the most inevitable thing in the world. The Gaullists were strong in the city: a Chirac follower had just won a smashing by-election victory in the 5th *arrondissement*, while two Giscardians had lost seats elsewhere in the capital. A plump-cheeked Norman count, d'Ornano did not fit naturally into campaigning in the city streets; Chirac, on the other hand, relished the endless round of glad-handing and small talk in the shops, markets and cafés. It was said that his palms became so sore that he had to wrap them in soothing bandages at night. There was a challenge from the left to be fought as well, but the opponent who mattered for Chirac was not on the list of candidates. The RPR leader might be crossing swords with d'Ornano day by day: his real target was the man in the Élysée.

On 25 March 1977, seven months to the day since he had resigned as Prime Minister, Chirac was elected Mayor of Paris. He and his

RPR were triumphant; Giscard was humiliated. The ex-Premier now had a mighty double power-base, made up of a mass party and control of France's greatest city, and he was ready for the ultimate challenge.

The presidential election of 1981 brought together themes which had run through French politics since 1965. In the left-hand corner, François Mitterrand was stronger than ever, with the solid backing of a resurgent Socialist Party plus the Communist regiments from the Red Belt suburbs and its provincial redoubts. The opposition had come close to winning parliamentary elections and was steadily extending its power in the regions. After a bout of internal feuding, Mitterrand had stitched together enough of the rival Socialist factions to ensure that he would face no internal challenge to his third presidential bid. On the right, in contrast, the two young allies of 1974 were fighting one another as much as they were combating the left.

For most of the previous five years, Chirac's RPR deputies had waged guerrilla warfare against the government in the National Assembly. Giscard's presidency was bogged down in low growth, rising unemployment, uncertainty about France's international standing and recurrent rumours that the President had accepted diamonds from the self-proclaimed Emperor Jean Bedel Bokassa in Central Africa. Social tension was rising: far from seeing their country becoming a fairer place, as Giscard had pledged, the French watched as inequalities rose and growth fell after the oil price crisis. The smoothly aloof man in the Élysée came to epitomise the haves to the growing ranks of the have-nots. When he attempted a reprise of his triumphal 1974 television debate with Mitterrand and asked about currency rates, the Socialist sat back and smiled: the next day, one of his staff told journalists that his boss had thought of asking whether Giscard knew the market rate for diamonds, but had held back out of respect for his office. The unspoken remark shot around town. Seven years of power had not been kind to Giscard; the unstoppably bright young man of 1974 had become the brittle autocrat of 1981. Eight months before the election, he held a 61–39 lead over Mitterrand in the polls. By the following March, the gap had narrowed to 51–49. Part of the reason was the challenge Giscard faced from his former Prime Minister.

Three years earlier, in the 1978 European elections, Chirac had shown his wild side with a Le Pen-like attack on the Giscardians as 'the party of the foreigners'. His only excuse was that he was in hospital after a car crash which may have affected his judgement. That kind of stridency cost the RPR dearly at the polls, but Chirac was unabashed. He was also more alone than he had ever been, having lost the counsel of his two original guides. It was said that his wife had issued an 'it's them or me' ultimatum, so Pierre Juillet went off to tend his sheep while Marie-France Garaud stood as an independent presidential candidate. Chirac's 1981 campaign made it plain that he was not fit to run the country. In the first round of voting, he won 18 per cent to Giscard's 28 and Mitterrand's 26 (Garaud scored 1.3 per cent). But the crude result was not the point. The RPR's leader was a killer force, a Clint Eastwood figure on a trail of bloody vengeance.

In public, Chirac had to say that he would vote for Giscard in the run-off fight with Mitterrand: as head of the biggest party of the right, he could not speak otherwise. But there was a deafening absence of any rallying call from Gaullist ranks. A minister recalled hearing Chirac say he would do all he could to ensure that Giscard was not re-elected. As for the RPR rank-and-file, five years of in-fighting had turned them against Giscard and his clan to the point at which some might let their hostility overcome their desire to keep Mitterrand out of the Élysée. The prospect of going fishing rather than voting on Sunday, 10 May 1981 held a large appeal for Chirac's supporters. The Communist leadership was equally ambivalent about backing Mitterrand, but their voters sensed a chance to install a government of the left at long last, and voted with their hearts.

As France's pre-eminent electoral strategist, François Mitterrand knew that he had to exploit the cancerous split between his two main opponents to the full. His best chance of winning lay in their ability to lose. Accordingly, he arranged a secret dinner for Chirac at the home of one of his most devoted supporters, Édith Cresson. As the evening ended, Mitterrand told the Mayor of Paris: 'If I am not elected President of the Republic this time, it will be a bore for me but, in the end, not too serious. I would go down as the man who took Socialism to 49 per cent of the vote. My place in history is already assured. I have left my mark. On the other hand, if Giscard wins again, you will have problems. I would not like to be in your shoes. He won't do you any favours, eh?'

It was vintage Mitterrand – setting his enemies against one another for his own good. The old fox knew who he was dealing with. Back in 1977, a guest at a dinner at the flat of a gadfly publisher, politician and short-lived Giscardian minister, Jean-Jacques Servan-Schreiber, had said: 'You may perhaps be surprised that I allow – or even cause – the election of Mitterrand, but it's the only way to get rid of Giscard. And we can't go on letting him sink France.' The speaker was Jacques Chirac. As for Mitterrand, before the first round of the election, he confided to a businessman friend: 'God save me from facing Jacques Chirac in the second round. If he is the candidate of the united right, I don't think I'll win.'

Mitterrand was spared that fight when Chirac was eliminated in the first round. But it was clearly going to be a very close battle with Giscard, and Mitterrand left no stone unturned. Among those he tipped over was the rock hiding the case of Michel Slitinsky, who, as a seventeen-year-old, had hidden in a cupboard and then escaped over the rooftops when two French policemen came to his family home in Bordeaux in the autumn of 1942 searching for Jews. After the Liberation, Slitinsky's sister, who had survived deportation, recognised the two policemen in the street. Slitinsky began legal proceedings against them, but they pleaded that they had been acting on orders from headquarters: they were never brought to trial. Researching into the complicity of the authorities with the genocide, Slitinsky found a sheaf of deportation orders signed by the head of the 'Jewish question' section in Bordeaux, Maurice Papon, who was now Giscard's Budget Minister. Slitinsky passed his documents to the investigative weekly, *Le Canard Enchaîné*, in the spring of 1981. According to Slitinsky, the journalist who wrote the documents up told him he had been in touch with Mitterrand before a front-page story appeared between the two rounds of the election under the headline, 'PAPON, AIDE DE CAMPS. When a minister of Giscard had Jews deported.' According to Slitinsky, the journalist, a former Socialist Party worker who now appears embarrassed and denies the tale, told him simply, 'Mitterrand agrees,' calculating that the revelation of Papon's role could swing 200,000 Jewish votes to him.

On a less public front, the champion of the united left sent a trusted friend, François de Grossouvre, to see the Mayor of Paris. De Grossouvre, an intriguer who spun schemes in the shadows for Mitterrand, had a special message to deliver. The left's electoral programme promised to introduce proportional representation to give smaller political groups seats in the National Assembly. This was acutely worrying for Chirac's RPR, which gained greatly from the winner-take-all system: in 1978, it had won one-third of the National Assembly with a quarter of the votes. De Grossouvre carried the message that, whatever his programme proclaimed, Mitterrand would keep the existing electoral system – if he said anything else in public, it was only to keep in with his Communist allies, who would benefit from a change in the voting method. Chirac appeared content. It was said that his visitor reminded him, pleasurably, of Pierre Juillet.

As the campaign reached its peak, François Mitterrand took to quoting the Paris mayor's public criticisms of Giscard in the late 1970s. Chirac did not rebut any of them. In a crucial television debate with the President, Mitterrand cited Chirac ten times. The Socialist and Gaullist might be on different sides of the political fence, but their mutual enmity towards Giscard brought them together. 'You have always been wrong,' Mitterrand told the Head of State in their television duel. He might have been speaking for Jacques Chirac. What role have the presence of the presidential ski instructor and straight-backed chairs at Brégançon played in the recent history of France? More, perhaps, than any policy debate in the National Assembly. Giscard's grandeur unwittingly hatched a complicity between the men to his left and right which was his undoing. Without it, Mitterrand would probably not have achieved 51.76 per cent of the vote, and France would not have spent the next fourteen years under his rule.

The first defeat of his life was traumatic for Valéry Giscard d'Estaing. President before he was fifty, he found himself rejected at fifty-five. In 1969, Charles de Gaulle resigned with a one-sentence communiqué and remained in seclusion in his country home. In 1974, Georges Pompidou died in office. In 1981, the third President of the Fifth Republic delivered a farewell message to the nation through his favoured medium, television. When he had finished speaking, he rose from his seat and walked off the set while the camera stayed symbolically focused on the empty chair. The implication that France had a vacuum at the very pinnacle of the state was yet another sign of Giscard's self-regard, a maudlin exercise by a man whose main public-relations failure had been that, after their first honeymoon, he had related less and less to the public.

The ex-President suffered the indignity of an abusive Socialist demonstration as he drove out of the Élysée for the last time. He did not read newspapers for months to avoid hurtful criticism, and said he found it hard to look at his own reflection in a mirror. He had banked so much on his own brilliance that he could not duck personal blame for defeat and the sweeping Socialist gains in ensuing parliamentary elections. At a private dinner the following year, Mitterrand told Giscard that history had been unfair to him. 'You are the best,' the new President added. 'I am sure we will meet again.' Soothing words, but little balm. By then, Jacques Chirac was rising in the opinion polls and Giscard's second Prime Minister, Raymond Barre, had emerged as the true incarnation of reliable conservative values. In the new trinity of opposition, Giscard ranked only third to his two former heads of government. No wonder he spoke of wearing widow's weeds.

Three years later, the ex-President was driving a bright green Peugeot through the narrow, winding roads of the central Auvergne to modest meeting places where he chewed over the problems of milk prices with farmers, sipped an aperitif in country cafés and showed a remarkable ability to remember the names of the pettiest of rural dignitaries. He told me that he had seen 7,300 people in his by-election campaign for a rural constituency in his home department of the Puy-de-Dôme. Giscard had come out of purdah: he spoke to small groups in villages and town halls facing the official portrait of his successor. This was where he had entered politics at the age of twenty-nine, displacing a very old member of his mother's family back in 1956. The setting might be modest for a man who had founded the European Monetary System and sat at summits with superpower leaders, but Giscard showed an unexpected common touch as he discussed agricultural subsidies and the water supply. In one café, he sat at a Formica-topped table and recalled what he had done for the mountain farmers during his years in power. 'I'm no longer President,' he told the thirty people in the room. 'I'm picking up life again, and so should you. Your purchasing power is falling, so are your livestock prices. You haven't been defended.' To make the farmers feel important, he pulled rabbits from the hat. One morning, seeing me at the back of a quarter-filled village hall, he veered away from rural matters and told the assembled audience that the eyes of the world were upon them. 'How you vote will be noted in Great Britain, in the United States. *The Economist* is here, watching you,' he informed the old men in caps and clogs. Nobody but Giscard could bring such attention to a village lost among the volcanic peaks of central France.

The ex-President was relaxed that autumn day. He won the by-election easily, and later wrote a book expounding the notion that, if only the sectarian political barriers could be surmounted, two-thirds of the French could agree on a programme of national consensus – whose natural leader needed no identification. He had, he told me, drawn fresh inner strength from his reflections in the heart of the countryside. He was now involved with real life, real problems. 'I am taking the heartbeat of France,' he said as he piloted his green Peugeot on the upland roads. Then I asked him what he thought of the resurgent Jacques Chirac and the rising star of his other Prime Minister, Raymond Barre. Giscard replied with a pleasantry, but his gloved hands tightened sharply on the steering-wheel and the car almost lurched off the road. The war was not over.

12

FRIENDS OF FRANÇOIS

As the face of the new President of the Republic scrolled up on
television screens across France at precisely 8 P.M. on 10 May 1981,
the left erupted in joy. Crowds danced in the streets to celebrate the end
of twenty-three years of rule from the right and centre. In the suburban Paris flat where I was having dinner, my host rushed into his
kitchen and re-emerged with a bottle of champagne and a sheaf of
Socialist red roses. Millions who had supported the left through decades
of Gaullism and Giscardianism suddenly saw their impossible dream
come true. François Mitterrand had proved that power at the summit
could change hands. Driving home late that night to our flat near
Socialist Party headquarters beside the Seine, I had to abandon the car
far from home because of the crush of people celebrating in the street.

No presidential victory had ever been so fêted by the winners or
feared by the losers. The Manichaean strain in French life was quickly
apparent. While joyous crowds milled through the night on the site
where the revolutionaries of 1789 had stormed the Bastille, alarmists
on the right warned that political police would soon be knocking on
doors. As businessmen smuggled their money over the Swiss border in
suitcases, the head of the French Rothschilds went into exile in New
York with the bitter phrase about being 'a traitor under Vichy, a
pariah under Mitterrand'. A Socialist congress compared such people
to the Royalist émigrés of 1789. A writer from the losing side reviled
France for having the stupidest right wing in the world. Having
shown that an alternance of power was possible, the left went on to

win an absolute majority in parliamentary elections the following month. Four Communists joined the government. In their first year in office, the Socialists brought in changes which equalled Roosevelt's New Deal or the British Labour reforms of 1945. A dozen major firms were nationalised. The death penalty was abolished, the working week was cut to thirty-nine hours, and everybody got the right to a fifth week's annual holiday. There was a wealth tax and an increase in the minimum wage. Welfare payments rose substantially, and the regions were promised decentralisation.

When the Finance Minister, Jacques Delors, suggested after six months that it might be time for a pause in the pace of reform, nobody took any notice. But the intimations of reality soon rose to the surface. In the first thirteen months of François Mitterrand's presidency, the franc was devalued twice, and inflation rose to 18 per cent. Despite all the reflationary measures, unemployment hit 2 million. The boom in purchasing power sent imports spiralling upwards. France was forced to raise billions of dollars in international loans to cover its soaring debts. In June 1982, the first knockings of what came to be known as the policy of *rigueur* were introduced with an evident incoherence as ideology met necessity: state spending was cut but the minimum wage was raised again. Economics and politics had rarely made such uneasy bedfellows.

Amid all these great events, it was not surprising that few people paid any attention to the affairs of a shock-absorber company called Vibrachoc. The firm had an array of foreign subsidiaries and a murky web of cross-holdings through the financial haven of Liechtenstein. At the start of the 1980s, it was not in the best of health. One big industrial group which looked at it as a possible takeover target estimated that Vibrachoc was worth a maximum of 65 million francs, and warned that a purchaser would need to pump in capital to keep it afloat.

Three months later, that same industrial group and the subsidiaries of two large banks paid 110 million francs for the struggling shock-absorber manufacturer. Part of the payment went to Liechtenstein; part was transferred to a company operating under Luxembourg law from the capital of Liberia. It was just the kind of transaction which the new President denounced in his fulminations against 'money which corrupts, money which kills, which rots consciences'. This made it all the more striking that the man who had sold Vibrachoc to such personal advantage was the President's oldest friend – and that the sale would not have been possible had Mitterrand not been in the Élysée.

Tell me who you frequent, as a French proverb goes, and I will tell you who you are. By that measure, François Mitterrand does not emerge with flying colours. The Bernard Tapie saga and the string of scandals linked to his peers have already been set out. But the story of Roger-Patrice Pelat takes the tale of moral decay a step further. It shows how the rot set in from the start of the Mitterrand era, and was not – as the President's defenders would have it – simply a function of old age in the last years of his reign. And, in its way, it provides another illustration of how little those at the pinnacle of power are even aware of the gulf separating them from the proper standards of everyday life.

Pelat had fought for the Republicans in the International Brigade during the Spanish Civil War. He met François Mitterrand when they were prisoners of war of the Germans. Later, they were colleagues in the Resistance. It was in Pelat's flat in Paris that Mitterrand first saw a photograph of his wife to be. Half a century later, Danielle Mitterrand told an interviewer that the friends who had never disappointed her and the President were people they had met during the war, such as Roger-Patrice. He was certainly most helpful to the Mitterrands over the decades. One of the future President's brothers worked as a manager of Vibrachoc in its early years. Between 1972 and 1980, the firm paid the politician an annual fee for advice. After 1981, the payments were directed to one of Mitterrand's sons, a Socialist deputy in the National Assembly: asked what the firm got in return, Vibrachoc's finance director said that the payments were simply a means of assuring the younger Mitterrand of 'a friendly annuity'.

Pelat was one of the few people allowed to call Mitterrand '*tu*'. Danielle spoke of his 'intoxication' when he was with François. On one occasion in 1988, Pelat made out a cheque for 150,000 francs to Mitterrand: questioned about it later, the Élysée explained that the money was reimbursement for old books which the President had bought for his friend on his foreign travels. Although the Head of State had a perfectly good home in the narrow Rue de Bièvre on the Left Bank, Pelat contributed 300,000 francs to a fund established to help him buy a new flat in case a right-wing electoral victory deprived him of a second term in the Élysée. On a visit to Paris, Mikhail Gorbachev was surprised when a large man walked calmly into the salon at the Élysée where he was conferring with Mitterrand. As recounted by a French journalist, the Head of State smiled and said: 'Let me introduce Patrice Pelat. He's an old friend.' Some came to call the former maker of shock-absorbers France's Vice-President. He was said to keep a dinner jacket in the President's wardrobe.

Whatever Mitterrand might say in public about the awful power of money, his old pal liked getting it and spending it – and avoiding as many taxes as possible. He acquired a company yacht in the Mediterranean. He and his sons drove Rolls-Royces; he owned a hunting estate and racehorses. Vibrachoc was Pelat's biggest killing, and, though it was not publicised at the time, there was really no mystery about how he managed to get such a good price for his stumbling firm. The main buyer was the Alsthom industrial group, and Alsthom's parent company had just been nationalised by the Socialists. The two banks which bought smaller stakes were also under state control. At the same time, Pelat had also begun to build up a relationship with a couple of men he called the 'two Bs'. One was Alain Boublil, an adviser on industrial policy at the Élysée. The other was Pierre Bérégovoy, Mitterrand's chief of staff. With those cards in his hands, it was not surprising that Roger-Patrice had been able to push through such a sweet deal. At least one Mitterrand viewed the matter in a different way, however: 'When François became President,' said Danielle, 'Patrice relinquished his main business in order to be more available and closer to his friend.'

It is October 1982. One of the most senior members of the government is on the telephone. May I say, he breathes into the mouthpiece, that your funeral address today was one of the most brilliant speeches I have ever heard? A short silence. Then the minister humbly suggests that the speech might be reprinted and distributed to every school in France for the edification of the nation's youth. With that, he ends his conversation with the President of the Republic and turns to tell me about his plans to reform France's welfare system.

Pierre Bérégovoy had entered the government as Minister for Social Affairs at the end of June, two months after Pelat cashed in his Vibrachoc chips. Once the euphoria of 1981 dissipated, even François Mitterrand had to acknowledge that something needed to be done to

rein in the galloping welfare deficit, and Bérégovoy seemed just the
fellow for the job. The President had no more faithful servant than the
man who had been his Secretary-General at the Élysée. 'Béré' strutted like a bespectacled bantam cock behind his master. His devotion
was absolute; thanks to Mitterrand, he had risen to the uplands of
power, and he clearly intended to scale a few more peaks before he
was through, which he could only do with the help of the President.

While Pierre Bérégovoy was drawing up plans to cut billions from
the social security budget, Roger-Patrice Pelat went on trying to add
to his fortune. His closeness to Mitterrand got him a seat on the
board of Air France, meaning unlimited first-class travel to any destination he liked, including a home he had bought in the Caribbean. In
the summer of 1982, he had tried to muscle in on a deal to sell uranium to India, but was repulsed. Six months later, he invited a select
group of guests to spend Christmas with him at a luxury hotel in an
oasis in Morocco. Among the guests were Alain Boublil and Pierre
Bérégovoy, who had his fortune told by a local wizard.

Back in France, away from the delights of Yuletide in the desert,
the government was fast falling out of favour. It fared badly at municipal elections, and the economy needed another dose of strong
medicine. In March 1983, as pressure on the franc became unbearable,
Mitterrand spent a long weekend debating whether France should
remain a full member of the European Community or should sheer
off in pursuit of Socialism in one country. Jacques Delors negotiated
the European course in Brussels while left-wing Socialists in Paris
urged the President to go it alone. Mitterrand took the tough but
inevitable course. The franc was devalued again. Returning from
Brussels, the Finance Minister introduced a full austerity plan; France
got a huge European loan; and the Communists were forced to quit
the government. By the following spring, job cuts were being decreed
in the newly nationalised industries which, a couple of years before,
had been hailed as guarantors of employment and national prosperity.
Delors was the man of the moment, but when he was offered the premiership, he overstepped the mark by making it clear that he wanted
to retain control of the Finance Ministry, which would have made
him as powerful as the President. Instead, he went off to head the
European Commission. A Mitterrand loyalist became Prime Minister,
and Pierre Bérégovoy moved to the Finance Ministry.

Amid all this turmoil, the President found solace in long, reflective walks around Paris with Roger-Patrice. The two elderly men called at antiquarian bookshops and strolled by the Seine, Mitterrand wearing his characteristic big black hat, Pelat in a cap. When his friend turned back to affairs of state, Pelat devoted himself to seeking out fresh avenues of profit. France's economic policy might have gone austere, but that did not mean that a man could not use his contacts to good effect, even if it involved one of the more bizarre enterprises France has ever undertaken. The story was fully unveiled by the journalist Jean Montaldo in a book stuffed with revelations about doubtful members of Mitterrand's entourage.

Shortly before his election to the Élysée in 1981, the Socialist leader had paid a little-publicised visit to the Stalinist outpost of North Korea. After his victory, the North Koreans pressed for an improvement in relations with Paris, and the idea of France building a prestige hotel development in their country gradually emerged. A French company took up the idea, but wanted export credit guarantees from the government in case anything went wrong. Given the nature of the North Korean regime and the country's dubious attractions as a tourist centre, French ministers were wary – among them, the new chief of the nation's finances.

Pierre Bérégovoy advised the Prime Minister, Laurent Fabius, against the state underwriting the North Korean project. But the contract for a 46-storey hotel with 879 rooms and 123 suites was still signed in the autumn of 1984, with export credits guaranteed up to 95 per cent. Building work started a year later. It soon ran into difficulties when the Koreans withheld payment. The project was eventually completed, thanks to the intervention of Pelat. Despite the reticence of his friend at the Finance Ministry, he had used his influence at the highest levels to get the state guarantee. In return, Montaldo established, a subsidiary of the company involved showed its gratitude by carrying out work on Pelat's country estate to the precise value of 24,655,462 francs and 60 centimes.

Soon after he moved into the Finance Ministry, Pierre Bérégovoy invited three foreign journalists to lunch. His new seat of power was housed in part of the Louvre palace, where elegant salons and corridors stretched further than the eye could see. We sat with the minister at a round table in his ornate private dining-room and waited for him to lecture us about the economy.

Instead, Bérégovoy picked up the plate set before him – it was probably Sèvres porcelain. Who could have thought, he said, that the son of a Norman café-owner and a Ukrainian immigrant, a man who had gone from school to work in a textile factory at the age of sixteen, would now be sitting in the splendour of the Louvre eating off the finest of antique plates? And now could we three journalists give him, the newly-appointed Finance Minister of one of the world's major economies, some tips on how he should behave at a meeting with his peers in Washington the following week? In anybody else, it would have been sickeningly insincere. But Bérégovoy really meant it. Throughout his life, he was so genuinely and touchingly struck by what he had achieved that he found it impossible to hide his delight, and not to invite others to be equally impressed. But he also always seemed in need of a helping hand, a reassuring word.

The dining-room in the Louvre was indeed a long way from the world into which Pierre Bérégovoy had been born in Normandy two days before Christmas in 1925. His mother ran a small café-cum-grocery shop in a suburb of Rouen. The original Ukrainian family name meant 'down by the riverside', and Pierre was nicknamed '*le petit russe*' at school. The four children were brought up by their grandmother in the countryside. His family politics were of the left, and it was said that, as a child, Pierre made models of the Popular Front leader Léon Blum. According to a younger brother, he always had the last word in arguments: not even his grandmother dared to contradict him. As teenagers, he and his brothers played a game called Allies. Pierre allotted the roles, and was always Churchill.

Once he had earned his school proficiency certificate, Bérégovoy went to work as a fitter and turner. Then he moved to the railways and, while training to be an engine-driver at the age of seventeen, joined the Resistance, derailing German trains during the invasion of Normandy. After the Liberation, he joined the state gas board and took out membership of the main Socialist party of the time, the SFIO. He attended night-school classes and was promoted to increasingly important posts at the gas company. He quit the SFIO in protest at its support for repression in Algeria, allied himself with the patron saint of the French non-Communist left, Pierre Mendès-France, and then, in 1973, gravitated into the orbit of François Mitterrand, negotiating electoral agreements with the Communists and rising to the number-two position in the Socialist Party machine.

Bérégovoy's *modus operandi* was clear and honourable, unlike the ways of many around him. He got a foothold with a modest position in a company or political party and then, by dint of hard work and intelligence, rose steadily on his way to the ornate dining-room in the Louvre. Some of Mitterrand's more urbane companions sneered at his earnestly upward mobility. But he got things done. Just as Jacques Chirac had been Pompidou's bulldozer, so Pierre Bérégovoy was Mitterrand's earth-mover, and he readily shouldered responsibility for policies that won the government growing unpopularity at home but which made him a pin-up boy of international finance as French inflation dipped down to 5 per cent in 1985 – less than a third of its level in the left's go-go years.

There was one prize waiting to be won, but Mitterrand held back. In 1983, Bérégovoy was said to have believed that he had a chance of becoming Prime Minister, and was ready to follow whatever policy was needed to secure the top ministerial job. But, when the President decided in 1984 to replace his first Prime Minister, Pierre Mauroy, he promoted his young protégé, Laurent Fabius. Loyal retriever Bérégovoy was informed that, at fifty-eight, he was too old for the job.

The Finance Minister's tight policies contributed powerfully to the triumph of the right at National Assembly elections in 1986, and the opening of two years of uneasy *cohabitation* between François Mitterrand and his third Prime Minister, Jacques Chirac. During their months together, the President took sly pleasure in tripping up the eager Gaullist head of government. On one occasion, he set out for a summit in Japan on his own in the official aircraft, forcing Chirac to follow in a commercial airliner. The two men tussled over privatisations and legislation as they shaped up for their real clash – the 1988 presidential election. Powerfully helped by his opponent's abject campaign, Mitterrand won a decisive victory, with 54 per cent of the vote; he even beat Chirac in the Gaullist's adopted department of the Corrèze. After moderately successful National Assembly elections, the President was now free to pick a new Prime Minister from among his own followers again.

For the second time, Mitterrand told Bérégovoy he was too old. The man he was forced to appoint by the balance of power on the centre-left, Michel Rocard, was only five years younger and had been around since the mid-1960s. The President's visceral and well-known dislike for Rocard – 'he's just about good enough to be a junior minister for the Post Office' – must have made the appointment all the more galling for Bérégovoy. The Finance Minister received some consolation in being ranked as a Minister of State. The new Prime Minister, who had been Mitterrand's main challenger in the Socialist ranks for a decade, was a reasonable man who believed in dialogue and wanted to establish a broad Social Democratic party on West German lines. But few from outside the ranks of the left agreed to join the experiment, and France grew bored with Rocard's painstakingly sensible approach. The Socialists did very badly at European elections and tore themselves apart at a fratricidal party congress. And all the while, money stayed tight, unemployment rose, taxes remained high, the National Front stirred up rancour, and the President played favourites with his courtiers.

Still, France's state companies could cut a dash on the world stage. On 11 November 1988, after three months of negotiations, the big nationalised metals company, Péchiney, reached a $1.2 billion agreement to take over a US firm, American National Can. On 14 November, Péchiney informed the government of the deal, which was made public a week later amid official celebration that French enterprises were still international players. Within a few weeks, the takeover had set off one of the great scandals of the Mitterrand era, involving a rich cast: a Middle East arms-dealer, a senior Finance Ministry official, banks in Switzerland, Luxembourg and Anguilla, sharp-eyed investigators from the Securities and Exchange Commission in the United States – and some of the President's men.

The Securities and Exchange Commission was intrigued by the pattern of trading that had taken place in the shares of Triangle, the company which controlled American National Can, before the Péchiney deal was made public. The value of Triangle stock had increased significantly when the sale was made public. Anybody who bought Triangle shares in the weeks before the deal ended up considerably richer. The US investigation prodded the control commission at the Paris Bourse into a similar probe. The joint inquiries revealed large buying of shares in Triangle by French and Middle Eastern investors, partly through Swiss banks. The purchases seemed to be linked to the progress of the secret talks: they had been particularly strong during the ten days between the deal being clinched in private and the public announcement in Paris.

As the scandal became known, Mitterrand went on television to denounce speculators, go-betweens and well-connected financiers. The snag was that the two main buyers of Triangle shares turned out to be his good friend, Roger-Patrice Pelat, and another businessman with close Socialist connections. Pelat was reported to have acquired 10,000 shares just one day after the government in Paris got its first confidential notice of the takeover agreement – and a full six days before the announcement. Then *Le Monde* revealed that Pelat or one of his sons had bought another 40,000 Triangle shares through a bank in Lausanne, giving them a total profit of $1.8 million.

The Péchiney affair was not the only such case of financial legerdemain: a group of businessmen linked to the government was alleged to have used insider information in a bid to take a strategic stake in a big bank during a takeover bid. There was also the matter of a sheaf of documents which various journalists were shown at the time. They indicated that France had tried to raise a $20 billion loan as the initial Socialist experiment went off the rails. It was never evident if the papers were real or forged; and, if genuine, whether they documented real negotiations or were an attempt to wring a large commission out of the government for a deal that never was. What made them tantalising was that one of those named in the documents was referred to as 'M. Patrick' – a name just one letter away from Patrice. Even if it was all a hoax, it was intriguing that the perpetrators had chosen to point in the direction of the President's best friend.

In the Péchiney case, there were no such uncertainties. Pelat had clearly indulged in insider dealing before the takeover was made public. The question was where he and his associates got their information. The answer led to the less illustrious of Pelat's 'two Bs', Alain Boublil. Short, tubby and cocky, Boublil was not a popular man. He exuded self-esteem and, as industrial adviser at the presidency in 1982, had contemptuously waved aside any suggestion that the subsidies and corporate engineering which the Socialists were implementing might not work. As losses in the state sector rose and jobs began to be cut, he showed not the slightest trace of self-doubt, switching seamlessly to the new orthodoxy like any good apparatchik. Moving to Bérégovoy's Finance Ministry, he strutted his stuff clear of the norms of mere mortals. He saw no problem, for instance, in accepting hospitality from a Lebanese wheeler-dealer, Samir Traboulsi, who was an intermediary between Péchiney and Triangle as well as being an investor in the ill-fated banking activities of Jean-Maxime Levêque and a man whose social life had gained him the nickname of the 'vizier of pleasures' – in 1998 he was named in a sensational Paris court case as having organised an evening with five or six high-class prostitutes for a Saudi Arabian prince, allegedly receiving $400,000 for his services. Boublil's defence was simple: he was being got at because he was 'neither a practising Jew, nor a freemason, nor a provincial, nor a member of the upper bourgeoisie, nor a member of the top civil service'.

When this inside-outsider and Traboulsi were sentenced to jail terms in connection with the Péchiney affair, nobody grieved. What was piquant, however, was that some of the insider information on which Pelat capitalised so avidly was divulged to him at Pierre Bérégovoy's fortieth wedding anniversary party, in a restaurant off the Champs-Élysées where the President's old crony sat at the top table. Boublil and Traboulsi were also present. Told about the guest-list at the party, Mitterrand was furious at Bérégovoy. 'He shouldn't have done it,' he exclaimed. 'He shouldn't have.' The Lebanese businessman was said to have put his private plane at Bérégovoy's disposal for election trips. A month before the anniversary party, the Finance Minister had presented Traboulsi with the Légion d'Honneur for his help in freeing French hostages in the Middle East: once again, Pelat had been present at the reception. Mitterrand had warned Bérégovoy against appearing in such company. But some things seemed to override even his master's voice for the minister who had found it so impressive to be eating off fine porcelain.

By the time Boublil went to jail for his involvement in the Péchiney affair, Roger-Patrice Pelat was dead. He had a weak heart, and died while awaiting trial. In conversation with his aide, Jacques Attali, François Mitterrand struck the self-pitying tone that he could affect when cornered. 'It's endless,' he said. 'Those people who are accused have no electoral mandate, no public job. They do not work with me. One cannot sanction them or sack them. I'm told I should do something, but I'm not going to put out a statement saying: "Tom is no longer my friend; I won't lunch with Dick any more; and I'm not going to go for walks with Harry."'

It was time for another change of Prime Minister. Yet again the President ignored the claims of Pierre Bérégovoy. He turned first to Jacques Delors, who spent a sleepless night considering whether to return to Paris but decided he preferred to continue running the European Commission. Rebuffed by France's most popular politician-in-exile, Mitterrand appointed France's first woman Premier, Édith Cresson. Bérégovoy promptly submitted his resignation from the Finance Ministry, where he had maintained the parity of the national currency through thick and thin. Mitterrand's reaction was typical. 'You'll get used to Cresson and you can hold the franc firm in the meantime,' he told his faithful servant, sweetening the pill by expanding Bérégovoy's empire to take in industry, trade and telecommunications. When asked how he was bearing up, the minister replied darkly: 'I just do what I'm told but I'm keeping my own records about everything.'

Powerful though he was, Bérégovoy showed signs of insecurity. He was always pulling opinion polls from his pocket to consult. The Finance Ministry moved to a huge new building down the Seine, where Bérégovoy delighted in showing foreign colleagues the extent of his domain. One caustic visitor remarked that it was typical of France to have a big new building but no new policies to run from it. The defender of the franc, whose notepaper was headed 'Former Mechanic, Minister of the Economy and Finance', grew shirty when it was suggested that he had known little about economics before 1981 and had been forced to take a quick lesson from the Governor of the Bank of France. He hated being the butt of the jokes which, as a politician, he should have learned to endure long before. The Interior Minister, Pierre Joxe – a superior fellow whose father had been a Gaullist luminary – once remarked that it was obvious Bérégovoy was an honest man because of the cheap red socks he wore. The story immediately did the Parisian rounds. It was said that his wife bought them at the low-cost Prisunic chain. Bérégovoy was furiously touchy about this: his staff was reported to have complained to *Le Monde* because its cartoonist, Plantu, always showed him with crumpled socks under baggy trousers.

When Cresson was sacked after a short and unhappy spell in power in 1992, it was obvious that whoever took over from her would be inheriting a rotten job. The National Assembly elections the following year were being written off in advance. It was lamb-to-the-slaughter time, and so the perfect moment to summon the final kamikaze. With Bérégovoy as Prime Minister at last, the Socialists slumped to 18 per cent in regional elections; unemployment rose to one-tenth of the labour force; and the Maastricht Treaty only barely scraped through a referendum despite being backed by almost the entire political establishment. On top of everything else, the spectre of Roger-Patrice Pelat fell across the Prime Minister's path from beyond the grave.

Bérégovoy was not a rich man, but his years in office had bred a taste for what the French, in one of their linguistic adoptions, call 'le standing'. In 1981, he had done all he could to get his hands on a fine official apartment in a historic building across the Seine from the Élysée. When he was given the job of bringing welfare spending under control, Bérégovoy insisted on having a private lift installed in his ministry. Later, he demanded a personal helicopter. He also bought a 100-square-metre flat in the smart 16th *arrondissement* of Paris. How was he going to pay for it? No problem: the President's pal stepped in. On 18 September 1986, a notary registered a loan for 1 million francs to Pierre Bérégovoy from Roger-Patrice Pelat. That covered nearly half the price of the apartment. And Pelat went even further – the loan was interest-free. Some doubted if it was ever meant to be repaid at all. And what would be the pay-back price for that, it might be wondered.

On 3 February 1993, seven weeks before the National Assembly elections, France's main investigative weekly reported the Pelat loan. Bérégovoy was immediately pursued by questions. Instead of coming clean, he gave ambiguous and halting replies. *Le Monde* recalled the existence of an anti-corruption code which insisted that officials must be clear and open about any loans they were granted; the code had been drawn up by a commission appointed by Pierre Bérégovoy. Such was the decline in the Prime Minister's status that even his parliamentary constituency in the city of Nevers – capital of the

Nièvre department, and a political gift from Mitterrand – was thought to be under threat for a time.

When the election results were announced, the Socialists had lost 203 of their 258 seats in the National Assembly. Fifteen ministers were beaten. It was one of the greatest thrashings any major French political party had ever undergone, the price of sustained austerity, scandal and boredom with the same gang of men and women in government. If anybody carried responsibility for that, it was François Mitterrand, but, in his aloof way and with two more years of his term to run, he managed to position himself above the crude political battle. As a result, the blame went to the man who had begun hacking into the social security deficit a decade earlier and who had kept his shoulder to the wheel ever since.

With 242 Assembly seats – a gain of 115 – the Gaullists were the big winners, but Jacques Chirac did not want to become Prime Minister for a third time, so he passed the baton to his close colleague, Édouard Balladur, while he concentrated on the coming battle for the presidency. On a sunny afternoon on 30 March 1993, Balladur drove into his new official quarters at the Hôtel Matignon. After conferring inside, he and Bérégovoy emerged at the top of the steps in the courtyard. They smiled for the photographers, and walked down the steps, arm in arm. The staff crowded to the windows to clap their departing boss. Bérégovoy turned to raise his hand in a final greeting.

Watching the scene, Balladur's press secretary saw it as a perfect illustration of the continuity of the republican state as government swung from one party to another. 'On the two men's faces, one read something like mutual respect, a common faith in national institutions, and a quasi-certitude that the story would not stop there for these two men who recognised one another's mutual value, even if the fortunes of public life had placed them in opposing camps.' As he drove out into the Rue de Varenne, the outgoing Prime Minister looked remarkably serene.

Six weeks later, Pierre Bérégovoy bought flowers for his wife and went through routine duties as Mayor of Nevers. It was the ultimately symbolic left-wing day of 1 May, and Bérégovoy had a meeting with trade unionists as well as giving out prizes at a cycling race. He had not heard from the Head of State since the election, though at least a word of comfort from on high might have been

appropriate. At the end of April, Bérégovoy had placed telephone calls
to the President who had dictated so much of his life. But there was
only silence from Paris. François Mitterrand had spoken publicly of
his esteem for Roger-Patrice Pelat when his friend was caught insider
dealing; in the spring of 1993, there was not a word for Bérégovoy.

So the son of a Norman café-owner, one-time gas-fitter, negotia-
tor with the Communists, former chief of staff to the President, Social
Affairs Minister, Finance Minister and Prime Minister of France got
into his official car and told the driver to take him to a canal outside
Nevers. When they arrived, he asked his driver and bodyguard to
leave him alone. Unseen by them, he took his guard's pistol from the
glove compartment of the car and walked to the side of the canal.
There, he shot himself in the temple.

Bérégovoy was flown to Paris in a critical state. President Mitterrand and Prime Minister Balladur rushed to the hospital. Bérégovoy
was dead on arrival.

In an interview recorded shortly before his death, the former Premier
had spoken of the 'unpleasant political climate' and of his share of
responsibility. As a loyal servant of the President, he gave no hint of the
depths of his despair, though there were reports that he had written to
another leading Socialist in terms that could have presaged suicide. For
all his devotion, Pierre Bérégovoy never quite fitted into what one
senior presidential aide described as 'a luxuriant jungle with some very
beautiful aspects to it, but a jungle all the same'. He was always just a
little too literal, a bit too ponderous on his feet, and never as amusing as
the bright stars and con men who rose and fell at the Élysée, a victim of
the system that enabled him to move from obscurity to the uplands of
power but, in the end, left him with nowhere to go. It was entirely in
character that Mitterrand should use his suicide for his own purposes,
attacking the press for investigating the tide of scandals lapping around
the regime. The President's voice choked when he lambasted the media
as dogs who had hounded an honest man to his grave.

Bérégovoy would have sounded a similar note. Shortly before he
killed himself, he told a group of journalists that he couldn't help feeling angry about the fuss over the Pelat loan. 'I'm sixty-seven and I
cannot even have a 100-square-metre flat,' he said. 'You know in
France, no one likes people who climb up the social ladder.' What
neither he nor many of the others around the Élysée could recognise

was that insider dealing, influence-peddling and interest-free loans
from dubious sources are simply things that those in power should not
indulge in. But then, despite all the rhetoric about the higher things
of life, morality was not something which was much prized at the
Élysée under François Mitterrand.

The Mitterrand presidency saw the emergence of a bright younger
class of Socialists. Some, like Lionel Jospin, remained resolutely serious and middle-class, intent on improving themselves and the people
they ruled over. Others – *la gauche caviare* – showed a taste for the high
life, and were ready to make the most of their positions. But behind
both these groups was a small cohort of men who had been with
Mitterrand over the long years out of power, and who formed his
praetorian guard. If Roger-Patrice Pelat was one of the more unusual
of these, and Pierre Bérégovoy the most stoic, others fitted more
readily into the traditional image of a political cabal. None more so
than a man who combined a career as one of the smartest lawyers in
town with a position as one of the key Mitterrandists.

On a snowy morning in 1956, Roland Dumas had taken the train
from Limoges to Paris. A former Resistance fighter whose father had
been shot by the Germans, Dumas had just been elected to the
National Assembly as a deputy for the Democratic and Social Union
of the Resistance for the Haute-Vienne department. He was met at
the Gare d'Austerlitz by an emissary who took him to meet a leading
figure of the soft centre-left of the Fourth Republic in a two-room
office on the Champs-Élysées. 'Your election was a surprise,' François
Mitterrand told the younger man. They soon became companions-in-
arms, with the ultimate aim of winning power for the older man.

Away from politics, the elegant, silver-tongued and well-connected
Dumas made a fair fortune as a lawyer for the Picasso estate, for Marc
Chagall and Herbert von Karajan. From time to time, he showed that
his heart was still in the right (that is to say, left) place by appearing in
major political cases, including one involving Mitterrand. His legal
office was in the narrow street off the Boulevard Saint-Germain
where his leader had a duplex apartment. As a 'tenor' of the bar and
part of the President's 'first circle', his standing was not diminished by
not being included in the initial Socialist governments. Meeting him

in the early 1980s, you knew that this was a man with a direct line to the presidency. When he did become Minister for European Affairs and government spokesman in 1984, one felt that the job was not quite up to him. Once, during lunch looking out over the Seine on the Quai d'Orsay, Dumas excused himself after the main course by explaining that he was required 'on the other bank' – that is, at the Élysée. He would drop references to what *le Président* was thinking into the conversation like truffles. When the Socialists returned to government in 1988, Roland Dumas became Foreign Minister, dealing directly with Mitterrand.

Naturally, such a man liked to live high on the hog, and felt little need for the reserve which might have cramped a less confident fellow. He lamented how his income had dropped when he joined the government. But he also claimed another side to his character: explaining why he kept large amounts of cash in his office, he said that it was out of 'a peasant's mentality'. A renowned ladies' man, he entertained close relations with the daughter of the Defence Minister of Syria, and with a Frenchwoman employed mysteriously by the Elf oil firm whom we met in Chapter 6. She said her job was to use her influence with the Foreign Minister on the firm's behalf. Despite their friendship and the incident of the 11,000-franc shoes she bought for him on her company credit card, Dumas denied having been swayed in any way. In particular, he denied most vehemently having anything to do with an intriguing U-turn in the mid-Mitterrand years.

Ever since De Gaulle established diplomatic relations with Beijing in 1964, France had been anxious to maintain a special link with China. But at the end of the 1980s this foreign-policy objective was threatened by another strand in the Gaullist legacy. Since the 1960s, arms exports had been one of the driving forces of France's economy. Mirage jets had helped to win the Six-Day War for Israel; French arms were sold covertly to South Africa; Exocet missiles equipped the Argentine forces. At a time of high unemployment, making weapons to sell abroad brought social as well as industrial benefits. So it was not surprising that the state-owned Thomson embarked on a big sales drive in 1989 for a new generation of high-technology frigates. The salesmen soon hit gold dust on the other side of the globe, in Taiwan, which undertook to buy six of the ships for 16 billion francs.

But, back in Paris, the Foreign Ministry vetoed the sale for fear of a hostile reaction from Beijing. Dumas was unequivocal: 'From start to finish, throughout the decision-making process, I gave an unfavourable opinion, as numerous official documents will show,' he insisted when the affair came to light.

Still, the sale went ahead. As we have seen, a judge investigating Elf's affairs questioned a woman friend of the former minister about an alleged payment of 47 million francs in return for her attempts to get Dumas to approve the deal. The probe also revealed regular cash deposits in his bank account totalling 14 million francs: Dumas, who had been made President of the Constitutional Council at the end of Mitterrand's rule, said the money came from the sale of art works and insisted that the whole affair was all an attempt to get at the memory of his late friend at the Élysée. But in mounting his defence, the normally discreet lawyer who was now the fifth-ranking personage in France said rather too much.

Yes, he told *Le Figaro* at the beginning of 1998, a commission had been paid. But it had not been the paltry sum mentioned in connection with his lady friend. According to Dumas, who was put under formal investigation in the spring of 1998, no less than $500 million had been involved. He, himself, had not been aware of it. Instead, the deal had been approved by none other than the President of the Republic – with the Prime Minister of the time agreeing. The contract, Dumas added, had also been authorised by Bérégovoy's Finance Ministry, and the details had been lodged in a secret file. What that file contained remained hidden, at least until its privacy could be breached for political or judicial reasons. But what emerged was at least the shadow of the biggest financial scandal of all, with the possibility that the paper trail might, this time, lead not just to a Roger-Patrice Pelat or a Samir Traboulsi, but even closer to the Head of State who so liked to denounce the power of money.

Eighteen months after the left's triumph in 1981, a man in a grey wig entered the Élysée Palace by a side door. Led upstairs, the visitor noticed the Pretender to the French throne sitting patiently in the passageway. What, he asked his host, was the Comte de Paris doing waiting there? 'General de Gaulle promised him France. I am giving him Africa,' was the reply. It was not plain what that meant, but in the early days of Socialist rule just about anything seemed possible.

Inside a corner office, the man in the wig, which he had bought from a fashionable hairdresser as a disguise for the occasion, listened politely as his host explained that he no longer had anything to do with an illicit Socialist Party funding operation. To prove it, the President's aide reached inside his desk drawer to produce a document showing that he had resigned his positions with the organisations involved. On top of the folder containing the document lay a large revolver.

A decade later, if one was to believe officials who fed friendly journalists with information, the same aide was roaming the corridors of the palace like a madman. Those who dealt with him in his professional duties said they found him quite sane. But the official informants told another story. One colleague who met him in a corridor reported that he was suffering from some kind of hallucination, and believed he was being tailed. Another said he felt as though he was being treated like a dog. Once, it was said, he burst into the office of the Élysée chief of staff without knowing where he was. He was reported to have told the President that he was losing his mind. Clearly, the man was growing old and suffering from diminishing physical and psychological powers. It was a sad end for one who had served so well, they all agreed.

François de Grossouvre had been as close to Mitterrand's secrets as anybody over the years; even Roger-Patrice Pelat probably did not know as much. The two François were both educated by Catholics. Each participated in extreme right-wing groups in the 1930s and had relations with both the Vichy regime and the Resistance – each saying that their collaborationist links were undertaken at the behest of their Resistance bosses. In the early 1960s, however, they seemed to have nothing in common. Mitterrand was a politician with a long past and an uncertain future; De Grossouvre was a doctor, farmer, a former company chairman and Coca-Cola's bottler in Lyon. But when they met, the two men fell for one another.

Though never a man of the left, De Grossouvre helped to organise Mitterrand's campaign against De Gaulle, and took an interest in the Socialist Party's finances throughout the 1970s. Wherever Mitterrand went, De Grossouvre was there, an elegant figure with his beautifully-cut suits and spade beard: the master and his very *parfait* courtier could have stepped from a late Renaissance Italian picture. De Grossouvre hated to see his name in the newspapers, and carried over a love for secrecy and intrigue from his days in the Resistance. He maintained discreet contact with wartime buddies who had moved into the covert shadows of Gaullism. For a while, he worked for France's espionage service under the codename of 'Monsieur Leduc'. De Grossouvre saw himself as a man of hidden spheres who got on with business, whether settling his chief's financial problems, warding off trouble, establishing deniable contacts – or just making sure the leader's overcoat was ready for him when he left a meeting.

Like Mitterrand, De Grossouvre was fascinated by the mechanics of power and the manipulation of people. Each operated on a need-to-know basis towards the rest of the world, including those who put their trust in them. Neither saw any need to tell third parties what they were doing. As they aged, the two men also discussed ways of staying young: De Grossouvre favoured ginseng from the Far East while Mitterrand preferred borage. The politician did not share his friend's love of hunting and riding, but De Grossouvre turned his passion to other ends – he used hunting pavilions for secret meetings between Mitterrand and his opponents. So it was no surprise that, when the Socialists won ultimate power, François de Grossouvre moved in to his corner office at the Élysée with the duties of looking after the intelligence service 'and various matters'. Later, the man known to associates simply as 'the hunter' was put in charge of the extensive presidential game estates: how much of a demotion this represented was not clear, but then things were often opaque with De Grossouvre. 'A well-informed, silent and secret man of business,' a police report said of him.

He was also a man who knew the value of his position – Pelat was not the only friend of François to cash in on his contacts. In one case, De Grossouvre received more than 300,000 francs for his services as intermediary between a French company and Middle Eastern interests; the money was delivered in three instalments in cash to his country home and to the concierge of his Paris apartment. A former President of Lebanon was a close family friend. De Grossouvre was said to have been a go-between with African dictators who supplied funds for French political parties. He made secret trips to the Middle East while his discreet visit to Jacques Chirac on behalf of his master in 1981 was the kind of mission he was cut out to perform. It was all highly deniable: the fact that, from 1988, his salary was paid by the Dassault aircraft firm and not by the presidency was kept extremely confidential. If more is known about De Grossouvre after his death than during his life, it is because the man in the grey wig – journalist Jean Montaldo – met him regularly in the decade after 1982 and wrote up their conversations in a best-selling book.

This makes it clear that, by 1994, something had gone terribly wrong between the two Françoise. Among other things, De Grossouvre claimed to be the only person to have slammed the door on a President of the Republic. He nurtured a hatred for Pelat and Tapie, and warned Mitterrand that he was surrounded by bandits.

'You cannot say that,' was the reply.

'Not only can I say it, but I can prove it.'

'I forbid you,' the President commanded.

So, said De Grossouvre, 'I slammed the door on him.'

To go with his Élysée office, De Grossouvre secured for himself an apartment on the Quai Branly by the Seine which Pierre Bérégovoy had coveted in 1981. It was a floor above the premises officially allocated to a loyal Mitterrandist senator, but De Grossouvre said its real occupant was the mother of the President's illegitimate daughter, who kept a bicycle parked on the first-floor landing. As well as anybody, De Grossouvre knew the extent of bugging employed by the French state – in their telephone calls, he and Jean Montaldo used codewords. But this man of the shadows felt able to talk openly in his apartment about Mitterrand and his mistress, despite the probable presence of microphones in the building. And, in Montaldo's account, De Grossouvre implied the existence of a corrupt financial network reaching up to Mitterrand himself.

It was an extraordinary indiscretion, but imagine that De Grossouvre knew that his conversations with Montaldo were being recorded by the buggers from the Élysée. He would also know that the transcripts of the recordings would be delivered to his former friend, the President, who would no longer talk to him. What better way, then, for a jilted devotee to speak to the one-time object of his fealty than through the microphones hidden in the Quai Branly? Mitterrand would have to read them. One François could speak to another.

'If something terrible happens to me, it will be that they have killed me,' De Grossouvre told Montaldo. 'They'll get me.' The former head of Mitterrand's secret 'black box' cell at the Élysée, Paul Barril, recalls him saying in 1993: 'They're going to gun me down. I know every-thing now. They're afraid.' Either De Grossouvre was becoming paranoid, or he had good reason to feel a net tightening around him. Certainly, his health was giving him problems. At seventy-six, age was catching up on this always active man. His sight was fading – a painful handicap for somebody devoted to hunting – and the detonation of so many rifles over the years had given him ear trouble. Unknown to him, Mitterrand had asked his personal doctor to examine De Grossouvre and arrange for him to be treated in a Paris hospital.

On 7 April 1994, François de Grossouvre lunched with one of his sons, put in a spot of hunting outside Paris and then drove to his office. He took with him a heavy revolver from the collection of almost 200 guns he kept in his official apartment. At around 6 P.M., he had a visit from his doctor. Seemingly mentally and physically dis-turbed, De Grossouvre turned the conversation to suicide and firearms, and referred to the buzzing in his ears. His doctor, an old friend, spoke of God and of the importance of keeping up one's spirits. De Grossouvre produced a small hunting badge and gave it to his guest, saying, 'Keep this in memory of me.' Then they talked of other things.

At 6:30 P.M., according to Captain Barril, De Grossouvre sent flow-ers to a former African Prime Minister with whom he was due to dine, saying that he would arrive at 8:30. He let his secretary leave, and spent half an hour alone. His doctor, meanwhile, had sent a mes-sage to Mitterrand warning him of De Grossouvre's state of mind. By then, however, the President's once-faithful servant had put the .357 Magnum pistol to his head and pulled the trigger. Blood splattered the walls, but the thick doors muffled the sound of the shot. His chauffeur discovered the body an hour later.

Paul Barril declared himself unconvinced by the official account. The message that had gone out with the 6:30 flowers hardly indicated a man who was about to end his life, he observed. There was no sui-cide letter. 'If he had, indeed, killed himself, the man I knew would have left a delayed-action bomb, files, the hundreds of notes he had sent to the President,' the Captain added in an interview given as he promoted his own memoirs. The dead man's archives would be 'not just a scandal, but Hiroshima!' In the halls of mirrors of the late Mitterrand era, it is impossible to separate truth from conjecture, book promotion from genuine questions. One thing was certain, however. In the last year of the previous century, a Head of State had died on the premises after over-exerting himself with his mistress, but François de Grossouvre went down in history as the first suicide at the Élysée.

It was raining on the morning of 11 April as the President of the Republic arrived at the church of Saint-Pierre in Moulins, capital of the agricultural Allier department in central France. A couple of Socialist former ministers were waiting for him. An ex-President of Lebanon stood to one side. Four hundred people filled the church for the funeral mass. After the service, a cortège of thirty vehicles drove with the coffin to the village of Lusigny, fifteen kilometres away, where François Mitterrand had sometimes stayed in the dead man's manor house set in a large estate. At the cemetery on top of a small hill, the coffin was carried down a sandy path to the family tomb. There, François de Grossouvre was laid to rest under the gaze of his former friend who stood holding an umbrella. For a brief moment, his eyes met those of the widow, standing surrounded by her children and grandchildren. Not a word was spoken. Accompanied by one of his ex-ministers, Mitterrand turned and walked away.

His closest friend gone from a heart attack in the midst of scandal, a former head of government committing suicide, an associate of three decades shooting himself in his corner office at the presidential palace; flying too close to Mitterrand's flame was a dangerous business. Particularly so because of the emotional power which the man was able to exercise over even strong-minded, successful individuals. The self-interest of a Bernard Tapie was understandable, but the depths of feeling which rejection by Mitterrand evoked in De Grossouvre or Bérégovoy was out of the ordinary. Politicians who came across him in his early provincial campaigns in the 1940s remembered his powers of seduction fifty years later. As his actor brother-in-law observed: 'Mitterrand aroused even more loving feeling among men than among women.' Which, given his sexual conquests, was saying quite something.

13

A FRENCH LIFE

The French were intrigued rather than shocked when the existence of François Mitterrand's mistress and illegitimate daughter became public knowledge late in his second term. His wife had known about them for a long time, but accepted the situation. 'So, yes, I was married to a seducer. I had to make do,' Danielle Mitterrand said later. 'She's his daughter, and François loved her enormously. They resemble one another like peas in a pod.' Asked about the young Mazarine towards the end of his life, Mitterrand shrugged the matter off. His widow was philosophical. 'We must accept that a human being is capable of loving, passionately loving somebody – and then, as the years go by, he loves in a different way, perhaps more deeply, and then he can fall in love with someone else. It is absolute hypocrisy to want to pass judgement on that.'

Such honesty spoke volumes about France. It was fitting from the widow of a man who, in so many things, personified his nation's history over more than half a century. By the time he became President, Mitterrand had already spent nearly four decades in politics. He was Europe's last ruler who had been in office in pre-nuclear days, and held his first government job when Truman, Attlee and Stalin were meeting to fix the shape of the post-war world. For most of his presidency he was known affectionately as 'Tonton' ('Uncle'). By the end, some followers had taken to calling him 'Dieu' ('God') if only for his seeming immortality. In everything from his childhood to the secrecy about his health, from his private life to the equivocations about his wartime years, from the twists of his career to his last New Year's dinner, François Mitterrand's odyssey was a parable of modern France. Beginning as a true Catholic believer, he ended up, in the words of one of his Prime Ministers, as a pure cynic. The man and his country moved in parallel from traditional roots to end-of-century malaise.

'My childhood, which was happy, has illuminated my life. When one is a child, when one arrives on this planet of which one knows nothing, everything is to be learnt, everything to be felt. The first sensations are so strong and dominant. They make their mark on a virgin canvas. I draw the largest part of my reserves of strength from my childhood. I have the impression that what I had at that moment and the little of it I have preserved (and I have kept some of it) represents the purest and cleanest part of my personality.'

Jarnac is an ordinary town of some 5,000 inhabitants surrounded by open countryside and rivers in the Charente department of western France. Before its association with François Mitterrand, it was best known for having given its name to the expression for a stab in the back, *'un coup de Jarnac'*, from a sixteenth-century incident in which one nobleman did the dirty on another. The future President was born there on 26 October 1916. His father was a station-master who later changed profession and became head of the vinegar-makers of the region. With four sons and four daughters, the Mitterrands were a close-knit family into which, François recalled, 'guests entered as if they were burglars'. They were austere and devout Catholics, who distrusted money-making and rarely displayed emotion.

François was sent to boarding school in the nearby big town of Angoulême. A withdrawn child, he had trouble communicating with others and made few friends. One lifelong character trait was established at an early age. 'I have never tended to confide in others,' Mitterrand remarked much later. 'In a big family, one has to develop zones of solitude.'

As a loner, the young Mitterrand enjoyed going for long country walks. He nurtured a taste for strolls along riverbanks, and wrote poems about their waters, starting with the Charente and the Gironde of his native region and going on to take the Rhine, the Rhône, the Nile and the Niger as inspiration. Seventy years later, he recalled with pleasure the sound of the wind blowing at night through the riverside trees. On his walks, the shy boy from the Catholic school spoke to imaginary crowds, haranguing them with rhetoric inspired by the revolutionaries of 1789 and 1848. Back at home, he climbed up to the attic, littered with maize husks, and launched vibrant speeches through the window overlooking the garden, 'changing the course of history according to my choices'.

'I think that there is only one role to play: to bring the directives and principles of our faith to the political groups to which it is necessary to belong and which are approved by the Church. The National Volunteers want a clean and strong France.'

If François Mitterrand always looked back with happy nostalgia to his childhood in the Charente, he was less forthcoming for many years about his early life in Paris. Arriving by train from Angoulême just before his eighteenth birthday to study politics and law, he felt lost and small in the big city – 'at the foot of a mountain that was to be climbed. I was without an identity.'

As the product of a Catholic education, it was natural for the youth from the provinces to seek a haven in a religious pension in the Rue de Vaugirard on the Left Bank. He quickly gravitated into reactionary politics, which was not surprising for somebody of his background in the fevered climate of the mid-1930s, when some dreamed of a Socialist–Communist revolution and others looked at Mussolini and Hitler as role models. He joined a group called the National Volunteers, the youth wing of a big extremist movement, the Croix-de-Feu. Mitterrand said he was 'seduced' by the Croix-de-Feu's leader, Colonel de la Rocque, but insisted that the Colonel was neither a fascist nor an anti-Semite – an opinion not shared by many. Above all, Mitterrand was influenced by his religion. He was put off the main extreme-right movement, Action Française, not by its political stance but because the Pope had declared an anathema on it.

Within a month of arriving in Paris he took part in his first demonstration. A photograph taken in February 1935 shows Mitterrand at a march against foreign students: a banner beside him proclaims, 'Go on strike against the wogs.' The future leader of the left wrote for a newspaper which admired Mussolini. He travelled to Belgium to visit the pretender to the throne of France, gave 500 francs to a campaign against the Socialist leader Léon Blum, and became head of a right-wing student group. At the age of twenty-one, he also fell in love.

'One Saturday, I had the blues. I went back to my room. On the table, I came across an invitation I had forgotten about. It was to a dance at the teachers' training college. I went. I saw a blonde with her back to me. She turned towards me. My feet were riveted to the ground . . . Then I asked her to dance . . . I was mad about her.'

Women were always important to François Mitterrand. Over the years there was as much speculation about his love-life as about his real political beliefs. He was said to have had a string of celebrated journalists as mistresses and a love-nest in Venice. He was reported to take particular pleasure in caressing the insteps of his lady friends. 'He was fascinated by Casanova,' according to a journalist whom Mitterrand picked to chronicle his last days. 'He couldn't go into a bar or a restaurant without seeking out the face of a woman, and giving his famous wink.' When he met the actress Juliette Binoche by chance in a bookshop, he asked her to give him a call. With undue modesty, she found the prospect too intimidating: 'How does one call the President of the Republic?' she wondered. 'It's like picking up the phone and asking for Father Christmas.' Others were not so reticent. Any attractive woman who rose to a high position in the Socialist ranks was suspected of having slept with him on the way up: when he told one of them that she might become a party secretary as a reward, she is said to have replied on the pillow that she didn't know how to type. A roman-à-clef in the 1980s suggested that Mitterrand had an illegitimate child as well as the sons born to his wife. The rumours were confirmed in 1994 when *Paris-Match* magazine printed photographs of the President stepping out to a twentieth-birthday lunch at a celebrated fish restaurant with his daughter, Mazarine, who had been conceived as he embarked on his second unsuccessful presidential campaign and who bore a striking resemblance to her father. Her mother was an archivist whom Mitterrand had met near his home on the south-western Atlantic coast. In *Premier Roman*, a thin novel that was scoured for autobiographical fragments when it became a best-seller in 1998, Mazarine wrote of her heroine's parents as 'long-time lovers, unmarried, leading their own lives, even while loving each other more than anything. They taught her that love was the only tie that triumphs over looks and judgements, convention and taboos.'

There was never any secret about Mitterrand's first love, even if the blonde Marie-Louise Terrasse had not been as struck by him as he was by her when his eye fell on her at the student ball. She did not give him her name because her mother forbade her to identify herself to unknown young men. In his mind, Mitterrand dubbed her 'Béatrice', as in Dante. He spoke incessantly about her to friends and watched her as she travelled between home and school. Finally, he accosted her. Defying her mother's command, she joined him at a café table and they shared a pancake. In the spring of 1940, when Mitterrand was called up to the army, they got engaged. In his letters to her from his army post, he referred to Marie-Louise as VM, for '*visage merveilleux*' (marvellous face).

As a sergeant during the Phoney War before the Nazis attacked, Mitterrand must have found the time slow. So, when not writing to VM, he turned his hand to a spot of fiction, with a short story entitled 'First Chord' about a young couple, Philippe and Elsa. She was 'supple and gay, sparkling as she awoke, a Persian at the sword, her pink curves like a jar of hair cream'. The prose slurped on. 'Every day of their brief love, she leaped from bed. As he lay about, she walked round the room dressed in her blue dream [*sic*]. She loved this hour of daydreams . . . Elsa never dared to parade naked in their room, for Philippe had a curious degree of modesty for a flirtatious man: odd habits, delights that remained ever elusive.' He was, after all, only twenty-three years old and, if only he had known it, was following in the footsteps of Charles de Gaulle, who had penned romantic fiction (equally unpublished) while convalescing from a war wound in 1914.

After France's defeat, the sergeant was taken prisoner of war together with thousands of French soldiers. As the months dragged by in his Stalag, VM's letters became rarer and rarer. Friends attributed Mitterrand's three escape attempts to his desire to get back to her. Again, there was a parallel with De Gaulle, who repeatedly escaped from German prison camps in the First World War, only to be recaptured each time. Mitterrand was more successful; his third break-out succeeded and he returned to France. But he found that the girl with the marvellous face no longer fancied the idea of marrying him. Early in 1942, the engagement was broken off. Many years later, as Catherine Langeais, Marie-Louise became more famous for a time than her former fiancé as an early television announcer. Some amateur psychologists believe that rejection hardened the young man's character and contributed to the growth of his pervasive cynicism. At the time, he spoke of the 'dryness of my feelings'. Decades later, he still sent Langeais flowers on her birthday.

Two years after being dropped by Marie-Louise, Mitterrand was in love again, this time with a photograph. In March 1944, when he headed a Resistance network, Mitterrand attended a party at the Paris home of his friend, Roger-Patrice Pelat. On the piano in the flat was a photograph of the sister of Pelat's partner at the time. 'I want to meet her, I will marry her,' Mitterrand said. A blind date was duly arranged at a restaurant on the Boulevard Saint-Germain. As with Marie-Louise, Mitterrand was not an immediate hit. Wearing an off-white raincoat and the large hat which became his trademark in later years, he also sported a pencil moustache. The overall effect made him look like a caricature of a tango dancer.

The young woman, Danielle Gouze, was in her last year at school. She found his acid tone irritating: Mitterrand only fell more deeply in love with her. He deployed to the full his powers of persuasion and seduction, and, within a couple of months, she agreed to marry him. There then followed a series of wartime adventures, including a train trip to her native Burgundy during which a friendly German soldier unknowingly ushered the young man through a police control that had him on its wanted list. They married in October 1944, after the Liberation of France (during which Mitterrand claimed to have saved De Gaulle's life by grabbing his legs as the General was about to be swept out of a window by an enthusiastic crowd in Paris). Over the wedding lunch, the groom announced that he was going off to a political meeting with former prisoners of war. The bride said she would accompany him. If you want to, Mitterrand replied. That was the moment at which she discovered her 'first and main rival: politics'.

Nobody outside the couple knows how much Danielle influenced her husband. Her own reflections on the subject indicate that she was content to watch him go his own way while she dedicated herself to good works and Third World causes. What she thought of her husband's decision to maintain close relations with some of Africa's worst dictators can be imagined; she, herself, showed lasting concern for human rights and stayed true to her old beliefs. She organised demonstrations for prisoners of conscience and remained a fan of Fidel Castro to the end, urging her husband to invite him on a state visit to France which earned them all a degree of mockery. She persuaded the shyster businessman Armand Hammer to agree to contribute $300,000 to her good works, though she never got her hands on the money. Danielle Mitterrand could have become an object of pity; instead, she remained dignified. After his death, she wrote: 'I see now how my husband excelled in the art of seduction towards the young girls who passed by. He was François the seducer.' That was part of life. A striking photograph taken at the Cannes film festival in 1956 shows a dark-suited Mitterrand gazing with more than passing interest at Brigitte Bardot while Danielle, in matelot jersey and sunglasses with her hands clasped behind her back, stares at the 22-year-old starlet as though at an anthropological specimen. 'Which woman can say, "I've never been cheated on" or that she never cheated in her own love-life?' Danielle Mitterrand once reflected. 'I stayed with him because he was different. With him life was never boring.' It was the matter-of-fact voice of the woman who, as a high-school girl, had hidden Resistance fighters at ultimate risk to herself. When warned by a friend that she should flee Paris because her photograph had been seized in a Gestapo raid on a Resistance hide-out, Danielle had replied: 'But what about my exams?'

'*I could have devoted my life to reflection, to have lived in the country in the company of trees, animals and a few loved ones. Perhaps that is a bucolic dream; still, I think I could have done it. But the stimulus of action was doubtless stronger than that of reflection, so in the end I launched myself into politics.*'

In October 1946, after an unsuccessful attempt to get elected in the Paris region, the thirty-year-old Mitterrand set off for the rural Nièvre department in central France to seek a seat in the National Assembly of the Fourth Republic. His first campaign in the department which was to become his electoral base for the next thirty-five years had its share of ironies given what was to happen three and a half decades later. The politician who would lead the Socialists and their Communist allies to the greatest power they have ever enjoyed in modern France first won his way to the National Assembly with the active backing of a network of conservative local notables. His speeches denounced the tripartite government of the left and moderate Catholics ruling France. Above all, the man who was to give the Communists their only taste of ministerial power under the Fifth Republic preached hard-line anti-Communism to rapt audiences in country halls.

The Nièvre, where the faithful Bérégovoy was to kill himself half a century later, went on electing Mitterrand throughout the Fourth Republic as he moved smoothly between ministerial posts – from ex-servicemen's affairs to the Information Ministry, then on to super-intend France's Overseas Territories before taking the powerful post of Interior Minister in 1954–55 and ending up as Justice Minister in 1956–57, at the time of the Suez expedition and France's war to hold on to its last big overseas possession across the Mediterranean. As a politician who knew the importance of patriotism, Mitterrand left no public doubt of his belief that Algeria must remain French. Heading a series of small parties and political combinations, he never had a strong popular following, eclipsed in intellectual ability by Pierre Mendès-France and in machine clout by the Socialist boss, Guy Mollet. In 1957, one of his associates told a Soviet agent that Mitter-rand was likely to become Prime Minister and would bring Mendès-France and Gaston Defferre into his government, wind up the war in Algeria, and strengthen the nation's finances.

If he never achieved the premier role he sought, Mitterrand still proved to be one of the most skilful exponents of the Fourth Republic game of ministerial musical chairs. The ever-shifting, un-ideological back-room world of French politics in the 1940s and 1950s suited him to perfection and shaped his style. Still, not everybody was impressed. I remember sitting at a dinner party of once-powerful provincial newspaper figures from the Fourth Republic who expressed universal distrust of the man. And the American ambassador to France, Douglas Dillon, wrote of the Interior Minister of the time in a classified despatch in 1954: 'My principal impression was his extreme cruelty. This man is very competent but dangerous.' The fail-ure of the Fourth Republic was, above all, a failure of its politicians rather than of its institutions, and François Mitterrand epitomised those for whom politics counted more than the nation.

When De Gaulle swept away the Fourth Republic in 1958, the shock was terrible. Mitterrand voted against the General's investiture. In the first parliamentary elections of the new Republic, he was defeated, and was said to have broken down in tears. But, as Douglas Dillon also noted, 'he is intensely ambitious and will do anything to reach his goals'.

After his defeat, Mitterrand wrote an article in his tame local newspaper, putting himself forward as a true republican standing up to De Gaulle's military coup. At the same time, as a supreme realist, he knew the need to try to dissociate himself from the system which had served him so well. 'For a long time, I have said "no" to complicated party combinations, to immobility, to colonial wars,' this archetype of the Fourth Republic and defender of French Algeria suddenly declared. If one constant ran through Mitterrand's long career, it was the ability to disown his beliefs of yesterday.

Such a man did not stay politically unemployed for long and, in 1959, the Senate – a body whose members are picked by local dignitaries – beckoned. Mitterrand dramatically announced that he had been the target of an assassination attempt, which appeared to have been a put-up job engineered to win sympathy. The episode earned him ridicule and reinforced the widespread belief that he was a man without scruples who would stop at nothing to advance his political career. He stayed in the Senate for three years, writing biting anti-Gaullist tracts before winning his way back to the more important National Assembly. At the same time, the one-time provincial boy strengthened his roots in the Nièvre by becoming Mayor of Château-Chinon in the hilly, wooded Morvan area of the department. On election days, he put up at the old-fashioned Hôtel du Morvan in the middle of the town to await the results. He would frequently eat lunch with the hotel's owners and always slept in the same room on the first floor. Lit by a single weak light-bulb, it was sparsely furnished with a lumpy bed, a straight-backed chair and a plastic-topped table on which Mitterrand wrote late into the night. There was a wash basin, but the lavatory was on the landing. A window looked out on to the surrounding hills – the latter-day equivalent of the attic window from which Mitterrand had once imagined himself addressing the nation as a boy.

'So what?'

During the long years of waiting for supreme power while the right fought its fratricidal battles, François Mitterrand collected an odd bunch of friends and associates, some of whom we met in the last chapter. But there was one acquaintance who would stand out as an especially strange man for the first President of the left to have entertained. A jovial rogue like Roger-Patrice Pelat might be explained away on the basis of wartime comradeship. René Bousquet was a different matter, and Mitterrand's relationship with him over more than three decades reflected another aspect of France which still stirs deep emotions half a century after the 1940 parliament voted full powers to Pétain, and Vichy agreed to collaborate with the Nazis.

The question of collaboration and complicity in genocide has, as we have seen, been an uncomfortable one which France has often preferred to ignore. Few of those who went along with Vichy and the German occupiers could have imagined the existence of extermination camps as such: they preferred vague formulae about work camps in Eastern Europe. Yet, even if they did not know of the extermination camps, anybody with eyes in their head could see that Jews were being forced to wear yellow stars on the streets of France before being rounded up and taken away. Later, even those who owned up to working for Vichy or the Germans denied that they had known about the more unpleasant things going on around them. A fair number insisted that their collaboration had, in fact, been a cover for clandestine Resistance work, leading the press baron Robert Hersant, who made no bones about his collaborationist record, to call himself 'the only Frenchman of my generation not to have been a hero of the Resistance'.

In much later years, nobody's war record was more subject to debate than that of François Mitterrand. Not only did he seem to have played a double game, but he also appeared unable to shake off the negative elements of the past, or even to admit that there might be anything questionable about them. Sometimes he grew indignant that anybody should presume to raise the subject, or else he put on a poker-face and muttered a dismissive 'So what?' If France preferred to blot out the memory of its equivocations about the years between 1940 and 1944, François Mitterrand stood as an example for the nation.

His role during those years reflected both sides of the country under occupation. There was no doubt that the future President had faced great personal danger as a member of the Resistance. He helped to organise underground networks among ex-servicemen, travelled to England for a frosty meeting with General de Gaulle, and was on the wanted list under his pseudonym of Morland. At the same time, he worked for the Vichy government as a civil servant, dealing with prisoners of war, which enabled him to save some French servicemen from concentration camps. Mitterrand said later that he did this with the blessing of the Resistance, which certainly found it useful to keep some of its people as moles inside the collaborationist regime. 'I was not part of the Vichy system,' he said in his posthumously-published memoirs. 'I was not a functionary but a contract worker.' He used the word 'press-ganged' to describe his employment, and added, as if it had some relevance, that he had filled a high-level post for less than today's minimum wage. The young man must have been good at his job because he was awarded the Francisque, one of the regime's top decorations, and was presented to the Vichy leader, Philippe Pétain. As President, Mitterrand continued the tradition of sending a wreath to Pétain's grave each Armistice Day in honour of his military leadership in the First World War.

If he was to be believed, Mitterrand, who prided himself on being a great humanist, managed to keep his eyes shut to some of the things going on around him. 'I didn't think about anti-Semitism at Vichy,' he once insisted. 'I knew that, unfortunately, there were anti-Semites who filled senior positions around Marshal Pétain, but I didn't follow the laws of the time and the measures that were being taken.' The 'unfortunately' jars, and Mitterrand's memoirs struck a somewhat different tone. 'Vichy was a weak regime, shapeless and lacking in soul, inspired by fascists, anti-Semites and determined ideologues,' he told a journalist who worked with him on his last reburnishing of history.

Still, as Head of State, he steadfastly refused to accept that there was anything amiss in his long relationship with a man who had signed the agreement with the Germans pledging the French police to round up foreign Jews, and who was the main organiser of the Vél d'Hiv atrocity in Paris in 1942. When it came to René Bousquet, Mitterrand said simply that he found the man to be a brilliant individual with whom he had interesting conversations. The President went on meeting the former police chief until 1986, five years into his rule and after well-publicised moves were made to get Bousquet tried for crimes against humanity. Despite having access to the full panoply of official French records, Mitterrand insisted that he had not been aware of Bousquet's wartime activities.

This was simply unbelievable. It was no secret that from April 1942 to December 1943 Bousquet had been Secretary-General of the police. As such, he was in charge of the national police, of economic policing and of 'supplementary police', which meant the anti-Jewish, anti-Masonic and anti-Communist crusade. He, too, claimed to have been involved with the Resistance, and was indeed arrested by the Germans in 1944, by which time any sensible collaborator would have sought a lifeline on the other side. After the Liberation, Bousquet was sentenced to five years of 'national degradation', but was later amnestied. Whatever his Resistance activities may or may not have been, there was no doubting Bousquet's key role in rounding up Jews. It was not as if Mitterrand needed access to official papers to know what Bousquet had been up to during the Occupation. His responsibilities had been outlined at the Nuremberg war-crimes trials in 1946 by the lawyer and politician Edgar Faure, another friend of Mitterrand.

Every time the President denied that there was anything wrong in his links with Bousquet, new information emerged. There is no evidence that the two men actually met while serving Vichy, but Mitterrand's evasions inevitably fuelled speculation. It was widely believed that his Resistance group, based on ex-prisoners of war, had unofficial contacts with the Vichy Ministry of the Interior and the police – and his membership of a far-right organisation was only a decade behind him. Whether Mitterrand found Vichy ideologically objectionable is a question which is unlikely ever to be answered, just as the true extent of his commitment to Socialism will always remain uncertain. No doubt he deplored Vichy's treatment of those it persecuted; but as a cool-eyed realist, his engagement in the Resistance may have been as much a matter of pragmatism as of political conviction, just as he could see clearly from 1965 onwards that the only way to win the presidency was to come at it from the left.

The links with the collaborationist right continued after the Liberation. When Mitterrand found himself briefly out of a job, he was taken under the wing of a cosmetics group founded by a tycoon who had financed pre-war terrorists of the far right, and who gave him a job running a beauty-care magazine. Back in politics after winning his place in parliament from the Nièvre, Mitterrand pushed an amnesty bill for collaborators which was said to have weighed on the judges' decision not to punish Bousquet more severely for his wartime activities. At that time, the former policeman was on the board of the Banque d'Indochine, which later merged into the Indosuez Bank. The bank financed anti-Gaullist politicians after the General's return to power in 1958. That year, Bousquet ran unsuccessfully for parliament – with the backing of a small political party headed by Mitterrand. Another of his associates was Robert Hersant, who had also been found guilty of collaborationist crimes.

During Mitterrand's first presidential bid in 1965, the Toulouse newspaper *La Dépêche du Midi* printed his leaflets for free, contributed half a million francs to his campaign funds, and ran an appeal by former Petainists and extreme right-wingers to vote for the anti-Gaullist candidate. Bousquet was on the board of the newspaper. The two men met again during Mitterrand's second presidential campaign in 1974. A magazine photographer snapped a lunch party at the candidate's country home in the south-west. Bousquet and his wife sat opposite Mitterrand: the caption did not identify the guests.

Research by a tenacious British journalist, Paul Webster, uncovered other links. Around the time Bousquet was being tried by the High Court of Justice, the rising politician named one of the former police chief's wartime staff as his press officer. At the Interior Ministry in 1954, with access to all the files, Mitterrand appointed three members of Bousquet's old entourage to his team. In 1965, he engaged as his parliamentary aide another of Bousquet's former subordinates – a man called Pierre Saury, who had worked on the deportation of Jews from Paris. Saury also acted as Mitterrand's link with former Petainists. When he died in 1973, his wartime and peacetime employers both attended his funeral. As President, Mitterrand did not break off contact with Bousquet until 1988. That was five years after France's leading hunter of Nazis and collaborators, Serge Klarsfeld, had published documents detailing Bousquet's eagerness to deport Jews. But still, the Head of State was unable to snap the link completely. After being booed by young Jews at a commemoration of the 1942 round-up in Paris, Mitterrand appointed his own lawyer, Georges Kiejman, whose father died in Auschwitz, as junior Justice Minister. Kiejman blocked legal proceedings against Bousquet in the name of national unity.

Towards the end of Mitterrand's rule, the Nobel Prize-winner Elie Wiesel was commissioned to write up a series of conversations with him. It was to be the President's philosophical apotheosis. When Wiesel, a Jew and a great admirer of Mitterrand at the time, raised the matter of Bousquet, the Head of State replied that he felt he had made no mistake.

'None?' Wiesel asked.

'None,' Mitterrand insisted.

'So,' wrote Wiesel some years later, 'there was no remorse, nor regrets. The anti-Jewish laws of Vichy? He didn't know.'

Trying to delve more deeply, Wiesel fired off faxes about Vichy and Pétain, the wreath sent to the Marshal's tomb, Bousquet and Mitterrand's Vichy medal. The President did not deign to reply, and then, unbelievably, insisted that he had been the one who had wanted to deal with the subject of Bousquet. All Wiesel could say was: 'I feel bad about that man.' He was not alone.

It was not even as if Bousquet was an isolated example. His wartime deputy was charged, but was never brought to trial and died in peace in 1989. Another senior official who oversaw all the prefects in the Vichy zone ended his days untroubled at his Riviera villa in 1992. And when it came to Maurice Papon, irony was added to neglect on the President's part. If the story told by the Jew who escaped death by hiding in a cupboard in Bordeaux in 1942 is true, Mitterrand owed part of his election against Giscard in 1981 to the revelation of Papon's wartime role. But, when the case came up in Cabinet, the President made it plain on several occasions that he was not in favour of reopening the case against a man he described as being 'of outstanding stature'. After *Le Canard Enchaîné* had broken the Papon story in 1981, Michel Slitinsky recalls that the journalist who wrote it told him that Mitterrand would certainly invite him to visit his country home, south of Bordeaux. Slitinsky never received an invitation, but René Bousquet did.

The fact that Mitterrand felt so little compunction about befriending Bousquet and protecting Papon was both a reminder of the extent of his own self-centred amorality and – once again – a sign of how

accurately he reflected the inner feelings of so many of his compatriots. There was also an obvious personal parallel between these two
Vichy-Resistants and his own wartime career. When Bousquet was
murdered in his Paris apartment in 1993, conspiracy theories flared up,
but the truth seemed to be that the killer was simply deranged. As he
was sentenced to ten years in jail for the shooting, he said he sought
pardon from God for breaking the commitment not to kill, from the
Jews for having prevented Bousquet appearing in court, and from the
dead man's family for having removed their father. A crazy gunman
had also deprived France of a chance to purge part of a dark stain on
its history, and the first elected President of the left ended his rule
under the shadow of the collaboration his country longed to put
behind it without going through the pain of exorcism.

'I think I'm going to mess up my exit by a couple of months.'

It was a sunny day in September 1994, and the President of the
Republic was talking to a guest at his home among the pine trees of
the Landes department on the south-western coast, where he felt
'the ocean in the forest'. They ate *foie gras*, lobster and grapes and
drank white wine. Mitterrand was in aphoristic mood, speaking of
'Nationalism, the opium of imbeciles' or producing the none-too-
profound observation that 'Socialism and Communism are branches
of the same tree – like Christianity and Islam'. He felt free to criticise
his opponents and his successor as leader of the Socialist Party with
impunity as birds whirled above and a bluebottle swooped on to his
forehead.

Three months later, the man whom some referred to as God was
asked what he expected the Father in Heaven to say to him when he
reached paradise. Terminally ill, Mitterrand sat stiffly in his chair as he
pondered his response. He had difficulty speaking; from time to time,
his right hand darted to the pocket of his jacket as if he needed to
touch a talisman. A confirmed agnostic who had rejected his Catholic
upbringing, he showed a shaft of wit as he answered the question.
'Now you know,' God would say. 'And I hope that He would add –
"Welcome."'

By then, the President had been living under the shadow of death
for more than a dozen years. In his 1981 election campaign, he had

pledged 'transparency' on the state of his health. There would be none of the secrecy which had surrounded the last months of Georges Pompidou's life, he promised. His doctor, Claude Gubler, issued two bulletins a year, giving his patient a good bill of health. They were, to say the least, highly economical with the truth. Every day for eleven years, the Head of State received secret medical attention. When he travelled abroad, he had treatment at night wherever he was: the needles and bottles of liquid were sealed in special suitcases and sent back to France in diplomatic bags for destruction. On trips to Communist countries, the injections were conducted in total silence for fear that the room might be bugged.

In 1992, the President was operated on for a decade-old cancer of the prostate, and the secret was out – or rather, in true Mitterrand fashion, part of it. Gubler had diagnosed the illness eleven years earlier. As the doctor recounted it, his patient's immediate reaction when told the news six months after moving into the Élysée had been that it must remain a state secret. After the first diagnosis, Mitterrand asked how long he had to live. The prognosis was three years; the President muttered under his breath: 'I'm done for.' But the treatment appeared to be working, and Mitterrand began to believe he had beaten the cancer. He did not consult Gubler before announcing that he would stand for re-election in 1988. France duly gave another seven years in power to a cancer patient in his seventies. Only he and his doctor knew the truth; the government and the electorate were kept in the dark. If it had known, would France have voted differently? Jacques Chirac ran a terrible campaign, but the facts about Mitterrand's state of health might have swung the balance or, even worse from the President's viewpoint, have encouraged the centre-left to throw its support behind his long-time antagonist, Michel Rocard. That could have shifted the course of history. But Mitterrand played the sphinx; he did not even tell his wife of his condition until 1991. In her usual understanding fashion, she said she did not regard this as untoward: 'He simply preserved our tranquillity of spirit.'

Even when the operation in 1992 destroyed the secrecy, the fact that the cancer had already spread was still kept quiet from the public. But radiotherapy, chemotherapy and a second operation diminished the man physically. In a book published immediately after Mitterrand's death, which was later banned and earned him a four-month suspended prison sentence, Dr Gubler reported that Mitterrand was so weakened that he was incapable of doing the job for the last six months of his time in the Élysée. His Gaullist Prime Minister of the time did not object since he was left to get on with running the country. The President apparently went straight to bed when he arrived at the Palace from his private home on the Left Bank at 9:30 A.M., and rested for most of the day. Nothing interested him except his illness and some of his grand projects, particularly the controversial new national library in Paris which was on its way to running six times over budget.

François Mitterrand spent the 237 days that would remain to him after he left the Élysée revisiting what he had most enjoyed in life – Venice and the booksellers of Paris, the countryside of Burgundy and political gossip with his old associates. Dying, he stayed in control. He saw out 1995 at separate Christmas and New Year celebrations with his wife and his mistress and their respective offspring. On his return from a trip to the Nile Valley with his second family, he told Danielle that he had decided to end his life by stopping eating. He asked his doctor what would happen if he ceased his medication. He would die three days later, he was told. Before that, he took a last delight in food. At a dinner over New Year, he started by consuming thirty oysters. He then ate an ortolan. This rare small bird is an officially protected species, but it is still caught while flying over the south-west and fattened on grain in a darkened barn for three weeks before being killed by a big shot of Armagnac liqueur. By tradition, the ortolan is eaten whole – wings, beak, innards and all. To ensure that not a whiff of the bird's unique aroma is lost, it should be consumed under a large napkin. At the end of the main course of the New Year dinner, one ortolan remained on the platter. Mitterrand took it and disappeared beneath his napkin for the second time that evening. After chewing the little bird, he lay back in his chair, beaming in ecstasy.

Then the man who had fought a solitary combat for half a century got ready to perish. He wrote out the instructions for his funeral – one grand state affair in Paris and a simpler ceremony in his native Charente department. He completed his memoirs. He wrote a letter to a long-time crony. And then, on 9 January 1996, at the age of seventy-nine, François Mitterrand died. A joke which did the rounds a few months later had the President arriving at the gates of heaven. You can't come in, says God, you are an adulterer – even worse than that, you think you are God and in this kingdom there is only one God. To which Mitterrand replies: 'When's the next election?'

His death was the occasion for a great outpouring of national reverence. A monument had gone; the Fifth Republic had lost its second great figure. His home town of Jarnac became a pilgrimage centre (though local tradespeople were disappointed when they tried to cash in on the Mitterrand legacy – a confectioner sold only 40 of 1,000 boxes of chocolates with the President's face stamped on them). Even a strident anti-Socialist like the former Gaullist minister, Alain Peyrefitte, opined that it was no time for polemics since Mitterrand had been France for fourteen years. There were bizarre touches; in Bulgaria, Mitterrand was hailed as the first foreign leader to draw attention to that country, and in China, it was recalled that the transliteration of his name was said by the supreme leader, Deng Xiaoping, to mean 'Enigma, all is clear'. Two months after his death, five of the ten best-selling books in France were about the late President: in all, at least four million books about him are reckoned to have been sold. One was by his widow; two were spoof memoirs in the name of his black Labrador dog, Baltique. A Swedish journalist wrote a book about her 'loving friendship' with the late President and their conversations on the Middle East, but she drew a veil over whether he was the father of her son. A woman who helped people to die peacefully told how she had eased the President through the last stage of his life, and how he had asked her to place a small stone for him near a Celtic cross below her house in the South of France. A former head of the secret service went into print to show that Mitterrand had personally approved the project to stop the Greenpeace boat *Rainbow Warrior* from sailing to protest against French nuclear tests in 1985, leading to an operation by French agents which cost a Portuguese photographer his life. A member of his intimate court unveiled Mitterrand's views on the great and the good: Margaret Thatcher had the lips of Marilyn Monroe and the eyes of the Roman Emperor Caligula, while Ronald Reagan 'has only a few records going round and round in his head'. In keeping with the paranormal tenor of the times, France's leading popular astrologer revealed that the late President had consulted her before making important decisions, greeting her with the query: 'How am I doing, and how is France doing?' and then asking where Helmut Kohl, Saddam Hussein and his own Prime Minister stood with the stars. When the French edition of *Penthouse* ran photographs of the astrologer from a pornographic film in which she had appeared in 1971, some wondered if the President's interest in her had ranged more widely than horoscopes.

Mitterrand's gooey wartime short story about Philippe and Elsa fetched 38,000 francs at auction. His family successfully sued Dr Gubler over the revelations about the President's illness, though they got less than half the damages they asked for. In December 1996, Jacques Chirac inaugurated the huge new national library building by the Seine. When he had been asked if he wanted the building to be named after him, Mitterrand had replied: 'If you had to take the decision and you asked me to take that decision, I would say "no".' Which most people took for a yes. So the huge 30-billion-franc building was duly named the Bibliothèque François Mitterrand. A poll carried out for *Le Figaro* at the same time showed that he was the second most popular President of the Fifth Republic. Despite all the woes and stress they had suffered under him, 65 per cent now said they had good memories of the Mitterrand years. As the newspaper remarked, 'He is greater dead than alive.'

Nobody had reflected the contradictions of the people he ruled more clearly. Nobody had done more to turn the Socialist movement into a party of government. Nobody had been more removed from the everyday world but more intimately involved in human affairs – Vichyite and Resister; the visceral enemy of the Fifth Republic who became its longest-serving Head of State and pronounced its presidential vestments greatly to his liking; intellectual and base schemer; a seemingly unworldly figure who never carried money but who presided over a scandal-ridden administration; a chronically unpunctual being who was also one of the greatest experts on the minutiae of French electoral geography. A man who liked to present himself as a great humanist and champion of freedom in the Third World, he had presided over a government which armed the genocide in Rwanda and propped up crude dictators in its former colonies. A driving force in the construction of Europe, he had proved unable to craft a role for Paris beyond the shadow of

Bonn. A man who prided himself on his grasp of history, he had failed to visualise the break-up of Yugoslavia or the unification of Germany. In the end, François Mitterrand was everything and, at the same time, nothing: his own greatest promoter and his own worst enemy, a solitary figure whose self-esteem and contempt for those around him seemed to know no limits. He was, he told his aide Jacques Attali, surrounded by dwarfs.

In the end, two things were plain: France's longest-serving President was not nearly as clever as he thought he was, and he had sacrificed the good of his country at his own altar. Commentators and those who had been seduced and abandoned by François Mitterrand wondered at his lack of any ethical dimension. In opposition, his amorality could be excused as necessary in the pursuit of power. But once he had reached the summit, it got even worse. He simply did not seem to care about any real values. His ultimate cynicism in power may have had a very simple root: from the end of 1981 onwards he knew that every additional day was a medical miracle. He was on the way out physically from virtually the moment he finally achieved supreme power. Life, in existential terms, held no promise, and so he would amuse himself by playing with power until the end came. The sadness for France as a nation was that the game lasted so long.

To the very end, there were two sides to the man.

Asked late in life if he had any regrets, Mitterrand was characteristically self-assured. 'None,' he replied. 'Not everything was perfect in my life; who can claim that it was? But everything I did, I can be proud of. I mean to say, as a man. I never bowed the knee in front of anything or anybody.'

But there was also another side.

A traveller comes across a group of men in his path.

'What are you doing?' he asks them.

'We are piling up stones,' they reply.

Further on, he meets another group, doing the same thing.

'What are you doing?' he asks them.

'We are building a cathedral,' comes the response.

'Well,' added François Mitterrand as he recounted the story to visitors before his death, 'I ought to have, and could have, built cathedrals. Often, all I did was to make piles of stones.'

14

THE JAWS OF VICTORY

La Rochelle, in the Charente-Maritime department of western France, is a pleasant place, with excellent fish restaurants, pedestrian zones and a fine yachting harbour. An English expedition sailed there in 1627 in a vain attempt to relieve the siege of the Protestant Huguenots, an episode immortalised by Alexandre Dumas and his musketeers. Three and a half centuries later, two of France's leading politicians flew to La Rochelle for a party congress to confirm who would become the next President of the Republic. The meeting was meant to be another step towards an effortless Gaullist restoration after François Mitterrand's fourteen years in the Élysée Palace. As things turned out, the weekend on the Atlantic coast set off the final battle in the Thirty Years' War of French politics.

The period since the left won power in 1981 had been a frustrating, unsettled time for the Gaullists under Jacques Chirac and the centre–conservative coalition headed by Valéry Giscard d'Estaing. Frustrating, because the right was not accustomed to being out of power – its leaders had been brought up to assume that the Fifth Republic belonged to them and, though they had won two major parliamentary elections in 1986 and 1993, they had been unable to best the man in the Élysée. Unsettled, because it was never quite clear who was in charge of the opposition to the so-called Socialist presiding over France.

After 1981, Jacques Chirac had rushed into the vacuum on his side of politics. Alone of Mitterrand's opponents, he had a real power-base as Mayor of Paris. Then the man who had succeeded him as Prime Minister back in 1976, the professorial Raymond Barre, emerged as the incarnation of true French values, too. Watching him tucking into a meal at Paul Bocuse's celebrated restaurant outside Lyon one stormy night in the mid-1980s gave one the impression that this was a man made to lead the traditional forces of France. On the menu that night was the truffle soup which Bocuse had named in honour of Giscard. The coolness that had set in since one man lost the presidency and the other the premiership did not affect Barre's appetite. As always, he acted as though he had time on his side. During the dinner, he mentioned a piece I had written in *The Economist* which contrasted his deliberate style with the livewire Chirac. He appeared quite content to have been portrayed as the tortoise moving at his own pace behind the Gaullist hare. Once described by Giscard as the best economist in France, his conservative manner disguises a sharp appreciation of the realities of modern finance. The portly Barre is never in a hurry; he doesn't feel the need to run, confident that he will get there in the end. He is certainly not a man lacking in self-assurance. Once, when a journalist queried the rightness of one of his policies, he simply told the man not to be so silly.

That approach struck a chord in the increasingly rudderless right of the mid-1980s, and the notion of both his former Prime Ministers moving to the front of the opposition ranks was enough to spur the deposed Head of State into action. Giscard thought he could outflank the impetuous Chirac without difficulty. But the idea that Raymond Barre might become President was a goad that could not be tolerated. Stirring the pot, Mitterrand promoted the idea that Giscard might agree to become his Prime Minister. A short time afterwards, he spoke approvingly of Barre as the kind of man he could easily work with. The right was in a mess, and Mitterrand knew how to make the most of it.

In the event, it was Chirac who was appointed to run the government after the left lost its parliamentary majority in 1986. In the presidential election two years later, Raymond Barre insisted on running and proved the emptiness of Charles de Gaulle's tirades against political parties. This most De Gaulle-like candidate had no organised movement behind him. Although he was clearly the best man in the race, he lacked an electoral machine to get the votes out, and so was eliminated with only 16.5 per cent in the first round. As one of his aides later said with a sigh, 'In France, the best never win.' When it came to the run-off ballot, Mitterrand beat Chirac by a handsome 54–46 per cent margin. It was a triumph for the old fox in the Élysée and a disaster for his opponent's shoot-from-the-hip style. Equally, it was fresh evidence of the right's continuing ability to auto-destruct through internal rivalries. Some drew the inevitable conclusion that Chirac was not the man to wrest power back at the summit of the state. For others, it was time to leave the battlefield. Raymond Barre moved to the sidelines to become a sage and happy Mayor of Lyon. As he put it to me, having operated at a national and international level, it was good to get down to earth. He seemed that rare animal, a one-time Prime Minister who was actually content with his born-again role in the centre of France, and chuckled with genuine pleasure as we talked in a Hong Kong hotel of *quenelles de brochet* and *poularde demi-deuil*.

So the war narrowed to the two companions-in-arms of 1974. It was an unequal conflict. Giscard's day was clearly passing: his ambitious younger followers paid him lip-service, but feuded for the succession. Recovering from a period of depression after his presidential defeat, Chirac consolidated his power by building up the Gaullist party. By the time of the left's collapse at the 1993 parliamentary election, the one-time protégé of Georges Pompidou was king of the heap. He had wobbled from time to time, notably during France's referendum on the Maastricht Treaty, but he and his cohorts were now on a roll, and the future seemed assured. No more internal wars, no Giscard, no Barre, no worries about the National Front. Having twice suffered as Prime Minister, Jacques Chirac was only too happy to leave his good friend and former Finance Minister, Édouard Balladur, to head the government while he concentrated on the apparently easy campaign to get to the Élysée. Two decades after knifing Chaban-Delmas in the back, life seemed to be simple at last. Blood simple, as it turned out.

Chirac and Balladur had met when the first was Pompidou's dashing lieutenant and the second the President's chief of staff. They stayed together through the years. From 1986 to 1988, Finance Minister

Balladur implemented privatisations and financial liberalisation for Prime Minister Chirac. The Gaullist leader regularly sent drafts of his speeches to his friend for comment and approval. Just as he had taken guidance from Pierre Juillet and Marie-France Garaud in the 1970s, so, two decades on, Jacques Chirac sought another source of benediction. For a man who lived for the roar of the crowd and who washed down his favourite dish of calf's head with Mexican beer, his choice was a strange one. Pierre and Marie-France spoke from the roots of France; Édouard floated free of terrestrial attachments.

Son of a rich trading family living in the Turkish city of Smyrna, he had pursued a career as discreet as that of his Gaullist friend had been public. Balladur was a born-again chamberlain of the Ancien Régime, a man of silk and velvet who could glide across a gravel courtyard without leaving the trace of a footstep. The Prime Minister hated loud noise and liked the company of soft-voiced noble ladies. He ate steamed sole and answered his telephone with a strange, fluting 'alloooo'. As Finance Minister, Balladur had insisted on moving his offices from a modern building down the Seine back to the Louvre, where major-domos walked backwards in front of him. The flashier members of the Mitterrand entourage were known as the 'caviar left'; there was no doubt that Édouard Balladur belonged firmly in the ranks of the caviar right. As President-in-waiting from 1993 onwards, Jacques Chirac waded through a hundred banquets, pumping hands, promising everything under the sun, a man seemingly with no aim in life except to campaign. As Prime Minister, meanwhile, Balladur lulled the nation into a comatose sense of peace, and watched with hooded eyes while his popularity soared. Everybody knew Chirac's latest opinion before his brain had fully formulated it; nobody had much idea of what went on behind the Premier's opaque exterior.

After the Gaullist triumph at the general election of March 1993, the deal had been clear: Balladur for Prime Minister, Chirac for President. Apart from freeing Chirac from the day-to-day business of government which he was convinced had harmed his previous presidential bid, the arrangement gave the Gaullist leader time to tour the country, to think and to seek his campaign themes. Balladur's reassuringly good links with big business would also be a help, counteracting the nervousness which Chirac aroused in that quarter. The two men might be very different, particularly in their public personae. But, if each kept to his appointed role, they could make a perfect team.

When he spoke to his Gaullist party congress at La Rochelle six months later, Chirac referred to their pact. As his eyes swept the hall, he saw Balladur looking up at the ceiling, avoiding his gaze. From a man as subtle as the Prime Minister, it was more than a signal. So the two companions-in-arms decided to take a stroll around the harbour. After that, Chirac later recalled, he 'understood that the presidential election might well not turn out as planned'. Balladur flew off in his official jet while the man who had headed his party for twenty years was left standing on the tarmac, waiting for his hired plane. At that moment, Jacques Chirac could be in no doubt that power had gone to his friend's head.

This was hardly surprising. Anybody with a surer strategic sense would have seen the danger coming: most French Prime Ministers nurture presidential ambitions at one time or another. Still, the rise and rise of Édouard Balladur had something unreal about it, as if he was touched by divine providence. Platitudinous and self-satisfied, the Prime Minister rose from peak to peak in the polls. He gave in to the threat of strikes and won more plaudits. He avoided decisions and became a hero. The *Financial Times* made him its man of the year. With Balladur, it was time to look forward to the past. Like his first patron, Georges Pompidou, two decades earlier, he epitomised a settled national existence. After the tremors of the Socialist years, his deliberate, courtly style struck a reassuring note. He seemed within reach of forging a new conservative consensus which would go beyond Gaullism and give France a single big centre-right party as a rampart against the Socialists. The Prime Minister personified the rule of the state, with pre-revolution echoes: *Le Monde*'s cartoonist showed him being carried in a sedan chair. Let them eat cake, he might have said as he sought to keep the populace happy by taking the easy way out. Adopting a phrase invented by Marie-France Garaud, satirists altered the last syllable of his name to dub him 'Ballamou' (*Balla-dur* = Balla-hard; *Balla-mou* = Balla-soft). But his hauteur created an illusion of living on a thoroughly superior plane, in which the nation could share – at least for a while.

As the Prime Minister soared in the polls, ambitious young conservatives also looked back at recent history. If Balladur was a second Pompidou, they could not help calculating, his presidency might spawn a bright young successor from outside the Gaullist ranks. So they lined up to be a second Giscard d'Estaing. Not to be outdone, some sharp young Gaullists deserted their party leader and joined the rush to the side of '*cher Édouard*'. It was, after all, only what Jacques Chirac had done in 1974. More surprisingly, the Interior Minister, Charles Pasqua, switched camps. In his ministerial job, Pasqua had access to political intelligence reports from around the country; so, some reasoned, if he had jumped ship, Chirac must really be done for. The Prime Minister's people began to talk of '*pauvre*' Chirac and the lost people around him.

This was a battle between two strands of politics, between straight-on, no-nonsense populism and genteel conservatism – calf's head versus caviar. While Chirac championed republican values, Balladur once told a lunch party that, overall, he thought that 1789 had been a bad thing for France. However great his airs and graces, President Balladur would run the government; however populist his appeal, President Chirac would leave day-to-day domestic business to his Prime Minister. Had there been a serious chance of the left winning, Balladur's ecumenical appeal might well have been irresistible. His base was broader, and he could easily have painted Chirac into a corner, accusing him of opening the door to another seven years of Socialism in a repeat of his performance in 1981. But once the only heavyweight figure from the opposite corner, Jacques Delors, decided not to run, the way was open for Chirac to stamp around the ring, facing Balladur with an impossible task in broadening his coalition.

There were plenty of precedents for this kind of fight on the right: the tussle between Giscard and Chirac; the struggle of Gaullists of the early 1960s against conservatives trying to hang on after the demise of the Fourth Republic; even, in its way, the contrast between the silent majority of the Second World War and the men of the right who actively engaged themselves on one side or the other. But there was also a new twist. From 1976 to 1981, the fight had been between Valéry Giscard d'Estaing and Jacques Chirac. In the 1980s, the battle had widened to take in Raymond Barre. Through all those years, Chirac's RPR party had always been a monolith behind its leader. Now, the Giscard–Barre camp had fled the field, and it was the great Gaullist army which was shockingly rent by internal strife on the verge of victory. In the past, whatever their differences, the General's followers had

usually managed to weave together their different wings. But now, it
was as if the imminence of the return to supreme power had infected
the movement with the old French virus of division. The Socialists
appeared terminally discredited; the centrists would not field a candidate; the Gaullists had only to push the door and the Élysée was theirs –
with all the symbolism which that entailed for the party of the man
who had founded the regime. But they nearly blew it. Another strange
tale of the ways of the men who presume to run France.

As the election came over the political horizon, Balladur was the
clear favourite, ready to move from his official residence at the Hôtel
Matignon to a much grander residence across the Seine, where he
could have as many major-domos as he wished waiting on him morning, noon and night. International finance and the French establishment knew who they backed. 'Chirac's fun, but Balladur's serious,'
one major fund manager told me. 'Chirac's time has passed; we're
ready for a time of real management,' echoed a French business
tycoon. 'It's simple,' said an international businessman. 'Chirac's mad.'
Given the later disclosures about Mitterrand's parlous state of health
and preoccupation with day-to-day survival, the Prime Minister's
authority was even greater than it appeared at the time. So much so
that Chirac showed uncharacteristic signs of hesitation about declaring his own candidacy – and, by one account, had to be encouraged
into making the announcement by none other than the old man in
the Élysée, who may have calculated that a wild performance from the
right could be the only faint hope left to the Socialists.

In fact, Chirac enjoyed strengths of which Balladur could not even
dream. He controlled France's strongest political party machine, and
had a thousand debts to call in. His praetorian guard was loyal, and he
had Paris. The Prime Minister might be the darling of the establishment, but elections are decided by voters – and, when it came to the
hustings, there was only one show in France in the spring of 1995.

Jacques Chirac hurled himself into his third presidential campaign
with all the *brio* of a man who knew that this was his last chance to win
the prize he had sought all his adult life. Incoherence incarnate, he
promised both wage rises and a decline in inflation. One day, he swore
his European fidelity; then he talked of a fresh referendum on the

Maastricht Treaty. He pledged tax cuts, but predicted an increase in the value-added levy. He was for modern business, but sent an emissary to ensure the latter-day support of the leader of the rioting small shop-keepers of the 1950s, Pierre Poujade. It was great theatre, with policy made on the hoof, arms in the air, rictus smiles freezing his face, a hundred hands pumped every hour. In contrast, Balladur was an also-ran, and some key figures read the way the wind was really blowing.

France's greatest political proponent of free-market economics, the Minister for Business, Alain Madelin, stayed loyal to Chirac: as an exponent of *libéralisme avancé*, he could see that Balladur was the re-incarnation of a consensus-corporatist spirit which even the born-again left rejected. The government's best cutting-edge, Foreign Minister Alain Juppé, also remained true to the man he had first served in 1983 in the Paris city government. And the main Gaullist Eurosceptic, the bloodhound-faced President of the National Assem-bly, Philippe Séguin, decided that, whatever their differences, Chirac was the man who should win the election. This trio, and the party machine, constituted such a formidable force that Balladur's chances ought to have been discounted as the election campaign got under way. But his bromide appeal was such that the media went on pro-moting him as the next Head of State – which only spurred the Mayor of Paris to greater activity.

As the election battle moved into top gear, one of the main pro-tagonists of the Thirty Years' War considered his options from the sidelines. The last non-Socialist President had every reason to hate Chirac for his tepid attitude in the 1981 presidential poll. But Mr Ex, as Valéry Giscard d'Estaing had come to be known, still had hopes for the future: if the European Union ever had a real President, who was better suited to fill the post than himself? At the same time, he wanted to preserve a domestic power-base, and he knew that Balladur was going right for his natural constituency, for the local notables who had kept him at the forefront of French politics through good times and bad. If the Premier won the election, Giscard might as well retire to his memoirs. Under Chirac, there might still be a role for him. So it was time to put aside old rancours for the sake of mutual survival.

As spring blossomed on the hillside behind his elegant country home in the Massif Central, Valéry Giscard d'Estaing announced his support for the man whose rivalry had cost him the presidency

fourteen years earlier. His hopes for the future were not to be fulfilled, however. He failed in a bid to become mayor of the Auvergnat
capital of Clermont-Ferrand, up the road from one of his châteaux;
and family pride was dented when a nephew was fined for involvement in a corruption scandal. Eventually, in a meeting-hall in Lyon,
the seventy-year-old wunderkind of the 1960s and 1970s was forced
to pass the leadership of the UDF to a former Defence Minister,
François Léotard. He was not the successor Giscard would have
chosen; the two men had long crossed swords. But the ex-President's
days of party political influence were waning. He could settle old
scores by influencing the choice of ministers on the right, entertain
dreams of becoming Europe's world spokesman and turn his hand to
a volume of soapy romantic fiction. He could rouse himself to indignation at the design of the British architect, Richard Rogers, for a
great motorway viaduct over the Tarn river, caress a project for a volcanic theme park in his native Auvergne, and speculate about the
benefits of devaluing the franc. But Giscard's time as a front-line general had passed: the war on the right had narrowed down to the
Gaullist ranks.

On the hustings, the Prime Minister cut an increasingly poor
figure. But who could have asked for anything more? Whatever one
might think of Édouard Balladur, he was always true to himself, and
his self did not include being at ease with the people. So when he
accosted teenagers in the street and tried to talk to them about
basketball, he clearly didn't have a clue what their replies meant.
Electioneering in a café, he was visibly ill at ease if he had to touch
anybody. Down in the Rouergue, a lamb peed on his jacket and the
farmers laughed among themselves. A satirical television show which
shaped public perceptions had great fun with skits in which His
Smugness the Prime Minister washed his hands after each electoral
handshake and told his wife that he had discovered some charming
new words – 'tu' and 'le peuple'. Such invention went down so well
because everybody believed it to be true, and the Prime Minister's
behaviour seemed to confirm it each and every day. As his press secretary put it later, Balladur had a problem with 'those French who are
called ordinary when one doesn't want to have too much to do with
them but who are the real people of France, those whose virtues one
praises as a group but whom one ignores as individuals'.

Suddenly, the man who had done so well in the polls seemed incapable of getting anything right. When low cloud forced his helicopter to land in southern France, the newspapers were fed a folksy story about how the Prime Minister had been picked up by a passing motorist, with two big dogs on the back seat, and how he had shown the common touch by chatting to the driver as she took him to the next stage of his trip. Some even reported the unlikely spectacle of Balladur standing by the road with his thumb in the air, hitching a lift from the lady. A couple of days later, he sent her a bunch of roses and a visiting card with his hand-written thanks. Unfortunately, it later turned out that the woman was the cousin by marriage of a Balladur adviser who was on the trip – and that he had telephoned to ask her to come to pick up the Premier. When the press learned of the spin that had been put on the tale, it reacted with a belly-laugh and a fresh dose of satire about the hitch-hike that never was. Things got even worse when it emerged that the supposedly ordinary motorist had been driving a large white Mercedes. (Coincidentally, Giscard d'Estaing had just published a romantic novel in which a man of a certain age gives a lift to a young hitch-hiker and embarks on an affair with her.)

The first round of the election duly propelled Jacques Chirac into the decisive second round and eliminated Balladur from the two-man run-off. Lionel Jospin, the last-minute candidate of the supposedly down-and-out Socialists, got the nomination after Jacques Delors ruled himself out of the running – as Mitterrand once said, Delors 'would like to be President without being a candidate'. Jospin showed how mistaken St Jacques had been by winning 23.3 per cent of the vote, to 20.8 for Chirac and 18.5 for Balladur. In part, that was not so surprising: Chirac and Balladur had, after all, split their party, and Jospin had managed to rally the Socialist faithful. If the orthodox right's scores at the first round were put together, and some of Le Pen's 15 per cent were added in, Chirac was well ahead for the run-off. But the Mayor of Paris could only be disappointed to have received just one-fifth of the overall poll. The combined scores of the two Gaullists still fell well short of the 50 per cent needed for eventual victory.

'This is the ultimate combat of his whole life, and he will not let himself fail,' one of Chirac's advisers said as we sat at a pavement café between the two rounds of voting. 'Anyway, the country wants a change. But it will be a hollow victory. We should have blown both Balladur and the left out of the water; we should have humbled Le Pen. We have the best candidate, the man to lead the nation, but we have to struggle to win over voters. They don't believe in us. They don't believe in anybody any more.'

As the second-round campaign unfurled, Chirac became somewhat more presidential; he even relaxed from time to time. His press office disclosed that in the afternoon of the Saturday before the final voting he went into the garden of the Paris City Hall to read a volume of Japanese poetry. Not everybody believed the tale, but it was a sign of how his staff were trying to spin an image of a mature, thoughtful politician with wide horizons. Balladur rallied more loyally to the flag than Chirac had done to the colours of Giscard in 1981. Some 85 per cent of the Prime Minister's first-round voters backed Chirac in the second round. So did a few from the left. As for the National Front, its leader told his supporters they might as well go hunting snails as vote; and 60 per cent of them did not support Chirac in the run-off. However one analysed the figures, there were a lot of non-Socialists who felt disassociated from the new President. Once again, Le Pen seemed to have his finger on the national pulse. Twenty per cent of the electorate abstained, and another 6 per cent cast blank or spoiled ballots. Snail-hunting might well seem more attractive than politics as practised by France's leaders over the past three decades.

If France is still a chauvinist nation when it comes to the sexes, imagine it as a woman in an old-fashioned tale. In 1974, she fell for the undeniable seduction of a brilliant, tall and slim young semi-aristocrat who promised so much but delivered a lot less, and ended up spending too much time away on safari. In 1981, she collapsed into the arms of an old roué who offered to lift her to better and brighter horizons. Despite his broken promises and self-absorption, she found herself unable to turn her back on him when the occasion came in 1988. Seven years on, she had become terminally disenchanted with the decaying and dying man and wanted a complete change of partner. For a while, she was seduced by the notion of a platonic, pursed-lip relationship with an unctuous eater of steamed sole. But, in her heart, she still believed that each advent of the seven-year itch should bring a fresh outburst of passion. The prospect of slipping into bed with Édouard Balladur was hardly calculated to give her a new lease of life.

After a long, lingering sigh for a wise and decent elder cousin from Brussels who decided she'd be too much trouble to handle, she finally went for a former cavalry officer who had been trying to sweep her off her feet for fourteen years. He was hardly the dashing new figure she dreamed of. But consider the alternatives. The professorial Socialist would give her lectures, and was hardly calculated to stir the juices. She might engage in a quick flirtation with the one-eyed rascal on her far right-hand side, give a quick smile to the engaging and stout Communist garden gnome, and even proffer a sisterly caress to a woman bank clerk who preached Trotskyite revolution in an endless presidential quest. But, in the end, she let her most assiduous suitor have his way with her at last, though not with any great joy. The groom grimaced in crazed excitement as he fought his way through the crowd to the wedding party on the Avenue d'Iéna on election night: a kilometre away, a clutch of political experts gathered round an early-morning dinner table in a restaurant off the Champs-Élysées and gave the marriage two months before it would begin to run into the ground.

The political experts were right. After an initial honeymoon, troubles mounted. Nuclear fury abroad was followed by the wave of protests at home against proposed reforms in the welfare system. The concentration on beating Balladur had been so intense that Chirac's men and women came to office without having been able to give sufficient time or thought to the job ahead. As the political editor of *Le Monde* put it, Chirac's only real election programme had been 'no to Balladur'. His campaign had aroused expectations of a new start, but, with a couple of exceptions, nobody around the Cabinet table had anything concrete to offer. Legislation which enshrined proposals made by candidate Chirac took a year or more to see the light, while other major policy changes had not been mentioned during the campaign. 'Now our difficulties start,' Alain Juppé told his staff encouragingly at their first meeting with the new Prime Minister.

The government made it known that the budget deficit was some

50 billion francs greater than it had been led to believe (a charge indignantly denied by Balladur). Privatisation revenue was a good deal less than expected. 'Our economy is good and healthy, our inflation is one of the lowest in the world, and our foreign trade is in strong surplus,' the new President declared. 'What is not working is our public finances.' Alain Madelin was sacked from the Finance Ministry after a running fight with the Prime Minister. Other ministries were all over the place. The President's ideas man, Emmanuel Todd, rounded on Chirac at the Élysée one day and accused him of having slammed the door on his electorate. As if to confirm Todd's suspicions, Juppé drew up his programme to reform welfare and state spending without any of the traditional consultations with bodies representing those who would be affected. After seeing 2 million demonstrators take to the streets and crippling strikes spread across the nation, even Super Énarque had to step back.

What was a month of strikes when the administration had seven years ahead of it to reform the country, mused Chirac. But the administration's unpopularity made it difficult to get anything done, let alone push through the deep reforms it had in mind. The President's standing in the polls dropped well under 50 per cent within a year as he alternately scolded the French for falling short of his expectations and then told them how wonderful they really were. His one-time companion-in-arms, Charles Pasqua, compared him to 'an unstable husband who beats his wife one day, then apologises the next day by showering her with compliments'. Such unions, Pasqua noted, usually go off the rails – 'the wife gets fed up, finds a lover and the marriage collapses'. Or else, the husband turns his weary eyes from problems at home and thinks about a trip abroad.

Not that Chirac's incessant international journeys weren't hard work: he threw himself into his role as France's top travelling salesman with all his usual energy. He also made some sensible decisions to set relations on a more realistic basis for the post-Cold War world. France even brought itself to admit 'without acrimony' that the United States was the sole superpower and that Paris now only ranked as one of the seven or eight most influential capitals. A closer relationship with Nato was developed. Missiles aimed at Russia were dismantled. The nuclear site at Mururoa was run down. Plans to reduce the overall strength of the military forces by more than 20 per cent were announced, with an end to conscription and army numbers cut by more than a third. Most of France's troops would be withdrawn from Germany, and the nuclear missile base on the Plateau d'Albion in the south-east shut. Surveying the cutbacks, a Gaullist deputy with strong military links mused that the losses were worse than at Waterloo. The army chief of staff, Philippe Mercier, revealed that, to help France meet the Maastricht criteria, spending on the army in 1998 was to be cut by 11 per cent. If such cuts continued, he warned, France would either have under-equipped forces, or would have to 'redefine a new defence tool' – whatever that meant.

By the end of his reign, Europe had become François Mitterrand's over-riding concern. That meant keeping in with Germany, and reciting the mantra of Maastricht. Jacques Chirac set out to re-assert a broader and specifically Gaullist and French approach to interna-tional affairs, aspiring to rekindle the glory years of the 1960s. But the overarching question which he studiously avoided was whether France could – or should – play its old role in a post-Cold War world. By balancing membership of the Western alliance with independence from Washington, Charles de Gaulle had been able to carve out a national niche in a bi-polar world. Now the globe was a much more fractured place and there was only one superpower. Chirac wanted to build up stronger relations with Washington; at the same time, he could not resist the temptation to try to ape the old Gaullist preten-sions. But, with united Germany the dominant continental power, any attempt to run a freelance foreign policy on behalf of Europe could only irritate France's partners, and make a less than convincing impression in Washington. Economic policy was shaped in Germany, and world policy across the Atlantic: where did that leave France? As the second most important member of the European Union, certainly. But on a wider world scale, as little more than a power which might or might not decide to join *ad hoc* alliances, and might be welcomed or barracked according to its decisions.

The key relationship, with Germany and Europe, might, in theory at least, offer a sphere for a resumption of classic Gaullism. With Britain having disqualified itself from being taken seriously by its behaviour in the later years of Conservative rule, the French Presi-dent was the only leader in the Union who could realistically challenge the German Chancellor on whether what is right for

Germany is necessarily right for its partners. As an American economist, Robert Levine, has pointed out, there is a parallel between the
potential French role in present-day Europe and De Gaulle's questioning of American influence in the 1960s. When differences briefly
flicked between Paris and Bonn over monetary policy, some saw a
glimmer of such an approach. After the Jospin government took
office, one of the first questions was whether it would establish an
alternative to Teutonic orthodoxy within the Community. There
are, after all, fundamental differences in the outlook of the two
nations. France is Eurocentric; Germany has looked across the
Atlantic since 1945. The Bundesbank's heart and soul are rooted in
the need to contain inflation for deep historical reasons; the politicians on the Seine, whatever their pride in having kept the economy
in line for a decade, are temperamentally more ready to flirt with
greater flexibility.

But it is also inconceivable that France should not be one of the
two key players in the future of Europe – which was the basic reason
why Jacques Chirac could not have joined the anti-Maastricht campaign in 1992 whatever short-term advantage he might have gained
from its victory. This means that Paris has to be viscerally tied to
Bonn, the Banque de France to the Bundesbank, the President to the
Chancellor. And, while Marianne may bare her breast with a smile,
Germania rarely relaxes.

So, while the economic criteria of the Maastricht Treaty snapped at
France's heels, the vicious circle of economic policy remained as tight
as ever, and took its political toll. The price of continuing low inflation and Euro-orthodoxy was low growth. But this kept down
government revenue, made the deficit reduction required by Maastricht that much more difficult to achieve, and turned the promised
tax cuts into a chimera. To try to boost its income, the Juppé government put up the sales tax, which hit the poor and the unemployed
whom Chirac had promised to defend. The number of firms going
bust rose, with almost 6,000 businesses shutting down each month.
Only a third of bosses of small businesses expressed any optimism
about the future, as unemployment edged up again to the record
levels of the worst days of the Mitterrand era. The President went on
television with a marathon programme whose audience dropped
embarrassingly low as viewers turned to a sexy film on the other

channel. 'The truth is that we live in a profoundly conservative country and that it is very difficult to change things,' he lamented. Perfectly
true, but he was in a fix of his own making. He had won the presidency by promising a new economic and social deal at home, and he
wasn't delivering. Or, rather, what he was serving up through his
Prime Minister was not the dish the nation had ordered. It had asked
for a rich stew; Chirac and Juppé were giving it gruel. No wonder
that a lot of people saw attractions in *l'autre politique*, a code-word for
reflation. Senior officials might speak proudly of the strong franc and
sneer at the floating pound, but the economic situation across the
Channel could look quite attractive to a long-term unemployed steel-
worker or a former Félix Potin manager searching for bargains at the
local discount store.

Through it all, Alain Juppé kept an iron grip on the business of
government. The political editor of *Le Monde* compared the President
of the Republic to an unidentified flying object – 'one no longer
knows quite who he is, where he is, what he wants'. But his Prime
Minister was always there. He put his imprint on anything and everything. Given the ministerial chaos around him, he had little choice,
but he went that mile further. In the midst of the national strikes of
1995, Juppé personally put in an urgent telephone call to the head of
the Communist trade union federation – to ask about the staff situation on one Paris Métro line. He did not admit to the slightest fault
in anything. Even when his grace-and-favour housing in a municipal
flat on the Left Bank cast a stain on his squeaky-clean technocratic
image, he waxed indignant at the fuss. A trusted aide moved across the
Seine to become chief of staff at the Élysée; other acolytes were put in
to run ministries, often showing more loyalty to the Juppé machine
than to their nominal bosses. The Minister of Justice, Jacques Toubon,
was moved to remark that there was a difference between a conduc-
tor and a one-man band. All this might have been fine if the
government was doing well, but Juppé had achieved the double feat
of getting very little done and breaking records for unpopularity.
Visibly, the Prime Minister didn't know what to do about it except to
call another meeting of experts. Some of those around him wondered
if he was losing his way. Even his boss sensed that it was time to do
something about the mess.

Chirac is a Bonapartist, a man who puts his trust in his direct link with the people, in his ability to incarnate the nation. Like the First Emperor, he believes in moving fast, living off the land, using concentrated force to achieve his ends. And, like the First Emperor, none of his victories has led to lasting peace. But that did not stop either of them having another go. So what Jacques did next should have surprised nobody. Like a general who has finally won his battle but finds peace hard to deal with, he went back to war.

Some of his advisers thought he should have done this two years earlier to finish off the job. The presidential victory had left Chirac with a dilemma: did he co-opt the supporters of Édouard Balladur by bringing them into the government or did he banish them from the regained Gaullist paradise? Sensible as the first option would have been in producing a dominant Gaullist-conservative bloc, the winners of 1995 were not in a forgive-and-forget mood: Chirac's wife was said to be unremittingly bitter about former supporters who had deserted their camp, and it was known that politicians who fell foul of the former Bernadette Chodron de Courcel had a short life-expectancy with her husband. But there was still a large Balladurian block in the National Assembly who were saying that the new President hadn't won, it had been they who had lost. This was not simply crying over spilt milk for, as Patrick Jarreau of *Le Monde* wrote, 'they had in their hands a deck of cards that appeared to be solid gold, with a large majority of deputies of the right in their camp, plus the most watched television channel in France, etc. . . . Given the result they arrived at, one has to conclude that they were really lousy players.'

So the logical course for Chirac in 1995 would have been to have called legislative elections immediately to clear out these traitors. Some of his top advisers pressed him to go to the country to finish off the anti-Balladurian job. The conjunction of presidential and parliamentary elections was well established: the Socialists had gone to the country after Mitterrand's victories of 1981 and 1988. But, like the allies in the Gulf War hesitating to invade Iraq to finish off Saddam Hussein, Chirac held back – in part because he had tied his own hands during the fight for the presidency. Balladur had pledged to call legislative elections if he won. That had been enough to produce a negative knee-jerk from Chirac, who brushed the idea aside and then, once in the Élysée, compounded his refusal with a high-minded observation about not using elections as a means of governing France.

Two years later, it was all he could think of. The government had fallen into impossibly deep discredit with the public. The task it had set itself was eminently necessary – to lift France from its late Mitterrandist gloom, to give it a new national and international élan, and to prepare it for the single European currency. That last objective was a suitably long-term goal for a seven-year presidency, but the imminence of the Maastricht Treaty deadline meant that Chirac and Juppé did not have much time to play with. On top of that, their bossy, elitist style was completely wrong for the times. As so often, it ain't what you do, it's the way that you do it. But the men at the top ploughed on in ever-decreasing circles. To make sure there was no weakening of resolve, the President established a four-man 'crisis cell' at the Élysée, consisting of himself, the Prime Minister and their two closest officials. 'Act without talking,' was their watchword.

They might act, but senior politicians warned Chirac that the long grind of reform risked undermining the administration and encouraging anti-European sentiment. Gloomy forecasts were piling up about unemployment, tax rises and spending cuts. Chirac's loyalty to Juppé ruled out the traditional presidential escape route of sacking the Prime Minister. His hostility to the Balladurians led him to veto Juppé's proposal to replace his lacklustre Finance Minister with a bright spark who had gone over to the other side in 1995. The chief of staff at the Élysée, Dominique de Villepin, proposed the old Gaullist recipe of a referendum. De Villepin, a member of the crisis cell who was known for having an iron first in an iron glove, was the ultimate Juppé–Chirac loyalist, having served the first when he was Foreign Minister and organised the presidential campaign of the second. When a journalist sourced a story on the President's circle, De Villepin told him curtly, 'I am the circle.' His referendum wheeze was, however, rejected since it entailed the risk of provoking a hostile line-up ranging from the left to the National Front, and taking in a fair number of Eurosceptic Gaullists along the way. So was the idea of a crisis government of the great and good, to include such luminaries as Giscard d'Estaing and Raymond Barre. Instead, at 3 P.M. on the afternoon of 17 April 1997, Chirac called half a dozen advisers to a room beside his office at the Élysée. Among those present was his younger daughter, Claude, who passed for an expert in public relations. The meeting agreed that the time had come for decisive action. Four days later, the President announced the dissolution of the National Assembly and two-round elections for 25 May and 1 June to give France 'a fresh impetus' for the challenges that lay ahead. On a visit to Beijing soon afterwards, he told the Prime Minister, Li Peng, that he had called the election because his majority was too large and uncontrollable. 'I will lose a hundred deputies, but they will be easier to handle,' he added. 'And Juppé will put everything in order.'

There was no denying the problem which Chirac and his men faced. But the way they attacked it was like the old joke – How do you get to the Eiffel Tower, asks a tourist. If I were you I wouldn't start from here, responds the Parisian. As often happens with politicians who hunker in the bunker, the men in the crisis cell were starting from the wrong point in several ways. They assumed that France was still set in the political environment of 1993–95, in the crushing defeat for the left at the last parliamentary election and the pre-eminent position of the Gaullists at the presidential poll. The débâcle of the late Mitterrand years seemed too close for the French to be ready to put their faith in the left under the leadership of the well-meaning but uninspiring Lionel Jospin. If the President and his men had lifted their eyes from their dossiers, they might have noticed how Mitterrand was not faring so badly in posthumous opinion polls, recalled how Jospin had revived the spirits of the left in 1995, and even recognised how his shadow team looked a good deal more attractive than the apparatchiks of the right. And some fearless aide might have pointed to a poll which showed that 59 per cent of those who had voted for Chirac two years earlier now thought that he talked a lot but that nothing concrete followed.

Another problem was not so much that the President was blatantly going back on his word about holding the election – the French were well used to being lied to by their leaders. It was rather that he and his head of government had nothing new to offer except fresh spoonfuls of Dr Juppé's purge. So why was he holding an election at all? If he won, it was more of the same. The only logical conclusion was that he was offering voters a chance to change policies. There was a fault here which the country was not slow to latch on to.

And then there was a difficulty which went to the heart of the political system. However low his popularity, a President of France has to appear to be in charge. At the depths of his fortunes, François Mitterrand always seemed capable of manipulating events. As for Chirac, his whole career had been based on leading from the front. But now he appeared to be in thrall to his Prime Minister. Even worse, Chirac looked like a man who was running scared on behalf of his government. And of what? Surely not the schoolmasterish Lionel Jospin: the Prime Minister had summed up the administration's contemptuous view of him when, a cigarillo between his lips, he asked a group of journalists at the start of the campaign what they thought of the Socialist chief and, before they could reply, supplied his own answer: 'He's really very bad, isn't he?' No, the demon at Chirac's back was the French people. He had won their highly conditional love in 1995, but now it was seeping away by the day. He had to regain it, haunted by a terrible frustration at having been unable to capitalise on winning the greatest prize of his life and by the fear of what might lie down the road. For the ultimate macho performer of French politics, this could only be a sign of failure foretold.

Now pause for a paragraph of what the French call *la psychologie de concierge*. Throughout his career, as we have seen, Chirac has sought guidance from others. Having won the supreme prize, he should have been his own man. But he still felt the need for a bond, and he chose Alain Juppé as the mast for his ship of state. The two men had worked together for more than a decade at the Hôtel de Ville in Paris. According to one account, they had another bond. Chirac's elder daughter was prey to suicidal depression. Reports of her death swept Paris from time to time: on one occasion, the Chiracs received thousands of condolence messages for a death which had not taken place. Juppé's youngest daughter fell prey to the same illness, and Chirac moved in to comfort and give advice. She survived in much better shape than Chirac's daughter. That gave a depth to their relationship which went beyond politics, and contained an echo of the way in which Georges Pompidou had run a foundation in memory of De Gaulle's Down's syndrome daughter. In a sense, the policies which Chirac and Juppé were jointly defending could be seen as being irrelevant. This intensely fragile President had put faith in his Prime Minister in a way that went beyond the usual relationship between the

Élysée and the Hôtel Matignon. In human terms, it was admirable. Politically, it paved the way for ruin.

The worst duly came to pass. The Socialists mounted a campaign which made some of their more thoughtful leaders blush in private – a little, at least. Under the slogan 'Dare to return to the left', they pledged to create hundreds of thousands of jobs without upsetting public finances, to cut the working week to thirty-five hours without any reduction in pay, to stop privatisations and to meet the requirements of the Communists, the Greens and any other allies they could find. Lionel Jospin emerged as the man France had been looking for – modest, determined, approachable and honest. Though an Énarque himself, he struck a welcome contrast to the superior technocracy of Juppé, De Villepin and their ilk.

As a power in the land under Mitterrand, Jospin had been as obnoxiously full of himself as the average French minister, a man who had undergone a charisma bypass somewhere along the path from his first career as a diplomat to the heights of the Socialist Party. I recall meeting him once at a 'summer university' outside Bordeaux and being taken aback by his condescension towards those he was introduced to. When the Prime Minister of the time, Michel Rocard, suggested that they might call one another '*tu*', Jospin was reported to have replied that the head of the government should remember that he was speaking to *Monsieur le Ministre de l'Éducation Nationale*, and ought to address him as such or by his even grander title of *Ministre d'État*. But a new marriage, and his unexpectedly good showing in the presidential poll, produced a definite change. His smarter colleagues complained that Jospin still dressed badly; however, he made the effort of buying some glad rags and a dinner suit from Armani – apparently he had a model figure, because the only alterations that had to be made were to the length of the trousers. He also learned how to smile. The nickname of 'Yo-Yo' given to him by a satirical television programme became rather endearing. He bought new glasses and a car with a convertible roof. Pictures of him smiling behind the wheel made Jospin look like a man who had discovered pleasure in life somewhat late in the day.

Showing the requisite degree of steel, he sidelined the political dinosaurs of the Mitterrand era and brought forward a new team, including Jacques Delors' tough and able daughter whose job would be to get to grips with unemployment. He kept the usual voluble Socialists quiet and disciplined during the month-long campaign, calculating correctly that their best chance of success lay in creating as few waves as possible and leaving their opponents to lose. Shedding their downbeat image of the early 1990s, the Socialists held out the comfort blanket of promises which the French wanted to hear, but they also radiated an impression of managerial competence. In keeping with the times, Jospin declared himself to be a man of ideas, not ideology. Even if those ideas sometimes looked less than realistic, and the move to a 35-hour week by the dawn of the twenty-first century seemed distinctly ideological, they were sold by men and women in sharp suits who spoke the language of modernity. And, unlike their opponents, at least they had some dreams to sell.

However well the Socialists fought, this was an election waiting to be lost by men who appeared to have acquired a death-wish. A saying from the 1980s that France had the stupidest right wing in the world suddenly came back into vogue. Travelling through France during the campaign that spring, I was struck by how many of those who rejected Alain Juppé retained a degree of respect for his fortitude, and how even those who backed the left raised their eyebrows when the talk turned to its economic programme. What people couldn't fathom was why those in power had given the country the chance to reject them. That questioning became even more pointed when Juppé proclaimed that he would unveil his programme for the future within forty days of the poll if he won. Why not do it straight away without needing an election? There was only one answer: what the Gaullists had up their sleeve must be so dreadful that they did not dare to reveal it before the voters went to the polls. In such circumstances, the prospect of flopping down at an oasis with Lionel Jospin rather than undertaking another forced march across the desert behind the unrelenting Juppé was all too alluring. So, at the first round of voting on Sunday, 25 May, the orthodox right got its lowest score under the Fifth Republic, abstentions soared, the National Front scored another triumph, and only one minister won an outright majority.

It was the greatest political shock Alain Juppé had ever suffered, his first major defeat. What made the awakening even worse was that he had ignored the storm signals. Such was the blindness at the top that, as France voted, the chief of staff at the Hôtel Matignon had been working on the inauguration speech for the Prime Minister's second government. The normally imperturbable Juppé was reported to have been unable to string more than a couple of sentences together when he met right-wing leaders on the Sunday evening. Later, he drove to the Élysée and mentioned the possibility of resignation: Chirac brushed aside the suggestion with a gesture of his hand. The following morning, the climate changed. Jacques Pilhan, the President's adviser on public relations, and Chirac's daughter, Claude, insisted that Juppé had to go. The Prime Minister's champion at the palace, Dominique de Villepin, was powerless to protect his man. Within ninety minutes the decision was taken. Some of the Prime Minister's faithful technocrats burst into tears when they learned the news. On Monday night, Juppé went on television to announce that, whatever happened at the decisive second round six days later, he would step down. Not for the first time, Claude Chirac's judgement was a matter of debate: for two years, the Prime Minister had taken the flak, but now her father was alone in the front line. As the Tiger of the First World War, Georges Clemenceau, said of his chief of staff: 'I fart; he smells.' Now nobody could deflect the odour from the President.

The following Sunday, 1 June, the left duly won its majority. The Socialists doubled their representation in almost half the departments of France. Rejected in his constituency near Toulouse in 1993, Lionel Jospin was returned this time with 63 per cent of the vote. In Bordeaux, Juppé, who later acknowledged how mistaken he had been not to have called a legislative election in 1995, won his seat – but with just 54 per cent of the vote in a constituency held by his predecessor in 1993 with 75 per cent. Ministers hurriedly removed their files from their offices; Jospin became the new head of government; and France entered a new era in its politics with a humiliated Head of State who still had five years of his term to run. On the other side of the world, the Chinese Prime Minister might have reflected on the strange ways of Western democracy.

The Socialists had staged a stunning comeback, but the reality behind the voting was somewhat more complex than it appeared – thanks to the genie in the National Front bottle. If the mainstream right had been humiliated, the combined forces of the left still fell short of a majority of votes, with 48.2 per cent in the second round. Without the ballots for Le Pen's men and women, Jospin would have had a significantly less convincing majority in the new Assembly. Once more, the divisions on the right had opened the door to the left. In the past, the division had been in the mainstream; now the wrecker came from the far bank.

Their strong score at the first round of the election meant that around 130 of the Front's candidates were entitled to stay in the field for the run-offs. As the party celebrated with glasses of sparkling wine at its headquarters in Saint-Cloud on 25 May, Bruno Mégret, the unnamed *dauphin*, preached entryism. He wanted to cut deals with the orthodox right under which each would withdraw some of its candidates to provide a straight run against the left. Driven by his hatred for Chirac, Le Pen took the opposite tack and insisted on maintaining as many candidates as possible for the second round. His mind was made up. Back in 1986, Le Pen had hoped to forge an alliance with the Gaullists during Chirac's second premiership, but had been coldly rebuffed. Now, a decade on, he had a chance to wreak his revenge – a dish, as the French say, best eaten cold, though the red-faced, jubilant Le Pen was hardly the epitome of cool that early summer night. There was no time for the long process of infiltrating the orthodox right as preached by Mégret. The only foe who counted was not Jospin but the man in the Élysée. The greater the chaos the Front could provoke, the greater the chances of the big bang in French politics which might open the gates of power.

In all, the Front put up seventy-six contenders for the second round. Although it won only one seat – in its bastion of Toulon, which it narrowly lost a year later – the party racked up 40 per cent in some straight fights with the left. The former OAS terrorist, Jean-Jacques Susini, scored 41 per cent in Marseille, and Mégret took 45 per cent in nearby Martigues. (After failing to find a safe constituency, Le Pen himself chose not to stand.) Even in triangular contests where they finished third, Front challengers clocked up 16 or 17 per cent of the vote. The split in the right-wing vote handed around a score of constituencies to the left. If they had gone to the right, Jospin's majority would have been cut from around sixty to around twenty-five. Not surprisingly, some less scrupulous members of the orthodox right began to talk about reaching local agreements with the Front. Le

Pen was said to be putting on weight because of all the secret meals right-wing Gaullists were having with him. Le Pen's go-it-alone tactics had proved his point in 1997, but even he was not immortal. The seductive power of Bruno Mégret's entryism lurked around the corner to snare those who would prefer to deal with the Front rather than to fight it.

As if all that was not sufficiently galling for Chirac, he also had to recognise that, by backing Jospin over Juppé, voters had snatched power from the Élysée, an ironic outcome for a Gaullist who stood, above all, for the imperial authority of the presidency.

It was not surprising that reports swiftly spread of Chirac sitting in his palace sunk in the kind of gloom that had enveloped him after his 1988 defeat by Mitterrand. It was a time for journalists to trot out phrases about the shipwreck of the presidency. Unlike De Gaulle or Mitterrand, Chirac was not a solitary man, and the sense of being alone must have weighed heavily on him. *Le Canard Enchaîné* quoted a friend of the President as saying: 'He's doing what he always does when things go against him. He's eating a lot of *charcuterie*, drinking a lot of beer and watching a lot of television.' Nothing seemed to go right – even the provenance of an African statue presented to him by his staff for his sixty-fifth birthday turned out to be of doubtful legality and had to be handed to a museum for safe keeping. Sympathising with a defeated Gaullist, Chirac remarked: 'You have had a slap in the face. I know something about that: it's often happened to me.' There were passages of arms between the Élysée and the new government over foreign affairs, jobs policy, and the role of government. Jospin took the President to task in Cabinet over the interpretation of the constitution, and Chirac used the traditional presidential television interview on Bastille Day to tick off the government on subjects ranging from immigration to the need not to tie down industry with 'obsolete and absurd regulations'. As if the rigours of the Juppé years had never existed, the Head of State insisted that the way to fight unemployment was to encourage small and medium-sized firms rather than to create artificial jobs. But when he called the passage to a 35-hour week 'a hazardous experiment', Chirac opened the door for the obvious response: with a nod at the legislative election, Jospin observed that hazardous undertakings were not unknown in politics.

But, for all that, France's third experiment in having a President of

one party and a Prime Minister of another got off to an unexpectedly
easy start. Whatever he had hinted at during the election campaign,
Jospin did not renege on the commitment to the Maastricht bud-
getary requirements which removed one potential threat to his dual
cohabitation, with a Gaullist in Paris and a Christian Democrat in
Bonn. Despite the 'no to privatisation' slogans of the campaign, the
sale of state assets was not abandoned, and new legislation on the sensitive subject of immigration struck a compromise between the
demands of the left and the fears of the right. Seven months after his
great victory, the Prime Minister even found himself confronted with
the militant demonstrations of the unemployed across the country,
supported by the Communists and Greens who both had ministers in
his government. He set up a billion-franc emergency fund to try to
soothe the protests, but also declared that he wanted France to be a
society of work, not charity. Dealing with the civil servants who
make up the bulk of its electorate, the government managed to get
union backing for wage increases limited to 1.3 per cent in each of the
two years before the 35-hour week comes into effect.

Given the long road to presidential and parliamentary elections
which did not have to be held until the year 2002, there was no rush
to start arm-wrestling over the Cabinet table. What became known as
the Siamese-twin period of French politics seemed very much to the
country's liking, though the challenge of the jobless soon began to eat
away at the Prime Minister's popularity. Watching the President rise in
the polls six months after his electoral débâcle, some of his remaining
fans noted how Bill Clinton had weathered a great setback in con-
gressional elections and gone on to win a second presidential term.
Like his flesh-pressing American counterpart, Chirac left Paris to do
what he did best – meeting the crowds and drawing strength from his
contact with them. He also took advantage of a trip to the city of
Troyes to spend the night in a bed specially elongated to accommo-
date General de Gaulle. For the first time in two years, he went to the
theatre. His standing in the opinion polls rose steadily, particularly
when he asserted France's traditional independence from Washington
by leading allied opposition to the bombing of Iraq at the beginning
of 1998. Regional elections a month later confirmed the disfavour
that had fallen on the right, but were not a complete disaster. With
35.6 per cent of the vote to the mainstream left's 39.6 per cent, the

Gaullists and their centre-right allies were not humiliated, even if they lost control of most regional councils. While the low turnout of 60 per cent indicated continuing disillusion with politics, the right could draw some comfort from the way in which voters had not stampeded to back the Socialists.

But there was no escaping the fate which Jacques Chirac had brought on himself and his followers. Short of an unforeseen national drama, the result of the regional elections ruled out an attempt by him to reverse the judgement of 1997, probably until the new century dawned. That provided Lionel Jospin with time to prepare a presidential bid, the National Front with the chance to play the pestilential power in regions across the country, and the right with a few years in which to pull itself apart again. When Chirac asked his former Finance Minister what his followers were saying about him, Alain Madelin was reported to have replied: 'They say that you always lead us to failure, Jacques. They believe you bring bad luck.' For some on the right, he simply became 'the President who brought back the left', a holdover from the past who belonged to the museum of French politics. And, as if that was not enough, the President faced another set of challenges which, in their way, were as significant for him as having to deal with the disarming Monsieur Jospin.

A photograph taken in the Paris Hôtel de Ville on the evening of 7 May 1995, as Chirac waited for the second-round results of the presidential election, shows the candidate, tieless and in shirtsleeves, looking anxiously up from his desk flanked by four men. The dominant figure is that of a heavy-set man with pouched eyes and the general air of a mournful bloodhound, who leans forward, his hands on the desk as he makes a point. Philippe Séguin had been a key actor in Chirac's electoral success. His demeanour and quick temper, his high intelligence and fine sense of strategy, had long marked him out from the polished ranks of the French political establishment. He was just the kind of enemy you don't want but, despite their collaboration in 1995, he and the President were set on a collision course.

Born in Tunisia into a family of teachers, the Gitane-smoking Séguin was an Énarque, but not one of the mandarins. Mayor of Épinal in the eastern Vosges department, he claimed to be the bearer of the true Gaullist faith – in the autumn of 1998 he even inveighed against Halloween as a dangerous trans-Atlantic import. Eight years earlier, Séguin and the rumbustious Charles Pasqua led an internal party revolt which was beaten back with only 30 per cent support from the faithful. Two years later, the pair headed the campaign against the Maastricht Treaty from the right in the close-run referendum. Watching them at work on the hustings, it was easy to see only two jowly, overweight politicians who were using the vote as a means of advancing their own fortunes within the Gaullist party, but the stakes they raised were enormous. As the ultimate political game-player, François Mitterrand hoped that the referendum would provoke a fresh split in the right between pro-European centrists and conservatives and nationalistic Gaullists. If Chirac had fulfilled such expectations and thrown his lot in with Séguin and Pasqua, France would have rejected the treaty, and Europe would have been faced with the unthinkable prospect of a future without its second most important power. But, for once, Mitterrand had misread his man, and it was Pasqua and Séguin who ended up as narrow losers.

Not that the Mayor of Épinal worried about being out of the mainstream. He was famously uninterested in building up a network of contacts and placemen similar to the one which had helped to ensure Jacques Chirac's control of their party for so long. As well as proclaiming the virtues of *l'autre politique*, Séguin had a habit of not mincing his words when it came to presidential matters. In 1988, he said that the RPR had other things to do than to support Chirac's repeated raids on the Élysée, and in 1994, he did not bother to attend the meeting at which Chirac launched his third presidential bid. But Édouard Balladur was even less to his taste. A broad and comfortable conservative coalition would have no place for the likes of him. So Séguin rallied to Chirac and became a star of the campaign, pressing the populist course which was to win the Élysée and making some of the best speeches of that summer. In a slip of the tongue, he referred to 'my' campaign. But, once Chirac had won, all the prizes went to Juppé, the organisation man, while the inspirer of victory was left to bide his time across the Seine as President of the National Assembly.

Although Séguin had been part of Chirac's election team, the new administration had no more eloquent critic. Back in the early days of the RPR, Chirac had flirted with the notion of 'Gaullist labourism'; now, Séguin promulgated 'social Gaullism'. Some of his job-boosting formulae might seem somewhat thin, such as his suggestion of fighting unemployment by abolishing electronic ticket machines on the underground and self-service petrol pumps to make way for human beings. His softening of his anti-European rhetoric aroused charges of trimming to the wind: he still denounced Maastricht as a bad agreement but said that, as a good democrat, he accepted the outcome of the 1992 referendum. What he wanted was Europe to fit the needs of France. It was a sign of the desperation of the President's position that, between the two rounds of the legislative election, the idea was floated of a new government to be headed by this arch opponent of Chirac's policies from the Gaullist left in tandem with the sacked free marketeer, Alain Madelin. That led one of Jospin's closest political friends to assure him that he was certain to become Prime Minister, since 'with you at Matignon, Chirac knows he will remain President; with Séguin, that's not certain'.

Even with Jospin at the head of his second government, however, Chirac was not safe from the only French politician who refused to take his telephone calls when he was in one of his periodic fits of temper. As he had moved on to even higher things, Chirac had passed the formal leadership of the party he had founded to Alain Juppé. Now that Juppé had been rejected by the French, it was time for what Séguin called 'a knife fight' at the RPR. The surviving Gaullist deputies rallied to the Mayor of Épinal, who took over the RPR and promptly twisted the knife by resuming relations with some of the prime Balladurian turncoats of 1995. Showing how serious he was about his new job by giving up his *mairie*, Séguin let it be known that 'Chirac lost because he didn't trust me'. Sounding some of his traditional themes, he warned of globalisation creating a vast casino, and called for a tax on international capital movements. But his first party congress also saw a lurch the other way, with calls for tax cuts, labour market flexibility and a slimming-down of the welfare state and the public sector. Free from the reserve which the President had to show in his criticisms of his Prime Minister if the business of government was to continue, the new RPR boss laid in to the Socialist government as having as much in common with Britain's New Labour as 'a bagpipe has with a sperm whale'. But he did not have things all his own way as he sought to reinvent the party.

As it came to the end of its sixth decade, Gaullism faced the challenge of defining its own meaning. Did it just exist to glorify its leader and get him elected, or did it have an ideology to set against the Socialists? Given the strength of the party machine and the party's inchoate combination of populism and big business, nationalism and Europeanism, the first definition seemed the more plausible. But, if that were the case, a second question loomed: was the RPR to continue to be the one-man band it had always been except for the brief Balladurian ascendancy? Despite the bruising experience of 1997, Chirac's qualities as a political Lazarus were legendary, and Philippe Séguin was soon reminded of them: his attempt to change the party's name failed, and his first major speech at a party congress was interrupted by a thirteen-minute ovation from the floor for the President, who was not even present. That did not answer the question of what Gaullism was for, but at least it gave the party a rock to cling to in difficult times – in stark contrast to the shifting sands that have set in among its allies.

Established in 1978 to back Valéry Giscard d'Estaing, the Union de la Démocratie Française was a mishmash coalition of regional dignitaries linked only by a broad pro-Europeanism, a lack of ideology, a desire for power and a web of intense personal rivalries. The coalition's scope was so broad, in fact, that the leader of one of its constituent parties served in a Socialist government while another flirted with the National Front. Like medieval dukes, its bosses relied on their provincial domains for their national status. For them, running a major region was as important as occupying a ministry in Paris, but in the spring of 1998, some of the UDF's provincial leaders suddenly found themselves short of foot soldiers to defend their territories.

On the very day of the Ides of March, elections were held for the twenty-two regional councils of metropolitan France where the right had won overwhelmingly in an anti-Mitterrand backlash in 1992. It was hardly the most ringing of elections: the biggest winner was the abstention ticket which attracted 42 per cent of those registered to vote. The proportional representation system used meant that there were only two outright results. After horse-trading in seventeen others in the following days, it became evident that, once again, the electorate had hedged its bets. By giving the left seven councils, voters had blunted the Socialists' legislative success of the previous summer – though they did gain the country's richest region, the Île-de-France.

Holding on to ten councils, the right could heave a sigh of relief, particularly after a similar pattern emerged soon afterwards on an even more local level in cantonal elections in which the left gained ground but still remained outnumbered by the right. But what counted that spring was what happened in five provinces previously held by the UDF where the balance of power was now in the hands of the National Front.

The night after the election, Bruno Mégret appeared on the evening news programme of the main state television station. The *dauphin* of the National Front had every reason to be pleased with himself. The National Front had taken 15.5 per cent of the vote – more than 3 million electors. At a tense meeting that morning, Mégret had convinced Jean-Marie Le Pen that the time had come to drop the old hard-line approach, and to offer the orthodox right an alliance to block the left. Poised and unthreatening, Mégret insisted on the Monday night news that the Front was a reasonable party which would not make the full adoption of its programme the price of an understanding.

True to their beliefs, Philippe Séguin held the RPR firm on an anti-Front line while Chirac thundered against the 'racist and xenophobic' party. A dignitary who talked enthusiastically to *Le Monde* about Mégret's offer in a motorway pizzeria was promptly expelled. A leading figure from Bordeaux who proposed opening the door to the Front got an angry telephone call from Séguin: an hour later, he was insisting that he had been misunderstood. Like any good electoral machine, the RPR does not fool about when it comes to discipline.

Discipline, however, was a quality the UDF always lacked. The day after Mégret's television appearance, its leaders agreed to reject the idea of collaboration with the Front, with Jean-Claude Gaudin from Marseille warning from his own experience of the dangers of making a pact with the devil. But, whatever the line laid down in Paris, some of the UDF's dukes were ready to listen to the siren song from the reassuringly reasonable lieutenant of the robber baron of French politics. These were not fly-by-night freebooters. Charles Millon, president of the Rhône-Alpes regional council, had been Defence Minister; Jean-Pierre Soisson, president of the Burgundy council, had been a Minister of State under the Socialists; Jacques Blanc was the long-time leader of the right in Languedoc-Roussillon. They made no secret of what they were doing – Soisson met the Front's local representative in a restaurant in Dijon and gave him a lift back to the city centre after assuring him that the region would be run by a 'right wing that has finally been brought together'. Millon first tried to build a majority without the Front and sought the unhelpful counsel of Giscard d'Estaing, but ended up reaching an agreement with the party's local boss. As a result, five days after the regional poll, Blanc, Soisson and Millon were elected to preside over their councils with the backing of the Front, as were two lesser-known UDF figures in Picardy and the Centre. The UDF's nominal leader, François Léotard, who had hoped to lead the Provence-Alpes-Côte-d'Azur council, left a session of the regional body in Marseille to order all five men to be suspended from the party on the spot. Back in the council chamber, Léotard had a problem of his own as Le Pen pushed his claims to the regional presidency, claiming that the UDF should back him in return for Front support elsewhere. In yet another demonstration of how the Front could force ideological opponents together in self-defence, the conservatives stepped aside to let in a Socialist as the price of blocking Le Pen.

The leaders of the UDF's constituent parties split off in different directions. One of the most prominent, former Education Minister François Bayrou, announced that he was going to establish a new movement to occupy the central ground of French politics. The free market champion Alain Madelin appeared ready to entertain some association with the Front while Charles Millon launched a new movement called simply La Droite ('The Right'), which he said would bring everybody together, but which did not save him from being voted out of his regional presidency in a re-run election at the beginning of 1999 by a UDF candidate backed by the Socialists. By then, François Léotard, who was under investigation in yet another party funding affair, had resigned as party leader while Hervé de Charette, a former Foreign Minister, simply spoke of the 'ruin of the right'.

No wonder the UDF leaders greeted the break-up of the National Front with such delight less than a year after it had caused them such grief. But the prospect of getting together with the RPR looked as distant as ever. Not that the Gaullists were as united as they liked to pretend. One of Chirac's most faithful followers, the former Justice

Minister Jacques Toubon, set up a new front in the recurrent civil wars on the right by forming a new political group in Paris to challenge the Gaullist mayor of the city. The President and Prime Minister might talk grandly about the need for fundamental reform of political life, but the incoherence – first on the right, then on the left and now on the right again – seemed to have no end. Even if the National Front had run itself onto the rocks, the question has to be posed ever more starkly as to whether the country and its leaders are capable of shifting into a new gear for a new century, or whether the people and their politicians will shoot off down yet another set of side-roads which will lead them ever closer to the precipice.

15

ON THE BRINK

There is, of course, another way of looking at France. The lure of the country remains as strong as ever. The British colonise the Dordogne and Provence, not to mention the Channel Tunnel hinterland of the Pas de Calais. Hong Kong financiers buy Rivieraland homes. A village in the Drôme becomes a corner of Belgium, and reports of prehistoric beings emerging at the foot of the gorges of the Ardèche turn out to be Dutch nudists cavorting in the river. Surfers ride the waves off Cap Breton, and mountaineers essay Mont Blanc. The success of Peter Mayle's books shows the folksy pull of country life in the south, and where did the last governor of Hong Kong go to write his Asian memoirs and cross swords with Rupert Murdoch but in a village by the Gorges de l'Aveyron? Foreign holidaymakers flock to the Côte d'Azur, the Loire Valley, Paris and the long western coast. So where's the worry? *Tout va très bien*, and a tribe of official spokespeople will always tell you how the nation has pulled itself out of its difficulties and is set to help lead Europe into the next century. To ask too many questions is seen as an annoying Anglo-Saxon attempt to shoot holes in the glorious Gallic balloon. When I mentioned the uncertainties of the 35-hour working week during a dinner one night, an official told me curtly that I should look on the bright side and not deliver below-the-belt blows. Some might see the enormous range of governmental forecasts of the number of jobs to be created – anywhere from 300,000 to 1 million – as an indication of a certain lack of reliable forecasting, but the scheme's proponents prefer to extol the breadth of the horizons they are opening up.

That is in keeping with the rosy side of France, which may have been too obscured in the previous chapters. Whatever its travails, the Hexagon always has a rosy side, and one would be a fool not to make the most of it. Moving away from the famous attractions, take a trip to the big heart of the country from which only the most committed Francophobe could remain immune. The high-speed train from the Gare Montparnasse whisks us to a station outside Tours on the Loire. There is champagne before a family dinner in a sixteenth-century château overlooking a small lake where dozens of fish have just been caught. The last bottles of 1982 Lynch-Bages claret from the cellar in the limestone cliffs are brought across the courtyard in a plastic milk-bottle carrier by the château-owner, to accompany jellied chicken, roast lamb and goat's cheese. Strangely, he serves his wine in small tumblers, like shot glasses, rather than the usual expansive *verres à vin*. As we eat, he recalls how, as a teenager in the Resistance, he had helped in the first assassination of a Gestapo officer and rose to command a unit alongside André Malraux in 1944. He had helped people escape across the demarcation line not far from where we sat, and still keeps his *nom de guerre*. Many years later, having turned down offers of a political or journalistic career and established himself as a successful businessman, he took clients shooting in the Loire Valley and saw this small château. He asked about buying it, but was told that the path of a planned motorway would go through its grounds. The owner wanted to sell, but who in their right mind would buy? From time to time he talked about the place to friends from wartime days. One day, one of them, an official in a position to know, telephoned to say that the motorway had been moved. Our host drove round that afternoon, and bought the château in cash for a knock-down price. Corruption? Or a reward for risks taken so long ago? A dyed-in-the-wool capital-ist, he is a close friend of a Communist Resistance leader who lives down the valley.

Then comes an easy drive through the verdant hills of Indre-et-Loire and the Haute-Vienne to a country hotel in a converted mill, with ducks on the pond, a gentle path through the woods and two excellent meals from the wellsprings of French gastronomy. After that, a touch of grim history at the martyr town of Ouradour-sur-Glane, where the retreating Reich Division massacred 642 inhabitants, includ-ing 500 women and children, in 1944. And then, in a more sunny mood, a visit to the beautiful red sandstone village of Collonges-la-Rouge before driving gently down the highland roads to the town of Figeac, home of the great Egyptologist, Champollion. Finally, the journey ends at a small village where the hardy Auvergne meets the softer Rouergue for five days of French country life, walking, eating, drinking, trying to soak up some of that old-time country wisdom, and marathon sessions of the archetypal French card game of *belote*. Pigs roam free by the woods; mushrooms sprout beneath the trees; the calves have never had a mad mother. We wake one morning to the rich smell of *foie gras* cooking below our bedroom, and our host presents us with a huge terrine to be consumed at a single lunch. In contrast to the château in Touraine, the wine from the cellar below us is poured into glasses large enough to take a whole bottle. In the nearby small town of Maurs-la-Jolie, market day brings out more than two hundred stalls. Two elderly couples – one man with a beret, the other with an old straw hat, one stout woman in a floral dress, the other wearing her apron – sit outside a café sipping *pastis* and soft drinks as if posing for a postcard. An elderly woman sells punnets of wild mushrooms. A grizzled farmer weighs his vegetables on a hand-held scale. A young woman stands behind a table covered with jars of snail pâté. The smell of melons is in the air. The only thing missing is the tourists.

At the start of the trip back to England, the shrine of Rocamadour is as beautifully impressive as ever on its cliff-face; nearby a fairy-tale château rises above our hotel and the *carpaccio de canard aux truffes* served in a gravelled courtyard by a river could not be bettered. The train to the north from Brive-la-Gaillarde is on time at both ends. In Paris, under the summer sun, the Natural History museum in the Jardin des Plantes is a wonder to visit. Friends and relations are fit and happy on their return from holidays in Brittany. There is even some good news in the air: the Health Ministry reports that new AIDS cases and deaths have dropped by more than half in a year. A French pair reach the final of the world ping-pong championship. Wine exports are booming. For the umpteenth time, politicians say that they can even see a decline in unemployment not too far around the corner.

At the Café Croissant behind the Bourse, where the Socialist hero Jean Jaurès was assassinated in 1914, the Père Duval *andouillette* tripe sausage is, as they say, grilled to perfection. Badoit mineral water is served in its proper light-green glass bottle instead of the more usual plastic. The political gossip over lunch is as fascinatingly in-bred as ever, and there is yet another project to start the newspaper France really needs. Then comes a lingering walk through the Marché Saint-Honoré, where the revolutionary Jacobins of 1790 planned the modernist centralisation of the nation in the library of a convent. Down the street, past the Rubis bar with its tasty Loire wines, stands the dimly-lit church of Notre-Dame-de-l'Assomption, which was given to the Polish community of Paris in 1850 and to which we used to take aid bundles for Solidarity. Three people worship in the gloom inside, and a pigeon flies in and out with me. Along the Rue Saint-Honoré, the ornate jewelled eggs that once delighted the Tsarist court still decorate the Fabergé shop. Maxim's, the epitome of outmoded style fallen from fashion, lies to the left, just before the Place de la Concorde where Louis XVI and Marie-Antoinette, Robespierre and Danton lost their heads. In the other direction is the neo-classical pillared temple of the Madeleine and the ornate *boiseries* and 1,000-franc meals of Lucas-Carton. A genteel ladieswear shop has the English name of W. Beresford picked out in curling white lettering on a grey background. An old-fashioned glazier in blue overalls crosses the road with the glass slotted into a wooden frame on his back. The cars hoot, but he moves at his own pace.

Clustered round the crossing with the Rue Boissy d'Anglas stand the shops of the great fashion names – Hermès, Lanvin, Lagerfeld to start with, and then, on one side of the street, Givenchy, Guy Laroche, Yves Saint-Laurent, Jacques Fath; on the other, Cartier, Gianfranco Ferré, Oscar de la Renta, Valentino. The chauffeurs waiting outside the smart Cercle Interallié club have parked their cars on the pavement, all the way up to the Japanese, British and American embassies. Dior and Versace put in a last fashionable appearance before you arrive in front of the Élysée Palace, peering through the high metal gates at the glass front on the other side of the gravel courtyard where we reporters used to crowd round ministers and presidential visitors for a soundbite to enlighten the waiting world. Across the narrow street, you looked up at the whitewashed buildings and wondered whether there was a Jackal-check on their inhabitants.

Just up the road, across the Place Beauvau with its Pierre Cardin outlet on the corner, sits another formidable centre of French politics, the Interior Ministry, housed behind its own impressive set of gates in a fine old aristocratic town-house. This is where the police get their orders, elections are organised and the inter-ministerial telephone system is centralised. The walk ends a hundred yards further on, at perhaps the most soberly stylish of Parisian hotels, the Bristol, where some bathrooms are as big as the bedrooms, where a Rothschild strangled himself, and where a German Defence Minister left a sheaf of secret Nato papers in the bar after a long night of drinking.

There are a hundred other excursions through Paris, each with its own character. The capital's compact size and variety make it a great place for urban walking. To take any one part of the city is to taste only part of its essence, just as to take Paris as representative of the nation is to miss most of what makes France the country it is. Personally, as you may have guessed, I prefer to flee high fashion – *dîner au champagne* is not my cup of tea, as it were. I'd rather wander through the market in Maurs-la-Jolie, drink a *pastis* in Calvinet or eat *truffade* in the kitchen. But, when it comes to visible signs of style on the street, a stroll down this stretch of the Rue Saint-Honoré gives more than a clue to why, for all its present vicissitudes, France still has a special face to show the world.

So, is everything really all right, Madame La Marquise? Has France just become a national incarnation of Molière's *Malade Imaginaire*? Not if you listen to somebody with a special claim to know about what lies behind that special face:

> France is suffering from an illness that goes deeper than the political class, economic leaders, fashionable intellectuals or the media stars realise.
>
> The people have lost confidence. Their feeling of helplessness inclines them towards resignation; it also risks arousing their anger.
>
> More than half the French population is neither listened to nor defended. Five million live in a precarious condition; hundreds of thousands of young people search in vain for something to nourish what remains of their hopes.
>
> The poor get poorer, those on low salaries stagnate. Shopkeepers, artisans, professionals, small business people face growing problems. More and more households have trouble meeting the rent or repaying loans; more and more small firms, with little or no support from

the banks, are forced to declare themselves bankrupt or to cut staff.

In some rundown suburbs of big cities, whole districts are outside the law. The police cannot intervene effectively. A Mafia-style economy flourishes with impunity – drugs, prostitution, looting. For those living there, insecurity is a daily experience. They are afraid. The contagion born from this fear threatens our society.

Too many of the French feel that they are not understood, and are looked down upon. They, too, are afraid. Fear of unemployment which a return of growth will not be enough to conquer. Fear of losing their social benefits, their retirement rights, the possibility of giving their children a better future. Fear of feeling like orphans in a world without moral standards, and fear of being passive spectators of the decline of France.

Everybody knows that fear breeds paralysis. The political, economic and social workings of our country are affected by paralysis. All the indicators show up the symptoms – but no therapy is forthcoming because too many of our leaders work on the basis of statistics, not real life. And the statistics, in themselves, do not express the gravity of the social fracture which threatens national unity.

The gap is widening dangerously between the man in the street and a political class which offers the French people the spectacle of an interminable costume ball at which the waltzers parade in front of the cameras before going off to foment their little plots.

The reasons for this disrepute are not difficult to grasp. While the number of people excluded from society rises each day, speculators enrich themselves, the privileged class displays its venality and makeshift clans nurture ambitions which knowingly gloss over the increasingly sombre reality.

France is being sucked down because it is exploiting its trump cards badly. The French people have a wealth of intelligence, combativity and virtues. What our elites lack is the intellectual courage to call into question outdated beliefs and obsolete practices.

If the French give in to the temptation of conservatism, the worst can be feared. A great country can step out of history in the space of a generation, and experience a lasting decline. Nations can die. Let us hope that our compatriots choose hope, and thus change, and that France will remain a united, prosperous, peaceful and respected nation.

Or take another, shorter, diagnosis:

The earthquake is everywhere. On the left as well as the right. The
change in parliamentary majority is not a perspective which enthuses
the French. The voters expect nothing. It's the whole system that
they contest, and very rightly so. It is the job of politicians to know
how to manage this protest. There has been no ideological debate on
Europe since the referendum of 1992. In truth, the French recognise
two matters of fact. To begin with, that, for the first time for decades
and decades, their children will not perhaps live in a better world
than they do. That's a damn shock! They ask themselves why, and
nobody answers their question. Then there is the fact that they find,
facing them, men and women elected from the right, the left, the
centre who are like little green birds that have less and less grip on
things. Politics cannot improve people's lives. Our democratic system
is operating in a complete void.

The warnings did not come from professional doomsayers or outsiders
inveighing against the tide of events which we have seen in this book.
The first was written by Jacques Chirac as he fought his third battle for
the Élysée, the second by the man who would like to succeed him, and
was already leading France's biggest party of the right, Philippe Séguin.
Inspired by advisers alert to the divisions in French society, Chirac
had hit a large nail plumb on the head while Séguin drew a conclusion from the election which reached beyond the bounds of conventional politics. They each know that France badly needs the vision
thing – a means of rallying the bulk of the people behind a leader who
can offer a realistic prospect of reaching the end of the rainbow and of
restoring the vital fit between the Head of State and the country.
Short of a resurrection of that togetherness, the French cannot be
expected to do anything but fall prey to the divisions and pressures
crowding in from many sides. It is no longer a question of month-to-
month politics or of instant fixes, but of how to pull France back from
the cliff on which it finds itself.

It is illusory to expect France and the French to change their natures.
They will remain by turn charming and haughty, patriotic and chau-

vinistic, petty and grandiose, charming and brusque, witty and yet strangely lacking in a sense of humour. Still, the shift in the reality within which they live is undeniable. They are not an introspective people like the Germans, nor are they given to Slav melancholia or to the insularity of the British. But, like their fictional national templates from the musketeers onwards, they are self-regarding. How they see themselves is important, and what is currently on view in the national mirror is not greatly to their taste, for all the reasons set out in this book.

The glass is cracked; the frame of the state is fractured. Apart from the facts at issue, the Papon trial took on a special importance for the way in which it undermined the orthodox view of the most sensitive period of twentieth-century French history at just the wrong moment: when the present is so uncertain, the last thing you want is for the accepted wisdom about the past to be upset. In a different dimension, the tragic farce of Corsica shows the mother of all states being treated with derision by a bunch of hoodlums. The privileges of the elite stand out in ever-greater contrast to the exclusion of an ever-increasing number of ordinary citizens from the kind of life that modern society owes them. And it is not as if the Énarques and their peers have shown themselves invariably skilful at applying what they preach: for the years between 1995 and 1997, the social security deficit was almost double the official forecast. The wave of scandals has shown the depths of corruption and profiteering. The bigger the state grows, the less it seems able to perform its proper function: when truck-drivers and other professions ready to exercise their ability to tie up the country and hold it to ransom, comparisons with a dinosaur are inevitable. Pandering to pressure groups undermines the democratic rights of the majority. The commentator Jean-François Revel thunders against 'a country which is more and more statist, and less and less governed'. What the sociologist Alain Touraine sums up as corporatist resistance to change, and a senior civil servant stigmatises as a climate of civic and moral disintegration, produces a readiness to take direct action that splinters the system into myriad competing interest groups. Too often, high rhetoric about solidarity is a mask for corporatist selfishness, buttressed by the brutality of management which sees conflict as a natural way of running a business. Everybody lowers their expectations of others, all the way from the little frauds of everyday life to the pickings of the great and good. The resulting demoralisation discredits the state as much as it discourages and frustrates its citizens.

Some on the left draw a Marxist conclusion and detect a pattern of social conflict developing into a rolling cycle, affecting one sector of national life after another; others see France as being in an almost pre-revolutionary state of rebellion and paralysis. A leading historian, François Furet, explained the success of the Fifth Republic as springing from its artful synthesis of the pre-1789 Ancien Régime and the Revolution, combining the quasi-monarchical authority and the recognition of individual liberty, centralisation and regionalism under the umbrella of l'État. Now, the fear is that an imbalance has set in between the state as liberator and the state as dominator. In 1884, Georges Clemenceau warned: 'Yes! We have guillotined the King, long live the State-King! We have dethroned the Pope, long live the State-Pope! We have chased out God, and these men of the Right say, long live the State-God! . . . The state, I know it well, it has a long history, full of murder and blood. All the crimes that have been accomplished in the world, the massacres, the wars, the breaches of sworn faith, the stakes, the punishment, the tortures, all have been justified in the interests of the state, the *raison d'état*.' A century later, the State-King has fallen far below the presumptions which should give it legitimacy. It may not go for too many tortures, but appears to have played its role in massacres in the middle of Africa. The State-God has become nakedly politicised, and the supposed independence of its State-Papal civil service wanes by the year − 'the whole system politicises the officials, and encourages behaviour and scandals which the civil servants should not go along with', says one Énarque who has opted out of the system. 'France is not a banana republic, but, in some ways, it's heading in that direction.'

Above all, and in the worst of all worlds, this top-down society constructed on rules and hierarchies finds itself with a ruling class that, in the fashionable phrase, had become 'delegitimised' − and a President who humiliated himself in the most public manner imaginable. 'France,' says the political journalist, Alain Duhamel,

> is living in a culture of power which distinguishes it from other democracies and handicaps it. The crushing primacy of government on parliament − unique in Europe − the privileged position of mayors in relation to their municipal councils, of the presidents of

regional councils to their regional assemblies, and also, until recently, of the chairmen of public and private enterprises to their boards, all that bestows a great advantage on the executives *vis-à-vis* those who are meant to control them and act as counter-balances. France is afraid of the free market society. The judiciary is fighting step by step to win its independence. The regions are regarded as a threat to national unity. The level of social contributions and public spending reaches unprecedented proportions. The proliferation of rules and regulations is self-perpetuating. The passion for equality smothers risk-taking. This dependency culture, this fascination with the state – the protective big brother – nourishes the perpetual and puerile power of 'the French specialness'. What if this omnipresence was, on the contrary, the French handicap?

Hence the importance of the judiciary in providing some real control on those in power, as medicine for a sick democracy. The distance which Lionel Jospin had put between himself and the corruption of the late Mitterrand era gave him a strong moral card when he moved into the Hôtel Matignon, and the appointment of a Minister of Justice set on drawing a line between politics and the law gave cause for hope, particularly for those on the left who had made the wrenching conversion to market economics and were searching for a means of ensuring the equality of rights between rich and poor. Still there were hangovers from the past. The new Chairman of the National Assembly Finance Committee had, it should not be forgotten, been sentenced to two suspended jail terms for illicit fund-raising activities.

As a country which has always put great store on ideas while getting on with everyday life, France finds itself rudderless in this pragmatic end of century. If the old verities no longer hold much water, new ideas are often marginalised or not adopted in the first place. Jean-Marie Le Pen is not alone in condemning the ways of market-minded foreigners. A best-selling book entitled *L'Horreur économique* traces France's employment woes to the way in which 'cosmopolitan foreign thought has taken over our familiar world, and destroyed it'. Politicians and commentators attack *la pensée unique* – the single-minded marketplace approach to be found across the Atlantic and the

Channel which, according to some French pundits, could be blamed for the death of Diana, Princess of Wales. A couple of sentences from the omnipresent sociologist and historian Emmanuel Todd provide as good an example of the way in which French superiority banishes reality in pursuit of comforting images: 'As the French have watched the United States and Britain over the last twenty years, they've seen a society where there is mounting insecurity,' he writes. 'They see a deregulated society where unions have been eliminated, where the population is divided into winners and losers, and where the needs of those who are left out are increasingly neglected.'

What Todd and others are propounding is a view which may be paraphrased as follows: we are in trouble, but others are worse off. Our unemployment rate may be three times as high as in the United States, but ignore that: we are French and will find our own way ahead. 'We have our model and we plan to stick to it,' as Jacques Chirac told a summit of industrialised nations. 'We say yes to the market economy, but no to market society,' added Lionel Jospin in a speech in 1998 in which he called for a Europe-wide war against unemployment and social exclusion. Just as General de Gaulle set out to chart a 'third-way' international politics between East and West in the 1960s, so France will stand apart from the gadarene rush of the global market, and come up with 'the French exception' to light its way into the next millennium. No matter that, just as nobody else followed De Gaulle's road, so even a cursory examination of what is on offer from the proponents of the French model reveals an array of logical flaws that should have any true Cartesian blushing in shame.

Start with Todd's first point, insecurity. If there is one thing the French worry about it is insecurity in the workplace, in the streets, in their lives as a whole. Move on to the 'elimination' of unions – their membership as a proportion of the labour force is actually higher in both the United States and Britain than it is in France. Then comes the division into winners and losers: according to France's National Statistics Institute, incomes stagnated among the lowest-paid in the first half of the 1990s, grew rather more among those in the middle and jumped most among the best-off. Crucially, it is difficult to point a finger at other countries when you have one of the biggest groups of 'losers' in the developed world in the shape of more than 3 million unemployed and double that number in a state which researchers describe as 'precarious'. As for those who are left out of mainstream society, France is not exactly a model when it comes to the 'new poor', the men and women in their twenties who have never had a proper job in their lives, the 18 per cent of young households living in poverty, the three-quarters of a million unemployed – some of them heads of households – whose benefits put them below the official poverty line for a single person. The French may sneer at 'McJobs', but they haven't come up with much in the way of an alternative except to pump yet more tax-payers' money into job-creation that has no real work to go with it. When the MORI polling organisation conducted a European survey of what worried people most, the French were at least twice as concerned as the British about poverty, homelessness and race relations.

In the real world of the late twentieth century, France's protesta-tions that it has a special protective prescription to remedy its ills sound horribly like the announcement in 1986 that 'we will stop the Chernobyl cloud; it will not pass over France'. That cuts little ice with the unemployed, who see their plight evolving into a form of apartheid separating them from mainstream society and politics. Neither will it shield the big state monopolies from the opening-up of Europe's telecommunications, aviation and energy industries. In its purest form, says the economist Guy Sorman, the French model is 'a society with no money, no risks, no victims and where chance plays no part'. Or, as another economist, Pascal Salin, puts it: 'The failure of classical liberal ideas in France is not a case of these ideas being abandoned so much as them never having been really understood.'

Unconcerned with linguistic purity, some of the media fawn over 'les Golden Boys' of French business, but the head of one big bank could not restrain himself from noting how government policies were encouraging those whiz-kids to cross the Channel to England's more business-friendly environment. Tens of thousands of others have headed for Silicon Valley, along with some of France's high-tech firms – France, one of the emigrants told *Fortune* magazine, 'is a very enjoyable country to live in – if you don't have to work'. When *Business Week* drew up a list of Europe's fifty hottest small- to medium-sized firms which were creating jobs as well as sales, just six came from France. The government of Lionel Jospin is so worried about entrepreneurs moving to more tax-friendly countries that it wrote a 'poison pill' into the 1999 budget to put a 26 per cent capital gains levy on anybody who acted so upatriotically – at the same time, the administration postponed a move to cut the 40 per cent tax rate on share options under pressure from the Communists who denounced the idea of giving 'presents to the privileged'.

The Governor of the Bank of France may well call for his country to create its own Bill Gates, but imagine, as *Business Week* did, what Gates might find if he went to Paris to set up a business. In his morning newspaper, he reads of staff at a failed bank taking their boss hostage to avoid closure. Then he sees in a magazine that half France's youth dreams of joining the civil service. He watches a demonstration by transport workers demanding retirement at 55, learns that some public sector staff are on a 32-hour working week, and notes the number of failing firms bailed out by a government whose budget deficit tops $57 billion. 'Get me out of this place!' Gates cries, and tells his banker back home to invest in Poland instead.

Labour flexibility is a term the French dislike because of its 'anti-social connotation'. France may want to spawn innovative companies to provide both new hope and fuller employment, but it quails at the price to be paid, which many already find too high: more than half the jobs offered to the under-25s are on limited contracts. The overwhelming reaction to such trends is to seek a return to the old ways. 'Everything has its limits, including economic realism,' as the Chairman of the National Assembly Finance Commission put it, in an opinion which appeared somewhat double-edged when he was forced to resign his parliamentary seat shortly afterwards because of his involvement in an illegal funding scheme. France is not wrong to wish to enjoy job security as a right, to hanker for the solidarity of workers and to see shareholder pressure as a threat to its traditions. A study by three economists has confirmed the worst French fears about the American model – low-skilled, middle-aged workers in the US are eight times more likely to lose their jobs than similar people in France. But the sting in the tail of this study points to one reason for France's high unemployment: hirings per worker were six times higher in the US than in the Hexagon, so people who do lose their job are more likely to remain out of work in France than in America.

'When people ask the reason for my journeys, I usually reply that I know what I'm getting away from, but not what I am looking for.'

The remark by the sixteenth-century sage Michel de Montaigne might apply to France at the end of the twentieth century. It knows what it wants to escape from, but not what it seeks – or what it is ready to leave behind. There is too much posturing. The left is harpooned by the illusions born from its electoral promises, and the right drifts in disarray. Fear stalks the land. When the chairman of the employers' federation proclaims himself to be a 'killer of false ideas and illusions', it is the first word which grabs the headlines.

The prospect of a long *cohabitation* between a Gaullist President and a Socialist Prime Minister has presented a unique opportunity to forge a new form of government. Such an outcome would fly in the face of the divisions that had so characterised the nation and the politics of the previous twenty-five years. In that sense, it would be abnormal. But, if the current French model has reached the end of the road, it could offer a real alternative to continuing business as usual – if those concerned were ready to grasp the chance that the electorate had served up to move into a different gear. The dangers of an artificial consensus born of a conniving dictatorship of right and left are obvious. It could produce the ultimate victory of the hermetic political class, to the even greater disadvantage of the nation and its people. But the broad central *entente* running from the Gaullists to the mainstream left now looks strong enough to form the foundation for a different kind of politics, which would be much less ideological, less a prisoner of the state, more open-minded – and, dare one hope, less personalised.

This could enable the French to reconcile their individualism with their role as citizens, and their politicians to shed the equivocations that made life so easy for Le Pen, banishing the hydra-headed National Front to the margins. It could enable France to come properly to terms with its past as a flood of regret from professional bodies at the time of the Maurice Papon trial suggested that many may now be readier to do than when they were ruled by men who liked to pretend that Vichy was not France. It could reconcile the French left with the modern world. More broadly, it could enable the politicians to accept that the job of reducing unemployment, healing the social fracture, absorbing the effects of monetary union and making the immigrant community a real part of French life is a long-term task that can only be achieved if they put the petty, personalised warfare of the past behind them. If they were able to go even halfway along such a road, France would, truly, be forging a new and exceptional model to present to the world and, far more important, to itself.

Much of what has been written in this book might lead to the conclusion that any such attempt is yet another instance of the self-deceptive, dreaming 'national Bovaryism' we picked up on in the first chapter. The mirror in which the French look at themselves may, indeed, be badly cracked; still, it can be repaired if the will is there. As a start, they have to rub the glass to get a clear image of where they are. For all the books and magazine covers on the ills besetting France, there is still a strong strand of national denial when it comes to recognising how the world has changed. But the French have to confront the implications of a future which lies in an increasingly integrated continent, bringing with it responsibilities and challenges. For all the pull of rural life and tradition, they have to come to grips with the modern nature of their nation. The state and the politicians have to free themselves from the grasp of lobbies, and to be ready to face down sectorial interests in the name of the people as a whole. Public morality has to triumph over corruption, requiring higher standards from those in power and restoring the notion of fraternity to the land of the Revolution. Lionel Jospin has made an encouraging start in the right direction, but he remains inhibited by some old habits that are proving all too powerful. The role of the state has to be re-thought – in the words of the economist Alain Minc, to be 'less of a shield and more of a sword of justice'. Government has to see itself an enabler of the individual genius of its people. The political class has to rediscover its public service role. The elite has to become more open to the world and its ideas. For, despite the uncertainties crowding in on it, this nation does remain special, and special places need to be able to rise to special heights to remain exceptional. It is time for a fresh revolution following a non-violent but sharply determined path which embraces the modern world while preserving the best of the past. Otherwise, the beacon from this lighthouse nation will grow dim as France implodes on the problems it cannot bring itself to face – and Europe and the world will be poorer places as a result.

BIBLIOGRAPHY

Alexandre, Philippe, *L'Élysée en péril* (Paris: Fayard, 1969)
——, *Le Duel De Gaulle–Pompidou* (Paris: Grasset, 1970)
Alexandre, Philippe, with Priouret, Roger, *Marianne et le pot au lait* (Paris: Grasset, 1983)
——, *Paysages de campagne* (Paris: Grasset, 1988)
Ardagh, John, *The New France* (London: Penguin, 1977 and later editions)
Attali, Jacques, *Verbatim* (Paris: Fayard, two volumes, 1993–96)
Bacqué, Raphaëlle, and Saverot, Denis, *Seul comme Chirac* (Paris: Grasset, 1997)
Barnett, Correlli, *Bonaparte* (London: Wordsworth, 1997)
Benamou, Georges, *Le Dernier Mitterrand* (Paris: Plon, 1997)
Booth, Martin, *Opium* (London: Simon & Schuster, 1996)
Bredin, Jean-Denis, *L'Affaire* (Paris: Julliard, 1983)
Brigouleix, Bernard, *Histoire indiscrète des années Balladur* (Paris: Albin Michel, 1995)
Brogan, Denis, *The Development of Modern France* (London: Hamish Hamilton, 1940)
Chirac, Jacques, *La France pour tous* (Paris: Nil, 1994)
Colombani, Jean-Marie, *La France sans Mitterrand* (Paris: Flammarion, 1992)
——, *Le Résident de la République* (Paris: Stock, 1998)
Dallas, Gregor, *At the Heart of a Tiger* (London: Macmillan, 1993)
de Gaulle, Charles, *Le Fil de l'épée* (Paris: Berger-Levrault, 1932)
——, *Mémoires d'espoir* (Paris: Plon, two volumes, 1970–71)
Domenach, Nicolas, and Szafran, Maurice, *Le Roman d'un Président* (Paris: Plon, 1997)
Dubief, Henri, *Le Déclin de la IIIe République* (Paris: Seuil, 1976)
Duhamel, Alain, *La République giscardienne* (Paris: Gallimard, 1980)
——, *La République de Monsieur Mitterrand* (Paris: Gallimard, 1982)
——, *Le Complexe d'Astérix* (Paris: Gallimard, 1985)
L'État de la France (Paris: La Découverte, 1992)

Ferniot, Jean, *De Gaulle et le 13 mai* (Paris: Plon, 1965)

Forrester, Viviane, *L'Horreur économique* (Paris: Fayard, 1996)

Giesbert, Franz-Olivier, *François Mitterrand, ou La Tentation de l'histoire* (Paris: Seuil, 1987)

——, *Jacques Chirac* (Paris: Seuil, 1987)

——, *Le Président* (Paris: Seuil, 1990)

——, *François Mitterrand: Une Vie* (Paris: Seuil, 1997)

Giscard d'Estaing, Valéry, *Démocratie française* (Paris: Fayard, 1976)

——, *Deux Français sur trois* (Paris: Flammarion, 1984)

——, *Le Pouvoir et la Vie* (Paris: Interforum, 1988)

Gubler, Claude, *Le Grand Secret* (Paris: Plon, 1996)

Hayward, Susan, and Vincendeau, Ginette, *French Film* (London: Routledge & Kegan Paul, 1990)

Hobsbawm, E. J., *The Age of Capital* (London: Weidenfeld & Nicolson, 1975)

——, *The Age of Empire* (London: Weidenfeld & Nicolson, 1987)

Horne, Alistair, *To Lose a Battle: France, 1940* (London: Macmillan, 1969)

——, *A Savage War of Peace* (London: Macmillan, 1977)

Imbert, Claude, and Julliard, Jacques, *La Droite et la Gauche* (Paris: Laffont/Grasset, 1995)

James, Colin, *France* (Cambridge: CUP, 1994)

Jamet, Dominique, *Demain le Front?* (Paris: Bartillat, 1995)

Jarreau, Patrick, *La France de Chirac* (Paris: Flammarion, 1995)

——, *Chirac: La malédiction* (Paris: Stock, 1997)

Jarreau, Patrick, with Kergoat, Jacques, *François Mitterrand: 14 ans de pouvoir* (Paris: Éditions Le Monde, 1995)

Jeanneney, Jean-Noël, *L'Argent caché* (Paris: Fayard, 1981)

Johnson, Michael, *French Resistance* (London: Cassell, 1996)

Julliard, Jacques, *La Cinquième République* (Paris: Seuil, 1976)

Klein, Richard, *Cigarettes are Sublime* (London: Picador, 1995)

Lacouture, Jean, *De Gaulle* (Paris: Seuil, three volumes, 1984–86)

Lavigne family, *Cousins d'Auvergne* (Aurillac: Association Cousins d'Auvergne, 1995)

Lévy, Claude, and Tillard, Paul, *La Grande Rafle du Vél d'Hiv* (Paris: Laffont, 1992)

Maîtres Cuisiniers de France, *Les Recettes du terroir* (Paris: Laffont, 1984)

Maspero, François, *Les Passagers du Roissy-Express* (Paris: Seuil, 1990)

Mauriac, François, *De Gaulle* (Paris: Grasset, 1964)

McLynn, Frank, *Napoleon* (London: Jonathan Cape, 1998)

Mermet, Gérard, *Francoscopie* (Paris: Larousse, 1994 and later editions)

Minc, Alain, *Le Nouveau moyen âge* (Paris: Gallimard, 1993)

Minc, Alain, and the Commissariat Général du Plan, *La France de l'an 2000* (Paris: Odile Jacob, 1994)

Mitterrand, Danielle, *En toutes libertés* (Paris: Ramsay, 1996)

Mitterrand, François, *Le Coup d'État permanent* (Paris: Plon, 1964)

——, *Ma Part de vérité* (Paris: Fayard, 1969)

——, *La Rose au poing* (Paris: Flammarion, 1973)

Mitterrand, François, *La Paille et le Grain* (Paris: Flammarion, 1975)

Moïsi, Dominique, 'The Trouble With France' in *Foreign Affairs* (New York, May/June 1998)

Le Monde, *La Droite sans partage: Élections législatives, 1993* (Paris: Éditions Le Monde, 1993)

——, *La Cinquième République* (Paris: Éditions Le Monde, 1995)

Montaldo, Jean, *Mitterrand et les 40 voleurs* (Paris: Albin Michel, 1994)

Monnet, Jean, *Mémoires* (Paris: Fayard, 1976)

Nay, Catherine, *Le Double Mépris* (Paris: Grasset, 1980)

——, *Le Noir et le Rouge* (Paris: Grasset, 1984)

L'Observatoire français des conjonctures économiques, *L'Économie française, 1997* (Paris: La Découverte, 1997)

Paxton, Robert, *Vichy France* (New York: Columbia University Press, 1972)

Péan, Pierre, *Une Jeunesse française: François Mitterrand, 1934–47* (Paris: Fayard, 1994)

Peyrefitte, Alain, *Le Mal français* (Paris: Plon, 1977)

——, *Quand la Rose se fanera* (Paris: Plon, 1983)

Pingeot, Mazarine, *Premier Roman* (Paris: Julliard, 1998)

Pompidou, Georges, *Pour Rétablir une vérité* (Paris: Flammarion, 1982)

Rol-Tanguy and Bourderon, Roger, *Libération de Paris* (Paris: Hachette, 1994)

Ross, George; Hoffmann, Stanley; and Malzacher, Sylvia, *The Mitterrand Experiment* (Oxford: Polity, 1987)

Tournoux, Jean-Raymond, *Pétain et De Gaulle* (Paris: Plon, 1964)

——, *La Tragédie du Général* (Paris: Plon, 1967)

Viansson-Ponté, Pierre, *Histoire de la République gaullienne* (Paris: Fayard, two volumes, 1970–71)

Weber, Eugen, *Peasants into Frenchmen* (Stanford, CA: Stanford University Press, 1976)

Werth, Alexander, *De Gaulle* (London: Penguin, 1965)

Willard, Claude, *La France ouvrière* (Paris: Editions Ouvrières, 1995)

Williams, Charles, *The Last Great Frenchman* (London: Little, Brown, 1993)

Williams, Philip, and Harrison, Martin, *Politics and Society in De Gaulle's Republic* (London: Longman, 1971)

Winock, Michel, *Histoire de l'extrême droite en France* (Paris: Seuil, 1993)

——, *Parlez-moi de la France* (Paris: Plon, 1995)

Zeldin, Theodore, *France, 1848–1914* (Oxford: Clarendon Press, two volumes, 1973–77)

——, *The French* (London: Collins Harvill, 1983)

I have also drawn extensively on the French press. Apart from the daily recording of events by *Le Monde*, *Libération* and *Le Figaro*, various passages in this book owe a particular debt to the reporting by *L'Express* during 1997–98.

The annual *Quid* almanac is a unique reference book. It has been invaluable to me in a hundred or more ways. I remain astonished by the way that a country whose books rarely contain even the most cursory of indexes can have created such a treasure. But then, this is a land of paradoxes.

INDEX

Académie Française, 28–9
accordions, 85
Adidas, 173
Africa, 34–9, 164–5, 170, 199, 202–3
ageing population, 43, 50
agriculture: in Corsica, 308–9; farm
    incomes, 117–18; intensification,
    110–11; rural life, 95, 99–101, 106;
    rural depopulation, 110–11;
    subsidies, 117–18, 119; *see also* food
Agriculture Ministry, 99–100, 281
Aimargues, 187
Air France, 6, 69, 81, 150, 311, 347
L'Air Liquide, 143
Alcatel–Alsthom, 153–4, 156, 158–9,
    172
alcohol, 21, 89–91
Algeria, 138, 185, 195, 196, 203, 214,
    270, 272
Algérie Française, 241, 270, 323
Alps, 103–4, 106
Alsace, 285, 286
Alsace-Lorraine, 314–15
Alsthom, 346
American National Can, 351
Amiens, 183–4
Amri, Imed, 190, 193
Andorra, 4, 305
Angola, 165
anti-Semitism, 215–28, 235, 268, 269,
    376

Arabs, 194, 198–9, 203–4, 206–7, 208
Aragon, Louis, 137
ARC (cancer charity), 63
Argenteuil, 190
Ariane estate, Nice, 186–7
arms industry, 154–5, 359–60
Arnault, Bernard, 143
Arnoult, Éric, 36
Atlantic Arc, 285
Attali, Jacques, 20, 74, 353, 385
Aubry, Martine, 42
Audit Court, 160, 161, 166–7, 331,
    332–3
Auschwitz, 216, 222, 224
Australia, 248–9, 250
Auvergne, 110
Avallon, 127
Aveyron, 102–3
AXA–UAP, 7, 44, 143, 144, 158

baguettes, 82–4
bakers, 82–4
Balladur, Édouard, 171, 264, 357, 414;
    background, 71, 390; and Chirac,
    389–92, 403, 404; loses farm votes,
    100; presidential ambitions, 233,
    391–3, 394, 395–6, 397, 398; as
    Prime Minister, 356, 390, 391;
    privatisations, 157
Balzac, Honoré de, 84, 95, 97, 256, 263,
    273

Bank of France, 46, 48, 78, 121, 401, 432
banks, 44–5, 145–9
banlieues, 180–208
Banque Nationale de Paris, 156
Barbie, Klaus, 218, 219, 268
Bardot, Brigitte, 11, 196, 372
Barre, Raymond, 295, 310, 341, 342, 388–9, 392
Barril, Paul, 364
Basques, 305
Bastille Opéra, 25, 54
Bayrou, François, 418
Beaujolais, 90
Beaune, 91
Beauvoir, Simone de, 41, 269, 289
Bébéar, Claude, 158
Benguigui, Yamina, 203–4
Bérégovoy, Pierre, 346–7, 348–51, 353, 354, 355–7, 358, 363, 365
berets, 81–2
beurs, 203–4
Bidermann, Maurice, 163–4, 166, 167
bidets, 92
Billancourt, 130–1, 132–3, 134
birth rate, outside marriage, 50
Blair, Tony, 53, 60, 253, 261, 262, 282
Blanc, Jacques, 417–18
Blois, 184–5
Blum, Léon, 121, 349, 369
Bokassa, Emperor Jean Bedel, 34–5, 64, 337
Bonassoli, Aldo, 331–2
Bongo, Omar, 38–9, 52, 165, 167, 170–1, 334
Bordeaux, 91, 179, 225, 279, 285, 294
Bosnia, 4, 19, 196, 197
Botton, Pierre, 177
Boublil, Alain, 346, 347, 352–3
Bousquet, René, 375, 376–7, 378–80
Boutros-Ghali, Boutros, 30–1
bread, 82–4
Brest, 287
bribes, 64, 65, 67, 158, 161, 168–9
Britain: Common Market membership, 12; and European Union, 400; relations with the French, 250–66
Brittany, 94, 286, 305

Budget Ministry, 174
buildings, disrepair, 24
Bundesbank, 48, 317, 401
bureaucracy, 77; *see also* civil servants
Burgundy, 90, 91

cafés, 84–5, 87
Calvet, Jacques, 72
Calvinet, 112–16
cancer, lung, 86
Cannes, 65
Cantona, Éric, 11, 261
capital gains levy, 431–2
Carignon, Alain, 66, 67
cars, 15–16, 130–5
Catholic Church, 21, 22, 63, 194, 221, 267–8
Caze, Christophe, 196–8, 201
Central African Republic, 34–5, 38, 64, 337
Cévennes, 101–2
Chaban-Delmas, Jacques, 293, 294, 295, 322, 323, 325, 327, 389
Chagall, Marc, 298
Chalandon, Albin, 331–2
Chambon-sur-Lignon, 271
Champagne, 91
Channel Tunnel, 252, 261
Charente, 96
Charette, Hervé de, 418
charities, 62, 63
Château-Chinon, 294, 374–5
Chavet, Christine, 41
cheese, 302–3
chefs, 93, 101–3, 304
Chevènement, Jean-Pierre, 73, 123
Chiappe, Jean, 307
China, 359–60, 383
Chirac, Bernadette, 97, 403
Chirac, Claude, 405, 409
Chirac, Jacques, 31, 45, 51, 95–6, 151, 268, 270, 276, 356, 387–91, 426; accepts guilt of Vichy regime, 222; affairs, 251; and Africa, 36, 38; and agriculture, 100; allegations of scandal, 68–9; and the role of the state, 282; baguette consumption, 84; and Balladur, 389–92, 403, 404;

Chirac, Jacques – *cont.*
 character, 57–8; *cohabitation*, 274,
  350, 411–12, 433; Corsican
  support, 286; and Elf oil company,
  164, 165, 171; and ÉNA, 71, 76;
  European policy, 47, 75; and
  Giscard d'Estaing, 328, 330–1,
  333–4, 336–7; and immigration,
  207–8; on importance of the state,
  277; Mayor of Paris, 287–8, 290–3,
  295, 336–7; 1981 presidential
  election, 338–40; 1988 presidential
  election, 388–9; 1995 presidential
  election, 232, 233, 393–4, 396–7;
  1997 legislative elections, 47–8, 49,
  59–60, 140, 405–9, 411; 1998
  regional elections, 417; nuclear
  tests, ix–x, 59, 243, 244, 245, 247,
  248, 265; prefers beer to wine, 89;
  as President, 56–60, 398–415;
  privatisation, 149; relations with
  Germany, 316; rise to power, 318,
  326–8, 341, 388; and the RPR,
  334–6; rural roots, 97–8; transport
  policy, 163; unpopularity, 114; and
  urban problems, 183–4
Churchill, Winston, 257
CIC bank, 150
cigarettes, 86–9
cinema, 4, 16, 26–7, 89, 121, 179, 297
cities, 179–208
Citroën, 15–16
civil servants, 71–9, 150–1, 278–9,
 281–2
Clemenceau, Georges, 281, 409, 428
Clinton, Bill, 12, 38, 59, 71, 251, 412
Club Méditerranée, 24, 93, 246
cohabitation, 55, 149, 213, 274, 350, 412,
 433
coins, 92
Colbert, Jean-Baptiste, 144, 277
Cold War, 12, 245
Colley, Linda, 255
colonies, 32–9
Comiti, Pierre, 307
Common Agricultural Policy, 117
Common Market, 12, 46, 258–9
Communist Party, 135–42; in local

government, 295; in Marseille, 299,
 300; Mitterrand defeats, 139–40,
 323; 1997 elections, 49, 141; and
 the Resistance, 122; under
 Marchais, 138–9
Compagnie Générale d'Électricité, 153
Compagnie Générale des Eaux, 153,
 154
companies, 431–2; empire-building,
 152–5; ÉNA and, 75; executive pay,
 157–8; foreign investment, 156–7;
 international competitiveness,
 143–4; privatisation, 149–51;
 scandals, 158–9; shareholders,
 155–6; stock market value, 43–4;
 taxation, 144–5; *see also* economy;
 industry
Competition Council, 161
computers, 45, 283
Confédération Générale du Travail
 (CGT), 137, 299, 300
Congo, Republic of, 164–5
conservatism, 52–3
Constitutional Council, 311
Corbeil-Essonne, 180–1, 196
corps d'état, 71
corruption, 64–70, 158, 161, 168–9
 Corsica, 286, 305–14, 427
Côte d'Azur, 93
Coty, René, 221
Council of State, 162
country life, 95–119
Crédit Agricole, 44, 314
Crédit Lyonnais, 145–9, 166, 172, 173,
 176
Cresson, Édith, 39, 40, 42, 338, 354, 355
Creuse department, 109, 110
crime, 19, 92, 189, 193, 196, 231, 291
Croix-Chevalier estate, Blois, 184–5
Crozemarie, Jacques, 63
cults, 22
culture, 26–7
Culture Ministry, 26
Cuq, Henri, 200

Daladier, Édouard, 257, 293
Daniel, Sara, 198
Danone, 143

Dassault, Serge, 180, 182
de Gaulle, Charles, 1, 2, 3, 275, 297,
  329, 370, 371, 406; and Algeria,
  270; chauvinism, 144; and divisions
  in French society, 270–1, 274, 280;
  Fifth Republic, 374; foreign policy,
  138; and France's international role,
  11, 400, 401, 430; Free French,
  11–12, 257, 268; on importance of
  the state, 277; loses power, 318–21,
  340; 1968 unrest, 135; nuclear
  weapons, 243, 244; as President, 55;
  relations with Britain, 258–9, 260;
  and the Resistance, 122, 226;
  unifying role, 317; women's rights,
  40; working-class support, 123
death rates, 86
Debré, Michel, 72
defence industry, 154–5, 359–60
Defence Ministry, 25, 155
Defferre, Gaston, 296, 298–301, 321,
  373
deflation, 61
Delors, Jacques, 42, 123, 259, 322, 344,
  347, 354, 392, 396, 407
democracy, 45–6, 51
demonstrations, 46, 79, 106, 286–7
depopulation, rural, 109–11
deputies, 293
Desplechin, Arnaud, 236
Dessange, Jacques, 127
Deutsche Bank, 147
Devedjian, Patrick, 215, 280
discount shopping, 127–9
divisions in French society, 267–77, 317
dogs, 193, 288
Doisneau, Robert, 84, 85
Dom-Toms, 32–4
Doriot, Jacques, 137, 139
d'Ornano, Michel, 336
Drancy, 216–17, 220, 226
Dreux, 131–2
Dreyfus Affair, 226–7, 268, 275
La Droite, 418
drugs, 21, 45, 192, 197, 198–9, 298, 308
Duclos, Jacques, 137, 138
Duhamel, Alain, 428–9
Dumas, Roland, 169, 358–60

Durafour, Michel, 227

École Nationale d'Administration
  (ÉNA), 71–80, 311
École Normale Supérieure, 75
economy: deficit-reduction measures,
  48; Maastricht Treaty, 401, 412; in
  Mitterrand's presidency, 347;
  problems, 42–5, 61–2; successes, 6,
  42; taxation, 151–2; under Chirac,
  401–2; and unemployment, 42–3
ÉDF see Électricité de France
education, 27–8; École Nationale
  d'Administration, 71–2, 77–8;
  Grandes Écoles, 70–2, 74; lycée
  schools, 2, 27; Muslim schools, 194,
  195; the state and, 281; violence in
  schools, 189; and youth crime, 193
Education Ministry, 27–8, 189
elections, 45–6, 49, 51
Électricité de France (ÉDF), 151
Elf Aquitaine, 38, 44, 135, 143, 156,
  164–72, 331–3, 359, 360
employment: job insecurity, 43, 61–2,
  430, 432; racism, 208; rural
  depopulation, 110; working hours,
  42, 48, 432; see also unemployment
ÉNA see École Nationale
  d'Administration
Énarques, 72–80, 427
Épinay-sur-Seine, 188
Eridania Béghin-Say, 71
Érignac, Claude, 306, 309, 312, 313–14
'l'État', 73, 277–83, 295, 428, 434
European Central Bank, 13, 46
European Commission, 148, 248, 259
European Community, 347
European Investment Bank, 74
European Monetary System, 328
European Parliament, 175, 177, 230
European Union, 31, 46–9, 400–1
Eurotunnel, 156; see also Channel
  Tunnel
Ex-Servicemen's Ministry, 281
executive pay, 157–8

Fabius, Laurent, 71, 77, 156–7, 348, 350
Fagegaltier sisters, 102–3, 303

Fargue, Léon-Paul, 84
farming see agriculture
fashion, 10–11, 423
fast food, 85–6
Faure, Edgar, 377
Fifth Republic, 123, 136, 138, 321, 328–9, 374, 387, 428
films, 4, 16, 26–7, 89, 121, 179, 297
Finance Ministry, 74, 354
financial institutions, 44–5, 118, 145–9, 155
First World War, 109, 120, 225, 244, 297, 307, 376
fishing, 111
Foccart, Jacques, 35, 37, 38, 165
Folz, Jean-Martin, 71
food, 4, 9–10; agriculture, 100–1, 106; bread, 82–4; British attitudes to, 262–3; cafés, 84–5; fast-food outlets, 85–6; foie gras, 18, 92, 114; French fries, 93; garlic, 92; regionalism, 271, 301–3, 304; restaurants, 93, 100, 101–3, 272, 286, 301, 304; rural food, 101–3
force de frappe, 243–50
foreign investment, 6, 156–7
Foreign Ministry, 34
Fourth Republic, 122, 135, 269, 373–4
France, Anatole, 271
France Telecom, 150
franchises, 127
La Francophonie, 29–31
Free French, 11–12, 257
Fresnes-sur-Escaut, 124
Fried, Eugen, 136–8, 139
frontiers, 304–5, 314
Frossard, André, 264
Fry, Varian, 297–8

Gabon, 38, 165–6, 167, 170–1, 334
Gaddis, William, 290
Galéron, Roger, 222–3, 224
gangs, 187, 189, 190–2, 206
Garaud, Marie-France, 322–3, 325, 327–8, 329–30, 334–5, 336, 338, 390, 391
garlic, 92
Gates, Bill, 45, 432

Gaudin, Jean-Claude, 186, 301, 417
Gaulle, Charles de see de Gaulle, Charles
Gaullism: and Balladur, 392–3; Chirac and, 327–8, 387, 388, 400–1; divisions within, 273; Giscard d'Estaing and, 329; lack of ideology, 415–16; 1997 legislative elections, 408; and the RPR, 335
Gauloises, 88
Gauls, 283, 317
Germany: and Anglo-French relations, 256–7; Chirac and, 400–1; relations with France, 265, 314–17; see also Occupation
Giscard d'Estaing, Valéry, 387, 388, 396; affairs, 251; and Chirac, 328, 330–1, 333–4, 336–7; economic crisis, 61; and ÉNA, 71; 1981 presidential election, 337–41; 1995 presidential election, 394–5; and Omega device, 331–3; as President, 55, 328–34, 337; Puy-de-Dôme by-election, 341–2; rise to power, 318, 323–6; scandals, 64; and the UDF, 416
Gitanes, 88, 89
Givors, 189
government: cohabitation, 55, 149, 213, 274, 350, 412, 433; corruption, 64–70; disillusion with, 45–9; Énarques, 72–80; Presidents, 54–60, 274, 317; Prime Ministers, 274; and privatisation, 149; the state, 277–83; women ministers, 28–9, 41; see also local government
Grandes Écoles, 71–2, 74, 154, 281
Greene, Graham, 66
Greenpeace, 383
Grenoble, 66, 67
Grigny, 188
Grossouvre, François de, 340, 361–5
Gubler, Dr Claude, 381, 382, 384
Guigou, Élisabeth, 39, 40, 42
guns, 188, 190, 191
Guyana, 7, 33–4

Haberer, Jean-Yves, 148
Hachette, 143
hairdressers, 127

Halter, Marek, 235
health care, 21
Heath, Edward, 259
Hersant, Robert, 375, 378
Hitler, Adolf, 121–2, 137, 138, 238, 257, 265
holidays, 93–4, 121, 263
Holocaust, 217, 227, 228
homosexuality, 50–1
Horowitz, Jules, 332
housing estates, 180–7, 188–92, 207
Hue, Robert, 140, 141
hunting, 96
hypermarkets, 126–7, 128

Ibsa, 145–6
Île-de-France, 287, 291, 416
immigration, 199–208; Arabs, 194, 198–9, 203–4, 206–7, 208; *banlieues*, 131–2, 202–3; Jews, 224; National Front and, 51, 211, 212, 213–15, 226, 229–30, 233–4; racism, 19, 51, 187, 196, 201, 205–8, 226; religion, 200–1; slang, 204–5; treatment of immigrants, 199–200; unemployment and, 123–4, 132
income tax, 151–2
Independent Republican party, 324, 329
Indochina, 214, 308
Indre department, 110
industry: car industry, 130–5; defence industry, 154–5; foreign investment, 6, 156–7; multinational companies, 6–7, 44; privatisation, 132, 149–51; unemployment, 123–4, 125; *see also* companies
Inspecteurs des Finances, 73, 133
Interior Ministry, 423–4
invasions, 304–5
Islam, 194–7, 201, 272, 288
Ivory Coast, 168

Jaffré, Philippe, 171
Japan, 247–8
Jarnac, 367, 383
Jaurès, Jean, 227
Jews, 63, 201; anti-Semitism, 215–28, 235–36, 268, 269, 376; Bousquet

and, 377, 379; German Occupation, 103–5, 279, 375; immigration, 199; Papon and, 339; *see also* Dreyfus Affair
Joan of Arc, 11, 22, 25, 211, 254, 260
Johnson, Douglas, 121
Joly, Eva, 167–72, 177
Jospin, Lionel, 53, 55, 241, 268, 358, 429, 431; character, 407; *cohabitation*, 274, 411–12, 433; and the Communists, 141; and Dreyfus Affair, 226–7; and ÉNA, 71; holidays, 93–4; 1995 presidential election, 396; 1997 legislative elections, 49, 60, 405, 406, 407–8, 409–10, 411; reduces *cumul des mandats*, 293; working hours reduction, 48
Joxe, Pierre, 354
Juillet, Pierre, 322–3, 325, 327–8, 329–30, 334–5, 336, 338, 340, 390
Juppé, Alain, 71, 151, 398; and Chirac, 69; and Corsica, 311; economic policy, 401, 402; immigration policy, 213–14; as Mayor of Bordeaux, 294, 295; 1995 presidential election, 394, 414; 1997 legislative elections, 406–7, 408–9, 411; as Prime Minister, 402; unpopularity, 79–80, 289, 291; urban problems, 183; women ministers, 41
Justice Ministry, 41–2

Kelkal, Khaled, 185, 195, 201, 238
Kennedy, John F., 12, 259
KGB, 68, 139, 290
Kiejman, Georges, 379
Klarsfeld, Serge, 218, 378
Kohl, Helmut, 170, 316, 384

Lacharrière, Marc de, 72
La Martellière, 105
Lang, Jack, 26, 228
language, 17, 28–32, 204–5, 261–2
La Rochelle, 294, 387
Laval, Pierre, 187, 225, 269
Lavigne, Joseph, 112

Le Chambon-sur-Lignon, 103
Le Chevalier, Jean-Marie, 235
Leclerc, Édouard, 129
Le Floch-Pringent, Loïk, 163–4, 166–9,
    172, 177
Léotard, François, 395, 418
Le Pen, Jean-Marie, 66, 174, 226–42,
    243, 250, 305, 429, 433; anti-
    Semitism, 226–8; character, 233–4;
    growing popular support for
    National Front, 51–2, 209–15,
    230–3, 242; and Mégret, 239–40;
    1995 presidential election, 232–3,
    396, 397; 1997 legislative elections,
    410–11; 1998 regional elections,
    417, 418; public meetings, 209–11
Le Roy-Ladurie, Emmanuel, 2, 96, 277
Lesnes, Corine, 124
Levêque, Jean-Maxime, 145–6, 177, 353
Liberation, 121–2, 138, 217, 269
Lille, 159–61, 179, 197, 315
Limousin, 271
literacy, 28
literature, 5, 27, 95–6, 179
local government, 293–5; corruption,
    64–6; Paris, 290–1; regions, 286;
    under National Front, 234–7
Loire Valley, 184
Longo, Jeannie, 40–1
L'Oréal, 143
lottery, 159, 177
Louis XIV, King, 2, 86, 144, 267
Louvre, Paris, 56, 288, 292–3
Lucet, René, 299–300
lung cancer, 86
LVMH group, 7, 143
lycée schools, 2, 27
Lyon, 51, 179, 187, 189, 195, 224, 233,
    282, 295

Maastricht Treaty (1992), 47, 48, 140,
    152, 210, 258, 276, 355, 389, 394,
    400, 401, 404, 412, 414, 415
McDonald's, 85–6, 114, 127, 265
Macmillan, Harold, 12, 258–9, 270
Madelin, Alain, 76, 280, 394, 399, 413,
    415, 418
mafia, 64–5

Major, John, 59, 255
Malraux, André, 26, 88, 264, 421
Mammouth, 127
Manichaean heresy, 267, 271
Marchais, Georges, 138–9, 140, 141
Marcon, Régis, 101
Marianne, 2, 278
Marlboro, 88
marriage, 50
Marseille, 174, 179, 185–6, 187, 196,
    201, 233, 287, 296–301, 308
Masons, 272
Maspero, François, 203
Massif Central, 101
Mauroy, Pierre, 159, 162, 295, 350
Maxwell, Robert, 145, 147
mayors, 293–5
Médecin, Jacques, 65–6, 295
Médecins Sans Frontières, 4, 247
media, 283
Mégret, Bruno, 236, 238–40, 241, 410,
    411, 417,
Mendès-France, Pierre, 226, 269, 321,
    350, 373
Mercier, Philippe, 400
Merisiers estate, Trappes, 184
Metz, 20, 51, 179
MGM (film studio), 45, 147
Michelin, 92, 125, 143
Milice, 219, 225, 242
Millon, Charles, 417–18
Minc, Alain, 64, 66, 80, 434
Minitel, 22, 45, 111, 283
Mitterrand, Christophe, 36
Mitterrand, Danielle, 345, 346, 366,
    371–2, 381, 382
Mitterrand, François, 255, 268, 283,
    366–86; and Africa, 35–6; and
    agriculture, 99–100; Bastille Opéra,
    25; and Bérégovoy, 350–1, 353, 354,
    356–7; and Bernard Tapie, 173,
    174, 178; building projects, 7, 56,
    382, 384; cancer, 380–3, 393;
    cohabitation, 274, 275, 350; and
    Communists, 136, 139–40; and
    Corsica, 310–11; and De
    Grossouvre, 361–5; death, 382–3;
    defeats Communists, 323; denies

state's responsibilities for Jews in the war, 221; early life, 367–72; economic crisis, 123; and Énarques, 73, 75; and Germany, 315, 316; Giscard defeats, 325–6; illegitimate daughter, 363, 366, 369–70; and the Louvre, 292; love-life, 369–71; Maastricht Treaty, 276, 414; marriage, 371–2; as Mayor of Château-Chinon, 294, 374–5; 1981 presidential election, 337, 338–40; 1988 presidential election, 388–9; nuclear weapons, 245, 246, 247; as President, 54, 56, 343–8, 350–65, 366–7, 381–6; proportional representation, 230, 237; and René Bousquet, 375, 377, 378–80; rise to power, 318–19, 326, 372–5; and Roger-Patrice Pelat, 345–8, 353–4, 355, 357; rural roots, 96, 99; scandals, 68; TGV, 159; war record, 370–1, 375–7

Mobutu Sese Seko, 37
Mollet, Guy, 373
monetary union, 48–9, 92, 258, 404
Monnet, Jean, 122
Montaldo, Jean, 348, 363
Montataire, 188, 189
Montchovet estate, Saint-Étienne, 185
Montereau, 94
Montpellier, 285
morality, 50, 62–70
Mortimer, John, 252
Moselle department, 238
motorways, 23
Mouillot, Michel, 65
Moulin, Jean, 122, 268
Moulinex, 144
Mulhouse, 20
multi-culturalism, 201–2
multinational companies, 6–7, 44
Mururoa, 245, 246–7, 249, 399
Muslims, 194–7, 201, 272, 288

Najac, 284–5
Nancy, 51, 179
Napoléon I, Emperor, 2, 3, 11, 14, 17, 40, 255, 260, 261, 264, 277–8,
306–7
Napoléon III, Emperor, 256
National Assembly, 46, 207, 293; Communists in, 140; National Front in, 230–1, 237; 1997 elections, 49, 60, 405–9; scandals, 68; women members, 39, 41
National Council of French Patronat (Movement of Enterprises of France), 154
National Front, 174, 433; anti-Semitism, 226–8; and Bruno Mégret, 238–40; in Dreux, 132; electoral support, 19, 51–2, 237–8, 240–2; Le Pen and, 209–15, 229–34, 240–2; in local government, 234–7; in Marseille, 300; in National Assembly, 230–1, 237; and 1995 presidential election, 397; 1997 legislative elections, 60, 408, 409–11; 1998 regional elections, 417–18; racism, 196, 207, 208
nationality, 205
Nato, 249–50
Nazis, 104, 121–2, 131, 137, 194, 215–16, 218–19
Neuilly-sur-Marne, 188
newspapers, 283
Nice, 186–7, 282, 285, 287, 295, 314
Nique Ta Mère (NTM), 205, 235
Noir, Michel, 66–7, 177
North Africa, 195, 203–4, 297
North Korea, 348
nuclear power stations, 23–4
nuclear weapons, ix–x, 4, 58, 59, 243–50, 399

Occupation, 103–5, 121–2, 131, 137–8, 215–26, 268, 278, 375
oil industry, 164–72, 330–3
Olympique de Marseille (OM), 173, 174, 175, 176
Omega device, 331–3
Orange, 234
Organisation for Economic Co-operation and Development (OECD), 42, 149, 152
Ouradour, 126

overseas departments and territories, 32–4

Pagès, Patrick, 101–2
Pagnol, Marcel, 121, 297
Papon, Maurice, 219–20, 221, 227, 278–80, 311, 339, 379, 427, 433
Parretti, Giancarlo, 147
Paris, 179, 278, 287–93, 422–4; arrondissements, 286; Chirac as mayor of, 68–9, 287–8, 290–3, 295, 336–7; crime, 196; as cultural centre, 25–6; gentrification, 289, 292; government, 290–1; immigrants, 202–3; restaurants, 286; revenues, 292; shops, 126; tourism, 7–8
Paris, Comte de, 202, 203, 272, 360
Paris Bourse, 6, 43–4, 351–2
Parti Communiste Français (PCF) see Communist Party
Pasqua, Charles, 76, 164, 171, 213, 392, 399, 414
Pau, 82
Paxton, Robert, 218
Péchiney, 71, 351–3
Pelat, Roger-Patrice, 345–8, 352, 353–4, 355, 357, 358, 361, 363, 371, 375
pensioners, 43
Pérec, Marie-José, 204
Perpignan, 20
Pessimism Index, 42
Pétain, Marshal Philippe, 221, 269, 278, 376, 379
pétanque, 14, 92
Peugeot, 72
Peugeot–Citroën, 134–5
philosophy, 26
Piat, Yann, 64–5
pieds noirs, 270, 272, 297
Pierre, L'Abbé, 62–3
Pilhan, Jacques, 409
Pinault, François, 148
Pinay, Antoine, 293, 331
Poilâne, Lionel, 83
Point, Fernand, 87
Poliakov, Léon, 218
police, 187–9, 191–3, 205, 224, 237

Polynesia, 33, 59, 246–7, 249
Pompidou, Georges, 28, 136, 329, 391, 406; affairs, 251; and Britain's entry to Common Market, 259; and Chirac, 326–7; and De Gaulle, 19–20; death, 321–2, 325, 340, 381; 1968 strikes, 123, 319; as President, 321
Poniatowski, Michel, 275–6, 324, 329
Popular Front, 121, 135, 137, 275, 287
population, 23, 50, 199; rural depopulation, 109–11
Post Office, 6, 151
Potin, Félix, 126, 127, 129–30, 172
Poujade, Pierre, 130, 394
poverty, 43, 124, 183–6, 431
Powell, Sir Charles, 253
Presidents, 54–60, 274, 317
Prime Ministers, 54, 274
privatisation, 132, 149–51, 412
prostitutes, 92–3
Protestants, 267–8, 271, 272
public-sector workers, 150–1

racism, 19, 51, 187, 196, 201, 205–8, 226
Radical Socialist party, 279
railways, 4, 6, 23, 151, 159–63
Rainbow Warrior, 56, 246, 383
Ramée, Joseph, 14
Raoult, Éric, 208
Rassemblement Pour la République (RPR), 241, 418; Chirac and, 58, 335–7, 338, 340, 392; funding, 69; Mégret and, 239; Séguin and, 414, 415–16, 417
Reagan, Ronald, 61, 383
referendums, 47
regionalism, 283–7; Corsica, 305–14; food, 271, 301–3, 304; local government, 293–5; wine, 303–4
Reims, 20
religion, 21–2, 194–7, 200–1, 202, 267–8, 272
Renault, 130–5, 156
Renoir, Jean, 121
Resistance, 121–2, 135, 218, 226, 244, 268–9, 279, 376, 377, 421

restaurants, 93, 100, 101–3, 272, 286, 301, 304

Réunion, 34

Revolutions: (1789), 39–40, 79, 120, 253, 255, 268, 275, 277, 280, 428; (1830), 120, 275; (1848), 275

Rhône-Poulenc, 71, 163

rigueur policy, 344

riots, 187–9, 206–7

Riviera, 25, 65, 93, 261, 263

roads, 4, 23

Rocard, Michel, 71, 73, 239, 268, 381; high-speed rail link, 159–60; and housing estates, 182–3; Mayor of Paris, 294; as Prime Minister, 351, 407; proposes twin-track elections, 273

Rocca-Serra family, 309

Roubaix, 197–8

Roux, Ambroise, 153–4

RPR *see* Rassemblement Pour la République

rural life, 95–119

Ruymbeke, Renaud van, 172

Rwanda, 34, 36

Saint-Amand, 268–9

Saint-André-de-Rosans, 106–9, 110

Saint-Bonnet-le-Froid, 101

Saint-Étienne, 20, 185, 238

Saint-Gobain, 71

salaries, executive pay, 157–8

Sampieru, 313

Sanai, Darius, 190–2

Sand, George, 9

Santé prison, 167–8, 177

Sarcelles, 202–3

Sarraute, Nathalie, 84

Sartre, Jean-Paul, 81, 131, 133, 138, 269, 275, 289

Saury, Pierre, 378

savings, 62

Schemla, Élisabeth, 205

Schmidt, Helmut, 328

Schneider industrial group, 172

schools *see* education

Schröder, Gerhard, 315–16

Schweitzer, Louis, 132–3, 134

Second World War, 103–5, 121–2, 131, 137–8, 215–26, 227, 244, 257, 268–9, 297–8, 370–1, 375–7, 392

Securities and Exchange Commission, 351–2

Séguin, Philippe, 394, 413–16, 417, 426

Seine, river, 94

Seita, 86

self-confidence, international, 12–14

separatism, 305, 309, 310

Servan-Schreiber, Jean-Jacques, 339

sexuality, 93, 251, 263–4

SGS-Thomson, 150

shareholders, 155–6

shops, 125–30

slang, 204–5

Slitinsky, Michel, 339, 379

smoking, 86–9

SNCF, 160–63, 167, 281

social security, 79–80, 144, 184, 347

Socialist Party: and Bernard Tapie, 173, 174; Communists and, 136, 137; divisions within, 273; and Dreyfus Affair, 227; electoral success, 172, 274–5; immigration policy, 214; in Marseille, 300; Mitterrand's presidency, 343–8, 355–6, 358; 1981 election, 123; 1997 legislative elections, 48, 49, 140, 407–8, 409–10; and privatisation, 150; scandals, 68

Société Générale bank, 7

Sofrès, 250, 253

Soisson, Jean-Pierre, 417–18

Sorbonne, 135

Soros, George, 6, 61, 76, 154

state (*l'État*), 73, 277–83, 295, 428, 434

stock market, 155

Stoclet, Denis, 127, 128

Strasbourg, 20, 77, 189, 207

Strauss-Kahn, Dominique, 43, 149

street culture, 204

strikes, 62, 123, 141–2

students: 1968 revolt, 99, 135, 172, 275, 276–7, 319; rising numbers of, 43

suburbs, 180

supermarkets, 128

Susini, Jean-Jacques, 410

Taiwan, 359–60
Talleyrand, Charles-Maurice de, 278
Tapie, Bernard, 173–8, 300, 345, 363,
    365
Tarallo, André, 170
Tartarets estate, Corbeil-Essonne, 180–1,
    190–2
Tati chain, 127–8
taxation: cafés, 85; corporate tax, 144–5,
    152; income tax, 151–2; indirect
    taxes, 152; rising levels of, 42, 43;
    tobacco, 86, 87
teachers, 281
telephones, 45
television, 85, 159, 179–80
terrorism, 132, 195, 201, 288, 310,
    311
Thatcher, Margaret, 13, 61, 71, 252–3,
    259, 383–4
Thiam, Anna Rose 'Lise', 168
Third Republic, 120, 275, 279
Thomson, 359–60
Thorez, Maurice, 135, 137, 138
Tiberi, Jean, 69, 291
tobacco, 86–9
Todd, Emmanuel, 76, 399, 430
Total, 71, 156
Toubon, Jacques, 70, 291, 402, 418–19
Toulon, 228, 234–5, 282
Toulouse, 179, 189, 210, 285, 378
Toulouse, Counts of, 284, 285
Tour de France, 5, 21, 87, 96, 173
Tourcoing, 198–9, 208, 238
tourism, 7, 24, 289–90, 309
Tours, 294
Touvier, Paul, 218–19, 226, 280
towns, 179–208
Toyota, 6, 44
Traboulsi, Samir, 353
trade, 44, 46, 61
trade unions, 122, 137, 141–2, 273,
    430
Train à Grande Vitesse (TGV), 6, 159–62,
    185, 195
Transparency International, 158
transport: car industry, 15–16, 130–5;

railways, 4, 6, 23, 151, 159–63;
    roads, 4, 23
Transport Ministry, 136, 140
Trappes, 184
Trautmann, Catherine, 42
Treasury, 148
Les Trente Glorieuses (the Glorious
    Thirty), 60–1, 122
Triangle, 351–3
Turks, 199

unemployment, 42–3, 430–1; among
    immigrants, 123–4; Communists
    and, 139; Islam and, 195; Jospin
    and, 412; in Mitterrand presidency,
    123–5, 344; in Paris, 291; and
    privatisation, 151; proposed
    reduction in working hours, 42, 48;
    and racism, 199; Socialist policy, 49,
    61; Tartarets estate, 181; under
    Chirac, 401; and urban problems,
    183–4, 186; *see also* employment
Union de la Démocratie Française
    (UDF), 52, 241, 301, 416–18
United Nations, 13, 31, 207
United States of America: and Africa,
    37–8; Chirac's relations with, 399,
    400; illegal drugs, 298; nuclear
    weapons, 244
urban culture, 180–208
Usinor, 71, 149, 150
USSR, 136–7, 138–9

Valenciennes, 175
Var department, 64–5
VAT, 152
Vaulx-en-Velin, 185, 189, 196, 202, 208,
    238
Veil, Simone, 218, 227, 228
Vendée, 271
Vialas, 101–2
Vibrachoc, 344–5, 346
Vichy government, 76, 218–19, 221,
    224–5, 242, 268, 269, 275, 279,
    375, 376, 377, 379
Vietnam, 30–1, 247, 269, 308
villages, 106–9, 112–16
Villepin, Dominique de, 404, 409

Villiers, Philippe de, 233
vineyards, 89, 90
violence, 187–93, 195, 309
Viorst, Milton, 203
Vitrolles, 236–7, 239, 240
Voltaire, 15
Wartski family, 105
Wiesel, Elie, 379
wine, 9–10, 89–92, 301–2, 303–4
women, 39–42, 96–7, 154, 273
working class, 120–1, 122–5, 135,
    141–2, 242

working hours, 42, 48, 432
World Cup (1998), 21, 49, 159, 215, 252

Yalibez, Sarah, 221–2, 225
Yonne, river, 94
youth crime, 189, 193
Yvelines department, 184

Zaïre, 37
Zidane, Zizou, 215
Zola, Émile, 275, 281